Care-Giving in Dementia

Care-giving in dementia is a new speciality with its own rapidly growing body of knowledge. Volume 2 of *Care-Giving in Dementia* expands upon some of the topics in volume 1 and contains entirely new subjects. This second volume contains contributions from a wide range of health care professionals and researchers from around the world and provides a hand-book for all those involved in 'hands on' caring, or in planning care, for persons with dementia. The book provides a rich source of information on most recent thinking about individualized long-term care both of dementia sufferers and of their families.

Key themes in volume 2 are: the subjective experience of dementia; the provision of care for family carers; differing cultural perspectives of dementia; and the crucial importance of life-history information for under-standing a person's reaction to their illness. Chapters on the 'search' for an ethical framework and the best environment within which to provide care are particularly timely.

Care-Giving in Dementia volume 2 is multi-disciplinary and multi-professional in its approach and will be of use to health care professionals, students, lay care-givers and to all those requiring practical guidelines for care of dementia sufferers.

Edited by **Bère M. L. Miesen**, Psychogeriatric Centre 'Mariënhaven', Warmond and the Department of Clinical and Health Psychology, Royal University Leiden, The Netherlands, and **Gemma M. M. Jones**, Neuro-psychologist Honorary Research Fellow at St Mary's Medical School Hospital, London.

Care-Giving in Dementia

Research and applications
Volume 2

Edited by
Bère M. L. Miesen and
Gemma M. M. Jones

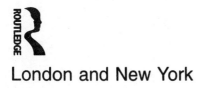

London and New York

First published 1997
by Routledge
11 New Fetter Lane, London EC4P 4EE

Simultaneously published in the USA and Canada
by Routledge
29 West 35th Street, New York, NY 10001

Typeset in Times by Keystroke, Jacaranda Lodge, Wolverhampton
Printed and bound in Great Britain by Mackays of Chatham PLC, Chatham, Kent

British Library Cataloguing in Publication Data
A catalogue record for this book is available from the British Library

Library of Congress Cataloging in Publication Data
A catalogue record for this book has been requested

ISBN 0–415–13844–2
      0–415–13845–0 (pbk)

For Michael Ignatieff, author of *Scar Tissue* (London: Vintage, 1993).

For Kenneth Solomon (1947–1994), who, through his cosmopolitan attitude, fought successfully against the blindness of therapeutic nihilism in geriatric psychiatry; whose contribution, especially to psychodynamic psychotherapy with the elderly, now inseminates psychiatry, psychology, social work, nursing and counselling.

For all care-givers who have stood by another person and tried to understand what they are seeing and meaning and feeling; behind the mirror of their memories, the words that won't be ordered, and the white knuckles on clenched fists.

Contents

Part V Environment, education and ethics

Figures

Tables

Contributors

Ilse Achterberg is an activity-therapist specialist at the Bernardus Nursing Home in Amsterdam. She works on a ward for the severely demented elderly and in the 'Snoezelcentre' which is a small education and PR department in the Bernardus Nursing Home. She went to a college of higher education, and is one of the founders of 'snoezelen' with the demented elderly. She writes articles and gives lectures and courses about 'snoezelen', and as a consultant she helps organizations introducing it on the wards.

Marco Blom is a psychogerontologist at The Netherlands Institute of Care and Welfare (NIZW), Utrecht, The Netherlands. He coordinates several projects within the programme 'Informal care and family care'. He has (co)published several articles and books on dementia, depression and family care-giving and was involved in the production of two videotapes on dementia. He is a board member of The Netherlands Society of Gerontology.

Kees Commissaris studied health sciences at the University of Maastricht, The Netherlands, and graduated in health education. In 1993 he completed his doctoral dissertation on 'Education about memory problems and dementia'. Dr Commissaris' current work at the Department of Psychiatry and Neuropsychology is part of the Maastricht Aging Study (MAAS). This longitudinal study, coordinated by Professor Jolles, is largely concerned with the age-related decline of memory and memory-related functions in normal people.

Carole Cox is Associate Professor of Social Work at the National Catholic School of Social Service, the Catholic University of America. She is the author of numerous articles and book chapters in the areas of ethnicity and ageing, hospital care, and care-giving. Dr Cox is also the author/co-author of several books and is currently conducting research on the longitudinal use of Alzheimer services. She is completing a study of community care for the elderly in Israel and the United Kingdom.

Pim Cuijpers is a clinical psychologist, and currently head of the Prevention Department of the RIAGG Westelijk Noord-Brabant, and outpatient mental health centre. He obtained his PhD from the University of Nijmegen. He wrote his thesis on support groups for care-givers of the demented elderly. He has published several books and many peer-reviewed articles on depression, care-giving, and prevention in mental health.

Rose-Marie Dröes is a Human Movement scientist who works as a senior researcher at the Department of Psychiatry of the Free University in Amsterdam. In 1991 she obtained her PhD in Medical Sciences from the same university. She was leader of several research projects in the field of psychosocial intervention for dementia patients living in nursing homes and at home. Dr Dröes is the author of *In Movement: On Psychosocial Care for Demented Elderly* (1991) and *Amsterdam Meeting Centers: A New Form of Support for Demented Elderly Living at Home and their Primary Care-Givers* (1994). Currently she is the leader of a research project in which the effect of Feil's Validation method on demented patients living in nursing homes is studied.

Mia Duijnstee, nurse and psychologist, is presently clustermanager at The Netherlands Institute of Care and Welfare (NIZW). In 1993 she was appointed part-time professor in the domain of 'Innovations in the field of home care' at the University of Utrecht, Faculty of Medicine, Nursing Science. She is (co)author of a number of articles, research and policy reports particularly in the area of home nursing. She has done research on the following subjects: the extent of family care, the problems of family carers and help being organized in The Netherlands for family carers.

Mary Fahrenfort studied social psychology and sociology. She specialized in doctor–patient communication and taught this subject at medical school for eight years. Her doctoral thesis, 'A doctor's romance', covered the same subject. During the past ten years she has been doing research and development for hospitals and nursing homes at the NZi, Institute for Health Care Management. At this Institute she is currently head of the department of Care for the Elderly. She has published extensively on matters of organization as well as communication in institutes for health care.

Bo Hagberg, PhD, was formerly Chief Psychologist at the Lund University Hospital. He has been Director of the Gerontology Research Centre since 1985 and Professor of Psychology, Department of Psychology, Lund University since 1989. As a clinician he has worked in psychotherapy, medical psychology and neuropsychology. He is author/co-author of scientific articles pertaining to personality and ageing, assessment and rehabilitation of dementia patients, life history reviews and longevity models.

Diane Hinshelwood qualified in activation and recreation therapy from George Brown College in Toronto. She is senior recreationist in the Geriatric Psychiatry Programme at Hamilton Psychiatric Hospital and has worked extensively with the special needs of the frontal lobe dementia patient.

Clemens Hosman, PhD, is Professor of mental health promotion and prevention of mental disorders at the University of Maastricht and Associate Professor of preventive psychology at the University of Nijmegen, The Netherlands. He has been working in the field of mental health promotions, prevention and social epidemiology since 1973. Over the last twenty years he has produced many publications on different aspects of prevention and prevention research. He chairs the European WHO Task Force on Mental Health Promotion and Prevention, and is director prevention of the Nijmegen research group on Prevention and psychopathology.

Reidun Ingebretsen is senior researcher at the Norwegian Institute of Gerontology, Oslo, Norway. She is a specialist in clinical psychology in the field of gerontopsychology and has published works on different subjects related to loss, grief-reactions, reminiscing and coping with life transitions in old age. She is co-author of books related to care-giving and dementia. In a current study, spouses of the demented elderly are followed up over a three-year period, with regard to their losses, attachment and coping during the dementia process.

Gemma M. M. Jones, PhD, neuropsychologist, is an Honorary Research Fellow at St Mary's Medical School Hospital, London, Department of Academic (Old Age) Psychiatry, St Charles Hospital, London. Her doctoral work was in the neuropsychopharmacology of Alzheimer's disease at the Institute of Psychiatry, University of London. She is a freelance consultant and educator about care-giving in dementia and long-term care facility design. She holds degrees in nursing and cell biology, and has written and lectured extensively.

Christopher King is a PhD candidate and research assistant with the Centre for the Body and Society, Deakin University, Australia. He received his MA in social welfare policy studies from Osaka City University, Japan. His current research is on postmodern images of the life course in contemporary Japan.

Tom Kitwood is a Senior Lecturer in Psychology at the University of Bradford, and leader of Bradford Dementia Group. This group has several concurrent research projects related to dementia care and the support of carers, and has had a leading role in developing methods for evaluating the quality of care in formal settings. Dr Kitwood is author of numerous publications in psychology, including the book *Concern for Others* (1991). His particular interest is in the moral, psychological and neurological aspects of being a person.

Wilma Kok is a nurse-sister in charge of the ward for the severely demented elderly at Bernardus Nursing Home in Amsterdam. She is one of the founders of 'snoezelen' and is a 'snoezelen' specialist. She went to nursing-school and completed four years of management training. She also works at the 'Snoezelcentre' in Bernardus Nursing Home. She lectures and educates on snoezelen in daily care, publishes articles, and visits nursing homes in The Netherlands to help them implement snoezelen.

Carolien Lamers studied social gerontology at the University of Nijmegen, The Netherlands, and now works as a clinical psychologist for Sheffield Consulting and Clinical Psychologists, UK. Dr Lamers works in a Community Mental Health Team for older adults, a memory clinic and a hospital for people who suffer from a dementia syndrome and who exhibit challenging behaviour.

Caroline LeNavenec is an Associate Professor of Psychiatric–Mental Health and Family Nursing at the University of Calgary in Canada. She received her doctorate in sociology at the University of Toronto, where she majored in sociology of the family and sociology of mental illness. She is co-author of *One Day at a Time: How Families Manage the Experience of Dementia* (1996) and author of *The Care Process with Dementia Patients* (1988). Her current research programme includes status of indicators of quality of nursing care, attachment patterns of people experiencing a chronic illness, and the use of music and alternative treatment modalities for patients with dementia in their families.

Bère M. L. Miesen, PhD, is a clinical psychogerontologist, educated at Nijmegen University, and working for the Psychogeriatric Centre 'Mariënhaven', Warmond and the Department of Clinical and Health Psychology, Royal University Leiden, The Netherlands. From 1970 onwards he has worked with the demented elderly, their families and professional care-givers, and is (co)author/(co)editor of many books on psychological aspects of SDAT and dementia care-giving. He is involved in clinical work, counselling, education and research (for example, the Warmond Longitudinal POPFiD Study). He also writes poetry. He obtained the 1995 Psychogeriatric Award from the Association of Psychogeriatrics in The Netherlands.

Marie Mills recently obtained her PhD, with a study of emotion, memory and dementia, from the University of Southampton, where she is now a visiting fellow. She has a background of nearly twenty years in residential social work, the past fourteen of which have been spent in running her own residential home for the elderly which specializes in caring for older people with dementia. She has written a number of articles on aspects of dementia care and is also involved in education and training of care workers.

Joep Munnichs studied psychology at the University of Nijmegen, The Netherlands, from where he obtained his PhD for a thesis later published as *Old Age and Finitude* (Karger: Bazel, 1967 and Arno Press: New York, 1980). He has been since 1972, the first full-time professor in psychogerontology at that university and head of the department. He was given emeritus status in 1990. He is founder of the Dutch Journal of Gerontology and Geriatrics. He has published widely in the field of life-span gerontology, and now is especially interested in thanatology and biography.

Henk Nies is a psychogerontologist, currently appointed as a senior researcher/consultant at the NZi, Institute for Health Care Management, in Utrecht, The Netherlands. His main fields of interest are innovations in care for the elderly, collaborations between services, and policy on ageing. He has published various books and a great number of practice-oriented articles and reports. He obtained his PhD in social science and social policy at the University of Nijmegen, The Netherlands.

Anneke van der Plaats is a social geriatrician. She works with the frail elderly in their own homes and lectures on geriatrics in a High School for Nursing and Social Work. From 1976 onwards Dr van der Plaats has participated in multi-disciplinary research at the University of Nijmegen on ageing. In 1994 she completed a study about basic theoretical assumptions in caring for the frail elderly.

Cees Salentijn, RN, is manager of the Nursing Department of Bernardus Nursing Home in Amsterdam. He is co-author and member of the editorial board of the *Handbook of Nursing Diagnosis, Interventions and Outcomes*, and of a Dutch journal on nursing perspectives. He has published several articles on the development of nursing diagnosis, and was co-producer of educational videotapes about the nursing process and about 'snoezelen'.

Per Erik Solem is a psychologist and senior researcher at the Norwegian Institute of Gerontology, Oslo, Norway. He has published works on different gerontological subjects, such as ageing and work, retirement, reminiscence, death and dying, care of the elderly and dementia. He is co-author of the book *Psychological Perspectives on Dementia*, and is currently involved in a study on spouses of the demented elderly.

Susan Tainsh is an Associate Professor of Medicine and Psychiatry at McMaster University, Hamilton, Canada. She has directed the Geriatric Psychiatry Program at Hamilton Psychiatric Hospital since 1988. The Program assesses and manages severe behaviour problems in dementia. Dr

Tainsh now specializes in systems consultation, education and clinical research.

Myrra Vernooij-Dassen studied sociology at the University of Nijmegen, The Netherlands. There she is a lecturer and senior researcher in the Department of General Practice and Social Medicine. Dr Vernooij-Dassen has published on the sense of competence of primary care-givers of people who suffer from a dementia syndrome.

Ilse Warners works as a nurse in various fields of health care, both in direct care-giving and in nurse-education. Besides a number of articles on nursing she has published some twenty articles on the care for demented persons. She was co-organizer of various symposia on psychogeriatric themes and participated in a number of gerontological research projects in The Netherlands.

Editors' note

We are pleased to have been able to compile volume 2 of *Care-Giving in Dementia*. This has only been possible through the enthusiasm and demand for volume 1. Many contributors were approached to provide chapters for this current volume; they, in turn, knew of other noteworthy and novel projects, and now we find ourselves already working on volume 3.

The publication of volume 2 reflects the growing concern for the increasing numbers of elderly persons with dementia needing care in a variety of settings, but more specifically it attests to the recognition that this is indeed a speciality area requiring its own 'body of knowledge' and theory base. We acknowledge the importance of exploring all types of work which aims to improve and facilitate care-giving. To this end, we have selected some contributions which do not necessarily reflect our own views or practice approaches. We hope the work contained herein will help stimulate discussion, thinking and the practice of newer and/or more refined approaches and outlooks to providing care.

As in volume 1, we have not insisted on a particular term for referring to a person suffering from dementia. You will find 'patient', 'dementia sufferer', 'elderly mentally infirm' and 'person with dementia' used uniformly and interchangeably within any chapter. None of the terms is totally suitable, but until a better one arises, we will make do with these.

Introduction

Gemma M. M. Jones

This volume, as its predecessor (*Care-Giving in Dementia*, volume 1, ed. G. M. M. Jones and B. M. L. Miesen, Tavistock/Routledge, 1992), is again intended to be a practical volume, primarily for health care professionals and students. We hope that some family carers will also be tempted to read it.

The chapters come under five major headings: models and theories; interventions in care facilities; interventions in the community; interventions for the family; environment, education and ethics.

We have maintained the same sub-sections as in volume 1 with a slight expansion into the areas of 'environment' and 'ethics'. While some of the chapters are extensions of topics introduced in volume 1, the content is entirely new, and has been selected to enhance the first book. This volume can be read without reference to volume 1 – however, readers wishing to gain a retrospective taste could begin with chapter 9 which provides a summary of most of the methods covered in it.

While there have been many advances in the neurobiological undestanding of dementia in the past few years, particularly with regard to differentiating some of the sub-types, our attempts to describe the behavioural implications of these sub-types is still in its infancy. The chapters on frontal lobe dementia are a laudable effort to advance our assessment and treatment skills for persons with specific types of dementia. No doubt there will be more work along these lines in future.

Readers will note the wide range in professions represented by the pool of contributors. Likewise, the research written about varies widely from pilot projects through to post-doctoral work. We have endeavoured to select chapters on their merit or their contribution to an 'eclectic' volume that would stimulate the type of discussion and further research needed to advance the field of care-giving. For this reason, there will be notable differences in style and approach between the chapters.

Key themes arising from this volume are: trying to understand the subjective experience of dementia, and the awareness-context of the sufferer; providing care for family carers depending on their perception of the 'burden' they carry and on the stage of grieving they are at; differing cultural perspectives of dementia and what we can learn from them; and, last but not least, the increasing awareness that life history information is essential for understanding a person's reaction to his or her illness and for planning relevant, individualized, stage-specific care. The topic of the most suitable environment for patients is a welcome addition to this volume and certainly one that will be expanded upon in later books. The last chapter on ethics provides a strong ending to the discussion of these themes.

It is noteworthy that the newer interpersonal approaches to caregiving (for example the Validation Method and Psychomotor Therapy) are increasingly resembling one another in terms of emphasizing the individual's past, and in that they are incorporating a wide range of communication, counselling and activity based interventions. Although such convergence in thinking 'broadly' about psychosocial interventions was, in retrospect, predictable, it is a marked advance from the 'reality orientation for everyone' thinking that pervaded the 1970s. While some researchers continue to believe that 'any attention given to the elderly mentally infirm' is bound to do some good because they are so starved of attention, the weight of the empirical evidence is beginning to support specific interventions for specific types and stages of dementia. We await, particularly, further strategies for working with persons having the 'early onset' form of Alzheimer's disease.

The methodological problems involved in conducting quantitative research with dementia sufferers are enormous. The behavioural variability between sufferers, family carers and professional carers is huge. The difficulty of finding sufficient numbers of persons, and comparable control groups for a suitable length of time to establish good baseline, intervention and follow-up measurements is substantial. This is not to say that only qualitative research should be attempted, but rather to draw attention to the need for more sensitive test measures, analytical methods, and to the as yet hidden observations behind the statistically 'insignificant' significance levels. Qualitative research with dementia sufferers and carers is helping to make researchers more aware of individual differences and the complexity of the questions to which we are seeking answers. It has also opened up to us the small window of attempting to understand the subjective aspects of both sufferer and care-giver.

We hope that caring for persons with dementia will become a more attractive field to work in as it becomes recognized as a speciality in its own right. Furthermore, we hope that family, student and professional care-givers will take up the invitation to help develop this speciality by discussing, thinking, researching and/or trying out new ways of providing care. While it is true that some aspects of care-giving are intuitive, this book would be in vain if other aspects of care-giving could not be learned. Our efforts to do this are founded in the reality that to date cures or treatment for dementias still evade us. We must confront the misery of sufferers and carers alike by finding humane, individualized ways of providing care and understanding.

Part I

Models and theories

The concept of personhood and its relevance for a new culture of dementia care

Tom Kitwood

Before the term 'care' was annexed to the twin vocabularies of nursing and social work it belonged, essentially, to the field of ethics. In this context, to care for others means to value who they are; to honour what they do; to respect their unique qualities and needs; to help protect them from harm and danger; and – above all – to take thoughtful and committed action that will help to nourish their personal being. In such ideas there is a strong recognition of the interdependence of human life, the fact that no one can flourish in isolation; the well-being of each one is linked to the well-being of all. Moreover, the noun 'carer' did not exist. That was a later accretion, a kind of debasement.

There are no techniques for caring, in the original sense, for the highest that any person can give to another is on the ground of wholeness and spontaneity. Diagnosis, assessment, care planning, therapies, care interventions, and so on are, at best, mere aids or supports; at worst, they are 'fixes', mainly serving the function of evasion and buck-passing.

Behind the masks of confidence and competence, behind the proud ideology of individualism and self-determination, perhaps every human being yearns to be truly cared for and to care. The wisest parenting, the richest friendships, marriages, partnerships, seem to come close to this high ideal. Perhaps, as a highly social species, we are actually endowed with instinct-like tendencies to develop strong and affectionate social bonds. The work of Bowlby (1979) and others, drawing on insights from ethology and psychoanalysis, certainly suggests that this is the case. Even self-reliance, so highly valued in western societies, is based on relationships that are experienced as secure. If these assertions are true, it must also be said that whatever nature has given us is always completed, filled out with meaning, in a culture. Thus caring is facilitated in some cultural settings, and is marred and distorted in others. Paradoxically, then, we are faced with the task of creating environments in which caring feels natural, and so, eventually, bringing about a new culture of care.

Those who have dementia, we can say without a shadow of doubt, need to be cared for in the true and original sense. In fact, however, this need is very rarely met, either when they are being looked after by members of their family or in formal settings. The traditions that we have inherited from the past contain many false beliefs and inept practices: there is much to lay aside, and much learning to be done, in creating a new culture of care. Also we should take into account the possibility that we do not have instinct-like drives to help us when it comes to looking after those who are old and frail, whereas we do for looking after children. If motive is to be found, it may have to come primarily from a culture that embodies a very strong ethical ideal.

The concept of caring can be linked to another, that of personhood. Here too the fundamental matrix is ethical: it implies a standing or status that is accorded by others. Thus one can be a human being, and yet not be acknowledged as a person. We have all had experiences of this, to a greater or lesser degree: we have known occasions where we felt discounted, devalued, violated, used, abused. Fortunately, most of us have also had experiences of the opposite kind, where we felt that our personhood was acknowledged. Even if these have not been as frequent as we would have liked, we have a record of them in our emotional memory; we can draw on them in our attempt to recognize the personhood of others, and in our hope of developing into people who really know how to care.

TWO WAYS OF BEING AND RELATING

Perhaps the most profound account of personhood in this century is that given by Martin Buber (1923), in the small book originally translated into English as *I and Thou* (Buber, 1937). Here he makes a contrast between two ways of being in the world, two ways of forming a relationship. The first he terms I–It, and the second I–Thou. Relating to another in the I–It mode implies coolness, information-getting, objectivity, instrumentality. Here we engage without there being any commitment; we can maintain a distance, make ourselves safe. Relating in the I–Thou mode, however, requires involvement: a risking of ourselves, a moving out and a moving towards. 'The primary word I–Thou can only be spoken with the whole being. The primary word I–It can never be spoken with the whole being' (1937: 3).

It should be noted here that Buber is not telling us of the existence of two classes of object in the world: 'Thous' and 'Its'. He is describing two contrasting ways of relating. Thus, as we have already noted, it is possible for one human being to relate to another in the I–It mode, and, alas, this is all too common. Buber also suggests that it is possible to relate to a non-human being in an I–Thou mode: an old woman whose dog is her sole companion, perhaps, or a Japanese man who faithfully attends to his bonzai tree day by day.

Many languages make a clear distinction between 'Thou' and 'You'.

'Thou', when sincerely used, is a form of intimate address, as if whatever is said or disclosed is for one person only. 'You' is more general, and far less personal. In the English language 'Thou' has virtually disappeared, its last vestiges being still found in a few dialects and in the language of certain religious groupings. The Quakers were very reluctant to relinquish their use of 'Thou', and for good reason. It is a curious irony that the best-known translation of Buber's work into English bears the title *I and You* (Buber, 1970). Without 'Thou' the essence of his meaning is much harder to apprehend.

The connection between Buber's ideas and the concept of personhood is self-evident. We misunderstand him if we think he is telling us that every individual needs a 'Thou' in order for his or her life to have meaning. He is saying, rather, that to be a person is to be addressed as Thou. In other words, the I–Thou mode of relating actually constitutes personhood. We can approach this idea from another angle by considering Buber's famous dictum 'All real living is meeting' (1937: 11). What is the nature of this meeting? It is not that of one intellectual exchanging opinions with another; it is not that of a rescuer, doing something for a needy victim; it is not even that of two practitioners, co-operating on some task. The meeting of which Buber speaks is that of making contact with the pure being of another, with no distant purpose, explicit or ulterior. The words we might associate with such meeting are awareness, openness, presence (presentness) and grace. Grace is a gift not sought or bought, a benediction that simply happens because one is in the right place at the right time.

This brings us to the way Buber speaks of freedom. 'So long as the heaven of Thou is spread out over me, the winds of causality cower at my heels, and the whirlpool of fate stays its course' (1937: 9). Here he points poetically to one of the most rich and mysterious of all human experiences. When we are addressed as Thou – when all instrumentality and manipulation are removed – we experience a profound expansiveness and liberation. Here – perhaps here alone – we can grow beyond attitudes, habits, scripts, poisonous expectations – all that others have imposed upon us in their zeal for utility. In contrast to this, to live exclusively in the I–It mode, whether as giver or receiver, is to be perpetually at the point of death.

It should be noted that Buber is not offering a psychology, in the ordinary sense. There is no way of demonstrating empirically, through experiment or observation, the truth or falsehood of his basic assertions; attempts to do so would involve a trivialisation so gross that it would be a travesty. Buber's work might be taken, rather, as a prelude to a psychology, or perhaps as an underpinning; it should be viewed as metaphysical. The point is this: before any empirical science or any form of systematic inquiry can get under way, some assumptions have to be made. If they are made openly and with awareness, they may or may not turn out to be valuable, but at least they are open to criticism. If the task of examining assumptions is avoided (as has so often happened in psychology), there is the risk of building an edifice on weak or inept foundations. Sartre (1939), in his account of the emotions, suggested that much of psychology is doomed to failure because it seeks to achieve a definitive understanding of human nature as 'the crowning concept of a completed science'. The truth is that the given world will not order the facts for us. We cannot avoid making choices about how to view human nature, how to bring structure into the domain. If we avoid these issues, we may simply end up by making bad choices. Psychology must begin, then, with a clear commitment to a view about what it is to be human.

So, Buber is offering us some basic assumptions about our humanity. We cannot prove or disprove them; we can only give our assent or dissent, according to whether they seem coherent and whether they accord with our experience. Here, at any rate, is a clear conceptualization of personhood, a possible basis for a psychology of caring. And there is a very sobering fact to take into account, in relation to those who have dementia. It is that the most thorough assessment can be carried out, the most efficient 'care planning' undertaken, the most comprehensive service provided – totally in the I–It mode, without any of the meeting of which Buber speaks ever having taken place.

THE I–IT MODE

If Buber's ideas, formulated some seventy years ago, still strike us as revelatory, it is surely because the I–It mode of relating is so common that it is often taken as 'normal', and the I–Thou mode has been exiled to the margins. Psychiatry as it has developed during the twentieth century, principally under the influence of medical science, scarcely knows the meaning of Thou. The person who is suffering from mental distress comes under the objectifying gaze of a powerful professional, there to become an instance of a disease category. It is not uncommon for someone placed in this situation to feel the last remains of hope and self-esteem ebbing away to nothing. A person may indeed go through a full course of psychiatric intervention without ever feeling heard, acknowledged, understood, comforted; he or she is simply given a diagnostic label and passed on for a 'treatment' that is of a predominantly technical kind. There are, of course, many individual examples that go against the norm. It is encouraging to know that there is an informal affiliation of doctors who are committed to the 'medicine of the person', as originally set out by the Swiss psychiatrist Paul Tournier (1957).

Psychology, too, as it has self-consciously developed into a 'science', has virtually no place for the I–Thou mode of relating. For some psychologists in training, who had hoped to develop a profound understanding of persons, this can be a cause of great disappointment. In the main frameworks of observational and experimental work the human being is a 'subject' (read – 'subjected to a set of rules in whose making he or she had no part'). It is relatively rare that we find mainstream psychology really making an attempt to understand persons on their own ground, and it is virtually unknown for it to have any serious concern with meeting, in Buber's sense. The great exception, of course, is psychotherapy, at least in some of its more homely forms (for example Hobson, 1985; Lomas, 1992). In therapeutic work, despite many failures and abuses, there is a serious commitment to meeting. It is disturbing to note, however, that orthodox psychology tends to exclude and dismiss psychotherapy as hopelessly unscientific and 'subjective' (for example Eysenck, 1985). In other words, orthodox psychology does not have a sufficient commitment to the I–It mode.

The patterns of so-called caregiving that we have inherited from the past are contaminated in a very similar way. It is a strange and tragic paradox that so much 'care' has been practised without real meeting; and even today, in a relatively enlightened age, it features only to a minute extent on any official agenda. Those with dementia have been among the worst affected. It is as if the presence of what used to be called 'organic mental disorder' places some kind of veto upon normal human encounter, and justifies an I–It mode of relating. The malignant social psychology that I have detailed elsewhere (treachery, disempowerment, infantilization, condemnation, intimidation, stigmatization, outpacing, invalidation, banishment, objectification) epitomizes this disastrous devaluing of persons (Kitwood, 1993).

If we search historically, the reasons for this and parallel corruptions of the idea of care are easy to discern. For the institutional practices that were accepted in asylums, hospitals, nursing homes and the like are the product of a long evolutionary development. According to Foucault (1967), in his history of madness in Europe, we need to go back to the seventeenth century, the period when society in its modern form was coming into being. In order for the new, more centrally governed, more 'rational' state to function effectively, all that smacked of disorder must be suppressed. So in that remarkable phase which Foucault termed 'the great confinement' huge institutions were built; large numbers of the mad, the dissident, the flagrantly immoral, criminals, beggars and witches were locked away. The regime of the new institution resembled in many respects that of an old-time zoo. The inmates were forced to work or left to their own devices in violence and squalor – on view to a prurient public on high days and holidays. Later, mainly during the nineteenth century, initiatives were made to reform the institutions and convert them into places of moral correction. Where this occurred the regime was softened and humanized, even if its style was patronizing to the point of stultification.

Then, from around the turn of the twentieth century, a new way of framing disorder gained ground. What had previously been moral inadequacy became a medical condition, and a strenuous attempt was made to reclassify aberrant thought and behaviour into a category frame of diseases. Accompanying this, of course, was a search for corresponding lesions in the nervous tissue. The success of this project in some instances such as tertiary syphilis promoted the view that the organic disease process would be found in every case. Within psychiatry it was Janet, and later Freud, who questioned the universality of organic aetiology, causing a frisson of doubt about the validity of this project at its outset (Gay, 1988). The reverberations of this scepticism have never died away.

This is the complex and self-contradictory tradition of 'care' that western society has inherited. In each of the three main phases of the history of mental institutions (bestialization, moralization, medicalization) the norms of practice had virtually no place for the personhood of the inmate, no recognition of the necessity of real meeting if a human life is to flourish. Of course there were some who went against these norms, attempting to develop forms of practice liberated from the dead hand of the I–It mode (for example Laing, 1961). But they were no great threat to the system; under the prevailing regimes of truth it was easy to consign them to the ranks of eccentrics or subversives.

THE CRISIS OF POSTMODERNITY

This is not an easy time to create a new culture of dementia care. There are many signs that western civilization has now entered one of its major phases of dissolution and re-formation. In some ways this may be comparable to the change that ushered in modernity, when many of the social forms we know so well were coming into being: nation states, centralized government, global trade, machinofacture, capital accumulation on a large scale, subordinate women, powerful associations of doctors, lawyers and financiers. The formation of the asylums was part of this first transition; the end of the asylums is part of the second.

Now the recognition is growing that the grand project of modernity has been, in some respects, a failure. Technology, developed mainly under the joint imperatives of profit and war, has solved the basic problem of scarcity, while bringing a host of new environmental and social problems. The economic–political process for delivering sufficiency, security and peace to the world population has not yet been discovered. Very few of the institutional forms in which such high hopes were placed – for example medicine, education and welfare – have worked successfully. In many countries, the state, which had taken on such huge burdens, has been divesting itself of its responsibilities as fast as it can. The pursuit of social order has produced an underlying chaos. The pursuit of reason has produced a profound irrationality (Smail, 1993).

This is the context for the restructuring of social care, which has taken different forms from one society to another. Although it would be a great mistake to ignore the genuinely humanistic concerns that have contributed to some of the changes, there can be little doubt that the one main motive has been financial. In relation to those whose mental powers are frail and failing, the worst possibility that lies ahead is that new institutional forms will emerge, no more respectful of personhood than those they were designed to replace. An older person living at home, receiving so-called packages of 'care', may turn out to be just as imprisoned and depersonalized as the former inmate of an asylum – and possibly a great deal more isolated and alone. A new-style residential or nursing home, despite all its appearance of comfort and efficiency, may reproduce many of the worst features of the older institutions; and – in some cases at least – with the additional dehumanizing tendencies that accompany the relentless pursuit of profit.

Nothing, however, is fixed or fated. If the crisis of postmodernity presents dire possibilities, it also holds out new opportunities (Murphy, 1991). There is, undoubtedly, a new humanism around, even if it thrives at present mainly on the margins. The last twenty years or so have seen a vast growth in counselling and psychotherapy, a new and widespread concern with the interpersonal domain. The cynic may say that this has happened because of the need to contain the stresses of impossible social conditions. If people were to be made redundant, or extremely insecure, or exploited by the imposition of impossible burdens at work, or excluded from a valued future, their anxieties would need to be eased if the whole system was not to be called in question. The radical consequences of this new exploration of experience, however, will not be easily dismissed. For there has emerged a new recognition of personhood, a new knowledge about what makes for its weal or woe. The disappearance of morons, imbeciles, idiots, mongols and cretins is far more than an exercise in cosmetics: it bespeaks a genuine social change. The improvements that have occurred during the last ten years or so in the care of those who have dementia are part of a similar growth in compassion and responsibility. The uncertainty and lack of direction that provoke so much bewilderment also provide a space for the emergence of a new culture of care. The dismantling of some of the old structures, although deeply unsettling, has created the opportunity for a radical and more benign redistribution of power.

DEMENTIA AND PERSONHOOD

It is not possible to create a culture through utopian speculation, by some ungrounded act of the imagination. We can, however, already have some inkling of what a new culture of dementia care will involve, because enough has already been learned in action (Bell and McGregor, 1994). The chaos of the last few years has provided the condition for questioning long-held certainties, for challenging deeply embedded practices. Certain guiding themes related to personhood have now clearly emerged, each in its own way challenging a cherished tenet of modernity. I shall discuss three of them briefly here.

The uniqueness of each person

It is paradoxical that an epoch which has exalted individualism virtually to the supreme value should have had so gross a disregard for individuality. Behind the ideology it was, of course, merely an economic individualism that was espoused. The truth is that we have each of us, our own history, personality, likes, dislikes, abilities, interests, beliefs, values, commitments, and our unique identity is made up through some combination of these. In asserting this we are no longer on the ground of metaphysics, but of perfectly orthodox social psychology, where propositions are testable, at least to some degree (Harré, 1976). It is amazing how far the individuality of those who have dementia has generally been expunged, even where rigorous methods of record-keeping, assessment and care-planning have been in place. In the older traditions of 'care' it was as if the single category 'primary degenerative dementia' rendered obsolete all other forms of differentiation; there is a mind-set here that is very difficult to overcome. Now, however, we are gradually beginning to make the joyful discovery that the more we truly recognize aspects of individuality such as those that I have mentioned, the less important the dementia seems to be.

The strong recognition of individuality is, then, the ground of true meeting, of addressing the other as Thou. It is not a matter of having a large collection of facts; but rather, of having a diffuse awareness, of being open to the uniqueness of the other's way of being.

Subjectivity

This is the second theme, clearly related to the ideas we have just explored. This is to say that each person has his or her own special way of experiencing events, relationships, change, places, atmospheres, familiarity, newness, surprise – and so on. There are particular kinds of things that tend to cause anxiety or fear, particular sources of pleasure, joy and satisfaction. All this, and much more, is summed up in the concept of subjectivity. Each of us acquires our subjectivity as a result of the accumulation of layer on layer of experience. For some persons, subjectivity is rich in feeling and emotion, whereas for others this domain is very largely occluded. No one can know the subjectivity of another, although at times it may be possible to develop rudiments of an empathic understanding. The failure to recognize differences in subjectivity is a major cause of the breakdown of relationships. The modernizing project placed its emphasis, of course, on objectivity, with the consequence that those who saw this as disastrous folly tended to be forced into extreme positions of protest.

An emphasis on subjectivity has a particular poignancy for the care of those who have dementia, because they have been so often treated in ways that verge on objectification. It would seem that for many years the question was virtually never raised: 'What is it like actually to be experiencing a dementing illness?' Even members of the family seem very rarely to have asked it, if we are to judge by the majority of biographical accounts. Perhaps the question was too threatening, too destabilizing of a fragile *status quo*. More radically, the question might even have been unthinkable by those who were deeply alienated from their own subjective life. It is only on the ground of our subjectivity, and an appreciation of that of another person, that what Buber calls true 'meeting' can take place. 'The primary word I–Thou can only be spoken with the whole being.'

Relatedness

This is the third guiding theme. Again, this goes sharply against one of the main ideas of the present time, which is to see human beings as separate and separated, coming together primarily to 'do deals' of some kind or other, rather like the supposedly rational agents who feature in conventional economic theory. Personhood, however, is constituted differently. It requires a living relationship with at least one other, where there is a felt bond or tie. Without this as a minimum the human psyche disintegrates, except in the most exceptional cases. It is also necessary for an individual to have some place of significance within a human grouping, bound together on the basis of family, friendship, occupation, religion, neighbourhood or whatever. It is as if the group comes to exist within the individual, as well as the individual within the group. We easily forget that human beings emerged as highly social beings, living out their lives in fairly small face-to-face groups, where the confirmation of their being was continually bestowed by others, and the presence of interpersonal bonds was more assured. This is the kind of psychological milieu which is natural to our species. Neither the pursuit of self-determination nor existence in a nameless crowd can ever provide us with an authentic human existence.

It is one of the great failures of dementia care, in the patterns we have inherited, that the theme of relatedness has been so largely forgotten. Recent work, interpreting some of the distress of those who have dementia in terms of Bowlby's attachment theory, is a very important corrective (Miesen, 1992). For in the traditional institution people often lived out their lives in a kind of collective loneliness, desperately anxious in their isolation. Even today, some forms of intervention seem to have the nature of short-term fixes, without regard for lasting attachments. At the very point, then, where social being needed to be enhanced because of the lack of inner stabilizers or buffers, people with dementia often found that what remained of their social being was taken away. In contrast to this we might see a good care environment as a place of enhanced sociability, bearing in mind that this will have different forms for those whose dispositions tend to be more extraverted or introverted. In a sense this sociability is a kind of 'coming home'; for this is the habitat to which our nature is truly adapted.

RECONSIDERING 'NORMALITY'

In this chapter I have characterized the essence of personhood, relating it to the original concept of caring. I have also tried to sketch out a broad historical picture, describing how we have arrived at the present turning-point and the possibilities that lie ahead of us now. In relation to dementia our knowledge of what we ought to do has advanced tremendously over the last ten years or so. Despite the difficulties, there is much to urge us on our way.

If, however, we take a standpoint as searching as that which I have taken here, it is clear that we are dealing with much more than the specific issue of the care of those who have dementia. In a sense we are questioning the standard assumptions and practices of everyday life; we are challenging what commonly passes as 'normality'. Our social world, so easily taken for granted, might be regarded as bizarre, sub-human, pathological in many respects. The problems we face in relation to dementia care are part of something much larger. Whatever damaging influences there are in a society, they are likely to emerge most powerfully in what is done to those who are most vulnerable and needy. Conversely, if we make some vital rediscoveries about the meaning of personhood in this type of context, and are able to sustain these in new patterns of practice, this is a very hopeful sign for society as a whole.

So – does this emphasis on personhood really mean some kind of normalization: that is, bringing people with dementia back into our ordinary ways of relating? In one sense the answer is 'yes', because the concept certainly implies that each individual should be treated in the same way as all others; there is to be no 'us–them' divide. But in another sense the answer is 'no', because treating human beings consistently as persons is so rare in everyday life. The concept of personhood presents a huge challenge to our ideas of what normality means.

REFERENCES

Bell, J. and McGregor, I. (1994) 'Breaking free from the myths that restrain us', *Dementia Care* 2 (4): 14–15.

Bowlby, J. (1979) *The Making and Breaking of Affectional Bonds*, London: Tavistock.

Buber, M. (1937) *I and Thou*, English translation by R. Gregor Smith (first German edition, 1923), Edinburgh: Clark.

—— (1970) *I and You*, English translation by W. Kaufmann, (first German edition, 1923), New York: Scribner.

Eysenck, H. (1985) *The Decline and Fall of the Freudian Empire*, Harmondsworth: Penguin.

Foucault, M. (1967) *Madness and Civilization*, English translation by Richard Howard (first French edition, 1961), London: Tavistock.

Gay, P. (1988) *Freud: A Life For Our Time*, London: Dent.

Harré, R. (ed.) (1976) *Personality*, Oxford: Blackwell.

Hobson, R. E. (1985) *Forms of Feeling*, London: Tavistock.

Kitwood, T. (1990) 'The dialectics of dementia: with particular reference to Alzheimer's disease', *Ageing and Society* 9: 1–15.

—— (1993) 'Person and process in dementia', *International Journal of Geriatric Psychiatry* 8: 541–545.

Laing, R. D. (1961) *Self and Others*, Harmondsworth: Penguin.

Lomas, P. (1992) *The Psychotherapy of Everyday Life*, Oxford: Oxford University Press.

Miesen, B. (1992) 'Attachment theory and dementia', in G. M. M. Jones and B. M. L. Miesen (eds) *Care-Giving in Dementia: Research and Applications*, vol. 1, London/New York: Tavistock/Routledge.

Murphy, E. (1991) *After the Asylums*, London: Faber.

Sartre, J.-P. (1971) *Sketch for a Theory of the Emotions*, English translation by P. Mairet, (first French edition, 1939), London: Methuen.

Smail, D. (1993) *The Origins of Unhappiness*, London: HarperCollins.

Tournier, P. (1957) *The Meaning of Persons*, London: SCM Press.

Chapter 2

The dementias in a psychodynamic perspective

Bo Hagberg

INTRODUCTION

There are several reasons for introducing the psychodynamic aspect when trying to diagnose, understand and treat patients suffering from dementia. First, for early diagnosis, personality-related symptoms may be the most sensitive indicator of a dementing disorder. This is especially true since gerontological research indicates that basic personality traits are stable throughout the life-span. Moreover, some of the dementias, such as those affecting the frontal part of the brain, almost exclusively affect the personality in the early phases.

Second, on theoretical grounds, it is hard to uphold the antithetical position so frequently argued for in neuropsychology that one part of the individual reacts upon another part, for instance, memory loss without the reaction to that loss also being affected by cognitive decline. This positivistic orientation will benefit from being brought into a psychodynamic frame of reference. Thus, a global understanding of the individual position can be reached where the balance between resources and deficit, outer and inner demands, can be accounted for at each step or stage of the dementing process.

Third, the psychodynamic approach can offer a model to deal with the interaction among the various variables studied. In addition, it can offer a developmental model in which it is possible to anticipate the next step either in the progression of the dementia or in expectations of improvement during rehabilitation.

In a psychodynamic paradigm, changes in cognition vitally affect the balance within the psychic apparatus, both in terms of cognitive representations of reality and in its formal aspect.

The benefit of a psychodynamic frame of reference will be a better understanding of the symptoms and signs of the patient with dementia, a better understanding of the patient's total situation, especially in relation to environmental demands and possibilities. Such an approach will also provide a firmer starting point for rehabilitation and counteract the sometimes fatalistic attitude induced by an incurable disease.

As a background to this discussion, a conceptual clarification seems to be in order. From an epistemological point of view, it seems important to separate at least four levels in the analysis of dementia.

First of all, the patient presents a behaviour, some aspects of which, in deviating from normality, can be classified as symptoms of disease. Second, the symptoms combine in various syndromes that identify different types of dementia. Third, these types of dementia stem from brain damage that can differ in extent, localization and type of structural change. Fourth, the brain damage can have different aetiologies such as, among others, neuronal degeneration, vascular dysfunction, low pressure-hydrocephalus and metabolic changes. Or, seen from a causal point of view, a vascular infarction may cause brain damage or cerebral lesion which results in a quantitative and qualitative change in behaviour that in certain combinations is called a specific type of dementia. At present, it is not quite clear whether this causal direction is uni-directional or interactive. Research on rehabilitation after brain damage suggests an interactive relationship, that is, behaviour affects not only the outcome of the cerebral lesion but the cerebral lesion itself (Stein, Brailowsky and Will, 1995).

Furthermore, in rehabilitation with the dementia patient, actions can be taken on at least the first three levels and sometimes on all four in order to improve the patient's well-being at any given time. Consequently, the immediate environment of the patient must also be responsibly managed to optimize the functioning of the patient. This viewpoint does not support the so-called validation therapies with their emphasis on passively sharing the patient's experiences.

THE PSYCHODYNAMIC PERSPECTIVE

The most significant symptom in dementias is cognitive change. There are a number of concepts in dynamic psychology that relate to cognition. The importance of cognition and cognitive maturity is most easily shown in developmental psychology, but is by analogy equally significant in the reverse, that is, in its effects on personality structures when cognition is declining. In developmental psychology, cognition is readily recognized as one of many determinants of personality growth. Thus the developing thought process is considered an essential pre-requisite for acquiring secondary process functioning (Rapaport, 1960, 1967), ego-development in terms of primary autonomy (motility, perception, memory, etc.; Hartmann, 1939) and secondary autonomous functioning, that is, the enduring mental make-up which makes adaptive behaviour possible (Hartmann, 1947).

Basically, secondary process functioning can be regarded as widening the time range for action. For instance, the individual can form an intrinsic representation of objects, wait and see when to act, and thereby find an optimal and convenient way of satisfying his needs. Primary autonomy describes the successive, more economical way of performing that comes with development. Initially, single motor sensory acts, such as walking, talking, bicycling, etc., take up most of our conscious awareness and also most of our neuronal capacities. As time goes by and the performance is repeated, the function is successively more and more economically performed, utilizing less of both conscious awareness and neuronal capacity, hence achieving more of autonomy in functioning. At the same time, such an economical way of functioning frees resources for other developmental activities, usually in the form of more abstract ways of thinking and reasoning. These free resources are one of the essential individual assets for restoring brain function in rehabilitation work after brain damage.

The development of defensive structures is also dependent upon cognitive maturation (Freud, 1936) as is the development within the conflict-free sphere of the ego (Rapaport, 1951, Hartmann, 1964). Originally in the psychodynamic model, development occurred as a result of conflicting needs and/or conflicts between the needs of the individual and requirements of the environment. The defensive strategies or defence mechanisms were thought of as mediators in these conflicts. Cognitive development and maturity can solidify the character of these strategies, not only in childhood (Freud, 1936), but also during normal ageing (Vaillant, 1977), so that with experience, and given intact cognition, the 'solutions' become more and more sophisticated.

Partly in opposition to the classical Freudian concepts of conflict and defence, the post-Freudians introduced the idea of development within the conflict-free sphere. This meant that conflict was not necessary for development, but that development took place outside the conflict areas and thus was even more dependent upon cognitive capacities. Recently, this dichotomy between the classical and the neo-Freudian approach to development has been related to Erikson's stage development theory. This theory assumes that development within the conflict-free sphere perhaps more often promoted a positive, that is, generativity versus stagnation, integrity versus despair (Hagberg, 1990).

With this model in mind, the consequences of decline would be twofold. First, regressive behaviour, as shown by dementia patients, would both increase the conflict and reduce the capacity of patients themselves to reach a satisfactory solution. Second, the cognitive decline would shift the dynamics from the conflict-free sphere to the conflict area.

We can also assume that sudden cognitive change alters the balance of dynamic personality organization both in its formal aspects and with regard to content. Formally, the ego-structure could break or crack – which can be seen primarily in conflict situations resulting in regressive, primitive or childlike behaviour in which emotional outbursts are less likely to be controlled. At the same time, lack of defence strategies could uncover anxieties and fears that are overwhelming for the individual and have to be dealt with together with spouses or staff. Other ego-structures such as concentration, ability for abstract thought, planning ahead, slowness of thought and reactions to stimuli may simultaneously be affected.

Ego-content comprises ideas and concepts about one's self and the environment as well as memories from experiences throughout life. These configurations are generally called intra-psychic representations, and can take on a more threatening and sometimes archaic quality, for example ani-mation of objects. These changes have their most dramatic consequences when it comes to reality testing, and delusions and even hallucinations are common in all the dementia diagnoses. These general ideas form the background against which the symptomatology in the dementia will be discussed.

Having worked with patients with dementing disorders in a clinical setting for more than twenty-five years, and, as a member of the Lund dementia group doing research in the same field for the last twenty years, I would like to argue for the following thesis: The introduction of cognitive change within the organization of the personality has profound effects on the organization itself. From a dynamic point of view, it affects the topo-graphic aspect as well as the structural aspect of personality. On this level of conceptual complexity, we must look for the first signs of the onset of dementia, follow the change in homeostatic balance as the dementia develops, and use it as a guide to understand in a broad sense how inter-vention can alleviate the suffering for patients and for those who take care of the patients during the progression of the disease.

EXAMPLES

Let me start with some concrete clinical examples of patients in whom topographic organization, that is, the balance between the unconscious and the conscious, is affected. I will then turn to some examples of structural change.

The first example is a man with a slowly progressive dementia of the Alzheimer type. At the time of the investigation, this 70-year-old married caretaker suffered from severe memory deficit, disorientation, agitation, affective lability, moderate confabulation and lack of insight. His medical history revealed progressive dementia for the preceding two years with successively increasing memory failure and difficulty in handling the activities of daily life. At the beginning of the investigation, the patient had conjunctivitis, which was successfully cured. Marked anxiety and depres-sive reactions developed, as well as constant complaints about the health of his wife. In psychological examinations, his performance was low, that is, subnormal in most cognitive tests. He was tense and anxious. Each time he was confronted with his disability to solve the tasks, he started rubbing his eyes and finally complained of not being able to see. He was easily diverted and then regained adequate vision, but each time he had difficulty with the test items the ability to see clearly was gone.

Whether this behaviour was due to physiological or psychological changes is arguable, but the change in behaviour mimicking the earlier organic eye disease can easily be understood as a partly regressive primitivization and externalization of psychological defence (or defence manoeuvres). Similar examples can be found in patients who complain of an inability to hear when the dementia makes the stimuli hard to understand.

The next example is of a patient operated on for a carotid stenosis. This 51-year-old carpenter had his own company employing two to three men. He was married and had four children. He was tested before the operation for stenosis of the internal carotid artery on the right side. A primary intellectual level above average was found but with a slight impairment of verbal and spatial memory. The patient reported a memory deficit for the past two to three years, slight dyspraxia and increased fatigue. He was irritable, with a decreased tolerance of stress. He had attacks of anxiety and increasing sleep problems. During the preceding six months, he had had spells of double vision, intensive headaches and transient left-sided hemiparesis. The electroencephalography (EEG) and pneumo-encephalography findings were normal. When asked about anxiety and sleep problems, the patient reported that as a young fighter pilot in the Finnish winter war, he was wounded but managed to make an emergency landing on a frozen lake, the cockpit filling with snow as he landed. Since he could not move, he was frozen but was finally cut loose and rescued. After the war he had enjoyed psychological good health. Simultaneously with the memory deficit twenty-five years later, his sleep became disturbed by a recurring nightmare of being trapped and immobilized, and being cold and in a state mimicking death. As a result of this, the patient refrained as much as possible from sleeping. There followed anxiety spells during the daytime, which, as a result of questioning, could be traced back to the same theme of death anxiety as in the patient's dreams.

It is plausible to assume, in this case, the breaking through of an early traumatic experience arising partly from a reactivation of the death theme in the patient, partly from the weakening of the ego-functions, especially those involving compensatory defence, both of which appeared concomitantly with the cognitive impairment. At the post-operative follow-up two months later, the memory deficit was gone, the anxiety had diminished and sleep was improved. The patient has not been in need of medical care since then. Thus, for many patients, behaviour can seem chaotic at first, but once the biography is known and a psychodynamic approach adopted, it is found to be quite comprehensible.

Another example shows a less advanced dementia of the Alzheimer type. A 60-year-old employee, married and with one grown-up son, had suffered for a year from increasing fatigue, restlessness, sleep problems and memory deficit. Progressive dementia was suspected. He had had recurrent depressive reactions and showed a hysteroid personality. After the onset of his disease, he periodically manifested astasia–abasia in stressful situations. His intellectual level was well above average (stanine 9 in most cognitive tests) but he had a clear-cut reduction in performing verbal and spatial memory tests. His interests were in advanced photographic work, literature, classical music and painting. He had been a highly sociable person, much esteemed for his wit and sense of humour, but lately, he had given up many of his interests. He could no longer recognize the subtle distinctions in classical music and it had turned into an 'unbearable noise'. He was no longer able to achieve his earlier skill in advanced photography. Concomitantly he reported in an emotional manner how his social intentions had taken on a crude and vulgar form. For instance, when complimenting a hostess at dinner, he had made insulting remarks with allusion to sex instead of being conventionally polite. In this case, there seems to be a primitivization of a hysteroid personality, that is, a childlike acting-out behaviour as the dementia progressed, behaviour similar to that before the onset of the disease, but now, however, much more crude.

From a psychodynamic perspective we can understand the reactions that accompanied the cognitive impairment in the examples given above in the following way. In the first case, regressive defence manoeuvres were employed in order to stave off latent insight and affect, threatening to break through in face of the demand of the test situation. The second example seems to show memories surfacing to consciousness following reactivation of previously unconscious material, as well as a reduction in ego resources, which both accompanied cognitive impairment. The third case illustrates the regressive primitivization of behaviour, but also with continuity in the personality reactions. The earlier, sophisticated hysteroid manifestation remained hysteroid but now in a most vulgar shape and sometimes the patient had to resort to conversions.

In these examples we knew from the physical examination that the patients were suffering from dementia or a cognitive deficit. However, when their spouses were interviewed about the time they first suspected the pathology, they reported not on cognitive changes but on behavioural ones, particularly in complex behaviour and when the patient was under stress and/or tired. The awareness of change in behaviour could be very vague, simply a feeling of change in the contact or a reaction that was out of the ordinary or beyond what was normally expected. At that time it was not taken as an indication of illness, but with hindsight was understood as a first sign of the disease.

The regression in complex behaviour has been confirmed in analyses of all the data from the Lund Longitudinal Dementia Study (Johansson and Hagberg, 1989; Johansson et al., 1990) using personality tests showing different patterns of defence mechanisms in frontal lobe dementia (FLD), Alzheimer dementia (SDAT) and multi-infarct dementia (MID), all with similar degrees of cognitive decline and compared with a normal group. Both SDAT and MID showed less anxiety control than the normal group. Repression was less frequent and more primitive in all three dementia groups than among the normal ones, and most so in FLD. Both projection and depressive reactions were more frequent in FLD. Thus, it can also be shown with psychological tests on groups of patients with dementia that the adaptive patterns differ, both compared to non-demented individuals and between patients with different dementia diagnoses.

The necessity of the dynamic paradigm seems most important when we turn to the progressive dementia of the fronto-temporal type (FLD). From onset and fairly far into the development of the disease, the major symptom comes from changes of personality characteristics, and it is later that cognition fails. Sub-types of the disease have been described (Brun, 1987). One sub-type is dominated more by cortical atrophy and shows more expressive and acting-out symptoms. Another form is dominated by sub-cortical lesions and shows more passive symptomatology (or falling-off symptomatology). It goes without saying that for patients with these kinds of symptoms, a personality theory would be the theory of choice to understand or to make sense of the behaviour changes that occur.

Let me start by relating one example of a patient with a rather typical and later pathoanatomically confirmed fronto-temporal dysfunction. This patient was an unskilled worker, considerate towards his family and con-scientious in his work, although sometimes jealous and quick to anger. Forty-six years old, he started complaining of fatigue, emotional lability with spells of crying, and an increased susceptibility to alcohol. Four years later his wife reported a marked change in his behaviour. He had become restless, aggressive, hypersexual, unrestrained and unreliable. He drove his car at high speeds through traffic lights and was involved in several traffic accidents. He was unable to concentrate and became forgetful, but his remote memory was better preserved. He also complained of intolerable pain in his stomach and his legs, but showed no insight concerning his mental changes. At the first psychiatric investigation, when he was 57 years old, he appeared mentally slow, dysphoric, and emotionally blunt with sparse mimetic movements. His blood pressure was 140/100. EEG was nor-mal, but pneumoencephalography (PEG) showed a slight cortical atrophy. He was no longer able to work and was referred to a mental hospital, since he refused to give up driving his car. During the following years, his mental deterioration progressed and he became increasingly aspontaneous, bulimic, amimic and mutistic, only uttering short stereotyped phrases. He died at 73 years of age, after seventeen years of progressive dementia.

If this symptomatology is put into a psychodynamic frame of reference, it can be seen that the patient is exhibiting an ego-functioning breakdown or an ego-regression. If we parallel the symptoms attributed to the frontal lobes with a description of ego-functioning, we can, as in the previous examples, see how the symptoms could equally well have been presented in psychodynamic terminology – for example, changes in adult thinking, planning ahead, delay of action, organizing of thought, generating new ideas, control and regulation of emotions, flexibility, regulation of the internal state of the body, evaluation of own behaviour and appreciation and development of ethics. All these symptoms belong to strategic and social functioning in an ego-psychological conceptualization.

The advantage of favouring the dynamic conceptualization is that we get a global or holistic view of the disparate symptoms in dementia. It shifts attention to the fact that in dementia all the ego-functions mentioned above are more or less affected, not just the focal symptom for a specific diagnosis. Going through all the ego-functions, both dysfunctional and intact, in an assessment procedure, gives a nuanced and unique picture of the patient. Such an assessment will increase understanding of the patient's way of behaving, and this understanding in turn forms the basis for a more helpful attitude towards the patient. Moreover, we can follow the development over time in cognition, emotional control and conative function using either Erikson's eight-stage model, Anna Freud's defence mechanism developmental model, Piaget's cognitive developmental model, or Hartmann/ Rapaport's ego-developmental model. In doing so, we can also anticipate the course of the progression. Hence, we can better plan and carry out rehabilitation work in which we can support ego-functioning (externalized ego-functions) in order to mitigate the consequences of the regressive behaviour.

It would be fair to state that frontal lobe dysfunction (FLD) is perhaps the best example of the necessity to use psychodynamic conceptualization in order to relate behaviour to brain function on a comparable level of complexity for both function and behaviour. Enumeration of observed symptoms can only partly match the functional organization of the brain. One example of this strategy is Mesulam's (1981) description of frontal lobe function. He concluded that frontal lobe dysfunction is hetero-geneous:

- some are irresponsible, hyperactive;
- some lose spontaneity, feeling, drive, motivation;
- some show erosion of foresight, judgement and insight;
- some show impairment of abstraction, creativity, mental flexibility.

However, interpreted in terms of an ego-psychological model or structural model of psychodynamics, the picture is far from heterogeneous. Rather it describes a change in personality where the symptoms, as an expression of this change, are related to each other in a meaningful way.

For instance, erosion of character and personality frees affective activity, which in turn disrupts behaviour and then threatens to interfere in social relations. Or, considered another way, lack of temperament fails to drive the ego-organization thus lessening the regulating functions and resulting in disruptive behaviour, which again has consequences for social relations. In short, a psychodynamic assessment would be the best way to do justice to the person with a brain lesion, particularly when the frontal lobes are involved.

This conceptualization also corresponds with the neuropsychological dynamic localization theory as presented by Luria (1980), which assumes that the neurophysiological basis for complex behaviour can be explained by 'the graded localization of functions'. This means that rather than being determined by a narrowly localized complex, action is determined by a sequence of local cerebral activities forming a pattern in which it is necessary for all parts to be intact in order to achieve an adequate performance. Qualitative changes in behaviour would then result from lesions in parts of the pattern, while a reduction in performance or a breakdown in behaviour would be the result of a dysfunctional pattern. These changes can result from lesions in the cortical structures, in sub-cortical structures projecting to the frontal lobe, or lesions in the basal nucleus such as thalamus. The various interconnecting systems and their relation to psychodynamic concepts are described in more detail by Stuss and Gow (1992) and Stuss and Benson (1986).

Let me give one more example from the FLD symptomatology, for which a dynamic interpretation is even more appropriate. In an attempt to find a more general description of the frontal lobe symptom, it has been termed the 'environmental dependency syndrome'. This means a tendency or an inclination by the patient to use whatever objects are within his view, that is, when seeing a telephone, to feel the need to use it. Traditionally, the main responsibility of the ego is said to be 'reality testing', meaning that in the interface between the individual and his or her environment, the ego mediates different demands and needs to reach an optimal and realistic adaptation, often in terms of a compromise between internal needs, external demands and the individual's intentions. Weakening of the ego-structure means less reality testing, resulting either in an environmental dependency as described by Mesulam or in the acting out of primary processes and need-fulfilment; two modes of behaviour that are frequently seen in FLD.

The examples could be multiplied but these suffice to support the argument: a symptom definition in psychodynamic terms better depicts the complexity of behaviour dysfunction encountered in demented patients, especially among the FLDs.

ADAPTIVE STRATEGIES AND COPING BEHAVIOUR

Various ways or strategies by the patient, staff and/or spouses for handling the situation when cognition is failing, can be identified in different degrees in the progress of dementia. The three main dimensions under consideration are cognitive capacity, ego-functioning and social relations. Before going into the interaction between these three areas of observation, it is necessary to explain how they are defined and measured. Examples and results to demonstrate the above reasoning will be taken from the Lund Longitudinal Dementia Study, which has been presented elsewhere (Gustafson and Hagberg, 1975; Hagberg and Gustafson, 1985; Hagberg, 1987: 30; Brun et al., 1990: 34; Hagberg, 1994: 49).

The degree of cognitive reduction

In order to obtain an overall assessment of cognitive decline, test performance on verbal ability, inductive reasoning, verbal immediate memory, special memory, intellectual speed and motor speed have been compared to a normal ageing group. The comparison gives five distinct profiles, referred to here as C1 to C5. The profiles have been related to regional cerebral functioning as measured with rCBF. Each profile shows a unique relation to rCBF, both with regard to mean level of cerebral functioning and in terms of regional cerebral flow distribution. The profiles have a high validity for description of the cognitive decline in dementia (Hagberg and Ingvar, 1976).

C1. Dementia without quantitative signs of cognitive reduction

The sub-categories described under this heading are illustrated in Figure 2.1, p. 27, and explained in detail in the next section. This group includes patients with early dementia, who demonstrate qualitative changes in behaviour, for example concentration disturbances or concentration fluctuation, concrete behaviour, for instance rude language or affective change, loss of control, irritability and so on. Relatives usually describe one of two patterns of personality change: (a) symptoms of frontal lobe syndrome – lack of judgement, lack of vitality, lack of commitment; and (b) prodromal signs of sub-clinical cognitive reduction – depression or increased anxiety.

C2. Focal memory reduction

In this group we find patients with an isolated memory disturbance. In all other respects the patients seem to be cognitively intact but they experience difficulty remembering things that have just happened. It is a matter of memory disturbances that exceed what we normally call age-related forgetfulness or benign forgetfulness. This causes the patient problems to such an extent that it influences daily functioning and work performance. The extent and degree of disturbances can become so advanced that the patient reaches a state of complete inability to memorize new materials, as in Korsakov syndrome. In spite of this, conceptual and reasoning ability remains unchanged.

C3. General reduction with retained verbal performance

In this group we find patients who suffer from a general decline in intellectual performance. The cognitive reduction affects memory as well as conceptual competence and reasoning and spatial ability. It is typical that the verbal performance remains intact. The patient communicates well, reads and writes, but it is apparent that the patient has difficulty in following the reasoning in an ordinary conversation. The patient shows stereotyped repetition or perseverance in his way of expressing himself. Mistakes and errors in performance also reveal that there is a logical reasoning fault behind the action. Lack of spatial ability shows up early in difficulty in following spatial descriptions, for example road descriptions, but eventually in difficulty in finding their way around in well-known surroundings.

C4. General cognitive and verbal reduction

Patients in this group have, in addition to general intellectual reduction, difficulty in finding words and doing simple arithmetic. In their difficulty in finding the right word, they search for a long time and often use paraphrases. Language has also become concrete, so that abstractions or metaphors are not readily used. The difficulty with arithmetic concerns addition and subtraction. In the beginning, mistakes are made when regrouping two-digit numbers. Later on mistakes are also made in addition and subtraction of single numbers. The spatial ability of the patient is still intact as far as performance in copying simple geometrical figures, such as triangles and rhombs, is concerned. In spite of this, the patient cannot reproduce those figures from memory.

C5. General cognitive and verbal reduction with a aphasia, agnosia and apraxia

The patients in this group have expressive and receptive aphasia, but with different emphases depending upon the diagnosis. These symptoms occur in the framework of general cognitive reduction, which make them different from those of patients with focal lesions after a stroke. In the latter cases a relatively well preserved intellectual capacity is found behind the aphasia. The patient has, in varying degrees, difficulty in identifying or recognizing objects, persons, sounds, pictures and text (agnosia). Intentional and purposeful motor actions work poorly or even worse when there is more intention behind the planned performance (apraxia). For instance, sitting down on a chair can be complicated in an apractic way by an intentional movement in the opposite direction and this is stronger, the more the patient attempts to sit down. The spatial ability of the patient is now so distorted that he or she can no longer copy simple geometrical figures.

The C-groups describe types and degrees of dementia and patients with a progressive dementia usually progress to group C5. This development does not occur successively within the different C-groups. As can be seen, they are distinct in quality and the onset of dementia can occur in groups C1 to C4. There is certain diagnostic relation so that an onset of multi-infarct dementia (or cardiovascular dementia) is somewhat more usual in C2, an onset of SDAT somewhat more usual in C3 and an onset of FLD somewhat more usual in C4. The groupings have been made primarily to give a general assessment of abilities and disabilities in the patient. In so doing, they also give directions for rehabilitation, training programmes, activation programmes and placement within the complex of alternative care and services. They have also been used as follow-ups for progression and treatment effects.

Adaptive strategies

A number of adaptive strategies can be identified by factor-analysing the standardized psychiatric investigation of the patients in the Lund Longitudinal Study (Gustafson and Hagberg, 1985). The main categories are as follows:

Ixophrenia consists of the symptoms of affective stickiness, emotional loading up, mental rigidity, circumstantiality and obstinacy.

Hypochondria-hysteria. In addition to hypochondria and hysteroid traits the factor includes rumination.

Depression/anxiety contain symptoms of low mood, anxiety, affective shallowness.

The paranoia factor is characterized by paranoia, suspiciousness and paranoiac delusions.

The main symptoms of *affect lability* are pathological crying and laughing.

Explosivity/restlessness include symptoms of explosivity, irritability, restlessness, mental rigidity, obstinacy and anxiety.

The factor *psychomotor overactivity/euphoria* contains symptoms such as logorrhea, paraphasia, psychomotor overactivity, euphoria, affective bluntness and confabulation.

The symptoms and signs of the above-mentioned clusters are assessed by a psychiatrist at different stages of the disease and in patients of different ages at the intake interview. Thus, the symptoms and signs can be considered as an expression of three things: first, habitual personality; second, age-related changes in manifestation of the habitual personality; and third, as a strategy of dealing with the problem brought about by the disease.

Cerebral functioning

Regional cerebral blood flow technique was used to determine the cerebral functioning as to mean level and local deviations relative to the mean level using the 133 Xenon injection technique. The left hemisphere was measured in all patients with either eight or sixteen detectors. For detailed description of the measurement technique, see Risberg and Ingvar (1973) and Hagberg and Ingvar (1976). The wash-out of the isotope is approximately parallel to the functional properties of the respective regions of the brain at rest. The method is now being used in clinical practice for diagnostic purposes as well as for treatment evaluation.

A THREE-DIMENSIONAL VIEW OF DEMENTIA

Using these three dimensions or perspectives of dementia, we can combine information about the kind and degree of dementia (as expressed in cognitive decline with adaptive strategies as evaluated in a psychiatric interview) with information about the functioning of the left cerebral hemisphere as measured with rCBF. Unique patient profiles can be drawn up and the patient–staff relationship can be tailored accordingly. In Figure 2.2, p. 29, the dimensions discussed are brought together with an outcome which results in individualized care which enhances the patient's rehabilitation. The model is based on results from the Lund Longitudinal Dementia Study. References to previous publications are given in Figure 2.2.

In Figure 2.1, the cerebral icons sum up the level of cerebral functioning concerning the hemispheric mean (hatched area) and significant local deviation (single or double circles).

There are a number of observations that could be made about this categorization. First of all, in the more marked degrees of dementia, C4 and C5, we find no patients who combine the adaptive strategies of ixoidia, hypochondria, hysteria, depression and anxiety. In psychodynamic terminology, this could be understood in two ways. First, the so-called more mature adaptive strategies demand a higher competence than is represented

Psychiatric factors

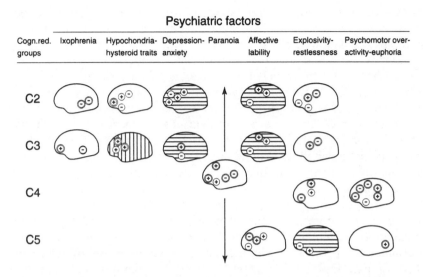

Cogn.red. groups	Ixophrenia	Hypochondria-hysteroid traits	Depression-anxiety	Paranoia	Affective lability	Explosivity-restlessness	Psychomotor over-activity-euphoria

Figure 2.1 Kind and degree of cognitive reduction, behaviour characteristics and functional level of the dominant hemisphere as measured by regional cerebral blood flow (rCBF). In rCBF, regional deviations from hemispheric mean are indicated by circles: marked/ moderate higher + / +, marked/moderate lower −/ −. Mean hemisphere reduction is indicated with striped areas.

in cognition groups C4 and C5, that is, a better adaptive ego-functioning. Zetzel (1970) formulated a similar interpretation in her study of the capacity for emotional growth. It is assumed that depressive forms of reaction require an ability to harbour conceptions and thoughts complex enough to form a content of the experience of depression. Of the depressive symptoms that Zetzel had in mind, it was primarily the emotional experience of guilt that had become attached to the original experience. This argument for conceptual complexity is most probably also true for other mature, adaptive strategies such as hysteria and hypochondria. Furthermore, these reactions are generated as the result of the conflict between opposing motives and desires. It is probable that for a dementia patient in group C4 or C5, many memories, ideas and earlier ambitions regarding life content and what could be expected out of life have been rejected and are no longer in conflict with what actually happens to the patient. Such an interpretation agrees with the usual observation among staff concerning patients in these groups. They indicate that as the dementia progresses, patients experience less suffering and come to appreciate a satisfying solution of the here-and-now situation as it relates to immediate care and services. This lack of concern with their previous life, family and friends is often a great disappointment to relatives when visiting, for the patient is no longer able to share in memories of the past.

Let us then consider the combination of moderate cognitive reduction, that is, C2 and C3 and ixoidia, hypochondria, hysteria and depressive symptoms in relation to rCBF. In patients with these forms of personality characteristics, we find a normal or moderately reduced mean hemisphere function (marked with striped or hatched area). The physiological measure of brain function is roughly parallel with the cognitive reduction (see also Hagberg and Ingvar, 1976). For the present discussion, however, the pertinent result is the shape of the hemispheric landscape. In four out of the six combinations, a relatively better or at least retained cerebral functioning is shown in the frontal and fronto-temporal areas. The results thus support an assumption that the frontal lobes play an important role for ego-functioning in general and in particular its adaptive regulating role. The 'landscapes' of a given area are calculated relative to the hemispheric mean. It seems more likely that it is the shape of the landscape in the frontal area, rather than the general level of hemispheric functioning, that determines the personality characteristics. It has been shown elsewhere (Hagberg and Ingvar, 1976) that a strong correlation exists between degree of cognitive decline and mean hemispheric functional level, while the specific kind of cognitive deficit was most often related to local post-central deviations in rCBF.

Let us then consider the right-hand side of the figure, where we find such reactions as affect lability, explosivity, hyperactivity and euphoria. Compared with the previously discussed characteristics, which might be termed adaptive, these have a somewhat acting-out quality about them. The results show that they exist on all levels of cognitive functioning, that is, in all C-groups. For the present discussion, again it is the shape of the landscape that is of interest. In six out of the nine combinations where there are patients to be observed, we find quite the contrary to the former combination, a frontal hypo-function. The results support the general hypothesis argued for here, that there is a correlation between the capacity of ego-functioning and frontal function of the brain. The more mature and adaptive function we find, the better frontal functioning and, in contrast, the more reduced frontal functioning the more primitive, acting-out behaviour is present.

The findings cannot be understood as if personality is localized in the frontal lobes of the brain, but frontal lobe functioning is an important pre-requisite for the maintenance of the maturity level and a continuity in the manifestation of personality, especially regarding the adaptive role of the ego. The interpretation of the frontal lobe dysfunction as a successive decline in ego-functioning is also in agreement with the staging of frontal lobe symptomatology as presented by Stuss and Benson (1984). The seemingly heterogeneous symptomatology in FLD can thus, from a psychodynamic perspective, coincide with a change in ego-capacity.

REHABILITATION AND CARE

Approaching the manifestation of dementia from a psychodynamic frame of reference has consequences for rehabilitation and for the care of the patient. Since there is no cure for the primary, degenerative dementias, rehabilitation and care become a matter of handling the progress of the disease in an optimal way both from the patient's perspective and with regard to staff and spouses.

In Figure 2.2, the main areas discussed so far are brought together with a focus on the staff/patient interaction. From left to right in the picture, we have diagnosis, type and degree of cognitive functioning, defensive reactions, dominant features and staff care-giving strategy. Based on the knowledge of primary and secondary symptomatology, it is obvious that the staff and the relatives, in their interaction with the patient, have to adopt different attitudes to the patient when carrying out various activity and training programmes. These are shown in the right-hand column. For a start, and as an aid to memory, we have called the attitudes like those of a coach, a mother and a father. This alludes to the traditional roles of mother and father as being emotional and instrumental respectively.

Looking at the figure, row by row, we find on the first row a dementia profile, which on the cognitive side is dominated by focal memory disturbance. It is our experience that an early multi-infarct dementia

COPING WITH DEMENTIA

Diagnosis		Cognitive function	Defensive reactions	Dominant feature	Staff care-giving strategy
MID/ CVD	C1	No cognitive reduction	Neurotic reactions	Multiple focalization Disorganization Maladaptation	Training Supporting Self-concept
	C2	Short-term memory reduction only	Depression–anxiety		
ALZ	C3	General intellectual reduction Retained verbal ability	Regression/projection Psychomotor over-activity	Lacking in understanding	Explaining Empathy
FLD	C4	General and verbal reduction Anomia and dyscalculia	Affective lability	Shortcomings in regulation and conative functions	Steering 'social supporting' and/or activation
	C5	General reduction with aphasia, apraxia and agnosia	Explosivity Restlessness		
		(Hagberg and Ingvar, 1976)	(Gustafson and Hagberg, 1975)	(Hagberg, 1986)	(Hagberg, 1990)

Figure 2.2 Coping with dementia: differential staff attitudes in caring for patients with different kinds and degrees of dementia.

often starts with the symptoms of the C1 or C2 categories, and that the adaptive strategies might be superimposed with neurotic, depressive and anxiety behaviour. The clinical picture is characterized predominantly by multiple cerebral lesions, disorganization of behaviour and adaptive difficulties. Staff care-giving strategy should emphasize mental, social and physical training, a supportive attitude, the building of self-concept and self-confidence, and motivational work, in order to optimize the total functioning of the patient. The attitude envisioned here comes close to what is generally called an ego-supportive type of psychotherapy, in which the activity programme is implanted. The approach is similar to that of coaching or training athletes or sportsmen, and hence this attitude is described as that of the coach.

In the second row, we find patients with simultaneous onset of memory and spatial disturbances. It is usual for SDAT to start with this combination of cognitive symptoms. Anxiety, regression, projection and restlessness are some of the characteristics of the way the problems are dealt with. Basically, the dominant feature seems to be a lack of understanding, both for what is happening around the patient and with the patient himself. Much of the anxiety and bewilderment arises from this lack of understanding. There are two key concepts for attitude here. First, repeated explanation to the patient of what is happening. When lack of understanding is combined with learning and episodic memory deficiencies, continued explanations of even trivial things to the patient become necessary. Second, an empathetic quality in relation to the patient is required, especially as verbal communication fades into aphasia and a great deal of the dialogue deals with intuitive understanding of the patient's intentions. In many ways the attitude has similarities with a mother's way of caring for an infant, especially before verbal communication has developed – hence the description of this attitude as 'mother' or 'mothering'. A good knowledge of the patient's own history is valuable both for empathetic understanding, but also for use in personal reminiscing to bolster the maintenance of the patient's identity (Birren and Deutchman, 1991; Hagberg, 1995).

The third row describes a patient with general and verbal cognitive reduction. This is where we eventually find the FLD patient, when the cognitive capacities start to decline. Adaptive capacities are lacking and the dominant features are inability to control and regulate behaviour, and sometimes also lack of drive to performance. Here the staff could best help the patient by adopting an attitude of external ego-function, that is, mediating between the patient's wishes and the environment. We have used the term 'social supporting' for this type of relationship, meaning both to steer, to evaluate and adapt behaviour, but also to activate when initiative is lacking. Verbal communication must be clear (univocal), attention must be paid to the difficulties in interpreting the patient's emotional reactions and the risk for aggressive outbursts. And most of all, patients should always be left with an opportunity to escape demands that go beyond their capacity to deal with. In a first attempt to name the appropriate attitude toward this patient, the name 'controller' was used. However, there were difficulties in using that term in staff education and the term 'father' has been substituted to draw attention to the instrumental quality of the relationship.

A differential attitude along these lines seems to give at least two advantages in rehabilitation and treatment of dementia patients. First, it will enable the patient to reach an optimal level of functioning within each level of disease. Second, it will increase job satisfaction among the staff in terms of understanding the patient and in terms of the results of this work. This progressive change in behaviour that characterizes the dementia patient requires a differential approach which staff and relatives can be taught with training and supervision. By and large a consciousness (awareness) of the unique qualities required in the relationship with the patients is a benefit for patients, staff and relatives.

Above and beyond the interactional and psychological aspect of the relationship between patient and staff, staff members also bring their ethical convictions to the meeting with the patient. This is often deeply rooted in a person as a way of life and must be respected. Most people who have been in contact with the dementia patient, have been confronted with the priorities: 'Do not harm the patient!' 'Keep the patient alive!' The problem is sometimes exemplified in the feeding of a hostile, negative patient in advanced stages of dementia who does not want to eat. It is hardly possible to keep the patient alive without feeding him, which is contrary to the patient's intentions but necessary for keeping the patient alive. The problem also occurs in many other caring situations, when patient and staff do not agree. For some staff members, 'Do not hurt the patient!' has priority over 'Keep the patient alive!' and for others the priority is reversed. The problem has been discussed by several researchers (for example, Åkerlund and Norberg, 1985) and a number of things have been suggested. First of all, it is stated that ethical attitudes have to be respected and dealt with accordingly. But it has also drawn attention to the recruitment of staff and their placement in different units within the caring system and for different patient categories. The problem has also highlighted the importance of continuous supervision for staff, and counselling for spouses individually or in groups, in order to handle the stress often experienced in caring for patients with advanced dementia. Most importantly, ongoing supervision serves as a safeguard against abuse when caring is given either by staff or by relatives (Grafström *et al.*, 1993).

THE LIFE-SPAN PERSPECTIVE

In a life-span perspective, ageing implies changes in many forms. There are purely biological changes such as weakening of muscle strength, shortness of breath, greying of hair, etc. There is also the onset of disease; many elderly people have between two or three different medical diagnoses. There is cognitive decline, as for example in benign forgetfulness or the onset of dementia, as well as changes in the social environment, such as retirement, the empty nest, etc. But there are also unique assets for the elderly in terms of life experiences. These are of immense value when handling changes brought about by ageing (Hagberg, 1995). In a life-span perspective, a general model can be created that includes type of change, individual characteristics, coping behaviour, adjustment in adaptation and the experience of quality of life (Hagberg, 1990). The model tries to explain the interaction between the ongoing variables. In this holistic life-span perspective model (see Figure 2.3), the changes brought about by the

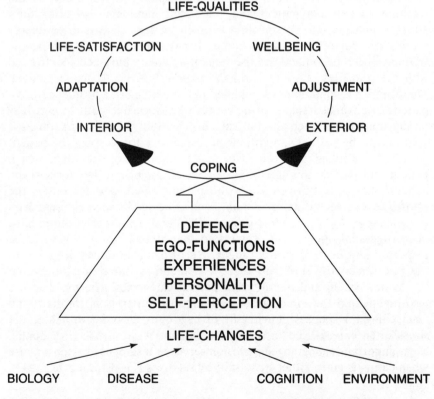

Figure 2.3 Coping in a life-span perspective: relating biological, medical, cognitive and environmental changes to life-quality as indicated by personality structure, preferred coping strategies and psychological attitude.

onset of dementia are assumed to be integrated by the patient through an adaptive process based mainly on previous learning and experience.

This can be understood as applying coping strategies of various kinds by which an optimal adaptation/adjustment is reached, the success of which will ultimately make a contribution to the experience of life satisfaction/ qualities. In addition to cognitive ability, this process is heavily dependent on personality-related factors such as ego-strength, defence mechanisms, neurotic behaviour, previous autobiographic experiences, and self-concept which to varying degrees has to be boosted by staff interventions using the different types of approaches described earlier. As the dementia progresses, the patient passes different stages with different competencies. The treatment is directed towards optimizing adaptation with the help of caring efforts from relatives and staff personnel, and to facilitating pharmacotherapy to have a positive effect. Let us consider for a moment one of the determinants of the model – previous experience in terms of life-history, life-review or autobiography. It contains the collected experience of a lifetime as remembered at any point in time. Being aware of his or her own life-story, if necessary supported by staff members and listened to by fellow elderly or patients, has been shown to enhance self-conceptualization and uphold the identity of the individual (Hagberg, 1995). Sharing these experiences between patient and staff is the best way to cope together with the problems that lie ahead as the dementia progresses. According to our experience, a reference frame of this kind greatly improves the patient's situation both in respect of his or her own well-being, as well as of the satisfaction of staff and of relatives' interaction with the patient. In a way, this model also tries to bring understanding to behaviour that otherwise would seem to be totally out of place when we do not know the patients' earlier experiences. It is also our experience that the quality of this interaction increases in significance as cognitive decline progresses. And finally, when the possibility of reaching the patients by way of instructions is lost, the attitude of the staff gained from a proper understanding becomes the essential therapeutic agent.

CONCLUSIONS

Most often psychological reactions from brain damage have been described as catastrophic reactions, indifferent reactions, protective reactions, compensatory reactions and other forms of defence manoeuvres against the patient's awareness of his or her disabilities and failures. Instead of stressing the reaction by the individual to brain damage, the viewpoint adopted here is that the person does not only react to damage but is affected by it in his capacity to organize and integrate new experience. It is also argued that the effects of cognitive impairment upon personality have consequences far beyond the immediate confrontation of disability and failure of a cognitive nature. Thus, there is reason to believe that changes in cognitive function vitally alter the balance within the psychic apparatus, which affects the organization of the total personality, especially the ego structures and their functional properties.

Such an approach in working with patients suffering from dementia would be advantageous. It would help to identify behaviour units of great enough complexity to be sensitive to an early change of behaviour – something which is necessary for early detection of the onset of dementia. From a rehabilitative point of view, it would make it possible to anticipate the progression of dementia using any developmental model, such as Erikson's model, Anna Freud's model of defence development, or Piaget's cognitive model, as well as Hartmann's and Rapaport's ego-developmental model. To be able to identify successive steps in decline also makes it possible to take supportive actions in order to lessen the impact in terms of regressive behaviour. It would also make rehabilitation work more specific and efficient because we know the phase-specific major problems in each developmental stage and know that rehabilitation and training must focus on those successive, emerging threat situations. Last, but not least, it would not only make the observed behaviour more comprehensible, but also make work with dementia patients more interesting for the caring personnel.

REFERENCES

Åkerlund, B. M. and Norberg, A. (1985) 'An ethical analysis of double find conflicts as experienced by care workers feeding severely demented patients'. *Int. J. Nurs. Stud.* 3: 207–216.

Birren, J. E. and Deutchman, D. E. (1991) *Guiding Autobiography Groups for Older Adults. Exploring the Fabric of Life.* Baltimore: The Johns Hopkins University Press.

Brun, A. (1987) 'Frontal lobe degeneration of non-Alzheimer type'. I. *Neuropathology. Arch. Gerontol. Geriatr.*, 6: 193–208.

——, Gustafson, L., Risberg, J., Hagberg, B., Johansson, A., Thulin, A.-K. and Englund, E. (1990) 'Clinicopathological correlates in dementia: A neuropathological, neuropsychiatric, neurophysiological and psychometric study'. In M. Bergener and S. I. Finkel (eds) *Clinical and Scientific Psychogeriatrics.* New York: Springer.

Freud, A. (1936) *The Ego and the Mechanisms of Defence.* New York: International Universities Press.

Grafström, M., Norberg, A. and Hagberg, B. (1993) 'Relationships between demented elderly and their caregivers. A follow-up study of caregivers to demented, previously reporting abuse when caring for their spouses and parents'. *Journal of Advanced Nursing*, 18.

Gustafson, L. and Hagberg, B. (1975) 'Emotional behaviour, personality changes and cognitive reduction in presenile dementia: related to regional cerebral blood flow'. *Acta Psychiatrica, Scand.*, suppl. 257: 39–68.

Hagberg, B. (1987) 'Behavior correlates to frontal lobe dysfunction'. *Arch. Gerontol. Geriatric* 6: 311–371.

—— (1990) 'Coping i ålderdomen – en begreppsmodell'. *Gerontologia* 4(2): 121–130.

—— (1994) 'Demenspatientens beteende i ett psykodynamiskt perspektiv'. In K. Engedahl (ed.) *Atferdsforstyrrelser ved aldersdemens. Norsk Alderspsykiatri.* Rapport 1.

—— (1995) 'The individual's life history as a formative experience to ageing'. In B. K. Haight and J. Webster (eds) *The Art and Science of Reminiscing: Theory and Practice.* Francis and Taylor.

—— and Gustafson, L. (1985) 'On diagnosis of dementia; psychometric investigation and clinical psychiatric evaluation in relation to verified diagnosis'. *Arch. Gerontol. Geriatric* 4: 321–332.

—— and Ingvar, D. H. (1976) 'Cognitive reduction in presenile dementia related to regional abnormalities of the cerebral blood flow'. *British Journal of Psychiatry* 128: 209–222.

Hartmann, H. (1939) *Ego Psychology and the Problem of Adaptation.* New York: International Universities Press.

—— (1947) 'On rational and irrational action'. In *Psychoanalysis and the Social Sciences*, 1, New York: International Universities Press.

—— (1964) *Essays on Ego Psychology.* New York: International Universities Press.

Johansson, A. and Hagberg, B. (1989) 'Psychometric characteristics in patients with frontal lobe degeneration of non-Alzheimer type'. *Arch. Gerontol. Geriatr.* 8: 129–137.

Johansson, A., Gustafson, L., Smith, G. J. W., Risberg, J., Hagberg, B. and Nilsson, B. (1990) 'Adaptation in different types of dementia and in normal elderly subjects'. *Dementia*, 1: 95–101.

Luria, A. R. (1980) *Higher Cortical Functions in Man* (2nd edn). New York: Basic Books Inc.

Mesulam, M. M. (1981) 'A cortical network for directed attention and unilateral neglect'. *Ann. Neurol.* 10: 309–325.

Rapaport, D. (1951) *Organization and Pathology of Thought.* New York: Columbia University Press.

—— (1960) *The Structure of Psychoanalytic Theory.* New York: International Universities Press.

—— (1967) *The Collected Papers of David Rapaport*, ed. M. M. Gill. New York: Basic Books.

Risberg, J. and Ingvar, D. H. (1973) 'Patterns of activation in the grey matter of the dominant hemisphere during memorizing and reasoning – a study of regional cerebral blood flow changes during psychological testing in a group of neurologically normal patients'. *Brain* 96: 737–756.

Stein, D. G., Brailowsky, S. and Will, B. (1995) *Brain Repair.* New York: Oxford University Press.

Stuss, D. T. and Benson, F. (1984) 'Neuropsychological studies of the frontal lobes'. *Psychological Bulletin* 1: 3–28.

—— and —— (1986) *The Frontal Lobes.* New York: Raven Press.

Stuss, D. T. and Gow, C. A. (1992) '"No longer gage": Frontal lobe dysfunction and emotional changes'. *Journal of Consulting and Clinical Psychology* 3: 349–359.

Vaillant, G. E. (1977) *Adaptation to Life.* Boston: Little Brown.

Zetzel, E. (1970) 'On the incapacity to bear depression'. In *The Capacity for Emotional Growth*, 82–114. London.

Chapter 3

Culture and dementia

Effects on care-givers and implications for services

Carole Cox

Many factors affect the ageing process and the ways in which society responds to the aged. Culture includes the beliefs, values and norms transmitted to people within a society. Passed on through generations, cultural ties and belief systems are important forces in shaping behaviours. As such, cultural norms are primary influences on social interactions and relationships as they dictate proper role behaviours and subsequent expectations. Individuals growing up in society are acculturated to the expectations of those around them.

Culture and ethnic ties remain important as persons age. Ethnic values determine the status of the elderly, their roles and expected behaviours. Consequently, traditional cultural values can support older persons in maintaining their self-concepts and integration in society.

However, the strength of culture is not immutable. Its power as a determinant of behaviours alters with generations, residence, socioeconomic status, language, and degree of assimilation (Gelfand and Fandetti, 1980). As individuals begin to live outside ethnic communities, the saliency of cultural beliefs often begins to weaken (Gelfand and Baressi, 1987). As persons confront the demands of living within culturally pluralistic societies, traditional values are often in conflict with those of the dominant society.

The impact of these conflicts can have an important bearing on the aged. As children begin to assimilate, their adherence to traditional values can subsequently alter. In addition, mobility, conflicting responsibilities, and economics can impact on intergenerational relationships. Norms of filial obligation and responsibility may therefore be threatened as their relevance to the lives of younger persons declines or as their ability to fulfil them becomes more difficult.

Certain factors, however, may sustain cultural values, particularly with regard to family roles and behaviours. Minority groups with histories of discrimination, inadequate services, and indifference also contribute to a reliance on family care. Distrust of institutions and formal services can strengthen what are perceived as 'traditional behaviours'. Thus, in populations which have been subjected to discrimination, the role of the family has remained strong. Discrimination reinforces reliance on the family as a primary source of support.

However, it is presumptuous to assume that families, even within these ethnic groups, are available to provide the assistance required by their frail relatives. Even when desiring to assist and to fulfil social expectations, they may lack resources to do so (Lockery, 1991). Moreover, with adult children frequently torn between meeting traditional expectations and other responsibilities, tension can develop in their relationships with their older relatives (Stanford et al., 1990). A frequent response to this tension is for the children to distance themselves from the older relative as a way of coping.

CULTURE AND DEMENTIA

As culture shapes perceptions and behaviours, it also shapes responses to cognitive impairments in the elderly. Data from a survey of dementia in ethnic communities indicates that it is often not recognized because of tendencies to regard the elderly's cognitive deficits and behavioural problems as being normal parts of ageing (US Congress, Office of Technology Assessment, 1990). Consequently, professional consultation and support may not be actively sought. Shame regarding the relative's behaviour and a stigma associated with mental illness can be further barriers to using formal services.

Families continue to provide the bulk of assistance and care offered to the elderly (Stone and Kemper, 1990). Moreover, in caring for the cognitively impaired, research findings indicate that families are even less likely to use formal services than those caring for the physically frail (Birkel and Jones, 1989).

Meeting the needs of relatives with dementia can cause particular strains on families. As the illness progresses, needs for supervision and assistance escalate. Care-givers' abilities to meet these needs may be sorely taxed as they attempt to juggle their own responsibilities with those of their older relatives. In addition, witnessing the gradual deterioration of a loved one can add to the stress encountered by these families. Adding to the burden that care-givers may experience is the combativeness and lack of gratitude often displayed by the patient.

Concern over not meeting expected obligations for care can cause further stress to care-givers. To the extent that they feel unable to meet care-giving needs and tasks they may experience guilt in that they are unable to fulfil expectations and roles. In addition, not fulfiling these roles may cause others to perceive them as deviant. Thus, the stronger the adherence of individuals to traditional cultural norms, the more likely they may be to experience stress when these norms are not being met.

Research on Hispanic care-givers of dementia patients (Cox and Monk, 1990) illustrates how cultural values and norms continue to govern familial relationships and the care of elderly relatives. The care-givers strongly adhered to norms of filial responsibility to their parents including the need to provide assistance and a reluctance to involve professional help with the care-giving. As measured on the CES-D scale, a self-reported instrument for measuring depression, these care-givers were very depressed. Moreover, this depression was more severe among those who adhered most strongly to norms of filial support and were most reluctant to use professional help.

The Hispanic care-givers appeared to accept the stresses associated with their care-giving as being a normal and expected part of the familial role. As such, they were unlikely to use support groups or seek counselling, feeling resigned to their burden. These findings suggest that cultural values and traditional norms may act as additional strains to care-givers particularly as they conflict with the use of formal services.

AFRICAN AMERICANS AND CARE-GIVING

Much has been written about the important role played by the family in African American culture. The extended family continues to be the primary source of support for the elderly, with the elderly themselves continuing to play important roles in the network. African Americans have been found to have high levels of kinship interaction and exchange (Mindel, 1980). Assistance is reciprocal between the generations with the elderly offering help with housing, babysitting, and maintaining emotional bonds, while children provide instrumental assistance. This kinship system serves its members most effectively as a source of mutual aid (Markides and Mindel, 1987).

Extensive research on the informal support systems of the African American elderly shows a pool of varied informal helpers that is not restricted to the immediate family (Gibson and Jackson, 1988). A major effect of this system, with its alternative supports, is that physical limitations are not likely to be as stressful to the elderly as they may be in other populations.

The network of elderly African Americans has been associated with low levels of education, income, occupational status, living in the South, and the willingness of the older relatives to take care of children (Mitchell and Register, 1984). This extended system increases the potential number of informal supports with kin and non-kin appearing to play varying roles in meeting the needs of the elderly. Kin are found to provide long-term, instrumental assistance based on an obligatory relationship while non-kin are more likely to provide socioemotional support and care for short-term needs (Taylor and Chatters, 1986). If formal help is used it tends to complement that provided by the family with the latter remaining responsible for the home and personal care (Mindel *et al.*, 1986).

When children are unavailable to assist the elderly, other relatives, particularly siblings, often provide care. In addition, elderly African Americans receive more support than other groups of elderly from a wider social network including church members and neighbours (George, 1988; Ralston, 1984). The type, amount, and frequency of help is on a sliding scale, with increases in disability contributing to increases in the number of available helpers and increased contacts depending on the proximity of the family (Johnson *et al.*, 1990).

Data from the Long Term Care and National Survey of Informal Care-givers were examined by White-Means and Thornton (1990) to determine how ethnicity may affect informal care to the elderly. The results indicated that the Afro-American care-givers spent more time care-giving and that the amount of time was determined by the availability of substitute care-givers and the functional status of the relative. The only factor constraining the care-giving hours provided by the Afro-American care-givers was full-time employment.

However, the capacity of the family to aid the African American elderly should not be overestimated. In a study of the support systems of poor inner-city African Americans, Johnson and Baher (1990) found that adult children, even when close to their elderly parents, often did not provide instrumental support because of strains and distractions in their own lives. Moreover, many elderly resisted being dependent on their children, preferring instead to use formal services such as home help and chore workers rather than being another distraction in their children's lives.

It is essential that the viability of the support network be viewed within the reality of the competing demands and pressures placed on the primary family care-givers, African American women (Gratton and Wilson, 1988). In addition, many elderly frequently have no immediate family living within their state and therefore depend upon more distant relations, friends, or church members for assistance (Gibson and Jackson, 1988).

Finally, the development and patterns of the informal networks need to be understood as historical responses to years of poor care, social inequities, and injustices (Belgrave, Wykle and Choi, 1993). Consequently, any perceived preference towards informal care must be viewed not necessarily as an immutable cultural value, but instead as a reaction to an often inaccessible formal system.

CARE-GIVING FOR DEMENTIA RELATIVES

Studies on the impact of caring for a dementia relative by African American care-givers remain scarce. However, research findings suggest that cultural values and norms continue to influence the care-giving experience.

In a study of the desire to institutionalize the Alzheimer patient, Morycz (1985) found that African American care-givers experienced an amount of strain equal to that of other ethnic groups but that this strain, unlike that experienced by white care-givers, did not predict a desire to institution- alize. Moreover, strain in the African American sample was not related to the availability of supports as it was in the white sample. Instead, it was associated with the increased expenses of care-giving.

In a subsequent study of variations in care-giving responses to Alzheimer patients, Morycz *et al.* (1987) found that among African American adult children, burden was related to the functional incapacity of the parents to perform the activities of daily living, with women report- ing more burden than men. However, among husbands caring for wives with Alzheimer's disease, their own health problems, rather than the functional status of the wives, were the strongest predictors of burden. No significant predictors of burden were found for wives caring for husbands. Institutionalization of the relative was most likely to be sought by wives when they felt a lack of both emotional and instrumental support, while no significant predictors of institutionalization for husbands caring for wives were identified.

The ability of these care-givers to cope has been at least partially attributed to strong informal support systems and to their own feelings of competency (Nierderhe and Fruge, 1984; Morris, Morris and Britton, 1989). The impact that these factors may have on care-giver well-being is further suggested by findings which show that when care-givers do turn to formal services, they commonly seek help with improving their coping skills, meeting the elder's needs, responding to family issues, concern over relationships, eliciting formal and informal supports, and resolving feelings of inadequacy and guilt (Smith, Smith and Toseland, 1991).

In the research described here, the roles of informal supports and cultural values in the care-giving relationship and on the subsequent well- being and needs of African American and white care-givers of dementia relatives were explored. The conceptual model providing the framework for this study perceives care-giver stress as a function of four domains: the care-giving background or context, the stressors, mediators of stress, and the outcomes (Pearlin *et al.*, 1990). In this study, background characteris- tics include the ages of the patient and care-givers, education, hours a week spent care-giving, and income. The stressors are the patient status and the demands on the care-giver while the mediators are care-giver supports and coping abilities. The outcome variables included depression, relationship strains, and activity restriction.

Particular attention in the study was given to the roles of the potential mediators, informal supports and competency, in the two groups. An underlying research question was to determine if the roles of these media- tors varied between the two groups. Furthermore, with much research attesting to the strong supportive systems of the African American elderly, the research was interested in examining if these systems were more protective of the African American care-givers than of a comparable group of white care-givers.

DESCRIPTION OF THE SAMPLES

The majority, 84 per cent, of both sets of care-givers was female, and of similar ages, 53 years for the African American and 56 years for the whites. Approximately one quarter of each were college graduates. The two groups were also comparable in their income status with the median between $16,000 and $25,000 per year. Although more African American (45 per cent) than white care-givers (30 per cent) worked full-time, the actual hours of weekly employment were comparable between the groups.

Both African American and white patients were moderately cognitively impaired, had moderate levels of disruptive behaviour and poor social functioning. Both groups required some assistance with the activities of daily living but were not totally dependent. Care-givers in both groups reported depressive symptomatology, feeling severely strained in their relationships, and being limited in their activities.

A striking difference between the groups of care-givers was found in their relationships to the patients. In each group the largest proportion of care-givers was adult daughters, 49 per cent of the African Americans and 50 per cent of the whites. However, the African American care-givers were composed of significantly ($p < .01$) fewer spouses while containing a more diverse set of extended relatives.

Even with these widely disparate relationships, the two sets of care-givers did not differ in the hours per week spent in care-giving – approximately 100 hours for the African American and 112 hours for the white sample. A slightly higher proportion of the African American group, 34 per cent, as compared to 26 per cent of the whites, was caring for someone in addition to the patient.

The informal network, predominantly children and other relatives, was the main source of assistance to the care-givers. Moreover, although the majority in each expressed feelings of filial responsibility, among the African American care-givers these feelings were significantly ($p < .01$) stronger. Thus, it is not surprising that the African American care-givers received significantly ($p < .01$) more hours of informal help than the white care-givers – 22 hours per week as compared to 14 hours. However, approximately one quarter of each group of care-givers received no help from either relatives or friends.

It is important to note also that even with this instrumental help the African American care-givers were somewhat less satisfied with this assistance and felt a significantly ($p < .01$) greater need for more assistance.

Evidence of the disappointment in the supports is also given by the finding that 90 per cent of the African Americans and 78 per cent of the whites felt that no one really understood their problems.

The two groups of care-givers differed significantly (p < .05) with regard to the persons with whom they had discussed the patient. Although both were likely to have discussed their relative with other relatives and with the physician, African Americans were more likely to have also discussed their relative with the clergy (p < .01) and their friends (p < .05). Most care-givers – 76 per cent of the African Americans and 78 per cent of the whites – felt fairly competent in their own care-giving abilities.

REGRESSION ANALYSIS

Further analysis, through the use of hierarchical regression, helped to specify the factors contributing to depression, relationship strain and activity restriction in each group of care-givers. The variables selected for inclusion were those found to be significant in earlier bivariate analysis with the first set being background characteristics, the second set the stressors, and the third set the mediators.

The background characteristics, care-giver age and hours a week care-giving, had no noticeable effect on depressive symptoms in the African American sample. Within the white group, the hours a week spent in caring significantly contributed to depression.

An important difference was found between the two groups with the introduction of the second set of variables, the stressors. The status of the patient did not affect the African American care-givers. However, among the white sample, two of the predictors, disruptive behaviour (p < .01) and cognitive status (p < .01) had significant effects and contributed to a significant change in the adjusted explained variance (r^2 – change = .38; p < .001).

The mediating variables had noticeably different effects on the two groups. A feeling of not being understood by others and feeling incompetent were predictive of depressive symptoms among the African Americans, contributing to a significant change in the adjusted variance (r^2 – change = .31; p < .001). At the same time, the mediators had no impact on depression in the white group.

Younger age among the African American care-givers significantly contributed to their feelings of relationship strain. The background characteristics did not contribute to strain among the white care-givers. With the stressors added to the equations, only one, disruptive behaviour by the white patients, significantly contributed to care-giver strain (p < .01), resulting in a significant change in the explained variance (r^2 – change = .31; p < .001). The stressors did not affect the strain in the African Americans.

The most important variable in predicting strain for the African American sample was their sense of incompetency (p < .0001) in coping with their relative, which significantly affected the change in the adjusted variance (p < .05). The mediating variables had no impact on relationship strain among white care-givers.

The examination of the factors predicting activity restriction also revealed disparities between the two groups. The background character-istics did not affect restriction among the African Americans. The hours a week spent in care-giving contributed to restriction within the white group (p < .05) resulting in a significant adjusted variance (r^2 – change = .18; p < .01).

In both samples, patient status contributed to activity restrictions although the particular predictors varied. Within the African American group, restricted activities were largely due to the functional status of the patient (p < .01) which significantly affected the adjusted variance (r^2 – change = .23; p < .0001). Within the white sample, care-givers were most affected by the disruptive behaviour of the patient (p < .05).

Within the African American sample, a lack of understanding by others contributed to activity restriction (p < .01), resulting in a significant change in the adjusted variance (r^2 – change =.15; p < .01). As with the other outcome measures, the mediating variables had no impact on the white care-givers.

PREDICTING NEED FOR ASSISTANCE

As the study was also interested in learning what factors were associated with a need for more assistance in the two groups, variables which were significantly related to this need in a bivariate analysis were entered into a regression analysis in order to identify the importance of each potential predictor.

Two of the background characteristics, a feeling by the care-givers that others did not understand their problems and self-perceived incompetence in dealing with the patient significantly predicted a need for assistance. However, after controlling these factors, the strongest predictor of this need was being an African American. Together, these variables explained 0.16 per cent of the variance (p < .008).

DISCUSSION

The findings of this study reveal many similarities, but also important differences, between African American and white non-minority care-givers of dementia patients seeking assistance. Care-givers in both groups are contacting the formal Alzheimer's Associations when the patients have at least moderate impairment. Both groups at the time of contact are also experiencing comparable levels of stress. At the same time, each group has a rather extensive care-giver history with substantial involvement as indicated by the hours a week spent in care-giving tasks.

Consistent with other studies of care-givers using Alzheimer's services (Chenoweth and Spencer, 1986), both sets of care-givers are well-educated and middle-class. The diverse relationships of the African American care-givers are also reflective of the extended patterns of informal support networks described in other research.

Based on the model underlying this study, the results indicate that the factors contributing to care-giver stress vary substantially between the two samples. The role played by the potential mediators is particularly intriguing. Although neither group felt that others understood their concerns, this dissatisfaction with the emotional support had a significant impact only among the African American care-givers, who actually received more hours of informal assistance.

Difficulties with informal supports by African Americans have been reported in other studies of care-giver well-being (Cox, 1993). In a study of hospitalized dementia patients, African American care-givers were significantly less satisfied than white care-givers with the assistance provided by their relatives and with the quality of these informal relationships.

This dissatisfaction may be partially explained by the fact that as African American care-givers maintain stronger adherence to norms of filial responsibility, they also have greater expectations of their supportive networks. The assistance that these supports provide may suffice in the normal course of care-giving but may not be sufficient to meet the demands of a dementia patient. Thus, when support needs are perceived as being insufficient, regardless of the number of hours of instrumental assistance, care-giver well-being may be affected. From this perspective, it is not surprising that this group experiences a greater sense of disappointment and need for assistance than their white counterparts. Supports, rather than acting as buffers to stress, may actually exacerbate it in as much as they fail to meet care-giver expectations.

The fact that competency was a significant predictor of stress only within the African American sample may also stem from cultural variations associated with filial responsibility. Given their stronger adherence to cultural values which prescribe care for the elderly, African American care-givers may be increasingly susceptible to stress when they feel unable to meet these responsibilities. As the patient's needs increase, the sense of incompetency may also increase, magnifying this stress. Again, rather than acting as a buffer in the care-giver process, cultural expectations may act to exacerbate the stress.

In contrast to the African American sample, stress in the white care-givers was not affected by the mediating variables. Most of the change in care-giver stress in the white sample can be attributed to the functional and cognitive status and to the hours a week spent in care-giving. It would appear that when these care-givers seek formal assistance, they have accepted the extent of involvement of their informal supports as well as their own degree of competency.

The strong influence that informal relationships have on the status of the African American care-givers implies that interventions which assist in strengthening these networks may be warranted. Helping care-givers to express their needs as well as their disappointments to their relatives may help to strengthen these networks and thus assist in reducing the stress experienced by the care-giver. Moreover, in light of the active instrumental involvement that these informal supports provide, counselling regarding the nature of the illness and the needs and limitations of the care-giver may be most effective if it encompasses several family members rather than just the primary care-giver.

The sensitivity to competence issues experienced by the African American care-givers suggests that they may benefit from specific interventions designed to enhance their skills and coping mechanisms. At the same time, counsellors should help them to understand and accept their limitations as care-givers. Without this type of intervention, they may remain vulnerable to stress resulting from perceived failures in meeting cultural expectations.

White care-givers seeking assistance may benefit most from interventions which teach them how to cope with specific behaviours of their relatives. Although competency was not a predictor of stress, the problems encountered with managing the behaviour of the patient and dealing with cognitive impairment imply that programmes which strengthen their coping skills can be particularly worthwhile. Individual and group interventions which enable them to express their limitations, receive support, and learn specific techniques from others may be most effective. In addition, their stress may also be alleviated by increased assistance in caring for the patient. Respite care, whether formal or informal, could offer significant relief.

The African Americans' greater propensity for discussing the relative with the clergy as well as with friends is further evidence of their interest in both obtaining support and increasing their coping abilities. Consequently, providing information about the illness and strengthening care-giving skills may be important in empowering these care-givers and decreasing the need for both informal and formal services.

SUMMARY

Cultural values continue to be important influences in care-giving relationships as they can affect behaviours, expectations, and well-being of care-givers. For many groups, particularly minority populations, these traditional values continue to act as salient forces as they underlie the nature of relationships as well as individuals' own self-concepts. However, the importance of these values may diminish among non-minority groups who do not share the same histories of discrimination and have therefore not relied so strongly on informal supports.

Understanding the nature of the stress experienced by diverse cultural groups and incorporating ethnic values into the design of services are pre-requisites for meeting care-giver needs. Without such understanding, sensitive and appropriate services cannot be offered and those most in need may continue to remain neglected by the service systems.

REFERENCES

Belgrave, L., Wykle, M. and Choi, J. (1993) 'Health, double jeopardy, and culture: The use of institutionalization by African-Americans', *The Gerontologist* 33: 379–385.

Birkel, R. and Jones, C. (1989) 'A comparison of the caregiving networks of dependent elderly individuals who are lucid and those who are demented', *The Gerontologist* 29: 114–120.

Chenoweth, B. and Spencer, B. (1986) 'Dementia: The experience of family care-givers', *The Gerontologist* 26: 114–120.

Cox, C. (1993) *Factors Associated with the Discharge Dispositions of Hospitalized Dementia Patients*, Final Report to the AARP Andrus Foundation, Washington, DC.

—— and Gelfand, D. (1987) 'Familial assistance, exchange, and satisfaction among Hispanic, Portuguese, and Vietnamese elderly', *Journal of Cross-Cultural Gerontology* 2: 241–255.

—— and Monk, A. (1990) 'Minority caregivers of dementia victims: a comparison of black and Hispanic families', *Journal of Applied Gerontology* 9: 340–354.

Gelfand, D. and Baressi, C. (1987) 'Current perspectives in ethnicity and aging'. In D. Gelfand and C. Baressi (eds) *Ethnic Dimensions of Aging*. New York: Springer.

—— and Fandetti, D. (1980) 'Suburban and urban white ethnics: attitudes towards care of the elderly', *The Geronotologist* 20: 588–594.

George, L. (1988) 'Social participation in later life'. In J. Jackson (ed.) *The Black American Elderly*. New York: Springer.

Gibson, R. and Jackson, J. (1988) 'The health, physical functioning, and informal supports of the African-American elderly', *Milbank Quarterly* 65 (Supplement 2): 421–454.

Gratton, B. and Wilson, V. (1988) 'Family support systems and the minority elderly: A cautionary analysis', *Journal of Gerontological Social Work* 13: 81–93.

Johnson, C. and Baher, B. (1990) 'Family networks among older inner-city African Americans', *The Gerontologist* 30: 726–733.

Johnson, H., Gibson, R. and Luckey, I. (1990) 'Health and social characteristics: Implications for services'. In Z. Harel, E. McKinney and M. Williams (eds) *African American Aged: Understanding Diversity*, Newbury Park: Sage.

Lockery, S. (1991) 'Caregiving among racial and ethnic minority elders: Family and social supports'. *Generations*, Fall/Winter, 58–63.

Markides, K. and Mindel, C. (1987) *Aging and Ethnicity*. Newbury Park: Sage.

Mindel, C. (1980) 'Extended familialism among urban Mexican Americans, Anglo, and Black Americans', *Hispanic Journal of Behavioral Sciences* 2: 21–34.

——, Wright, R. and Starrett, R. (1986) 'Informal and formal health and social support systems of black and white elderly'. *The Gerontologist* 26: 279–285.

Mitchell, J. and Register, J. (1984) 'An exploration of family interaction with the elderly by race, socioeconomic status, and residence', *The Gerontologist* 24: 48–54.

Morris, L., Morris, R. and Britton, P. (1989) 'Social support networks and formal support as factors influencing the psychological adjustment of spouse caregivers of dementia sufferers', *International Journal of Geriatric Psychiatry* 4: 47–51.

Morycz, R. (1985) 'Caregiver strain and the desire to institutionalize family members with Alzheimer's disease', *Research on Aging* 7: 329–361.

——, Malloy, J., Bozich, M. and Martz, P. (1987) 'Racial differences in family burden: clinical implications for social work', *Journal of Gerontological Social Work* 10: 133–155.

Nierderhe, G. and Fruge, E. (1984) 'Dementia and family dynamics: Clinical research issues', *Journal of Geriatric Psychiatry* 17: 21–56.

Pearlin, L., Mullan, J., Semple, S. and Skaff, M. (1990) 'Caregiving and the stress process: An overview of concepts and their measures', *The Gerontologist* 30: 583–594.

Ralston, P. (1984) 'Senior center utilization by black elderly adults: Social, attitudinal, and knowledge correlations', *Journal of Gerontology* 39: 224–229.

Smith, G., Smith, M. and Toseland, R. (1991) 'Problems identified by family caregivers in counselling', *The Gerontologist* 31: 15–22.

Stanford, E., Peddecord, K. and Lockery, S. (1990) 'Variations among the elderly in African American, Hispanic, and White families'. In T. Brubaker (ed.) *Family Relationships in Later Life*. Newbury Park: Sage.

Stone, R. and Kemper, P. (1990) 'Spouses and children of disabled elders: How large a constituency for long term care reform', *The Milbank Quarterly* 67: 485–506.

Taylor, R. and Chatters, L. (1986) 'Patterns of informal support to elderly black adults: family, friends, and church members', *Social Work*: 432–438.

US Congress, Office of Technology Assessment (1990) *Confused Minds, Burdened Families: Finding Help for Alzheimer's Disease and Other Dementias*, OTA-BA-403, Washington DC: US Government Printing Office.

White-Means, S. (1993) 'Informal home care for the frail Black elderly', *Journal of Applied Gerontology* 12: 18–33.

—— and Thornton, M. (1990) 'Ethnic differences in the production of informal home health care', *The Gerontologist* 30: 758-776.

Chapter 4

Memory, emotion and dementia

Marie Mills

INTRODUCTION

The issue of failing memory within the dementias appears to be the locus of loss and torment for sufferers and carers alike. In more recent years, this area of concern has been positively addressed by theoreticians and/or practitioners (Feil, 1985, 1992; Jones and Burns, 1992; Kitwood, 1990a, 1990b; Kitwood and Bredin, 1992; Miesen, 1992; Woods *et al.*, 1992). Their work, and others, has led to a variety of interventions designed to restore personhood and well-being in those older members of our society who live in the bewildering world of dementia.

These interventions, however, do not fully address the underpinning theoretical concepts inherent in their application. It is hypothesized that it is the relationship between memory, emotion and dementia which largely generates and supports the therapeutic process. However, our understanding of the phenomena involved in this tripartite relationship remains limited. Emotions, themselves, have been largely disregarded in scientific investigations, yet they have been an essential part of human beings throughout their long evolutionary history.

THE EMOTIONS

Humans share an emotional heritage with other animals (Darwin, 1872). At present there are over a hundred theories on emotion (Thompson, 1988). Some emotion theorists regard emotions as numerous and varied social constructs that owe their existence to the influence of culture, social experience, and learning (Averill, 1986; Harré, 1986). Other theorists regard them as psycho-evolutionary and fundamental to all human beings (Izard, 1991; Plutchik, 1980). The phylogeny and ontogeny of emotions would indicate that emotions have evolved because of their adaptive functions in the instinct for survival, which is the basis for all aspects of human behaviour (Darwin, 1872). It is the strength of this instinct which forms part of psychoanalytic theory (Freud, 1920), and which suggests that survival and the emotions are intertwined.

The psycho-evolutionary perspective states that emotions are fundamental and derived through evolutionary–biological processes (Izard, 1991;
Plutchik, 1980; Tomkins, 1981). Moreover, it is suggested that emotions,
in evolutionary terms, emerged prior to increased cognition (Tomkins,
1981). It is further argued that fundamental emotions have a distinct and
specific feeling that achieves awareness. The fundamental emotions that
meet these, and other criteria, are interest, enjoyment, surprise, sadness,
anger, disgust, contempt, fear, shame and guilt (Izard, 1991). If this theory
is correct, it is these emotions which should be found to exist in older people
with dementia.

Theoretical arguments suggest that dementia sufferers have a rich and
powerful emotional life (Kitwood, 1993). Moreover, it is suggested that
these emotions are not merely labile, but recognizable states that seemingly
correspond to present experiences and events (Mills and Walker, 1994).
However, much of the literature associates dementia with emotional problems. These include disinhibition and blunting of emotions, together with a
lability of emotions and lack of self-control (Bromley, 1990; Williams,
1987). Kitwood and Bredin (1992) suggest that many of the behaviours seen
in older people with dementia, which include emotional issues, are more
of a problem for their non-demented carers and others. Further, they
perceive sufferers of dementia as being 'generally more authentic' about
their emotions.

This neurophysiological–biological aspect of emotions allows some
understanding of the phenomena. Emotions do not rest unobserved within
brain structures and processes. They express themselves through our
actions and our felt experiences. Emotions can be seen as feeling states,
that allow us to exist in a state of well-being or ill-being. They colour our
perceptions, influence our reactions and our behaviours. 'Emotions are
with us always from the moment of birth until death' (Izard, 1991: 13).

COGNITION AND EMOTION

In recent years there has been a move within cognitive psychology to
theorize possible links between cognition and emotion. It is suggested that
emotional nodes in memory structures, connected to cognitive structures,
will be 'triggered' by similar emotional stimuli such as mood (Gilligan and
Bower, 1984). Other theorists posit the concept of interrelated/intertwined
systems of cognition and emotion (Singer, 1973, 1974), which, in some
instances, will allow emotional processes to function independently (Izard,
1984, 1991; Leventhal, 1984; Tomkins, 1962, 1981). Thus, within cognitive
psychology, there is an embryonic framework that links thinking to feelings
(Averill, 1986; Buck, 1988; Lazarus, 1982; Williams *et al.*, 1988). This
framework includes the relationship between mood and memory, and the
establishment of cognitive approaches in emotional disorders. There is,

therefore, within the cognitive school of thought, a posited association between memory and emotion (Baddeley, 1990; Bower, 1981; Bower and Cohen, 1982; Gilligan and Bower, 1984; Leventhal, 1984; Williams *et al.*, 1988).

EMOTION AND MEMORY

Studies suggest that autobiographical memories are closely intertwined with knowledge of emotion (Conway, 1990). Further, Brewer (1986) argues that all autobiographical memory is memory of information relating to the self. Bromley (1990: 233) also perceives autobiographical memories as strongly associated with emotional significance which have been organized into schema, in ways that permit ready access.

MEMORY, EMOTION AND DEMENTIA

This posited association between memory and emotion plays a significant part in the study of failing memory within dementia. Theoretical considerations have given some understanding to the notion that emotions are the 'fuel' that drives and supports humans to endure as physical and psychological beings. It is suggested, therefore, that emotions are strongly present within states of dementia, with their role becoming even more robust as cognitive abilities fade away.

A study of a small group of older people with dementia suggested that all who took part had many meaningful emotional memories available for recall. Their memories of past events held both personal significance and emotional intensity. This study was, however, small and took place over a period of three months (Mills, 1991). It was decided to investigate these phenomena in further detail. A larger study was undertaken which was designed to take place over a twelve- to eighteen-month timespan, with an increased number of participants.

METHOD

The setting

The study was conducted in a psychogeriatric day hospital situated on the outskirts of a small rural city in England. The setting cared for between twenty and twenty-five clients each day, drawn from a total client population of forty older people. All clients who attended the setting had some type of medically diagnosed dementia. Eight participants were selected from the total client group of nineteen women and twenty-one men, by the nurse in charge of the day hospital. The only criteria for selection was that the people asked to take part would be able to speak and would enjoy the experience of recalling their past lives on an individual basis.

Ethical considerations

Permission to undertake this study was given by the relatives of the participants, the hospital consultant and the nursing staff in the setting. Permission was also sought and obtained from the district ethics committee. All participants were also asked if they would like to take part. Although all agreed, permission was still asked of each, prior to commencement of each interview.

The sample

The group comprised two females and six males, aged between 65 and 85 years of age. At the commencement of the study, all participants, bar one, were living in the community with their spouses. The decision to use eight participants was not fixed at the commencement of the study as I was not sure how many participants could be managed at any one time. However, as the number of individuals grew to eight, this was felt to be an appropriate total, given the demands made by this type of inquiry on the interviewer and the setting.

Five of the participants, Mrs Abigail Woodley, Mr Ronnie Silverthorne, Mrs Bessie Pinks, Mr Robert Biddley, and Mr Melvin Rider, had severely impaired memories. Further, both Mr Ronnie Silverthorne and Mr Melvin Rider had severe speech impediments due to their illness. None of these five participants could ever recall my name, but all of them began to recognize me visually and would greet me with pleasure when I arrived in the interview setting. The remainder of the group, who had less impaired recall, were Mr Andrew Coxley, Mr Hugh Raft and Mr Charles Clerkenwell.

The methodology

The main methodology used during this study was the single case-study approach (Bromley, 1986, 1990; Runyan, 1982; Yin, 1989). This was deemed to be the most suitable method which would allow a close examination of participants' recollections of their past lives. All data were presented in the form of an individual story or case-study on each participant, using their actual conversations as the main focus of the report.

Method of data collection

Participants were seen at regular intervals of one to two weeks between April 1992 and January 1994. Most interviews were recorded on a small battery-operated dictaphone and subsequently transcribed. It was not possible to record all interviews, but the number of recorded and transcribed interviews with individuals ranged from thirteen to twenty-six, giving a total number of 141.

The approach used throughout the study

As with the pilot study, all participants were asked to recall their past memories with the aid of interviewer counselling skills. The use of this psychotherapeutic intervention has been a subject of some interest within dementia care (Gardner, 1993; Goudie and Stokes, 1989; Hausman, 1992; Mills and Coleman, 1994; Sinason, 1992). The approach used was based on Rogerian principles in which the use of active listening, empathy and unconditional positive regard played an active part. It is this type of approach which, suggests Tobin (1991), enables the past to be made vivid.

Analysis of data

Transcripts of the interviews were subjected to analysis using grounded theory, in which common emergent categories and themes were identified (Glaser and Strauss, 1967). All participants managed to recall emotional memories of the past. Further, exploration of the emotions, which were part of these memories, often encouraged additional recall. As the collection, organization and analysis proceeded, it gradually became apparent that all participants were giving fragments of information about themselves. Over time, these snippets of information began to cohere into parts of whole stories. All participants were actually recalling their own life-stories or their personal narratives. These stories of the self were often richly emotional and deeply meaningful.

Therapeutic considerations of the findings

The findings suggested both therapeutic and theoretical implications within dementia care. Prior to a later and more detailed discussion of the theoretical considerations, it is proposed to examine the therapeutic aspects of the findings both from a general and individual perspective as this is of some importance to sufferers of dementia and their care-givers.

General indications of well-being

An examination of the findings indicated that all participants experienced increased levels of well-being, albeit to varying degrees. The process of ageing, apart from dementia, is accompanied by many potential losses. All had stories of loss and grief, yet the recalling of these experiences did not produce overwhelming sorrow. Rather, participants spoke of their deeply felt and wounding experiences with great sadness and occasional anger.

Not all stories were sad stories. There were many that were joyous and nostalgic. They were often humorous. All participants loved to laugh. The interviews were frequently full of laughter, although grief and tears were often present.

Personal indications of well-being

Mr Clerkenwell, who had been a Japanese prisoner-of-war in Changi, was able to talk of his brutal experiences in some depth. Other griefs also emerged, but were accompanied by a sense of release. This was also a finding from the pilot study (Mills, 1993). Mr Coxley, too, spoke of his feelings of loss, but also of his love of the land. His days as a farm worker remained clearly in his mind and he happily recounted stories of this time. Mrs Bessie Pinks enjoyed the social aspects of the interviews. She found pleasure in talking to others and liked to find people who would 'chat along'.

At the beginning of the interviews, Mr Raft, who was mildly confused, was a deeply unhappy man. He told stories of an appalling childhood and of the miseries of his present life, but the telling of these times appeared to be cathartic. At the conclusion of the interviews he appeared to be a much happier person. Even participants who were more damaged by their illness found increased levels of well-being in a surprising manner.

Mrs Woodley, who was a very quiet and introspective person, eventually spoke of her troubled relationship with her mother. She saw herself as a very unworthy person, but, over time, this changed. She gradually began to develop more self-confidence and to feel a happier person. She laughed a lot more and began to initiate conversations with other clients in the study. These behaviours continued to be evident for some time after the conclusion of the study.

Others enjoyed speaking of their past achievements. Mr Silverthorne was able to recall his days as a manager in charge of a large workforce, together with the power and responsibility that accompanied this role. Although he said that 'those days had gone from glory now', he was still able to speak of the pleasure and pride he felt when members of his former staff team greeted him in the street. Yet another participant, Mr Rider, who was in the later stages of his illness, could recall some of his past academic achievements. 'Good, good days', he said.

The final member of the group

The eighth participant was Mr Robert Biddley whose narrative will be discussed in more depth. In many respects, he was not the most 'successful' participant, in that he did not retain well-being for long periods throughout the study, but he does give some indication of the general results. Further, a theoretical argument is strengthened if supported by its weakest results. Space precludes recounting his stories in their entirety, but it is intended to discuss a small number of themes, and to observe their content during the process of the interviews.

CASE-STUDY: MR ROBERT BIDDLEY (RB)

Background information

RB was seen between May 1992 and August 1993. He was a small, dark-haired, 66-year-old man who looked well dressed and very fit. He wore an ornate signet ring on the little finger of his right hand. At the first meeting, he appeared to have a pleasant and friendly personality with good social skills. RB had been recently admitted to a local authority home for the elderly. He had never married and he lived alone. Although at the commencement of the study he was diagnosed as having moderate dementia, clinical studies suggested that his age would hasten the progress of this illness. RB's condition did appear to deteriorate with a greater swiftness, compared to other older participants. This is indicated by the fewer interviews in this case-study. There was a total of thirteen recorded interviews with RB, although we met more frequently than this would suggest. He willingly agreed to be interviewed on a regular basis. He said he liked to be of help whenever possible.

RB had emotional memories available for recall, but did not appear to find it easy to disclose deep feelings. It is suggested that not all elderly people will wish to reminisce (Coleman, 1986). Equally, perhaps not all older people with dementia will wish to disclose deep and possibly painful feelings. The use of a psychotherapeutic approach, however, appeared to enable him to recall and repeat his stories in some detail.

The commencement of the interviews

During our first meeting RB chose to be interviewed in the empty dining room of the setting. When we were seated, I asked him if he would prefer to be addressed by his title or his Christian name. 'Oh call me Bob', he said. 'Everyone calls me Bob.' He had some clear memories of the past and recalled aspects of his childhood:

RB   I didn't want to get married. I'm one of seven children and that makes a big difference as well, doesn't it?

RB   What being . . . um one of seven children. . . . You're not going to get a lot given you. So you've got to get what you can! And that's it!

Memories of his mother were important. He said her name was Alice and it was her ring that he wore. With other members of his family he had helped to care for her during her long final illness.

RB   We looked after my mother, you know. They all did, all the children. We did what we could. We didn't have a lot, but we did the best we could! Mm. . . .

His experiences from this time, suggested that he felt he had to make his own way in the world. He had to work hard and be careful with money.

INT. Who did you work for?

RB British Rail!

INT. British Rail? Did you work for them for a long time?

RB Quite a bit! Yes yes.

As a worker for British Rail, RB was able to travel free on trains, all over Europe. He went on many holidays:

RB That was a perk for us because we were working for British Rail. . . . We just as well take advantage while you're at it, hadn't you?

INT. So you'd get the train over to the ferry and go on the boat would you?

RB And go to the various places that you want to get to. Yes, mm. . . . It's quite good.

RB saw having money as being the answer to most problems.

RB Because everything goes back to having money all all. . . . That's all it is! Got enough money . . . you can put everything right then can't you?

The main theme in his life story, however, was the desire to get on well with everyone. He saw acceptance of himself and other people as very necessary. Inherent in this social skill was the pleasure that he obtained from conversation and laughter in his interactions with others. This theme was to reappear throughout most of the interviews:

RB Oh, I've always em, have a chat with anybody, you know.

INT. I've seen that! You like chatting don't you?

RB Yes. If you don't do that, then what's life?

Further, RB seemed to be a person who accepted and welcomed the differences in other people. He indicated it made the world a more interesting place. He enjoyed laughing with other people:

RB Well, it's nice to have people . . . to have a laugh at each other.

INT. Oh yes!

RB You know, you know not the, you know, derogatory or anything like that!

He saw it as important to be able to laugh at himself:

RB Oh yes! But you've got to be able to laugh at yourself as well.

He saw no point in fighting or arguing:

RB No! But, you know, I er, to talk . . . I try to, you know, come to some sort of. . . . If they want to have an argument, they can have one. [He laughed.] But it doesn't do anything, does it really?

INT.   No.

RB   No.

INT.   Do you like arguments?

RB   Not all that much. You know, I mean, you get some people that er, really want to have a go don't they? They want to . . .

INT.   They do want to have a go . . .

RB   Pull you to pieces. . . .

RB saw laughter as very important. He concluded with a statement that was to become an important theme throughout most of the interviews:

RB   I think that if you can have a good laugh, that's a lot of goodness.

RB appeared to have a positive outlook on life. He seemed to be aware that his life was now different, and that he had to accept these changes:

INT.   That's the secret of getting older? Being happy when you're older?

RB   Could be! I don't know! I don't er, sell . . . try to have 'em out or anything like that, because it's gone! You're wasting time aren't you? You get to know people and that's it!

INT.   So you just take it as it comes?

RB   Yes, yes. . . . It's . . . if you try to alter everything, you know you can't! Well that's being stupid, isn't it?

INT.   Very sensible!

RB   Course to me, it makes sense you know.

He continued to expound on this theme:

RB   Yes, because most people in my predicament, they get to know the other people and, you know, they do the best they can! And that's all there is to it, isn't it!

INT.   So it doesn't make you angry?

RB   No! because I used to be as really sharp as a tack!

INT.   You used to be . . .

RB   I did. Yes!

INT.   I can well believe that!

RB   But I accepted it, I mean . . . [He gave a little laugh.] It's altered some, you know, as sharp as before you were! And it does. . . . Everybody helps you in any case!

INT.   But you accept things as they are. . . .

RB   Well it's no good trying to fight it, is it?

INT.   No. That's the secret. . . .

RB   You can't get anyone to er agree with you! . . . [He laughed but had tears in his eyes.] So you don't want to feel an outsider, do you?

He saw having friends as important:

INT. And have friends. . . .

RB That's it. . . . Yes.

INT. I've met a lot of people who know you and like you.

RB I expect you'll find quite a few more yet, I'm sure.

INT. I think you've spent all your life . . . um . . . enabling people to like you.

RB Well, I don't try to upset equals, if that's what you mean. . . .

RB People, lot of people. . . . Just because it's er, you're being *not* . . . being quite one hundred per cent, you know, it makes it's . . . it easier. There's a lot of people in the same . . . illness. The same predicament coming. . . .

INT. It *is* a predicament.

RB I used to be really sharp and do any job, you know. But er it's no good to apologize! Er . . . [There were tears in his eyes.]

INT. No. . . .

RB No. Not a bit . . . help . . . friends. Start again, don't you?

He was asked if he had had a good life. RB felt he had done his best:

RB Everything that I've done, I've done purposely and that's it! So I've no sense in . . . [He gave a little laugh.] . . . I shouldn't have done that, or I shouldn't have done this. . . . You just do the best things you can, don't you?

He spoke again of the need for laughter:

RB So long as you get a good laugh, why worry?

INT. That's your secret.

RB Laugh at yourself!

RB went on to crack a joke. He was very pleased to make me laugh. Laughter continued to be important to him. As with other cognitively impaired participants, RB could still make his meaning clear. Social relationships, including laughter, continued to hold particular significance for him:

INT. So it's relationships? Talking to. . . .

RB [Interrupts.] It is! Well tis, tis, I, I can have a chat with people, I . . . mean it's easier isn't it!

INT. I think it makes you feel happy, would you say that?

RB Oh yes! Oh yes!

INT. Makes you feel good?

RB Yes! Yes.

INT. Mm. . . .

RB I mean, if they get a bit stroppy and stamp on your corn or something like that, you can't love 'em can you?! [We both laughed.]

INT.   Oh no! Well you can't love everybody!

RB   You can't love 'em all can you?

INT.   You always make me laugh Bob. . . .

RB   Well it is a funny thing isn't it really? All this . . . all the other . . . things that people like trying to get on to some of this and that, . . . you know. And, em, you ask them about something special. They think, 'He's brash.' And, er, they don't know what to ask you . . . or . . . no conversation at all! Funny isn't it?

RB   I like the fun of talking to people that, you know, not trying, they're not trying to be big! Or anything like that. That's what I like, because they have a good laugh, and you have a good laugh . . . and that's the best thing isn't it?!

INT.   Do you like people that you think are the same as you . . . not too high [up]?

RB   I'm not too high, no. Well I'm very short aren't I? [We laughed.] . . . But when . . . but when I'm on me tip toes, I'm all right! [We laughed again.]

During a later interview and after a generalized discussion, I asked RB if he was the sort of person who tended to keep his feelings concealed from others:

RB   I wouldn't em . . . I wouldn't go up to them and give 'em a mouth of my, you know, all my mouth . . . er I don't think it's . . . it's . . . doesn't . . . doesn't do 'em any good!

RB still saw no point in arguing with other people.

RB   Yes! I'm . . . I always try to have things easier really! There's no . . . sense you know, trying to make it ten times difficult. . . . You don't . . . want that do you?

He still maintained that one should live and let live. Acceptance of others continued to be a strong personal principle. He seemed to feel there were people who thought of nothing but themselves. His words suggested that he felt it was a waste of time to try to change them:

RB   Some people usually come in . . . in a crowd even, you know. . . . And, em, they don't take any notice . . . any bad, the other person's likes or dislikes, or anything like that, you know. And they go their own sweet, you know! So. . . . you can't, you know, demand that they should do this, that, and that the other. That don't get you anywhere, does it?

INT.   No. . . .

RB   Does it?

INT.   So you think it's best to take things as it comes do you?

RB   Without a doubt! And em . . . there I've em . . . they're about the same as us really! Don't you think so?

During many of our interviews together we spoke of serious subjects, but RB always endeavoured to end the interview on a light note:

RB   So you've had a damn good laugh. . . . And I did as well!

INT.   So that's good isn't it?

RB   Yes, it is! Course it is! Yes, if we took it too serious, it would be terrible wouldn't it?

Towards the end of August 1992, RB's condition worsened. The staff from his residential home reported that he had begun to display increasing irritability towards others which quickly developed into aggressive outbursts. These incidents of aggressive behaviour began to increase in severity and it was decided to admit him to the psychogeriatric assessment ward in the hospital. It took a long time for his difficult behaviours to subside, and it was at this point in his illness that he began to pace the hospital corridors almost unceasingly. He tried to explain his need to walk continually:

RB   . . . Trouble is . . . with a walking stick! And I reckon I'll walk every day. The other serious bit is being . . . sitting on me . . . sitting doing nothing . . . something like that. . . . I presume it'll work out.

It was not long after this date that he was placed in the secure wing of a psychogeriatric nursing home. I visited him there on several occasions and he was pleased to see me. His social skills remained very good, although he was unable to hold conversations for any length of time. His pacing had become his main activity. When I visited him, we walked the corridors together. Towards the end of the series of interviews, I asked him if he had seen one of his relatives who was very pleasant:

RB   Yes, she is. . . . Nearly as nice as you. [We both laughed.]

INT.   You recognized me today, when I came in didn't you?

RB   It was good, wasn't it?

INT.   Yes. . . . That was nice.

RB   You only want one . . . one at times. . . .

INT.   One at a time?

RB   One at a time.

INT.   One visitor at a time?

RB   Yes. . . .

I asked if I might visit him again:

INT.   Can I come and see you again?

RB   Yes, I hope so.

INT.   Yes, I like seeing you.

RB   But the longer I'm there the less . . . you'll see of me, if you, if you know what I mean.

Unfortunately, RB's remark proved all too true. As with some other participants, I returned to the setting, after an absence of some months, in order to see if any fragments of his past stories remained in memory. This visit which took place in August 1993 was very short. He was fast asleep when I arrived at the nursing home. The staff reported that RB still continually wandered the corridors. He looked very frail and much older. The sister in charge reported that his behaviour was much as before. He said very little and continued to pace the corridors almost unceasingly.

All the staff in the setting displayed much compassion and concern for him. A member of staff lightly touched RB's arm, and told him he had a visitor. He immediately rose and walked across the room into the corridor. I accompanied him along the corridors, and gently led him into a discussion of his past major themes:

INT.   Do you remember when you worked for British Rail?
RB   Yes.
INT.   You do? Was that a good job? [Pause.] Was that a good job working for British Rail? . . . [RB did not reply.] Do you remember looking after your mum?
RB   Mmm!
INT.   Was her name Violet? . . . Was her name Violet? [RB nodded.] You looked after your mum for a long time. . . . [RB made no reply, and continued to pace the corridors.] But you remember working for British Rail?
RB   Yes.
INT.   A good job. . . . [RB did not answer. He continued to pace the corridors without pause.]

The dictaphone recorded the quick relentless sound of RB's feet hitting the floor as he walked. He appeared to be totally exhausted. This final interview would appear to indicate that, as with some other participants, only the merest outline of RB's stories remained.

Theoretical considerations of the case-study

A review of this case-study suggests that, as with other participants, Mr Biddley was recalling his own personal narrative. During the introduction to this chapter, it was suggested that the fundamental emotions might still be present in the memories of some older people with dementia. Mr Biddley's stories did contain associated emotions of interest, enjoyment, sadness, and hints of some suppressed anger. It is possible that he also experienced other fundamental emotions, but these were not made so evident.

Of some significance is the final interview in which only faint traces of his former memories can be seen. His life-story or narrative is of interest, because it gives some indication of the developing relationship between memory and dementia, during the later stages of the disease process. It is possible to trace the progress of some memories throughout the course of the interviews. These memories gradually faded and lost content, leaving only a faint trace. However, even at the very end of our time together, knowledge of Mr Biddley's past stories gave me some assistance in the framing of questions. During the interviews, he had recalled his own personal philosophy and personally significant life events. Not all of this information was available either in his social history, which formed part of his hospital notes, or from friends and relatives. Some type of record of the personal narrative in early dementia would, therefore, appear to be beneficial for both sufferers of this illness and professional carers. The importance of this concept will be discussed in more depth during the final section of this chapter.

RB's fragmented memories available for recall appeared to be those of his work, and of his mother. These memories, however, were much diminished when compared to those contained in earlier interviews. Nevertheless, these earlier interviews suggested that he still had his own particular stories to tell. His narrative contained much that was meaningful to his life, and allowed some light to be shed on his behaviour.

His early childhood experiences had led him to view his work and financial security as important. Other unknown experiences allowed him to develop good social skills. These skills permitted him to take pleasure in more casual social relationships. Although the relationship that remained in memory seemed to be of that between himself and his mother, this is not to deny his self-confessed need to interact well with others. Indeed this entire case-study reflects the importance that RB placed on getting on with other people, his enjoyment of conversation, and his love of laughter. His skills of acceptance, social interaction and the use of humour, still remained part of him for much of our time together. They gave meaning to his life.

Although dementia destroys many of the psychological defences which are so carefully erected during the course of a life, RB remained a relatively private person throughout our time together. Unlike some other participants, it was difficult to see him as an actor playing the central role in his own life drama. But for a period the sharing of his stories led to an increase in well-being and a sense of narrative identity.

As with other participants, the recalling of his past in the form of a life-story appeared to enable him to regain a sense of identity and personhood. This, in turn, allowed some understanding of the importance of his emotional memories, such as his sadness in trying to accept the cognitive changes imposed on him by his illness. RB's awareness of his loss corresponds to Miesen's (1995) argument that part of the symptoms of dementia, such as the fear, restlessness, sadness, aggression, inactivity, etc., which are so readily seen in this illness, could be explained as a reaction to loss and can be understood in terms of the awareness-context of the sufferer.

IMPLICATIONS FOR CARE-GIVING

Mr Biddley's case-study, together with a brief discussion of other participants, would suggest strong links between life and story (Widdershoven, 1993), together with the importance of the preservation of the narrative in dementia. The disappearance of the narrative appears to be linked to diminished personhood and well-being (Funkenstein, 1993). Within this study, the progressive ravages of this illness led to a lessening of this form of identity for many participants and to an eventual parting of our ways.

However, Gibson (1994) suggests that it is possible to put off this parting, by the use of therapeutic strategies. These strategies suggest a variety of methods which include reminiscence, life-review, and life-review counselling. The importance of the maintenance of the personal narrative in dementia cannot, therefore, be overestimated. There is a steady increase in the therapeutic use of life-recording methods for older people with, or without, dementia. However, most case notes of older people have a paucity of information on their social history, a comment that has been made elsewhere (Gibson, 1994; Johnson, 1976; Mills and Chapman, 1992).

Current research by Bornat (1994), together with Bornat and Adams (1992), indicates that the obtaining of a life-history of clients during assessments gives a more accurate understanding of present needs and wishes, both in the community and in long-stay settings. Further, an understanding of the attachment history of the client which will be related to the reaction to loss in the present, as will the awareness-context of the client, may explain current emotional states and behaviours. Moreover, this information will provide the basis for a range of interventions which may allow the grieving process to continue (Miesen, 1995).

Any recording of the narrative at an early stage of the illness, would enable carers to have some knowledge of their client's meaningful past. Gibson (1994) suggests that carers, in turn, can use client's life-histories to make sense of seemingly confused messages, and to remind/return this personal narrative to those in their care. This was an often successful strategy used during this study. There is a definite argument for encouraging care-giving relatives to construct a full social history with an emphasis on significant life events at an early stage of the illness. This history would prove invaluable in all aspects of present and future care management, which may involve the use of resources from many different agencies. Knowledge and understanding of the client would enable needs to be met more effectively. This information would provide topics for conversation and reminiscence, together with the awareness that, for the client, certain memories of the past might still resonate with some emotional pain.

It is of great importance to recognize and validate the emotions displayed by older people with dementia (Feil, 1992). It is also important to recognize the value of the emotions in these states of cognitive impairment. Sinason (1992) argues that strong emotional states in the present can unlock memory within dementia. Further, many of the participants' memories concerning emotional past events were very 'old' memories with proven durability. The exploration of the meaning attached to these memories appeared to fuel recall. This would suggest the strong presence of emotions within states of dementia, even as cognitive abilities fade.

However, the strategy of addressing the emotional message given by the participants appeared to power recall. This is open to a number of theoretical interpretations, but a simple explanation may be the most useful. It is probable that this understanding of feelings lessened anxiety, thus enabling memory to operate more effectively. Further, this understanding may have reduced some of the negative effects of attachment behaviours by allowing participants to feel safe and secure. There are few of us who are able to think clearly when worried, anxious, insecure and/ or fearful.

This strategy did not always involve verbally identifying the emotions that were expressed. It was often just enough to listen and accept these emotional messages. This form of acceptance appeared to 'hold' and support most informants in their efforts to recall and disclose very deep concerns. The findings suggest that not only was I able to encourage informants to tell their stories, but that I was also able to hold and support them as they began to lose the ability to remember their story. This, again, is of importance within dementia care work, especially for professional carers and care-giving relatives. Many of us seek to offer unnecessary and continual explanations to sufferers of dementia which allow us to feel useful and positive. Perhaps, at times, it is merely enough to say nothing, but to listen with warm attentiveness to their emotional messages and eventually to reflect their content in our replies. Thus we might say that they sound sad, anxious, worried, happy. This, in turn, leads to further exploration and further conversation in an illness which inhibits communication.

The understanding of the seemingly powerful relationship between memory and emotion appears to validate much of the therapeutic work within dementia care. Further, it is suggested that the sharing of the personal narrative within dementia reinforces carer attitudes of respect, understanding and acceptance. In this sense, therefore, the personal narrative of dementia sufferers is never lost. It continues its existence in the form of a treasure or bequest, which is bestowed on others to use how they will. It is hoped that we will learn to use it wisely and well.

REFERENCES

Averill, J. R. (1986) 'Acquisition of emotions during adulthood', in R. Harré (ed.) *The Social Construction of Emotions*. New York/Oxford: Basil Blackwell.

Baddeley, A. (1990) *Human Memory: Theory and Practice*. Hillsdale, NJ: Lawrence Erlbaum Associates.

Bornat, J. (1994) Introduction in J. Bornat (ed.) *Reminiscence Reviewed: Perspectives, Evaluations, Achievements*. Milton Keynes/Philadelphia: Open University Press.

—— and Adams, J. (1992) 'Models of biography and reminiscence in the nursing care of frail elderly people', in J. M. Via and E. Portella (eds) *Proceedings of the 4th International Conference on Systems Science in Health–Social Services for the Elderly and Disabled*, Vol. 11, Barcelona: A. Camps.

Bower, G. H. (1981) 'On mood and memory', *American Psychologist* 36: 129–148.

Bower, G. H. and Cohen, P. R. (1982) 'Emotional influences in memory and thinking: data and theory', in M. S. Clark and S. T. Fiske, (eds) *Affect and Cognition*. Hillsdale, NJ: Lawrence Erlbaum Associates.

Brewer, W. F. (1986) 'What is autobiographical memory?' in D. C. Rubin (ed.) *Autobiographical Memory*. Cambridge: Cambridge University Press.

Bromley, D. B. (1986) *The Case-Study Method in Psychology and Related Disciplines*. Chichester: John Wiley.

—— (1990) *Behavioural Gerontology: Central Issues in the Psychology of Ageing*. Chichester: John Wiley.

Buck, R. (1988) *Human Motivation and Emotion*, second edition. New York: John Wiley.

Coleman, P. G. (1986) *Ageing and Reminiscence Processes: Social and Clinical Implications*. Chichester: John Wiley.

Conway, M. (1990) *Autobiographical Memory: An Introduction*. Milton Keynes/Philadelphia: Open University Press.

Darwin, C. (1872) *The Expression of the Emotions in Man and Animals*. London, New York: Philosophical Library.

Feil, N. (1985) 'Resolution: the final life task', *Journal of Humanistic Psychology* 25 (2): 91–106.

—— (1992) 'Validation therapy with late-onset dementia', in G. M. M. Jones and B. M. L. Miesen (eds) *Care-Giving in Dementia: Research and Applications*, vol. 1. London/New York: Tavistock/Routledge.

Freud, S. (1920/1955) *Beyond the Pleasure Principle*. Vol. 18 of the *Standard Edition*, London: Hogarth.

Funkenstein, A. (1993) 'The incomprehensible catastrophe: memory and narrative', in R. Josselson and A. Lieblich (eds) *The Narrative Study of Lives*. Newbury Park, CA, London/New Delhi: Sage.

Gardner, I. (1993) 'Psychotherapeutic intervention', in A. Chapman and M. Marshall (eds) *Dementia: New Skills for Social Workers*. Case Studies for Practice 5. London/Pennsylvania: Jessica Kingsley Publishers.

Gibson, F. (1994) 'What can reminiscence contribute to people with dementia?' In J. Bornat (ed.) *Reminiscence Reviewed: Perspectives, Evaluations, Achievements*. Milton Keynes/Philadelphia: Open University Press.

Gilligan, S. G. and Bower, G. H. (1984) 'Cognitive consequences of emotional arousal', in C. E. Izard, J. Kagan and R. B. Zajonc (eds) *Emotions, Cognition and Behaviour*. New York: Cambridge University Press.

Glaser, B. and Strauss, A. (1967) *The Discovery of Grounded Theory: Strategies for Qualitative Research*. Chicago: Aldine.

Goudie, F. and Stokes, G. (1989) 'Understanding confusion', *Nursing Times* 85 (27 Sep.): 39.

Harré, R. (1986) 'The social constructionist viewpoint', in R. Harré (ed.) *The Social Construction of Emotions*. New York, Oxford: Basil Blackwell.

Hausman, C. (1992) 'Dynamic psychotherapy with elderly demented patients', in G. M. M. Jones and B. M. L. Miesen (eds) *Care-Giving in Dementia: Research and Applications*, vol 1. London/New York: Tavistock/Routledge.

Izard, C. E. (1984) 'The facets and interfaces of emotions', in R. Bell, J. L. Green and J. H. Harvey (eds) *Interfaces in Psychology*. Lubbock, TX: Texas Tech Press.

—— (1991) *The Psychology of Emotions*. New York/London: Plenum Press.

Johnson, M. L. (1976) 'That was your life: a biological approach to later life', in J. M. A. Munnichs and W. J. A. van den Heuvel (eds) *Dependency and Independency in Old Age*. The Hague: Martinus Nijhoff.

Jones, G. and Burns, A. (1992) 'Reminiscing disorientation theory', in G. M. M. Jones and B. M. L. Miesen (eds) *Care-Giving in Dementia: Research and Applications*, vol. 1. London/New York: Tavistock/Routledge.

Kitwood, T. (1990a) 'Psychotherapy and dementia', *Psychotherapy Section Newsletter* 8: 40–56.

—— (1990b) 'The dialectics of dementia: with particular reference to Alzheimer's disease', *Ageing and Society* 10 (2): 177–196.

—— (1993) 'Towards a theory of dementia care: the interpersonal process', *Ageing and Society* 13 (1): 51–67.

—— and Bredin, K. (1992) 'Towards a theory of dementia care: personhood and well-being', *Ageing and Society* 12 (3): 269–287.

Lazarus, R. J. (1982) 'Thoughts on the selection between emotion and cognition', *American Psychologist* 37: 1019–1024.

Leventhal, H. (1984) 'A perceptual motor theory of emotion', in L. Berkowitz (ed.) *Advances in Experimental Social Psychology* 17. New York: Academic Press.

Miesen, B. M. L. (1992) 'Attachment theory and dementia', in G. M. M. Jones and B. M. L. Miesen (eds) *Care-Giving in Dementia: Research and Applications*, vol. 1. London/New York: Tavistock/Routledge.

—— (1995) 'Psychic pain surfacing in dementia: from new to old trauma?' Paper presented at the European Colloquium on Therapeutic Work with Older People. University of Stirling.

Mills, M. A. (1991) 'Making the invisible visible: a qualitative study in the use of reminiscence therapy and counselling skills with dementing elderly people'. Unpublished thesis, University of Bournemouth.

—— (1993) 'Hidden wealth within dementia', in K. Tout (ed.) *Elderly Care: A World Perspective*. London/New York: Chapman and Hall.

—— and Chapman, I. A. H. (1992) 'Understanding the story', *Nursing the Elderly* 4 (6): 27–30.

—— and Coleman, P. G. (1994) 'Nostalgic memories in dementia: a case study', *International Journal of Aging and Human Development* 8 (1).

—— and Walker, J. (1994) 'Memory, mood and dementia: a case study', *Journal of Aging Studies* 8 (1): 17–27.

Plutchik, R. (1980) 'A general psychoevolutionary theory of emotion', in R. Plutchik and H. Kellerman (eds) *Emotion Theory, Research, and Experience*. New York/London: Academic Press.

Runyan, W. M. (1982) *Life Histories and Psychobiography: Explorations in Theory and Method*. New York/Oxford: Oxford University Press.

Sinason, V. (1992) *Mental Handicap and the Human Condition: New Approaches from the Tavistock*. London: Routledge.

Singer, J. L. (1973) *The Child's World of Make-Believe: Experimental Studies of Imaginative Play*. New York: Academic Press.
—— (1974) *Imagery and Daydream Methods in Psychotherapy and Behaviour Modification*. New York: Academic Press.
Thompson, J. G. (1988) *Psychobiology of Emotions*. New York, London: Plenum Press.
Tobin, S. S. (1991) *Personhood in Advanced Old Age: Implications for Practice*. New York: Springer.
Tomkins, S. S. (1962) *Affect, Imagery, Consciousness*: vol. 1, *The Positive Affects*. New York: Springer.
—— (1981) 'The quest for the primary motives: biography and autobiography of an idea', *Journal of Personality and Social Psychology* 41: 306-329.
Widdershoven, G. A. M. (1993) 'The story of life: hermeneutic perspectives on the relationship between narrative and life history', in R. Josselson and A. Lieblich (eds) *The Narrative Study of Lives*. Newbury Park, CA, London/New Delhi: Sage.
Williams, J. M., Watts, F. N., Macleod, C. and Mathews, A. (1988) *Cognitive Psychology and Emotional Disorders*. Chichester/New York: John Wiley .
Williams, M. (1987) 'Dementia', in R. L. Gregory (ed.) *The Oxford Companion to the Mind*. Oxford/New York: Oxford University Press.
Woods, R. T., Portnoy, S., Head, D. and Jones, G. (1992) 'Reminiscence and life review with persons with dementia: which way forward?' in G. M. M. Jones, and B. M. L. Miesen (eds) *Care-Giving in Dementia: Research and Applications*, vol. 1. London/New York: Tavistock/Routledge.
Yin, R. K. (1989) *Case-Study Research: Design and Methods*. Applied Social Research Methods Series, 5, revised edn. Newbury Park, CA, London/New Delhi: Sage.

Chapter 5

Awareness in dementia patients and family grieving

A practical perspective

Bère M. L. Miesen

The denial of empathy benefits no one. As mechanics we doctors always fail in the long run, but as counselors, teachers, healers and care-givers we can always contribute ... [even] at the moment of death. ...

(Siegel, 1986, p. 60)

... all hope is real in a patient's mind.

(ibid., p. 29)

INTRODUCTION

The first section of this chapter presents the concept of 'awareness-context' (AC), introduced by Glaser and Strauss (1965) in dying patients. It also occurs in dementing patients. It appears that Senile Dementia Alzheimer Type (SDAT) patients remain involved in their situation much longer than researchers have assumed before. From the AC perspective various dementia symptoms, particularly the secondary symptoms, can be considered as normal reactions of the sufferer to the experience of powerlessness, discontinuity and feeling unsafe, displaced, separated and isolated. From a psychological view SDAT can be understood as a chronic brain trauma which causes potential psychotrauma in the sufferer (Miesen, 1995b).

The second section explains that family care-givers of SDAT patients can drift into pathological grieving; into a grieving process which resembles the one which occurs in the case of a missing loved person. Family care-givers have to face an emotional separation and an actual spatial separation when an admission follows. In the case of dementia the emotional separation will only become definite as soon as the demented person is deceased. Living 'together' with a demented spouse implies living 'under the same roof' while feeling separated from each other. In such a separation situation it is obvious that the married couple will grow apart. The chance that both persons will (or can) communicate about their feelings is small.

The thesis of this contribution has practical consequences for the care-giving to both. The spouse who knows about the awareness-context of their dementing partner, will accept them more readily as an emotional equal. They may talk about these feelings longer, therefore, reducing the chance of pathological grieving. Hence, the (potential) isolation of the dementing person will be reduced.

THE SUFFERER

Awareness-context in dementia sufferers

Thirty years ago Glaser and Strauss (1965) introduced the term 'awareness-context'. They described AC in terminal patients, their family and the staff of the hospital. From their sociological perspective, they postulated four kinds of awareness that the oncoming death could have on the interaction between them. The core of their thesis is: those who don't know they are going to die, aren't even able to start grieving. Without information about the loss, there is no mourning process. Keeping this information away from the patient removes the possibility of saying goodbye and completing his or her life in whatever way. Formulating the core of their thesis in another way: one cannot interpret a terminal patient's behaviour correctly, and therefore interact with him adequately, without knowing what he has been told, or knows about his illness. To understand a patient's behaviour correctly one has to consider his AC.

Clinical observations and research (Miesen, 1993; Weinstein, Friedland and Wagner, 1994) have proven that SDAT patients still respond to their illness, even long after their 'illness-insight' has disappeared. Emphasis on the potential usefulness of dynamic psychotherapy (Hausman, 1992; Solomon, 1992; Solomon and Swabo, 1992) and recent focus on the perspective of the sufferers themselves (Gorman, 1993; Cotrell and Schultz, 1993) support this view. The clinical and empirical evidence of the existence of an AC in a dementia sufferer, suggests that SDAT patients remain involved (in a cognitive as well as an affective way) in the experiences which happen to them.

In research with dementia patients in different stages of the process (Miesen, 1990; 1993), a strong correlation was found between the phenomenon of parent-fixation (Miesen, 1985), the level of cognitive functioning and attachment behaviour. This was explained by postulating that remaining aware of one's cognitive dysfunctioning in dementia is like going into a 'strange situation' in which the person experiences feeling unsafe for long periods of time, powerless and with no structures to hold on to. Therefore the demented elderly have to cope with the same feelings that arise in situations which resemble separation, homelessness or displacement. The 'awareness-context' (AC) brings the sufferer in a chronic trauma (Miesen, 1995b). To understand a dementia patient's behaviour correctly one needs to consider his AC (Miesen, 1995a).

Clinical example of a dementia patient's awareness-context

Mr Wilkinson, born in 1935, got 'the' message in 1993. In the presence of his wife he was told in the hospital that it had been established without doubt that he was suffering from Alzheimer's disease. Ever since that day I have counselled them regularly. A selection follows from what he told me in the last half of 1994.

Is there still hope for me? No! I'm telling myself to hope, I don't want to be completely bowled over by it. But each day I have to fight it, to gain it back again. And that struggle makes me tired out, dog-tired.

I feel I cannot trust my engine any more. I'm still busy searching for proof to the contrary. But even a little evidence is hard to find. Someone sets so many different traps for me.

All the things I see here, I can smash them up. I nearly choke with fury. Why me? I don't have a scapegoat. There is nobody who gives me this pain. It's something inside myself, like my anger is. I know that, and I have to live with it.

General consequences of the awareness-context in dementia

1 The concept of AC compels us to differentiate very precisely between the real/primary symptoms of the disease (that is, behaviour/cognitive dysfunctioning directly related to brain dysfunctioning), and those reactions caused by the awareness of the symptoms. Without considering AC, all behaviour/symptoms become attributed to brain failure.
2 Assessing the AC requires additional assessment of the personality, wherein attachment history, coping style and life-history are examined. Personality can help explain the variation in individual reactions to the primary symptoms of dementia. Without this information one cannot understand the different reactions to the same primary symptoms, and cannot offer the most appropriate counselling or interpersonal care interventions (Miesen, 1992b). Hence, the AC requires a detailed assessment of the individual life-history. The AC implies, for some patients, that their present psychic pain will revive or trigger feelings of old unresolved trauma (Miesen, 1995a). Without this information one can never understand extreme outbursts to cognitive dysfunctioning.
3 The connection between AC on the one hand, and life-history and personality on the other, allows us to predict the individual's behaviour during the dementia process. Regardless of the aetiology of a primary dementia, the individual is involved in a process of cognitive (dys)-functioning. Therefore, a 'stage' model is a pre-requisite for planning care (Miesen, 1992c). Because the AC itself is related to cognitive

dysfunctioning (through decreased information-processing abilities), AC will change from a more or less 'continuous' to a 'momentary' state of awareness of their situation. In classifying dementia sufferers by aetiology alone, mistakes caused by not considering individual differences in AC occur. Together with a changing AC, individual reactions increasingly change from a cognitive to an affective level. The portion of the variation in demented behaviour explained by personality and life-course, will also change during the dementia process.

We don't yet know whether the effect of the life-course and personality of the sufferer is stronger at the beginning or at the end of the disease process. We could hypothesize that because of the progressive memory failure in dementia, first in short-term and later also in long-term memory, that life-history influences will gradually become less significant than innate personality factors.

General implications for care-giving

Dementia sufferers are, a priori, a very heterogeneous group: no one is the same (Jones and Miesen, 1992). Dementia sufferers are persons who are usually aware that something is amiss and that they are no longer functioning optimally (Miesen, 1992c). This implies that they react normally (to the abnormal condition of the brain) instead of abnormally (to a normal condition of the brain). Second, they are not only passive objects of their condition/situation, but active subjects of it. Considered from this perspective, dementia sufferers must always be thought of as serious partners in each interaction – be it a cognitive assessment situation, counselling or a research investigation. Considering symptoms such as fear, restlessness, sadness, aggression, inactivity, 'claiming' behaviour and so on, as reactions to loss, makes this behaviour accessible to change and therapy. Both care-giving and research must be directed at the cognitive and affective aspects of behaviour.

Mr Wilkinson's message

In August 1994 Mr Wilkinson's spouse stumbled upon a page of a lined notebook which was written upon on both sides (see Figures 5.2 and 5.3). Mr Wilkinson had had a higher education; there were no signs of a depressive state or Parkinson's disease. He was not taking any medication. In 1993 he was assessed and diagnosed with Alzheimer's disease and also for a hypokinetic rigid syndrome and myoclonia. Mrs Wilkinson finally reached the limits of her 'Strength Required to Bear' (SRB) (Duijnstee, 1992a; 1992b) only in May 1995. Her husband was then referred twice a week to psychogeriatric daycare.

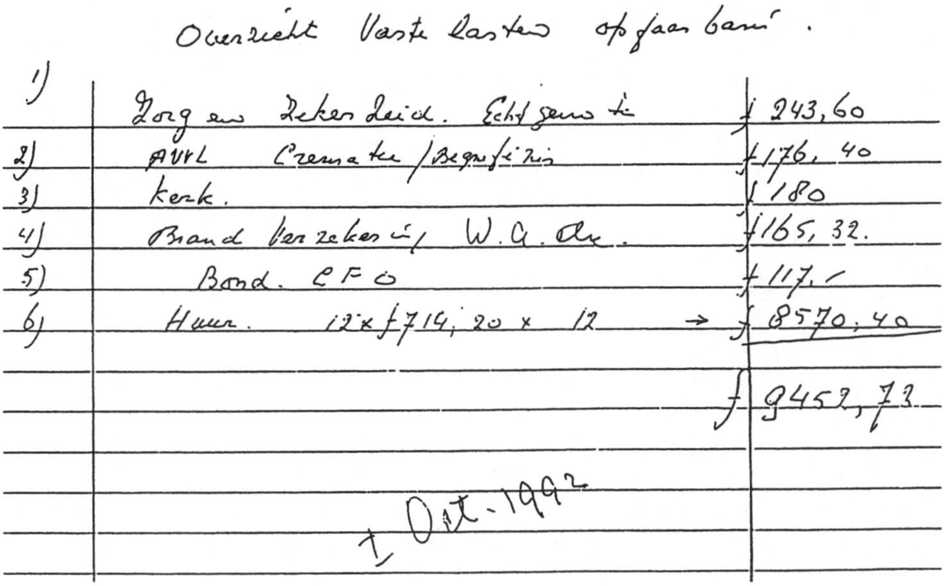

Figure 5.1 Facsimile of Mr Wilkinson's handwriting; October 1992

Formal features of the handwriting of Mr Wilkinson are language problems, both lexical and grammatical; expressive aphasia and agraphia; limitations of short-term storage of information: perseverations on several characters and on content; and restricted small peripheral movements. Content features of the handwriting of Mr Wilkinson are that it shows expressions of strong ideas and emotions (see Figures 5.2 and 5.3). Parts of the Dutch language can be translated literally as follows:

I love you
you have done it well
everything is so different
I am no longer able
I cannot do anything any more
there is nothing left of me
> (Figure 5.2)

you don't have to buy me clothes any more
but I hope you don't run out of me
for I still love you
> (Figure 5.3)

Figure 5.1, an outline of annually fixed charges of the family Wilkinson, serves as a comparison with more recent handwriting of Mr Wilkinson.

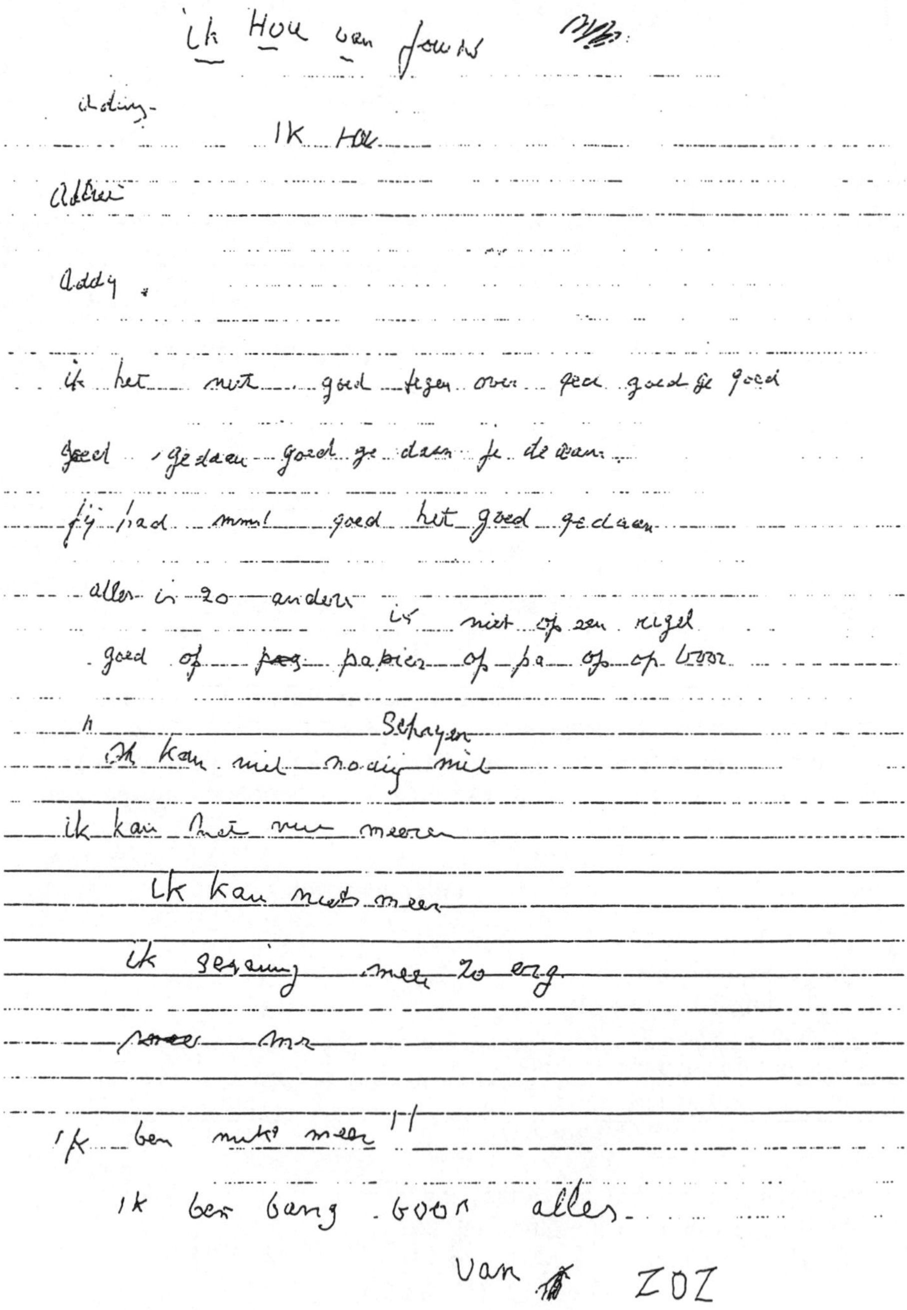

Ik Hou van jouw

adding-

IK Hou

adlui

addy

ik het niet goed tegen over jea goed je goed
goed gedaen goed ge daen je de aen
fij had mmml goed het goed ge daen
aller in zo anders is niet op een rigel
goed of pas papier op pa op op boor
h   Schrijven
Ik kan niel nodig niel
ik kan het niu meer
Ik kan niet meer
ik geseimg mee zo erg.
soee mr
ik ben niets meer
ik ben bang boon alles
Van ZOZ

Figure 5.2 Facsimile (top) of Mr Wilkinson's handwriting

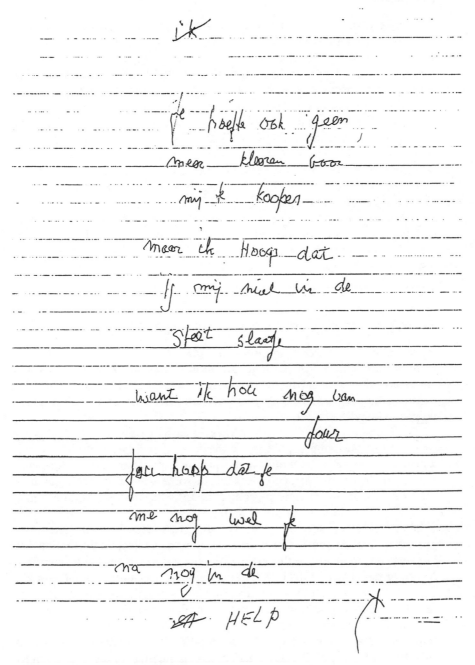

Figure 5.3 Facsimile (bottom) of Mr Wilkinson's handwriting

Conclusion

In assuming the very existence of an AC, one 'transforms' a 'dementia case' into a 'person consciously suffering, even fighting a chronic trauma'. This mental transformation turns a dementia sufferer, for example Mr Wilkinson, into a person one can talk with about his situation and the consequences of his disease. Hence, the AC changes our general mental image and opinion of the dementia patient. These changes need to permeate all levels of information/instruction to sufferers, relatives, professional care-givers, researchers and public. Without such a change one can never fully accept Mr Wilkinson's involvement in his dementia process or take him seriously. Without accepting the AC, one is taking a dementia sufferer's life while he is already losing normal brain functioning. Such metaphorical decapitation is unjust (Miesen, 1995b). If families could be taught or convinced that dementia sufferers did have an awareness of their situations (fear and other feelings) maybe this could further generate empathy and hence promote the grieving of both.

THE FAMILY CARE-GIVER

Family grieving: coping with a beloved, missing person

In addition to the practical problems, relatives of Alzheimer's disease sufferers are up against a range of emotional problems. Primary care-givers are often put on the spot. Sooner or later, they long for the actual death of the patient. How can we understand this wish and some of these behaviours and feelings?

The focus here is to develop a theoretical perspective for identifying one feature: the imperceptibility of the loss. This imperceptibility which makes the loss of a demented loved person a peculiar loss, is especially unfavourable for the grieving process. In some ways this loss resembles the case of a loved, missing person. This turns the family situation into a chronic, vague, unsafe emotional arena.

Many relatives, especially primary care-givers, experience the dementia process of a loved one as a burden. However, the subjective evaluation can be very different from the objective evaluation of the same burden. Recently, Duijnstee (1992a; 1992b) postulated three intervening factors to explain these individual differences in the 'Strength Required to Bear' (SRB) of primary care-givers. She identified variations in: 'How one handles the situation' (coping), 'Why one renders care' (motivation), and 'How one deals emotionally with the situation' (acceptance). It is evident that the last part of the life-span of the dementia sufferer is strongly connected with the SRB of the primary care-giver.

The SRB is affected by many factors; not only the kind and number of disabilities, but also the way the dementia sufferer copes with them. Other factors also influence the SRB, such as: health, information, informal help, financial status, living accommodation, professional care, the degree of understanding of the behaviour of the sufferer, emotional support, etc. Last but not least, the SRB is without doubt affected by the way the primary care-giver emotionally copes with the loss of the loved one. Primary care-givers are actively involved in a grieving process throughout the course of the illness.

General aspects of the grieving process

Dealing with loss is inherent to life. People have to experience loss, sooner or later. In general, old people have dealt with many losses. Identifying common aspects of normal (healthy) grieving, can help care professionals diagnose phases such as resistance, despair and detachment or shock, denial, anger, sorrow and acceptance. Bowlby (1980) too speaks of grieving phases. I prefer his description because he formulates the process in a psychological way. He speaks of the perplexity of the mourner; the long-lasting search for and strong longing for the lost person; the painful anguish and desperation when not succeeding; and finally, recovery and finding a way to live without the lost one. Though various communities and cultures have different grieving customs which deserve considered study, there is not scope here to do anything but acknowledge this reality.

Pathological grieving in general

When does one identify a grieving process as pathological? Three situations point to pathological grieving: (1) absence of grieving behaviour; (2) delayed grieving; and (3) chronic grieving behaviour. What causes these situations in which the individual behaves as if nothing has happened, reacts later on, or gets stuck in the process? Which factors amongst others can affect the mourning process in an unfavourable way?

(1) the intensity of the pre-existing emotional tie with the person, wherein ambivalence and exclusivism are relevant;
(2) the personality of the relative, including the individual style of coping with problems;
(3) the circumstances under which the loss happens or the person disappears;
(4) the attachment history of the relative (although connected with (1) and (2);
(5) the occurrence of unresolved old trauma/sores of the relative; and
(6) the perceptibility of the loss.

I want to focus on the idea that the last factor, the concreteness of the evidence of the loss, could complicate or prevent normal mourning and therefore could cause pathological mourning (Miesen, 1992a).

Examples of pathological grieving

Mrs Jones is the spouse of a moderate SDAT patient. She cannot handle her husband's behaviour as evidenced by her regular outbursts of aggression towards him. Counselling did not help her to cope with it.

Mr Johnson is the husband of a severe SDAT patient. He had strong feelings of guilt and compassion, while deciding to have his wife admitted to a nursing home. After the admission he visited his wife 'more than daily', for years.

Mr Williams is the husband of a SDAT patient who died after an SDAT process of ten years. For the last five years she stayed in a nursing home. He had a strong desire to date and to become involved with much younger women. In counselling he finally coped successfully with this unrealistic wish after he had prepared all the future funeral rites in advance of his spouse's death.

Mrs Wickland is the wife of a severe SDAT patient. Several years after her husband was admitted to a nursing home she remained overwhelmed by strong feelings of guilt while longing for a new mate.

The evidence of the loss in dementia

There is a great similarity in the experience of living with a dementia sufferer and in conditions of 'pathological' mourning behaviour in the case of a beloved missing person (for example in war, coma, sudden disappearance). One cannot perceive the person, yet there is no evidence of their actually being dead. Relatives often long for the evidence of actual death. Emotionally it is unbearable to live long with the uncertainty of not knowing what has happened. Any evidence of death or permanent separation offers at least the possibility of starting a grieving process. In the case of dementia, absence of the concreteness of the loss-evidence is a problem often underestimated by care-givers and health care professionals. When does one identify grieving as being pathological? In practice, this absence of evidence causes very long-lasting feelings of hope and guilt even 'against better judgement'. Letting go of 'the hope for improvement', is often felt as cheating the other or burying him or her alive. Often the relative of a dementia sufferer develops a strong desire for actual death. This wish can be understood as having three roots:

(1) knowing that actual death will end the trauma/pain of the patient;

(2) believing that actual death will stop the trauma/pain of the relative;
(3) hoping that actual death will provide concrete evidence of the loss, and will give the relative the real status of widowhood.

In addition to the negative influences on the grieving process, dementia represents a special kind of 'loss' in which the evidence of the loss often is contradictory and changes constantly. Hence, dementia is an 'a priori' unfavourable factor in the grieving process of the relative.

Conclusion

Relatives of SDAT sufferers have to cope with feelings which resemble those which arise in the case of a loved 'missing person'. Living together, but feeling separated, can have dramatic effects. Two older adults, living mostly in peace under one roof, are losing each other but are still staying in each other's proximity. This can be understood as an experience of separation which occurs slowly, but does not become definite while the dementing person is alive. Often it concerns the gradual loss of a usually strong attachment although the dementia sufferer is still close by 'in the flesh'. This is a frustrating contradiction, a dramatic antithesis. Relatives have to say goodbye slowly to a beloved person who is still there. This affects the acceptance of the primary care-giver; and so his or her coping and motivation (Duijnstee, 1992a).

The challenge for professional care-givers in dementia is to support relatives' 'Strength Required to Bear' by counselling them to become competent in 'slowly growing loose' from a beloved one. This loosening occurs under the difficult condition of fluctuating continuity in the relationship. Helping them to live with the perspective wherein the fact that the loss remains indefinite as long as the loved one is still alive, is crucial.

Family grieving could be facilitated if relatives were taught that dementia sufferers really have an awareness of their situation; have fear reactions and, therefore, are themselves involved in a grieving process; have increasing feelings of isolation and are in need of attachment to someone. This could renew empathy and understanding. This might generate healthy family grieving or might stop pathological grieving. The insight that the sufferer is in the same position of feeling separated and, therefore, has the same feelings, could prolong the process of communication and could promote a process of grieving together.

This perspective requires that health care professionals always have two care-plans: one for the sufferer and another for the family. However, in the grieving process of both, earlier coping skills, personality and unresolved losses affect the way of coping with the new situation. Knowledge of this will optimize the care-plan. In reality, family members have little desire to reveal past losses and coping skills, since they will not necessarily perceive themselves to be in need of help. Professional care-givers must be trained to deduce from the family's overt behaviour what stage of grieving they are in.

ACKNOWLEDGEMENTS

The author gratefully wishes to thank Gemma Jones for her comments, Han Diesfeldt for his specific assessment advice, and Petra Dekker for her help in preparing this chapter.

REFERENCES

Bowlby, J. (1980) *Attachment and Loss*, vol. 3: *Loss: Sadness and Depression.* London: Hogarth Press/New York: Basic Books.

Cotrell, V. and Schultz, R. (1993) 'The perspective of the patient with Alzheimer's disease: A neglected dimension of dementia research'. *The Gerontologist.* 33 (2): 205–211.

Duijnstee, M. (1992a) De belasting van familieleden van dementerenden. Dissertation. Nijkerk: Intro.

—— (1992b) 'Caring for a demented family member at home: objective observation and subjective evaluation of the burden.' In: G. M. M. Jones and B. M. L. Miesen (eds) *Care-Giving in Dementia. Research and Applications*, vol. 1. London/New York: Tavistock/Routledge, pp. 359–379.

Glaser, B. G. and Strauss, A. L. (1965) *Awareness of Dying.* New York: Aldine Publishing Company.

Gorman, M. (1993) 'The phenomenology of early stage Alzheimer's and related disorders'. Paper presented at the Fifteenth International Congress of Gerontology, Budapest.

Hausman, C. (1992) 'Dynamic psychotherapy with elderly demented patients'. In: G. M. M. Jones and B. M. L. Miesen (eds) *Care-Giving in Dementia. Research and Applications*, vol. 1. London/New York: Tavistock/Routledge, pp. 181–198.

Jones, G. M. M. and Miesen, B. M. L. (1992) (eds) *Care-Giving in Dementia. Research and Applications*, vol. 1. London/New York: Tavistock/Routledge, p. 481.

Miesen, B. (1985) 'Meaning and function of the remembered parents in normal and abnormal old age'. Paper presented at the Thirteenth International Congress of Gerontology, New York.

—— (1990) 'Gehechtheid en dementie. Ouders in de beleving van dementerende ouderen'. ('Attachment and dementia. How demented elderly persons experience their parents'.) Dissertation, Almere/Nijkerk: Versluys/Intro, p. 272.

—— (1992a) *Dement; zo gek nog niet.* Houten: Bohn Stafleu van Loghum.

—— (1992b) 'Attachment theory and dementia'. In: G. M. M. Jones and B. M. L. Miesen (eds) *Care-Giving in Dementia. Research and Applications*, vol. 1. London/New York: Tavistock/Routledge, pp. 38–56.

—— (1992c) 'Care-giving in dementia: review and perspectives'. In: G. M. M. Jones and B. M. L. Miesen (eds) *Care-Giving in Dementia, Research and Applications*, vol. 1. London/New York: Tavistock/ Routledge, pp. 454–469.

—— (1993) 'Alzheimer's disease, the phenomeon of parent fixation and Bowlby's attachment theory'. *International Journal of Geriatric Psychiatry* 8: 147–153.

—— (1995a) 'Attachment behavior in dementia: Parent Orientation and Parent Fixation (POPFiD) theory'. In: G. H. Pollock and S. I. Greenspan (eds) *The Course of Life*, vol. VII. Madison: International Universities Press Inc (in press).

—— (1995b) 'Psychic pain surfacing in dementia: from new to old trauma?' Paper presented at the European Colloquium on Therapeutic Work with Older People, Stirling (UK).

Siegel, B. (1986) *Love, Medicine and Miracles*. London: Rider.

Solomon, K. (1992) 'Behavioral and psychotherapeutic interventions with patients in the long-term care institutions'. In: G. T. Grossberg and P. A. Szwabo (eds) *Problem Behavior in Long-term Care: Recognition, Diagnosis and Treatment*. New York: Springer Publishing Co.

—— and Szwabo, P. (1992) 'The subjective experience of and psychodynamic psychotherapies for the patient with Alzheimer's disease'. In: J. E. Morley *et al.* (eds) *Memory Functioning and Ageing-Related Disorders*. New York: Springer Publishing Co.

Weinstein, E. A., Friedland, R. P. and Wagner, E. E. (1994) 'Denial/unawareness of impairment and symbolic behavior in Alzheimer's disease'. *Neuropsychiatry, Neuropsychology and Behavioral Neurology* 7 (3): 176–184.

Part II

Interventions in care facilities

Chapter 6

Practical management of frontal lobe dementia

Institutional perspectives

Susan Tainsh and Diane Hinshelwood

SUMMARY

In this chapter we discuss guidelines for the management of patients with frontal lobe dementias. These have been arrived at from an understanding of the clinical characteristics of these dementias derived from daily observations, over several years, in a cohort of patients. Management techniques were developed empirically to solve behavioural and cognitive problems encountered by the clinical team.

INTRODUCTION

Dementias of frontal lobe type have, probably by virtue of their lesser prevalence and poorly defined clinical criteria, received far less attention in the dementia literature than has Alzheimer's disease. That there has been a degenerative dementia specific to the frontal lobe and distinct from Alzheimer's disease, has long been recognized. Indeed, the original description of a neuropathological change such as in Pick's disease, was contemporary with that of Alzheimer's disease. Until very recently Pick's disease was thought to be rare, although prevalent estimates have largely been based on case series (Lishman, 1987: 391–393).

More contemporary work has suggested that frontal lobe dementias (FLD) may represent a much higher proportion of all degenerative dementias than previously recognized – especially those degenerative dementias occurring in the pre-senium. Indeed Neary *et al.* (1988) have maintained that FLD may comprise up to 25 per cent of degenerative dementias but that the prevalence has been underestimated largely because of misdiagnosis of FLD as psychiatric illness, or Alzheimer's disease. With the identification of the clinical pathological entity of frontal lobe dementia of non-Alzheimer's type (Gustafson 1987; Brun, 1987; Neary *et al.*, 1988; Gustafson *et al.*, 1990), coupled with studies suggesting higher prevalence than traditionally believed, both academic and clinical interest in FLD has increased.

Until recently, studies of this syndrome were hampered by lack of clear diagnostic criteria. However, the recently published clinical and neuropathological criteria for FLD (Lund and Manchester Groups, 1994) (see Table 6.1) will likely aid in the recognition of, and attention paid to this subset of dementias, which consume a disproportionate amount of increasingly scarce health-care resources. Under-diagnosis and misdiagnosis often result in inappropriate or detrimental management and magnify health-care resource consumption.

Table 6.1 Clinical diagnostic features of fronto-temporal dementia

Core diagnostic features

Behavioural disorder
- Insidious onset and slow progression
- Early loss of personal awareness (neglect of personal hygiene and grooming)
- Early loss of social awareness (lack of social tact, misdemeanours such as shoplifting)
- Early signs of disinhibition (such as unrestrained sexuality, violent behaviour, inappropriate jocularity, restless pacing)
- Mental rigidity and inflexibility
- Hyperorality (oral/dietary changes, overeating, food fads, excessive smoking and alcohol consumption, oral exploration of objects)
- Stereotyped and perseverative behaviour (wandering, mannerisms such as clapping, singing, dancing, ritualistic preoccupation such as hoarding, toileting, and dressing)
- Utilization behaviour (unrestrained exploration of objects in the environment)
- Distractibility, impulsivity, and impersistence
- Early loss of insight into the fact that the altered condition is due to a pathological change of own mental state

Affective symptoms
- Depression, anxiety, excessive sentimentality, suicidal and fixed ideation, delusion (early and evanescent)

- Hypochondriasis, bizarre somatic preoccupation (early and evanescent)
- Emotional unconcern (emotional indifference and remoteness, lack of empathy and sympathy, apathy)
- Amimia (inertia, aspontaneity)

Speech disorder
- Progressive reduction of speech (aspontaneity and economy of utterance)
- Stereotypy of speech (repetition of limited repertoire of words, phrases, or themes)
- Echolalia and perseveration
- Late mutism

Spatial orientation and praxis preserved (intact abilities to negotiate the environment)

Physical signs
- Early primitive reflexes
- Early incontinence
- Late akinesia, rigidity, tremor
- Low and labile blood pressure

Investigations
- Normal EEG despite clinically evident dementia
- Brain imaging (structural or functional, or both): predominant frontal or anterior temporal abnormality, or both
- Neuropsychology (profound failure on 'frontal lobe' tests in the absence of severe amnesia, aphasia, or perceptual spatial disorder)

Supportive diagnostic features
- Onset before 65
- Positive family history of similar disorder in a first-degree relative
- Bulbar palsy, muscular weakness and wasting, fasciculations (motor neurone disease)

Diagnostic exclusion features
- Abrupt onset with ictal events
- Head trauma related to onset
- Early severe amnesia
- Early spatial disorientation, lost in surroundings, defective localization of objects
- Early severe apraxia
- Logoclonic speech with rapid loss of train of thought
- Myoclonus
- Cortical bulbar and spinal deficits

- Cerebellar ataxia
- Choreo-athetosis
- Early, severe, pathological EEG
- Brain imaging (predominant post-central structural or functional deficit. Multifocal cerebral lesions on CT or MRI)
- Laboratory tests indicating brain involvement or inflammatory disorder (such as multiple sclerosis, syphilis, AIDS and herpes simplex encephalitis)

Relative diagnostic exclusion features
- Typical history of chronic alcoholism
- Sustained hypertension
- History of vascular disease (such as angina, claudication)

Source: After Lund and Manchester Groups, 1994

CLINICAL CHARACTERISTICS AND DIAGNOSTIC CONSIDERATIONS

While very few clinical investigators would agree that it is possible to differentiate between frontal lobe disease of the non-Alzheimer's type and Pick's disease, most investigators would agree that the frontal lobe dementias almost invariably manifest abnormalities in personalities, behaviour and social skills that antedate the recognition of cognitive changes. Indeed, it was found in one small case series that the social and behavioural problems preceded the onset of clinically apparent cognitive loss by several years (Miller *et al.*, 1991).

Two distinctive clinical sub-types have been described, the 'disinhibited' and the 'apathetic' (Blumer and Benson, 1975; Gustafson, 1987). A disinhibited type may present with manic-like symptoms such as grandiosity, impulsiveness, recklessness, jocularity, disinhibition and restlessness. He or she may also present with 'psychotic' symptoms not readily classifiable into one of the common psychiatric diseases. Patients have been referred to our specialized service from general psychiatric services where the treatment of 'mania' has been unsuccessful, and also from the criminal justice system. One patient came to us remanded for psychiatric assessment when his newly acquired habit of accelerating through red traffic lights could not be attributed to carelessness or deteriorating vision. Some patients with the 'apathetic' sub-type may present with apparent 'treatment resistant depression' because they exhibit apathy, anhedonia and reduced speech. Patients with frontal lobe disease, however, are apathetic rather than deeply depressed, and indeed it is a characteristic of frontal lobe disease that patients are rarely distressed by their condition and their symptoms are those of a 'pseudo-depression'.

The frontal lobe dementias seem to differ from the other dementias in that the behavioural symptoms which are their hallmark and which mimic psychiatric symptoms associated with affective or psychotic disorders, seem to be directly attributable to the dementing process as we understand it at present, and not to the emergence of a co-morbid psychiatric disorder as may be the case in Alzheimer's disease. Even alcohol or other substance abuse may be a visible manifestation of an underlying social disinhibition secondary to an emerging frontal lobe dementia.

KLUVER-BUCY SYNDROME

This syndrome, originally induced in primates by surgical ablation of both temporal lobes is characterized by hyperorality, emotional blunting, hypersexuality and utilization behaviour. It has been reported as occurring in frontal lobe dementia (Cummings and Duchen, 1981; Burns et al., 1990). Our own experience suggests that although aspects of the syndrome are prominent in our own patients, we have yet to see the fully expressed clinical syndrome.

It has been suggested that the frontal lobe dementias may have a lower age at onset than Alzheimer's disease (Heston et al., 1987). Indeed Risberg (1987), in a series of sixteen subjects, found a mean age at onset of disease of 56 years. In our own in-patient series, the mean age at onset has been 45.2 years (31–51). Our in-patient programme, however, admits those with severe behaviour disturbance in dementia and is likely biased towards admitting the 'disinhibited' rather than the 'apathetic' sub-type. It is not clear to us whether the disinhibited sub-type actually represents a more malignant form of frontal lobe dementia of an earlier age in onset than the apathetic type, or whether the apathetic sub-type, by reason of its lack of florid behavioural symptoms, comes to medical attention later in the course of the disease. Investigators agree, however, that the estimates of mean age at onset in dementia are conservatively arrived at, with the disease having been present for months to years before being obvious to family and friends. Since the 'apathetic' sub-type of frontal lobe dementia can masquerade as, and be misdiagnosed as, a treatment resistant depression, it seems tempting to speculate that (if the disinhibitive and apathetic sub-types are indeed aspects of the same disease) the mean age at onset may be even lower than hitherto believed.

The relative youth of patients with frontal lobe dementia implies an intrinsically fit and healthy population without the medical co-morbidity that is common in the Alzheimer's disease population. Whilst this undoubtedly allows for study of the natural history of the disease, it causes problems within a care system designed for the frail or infirm elderly with dementia and is problematic in the provision of long-term care. The disturbed behaviours accompanying this disease may not endear these patients to formal care-givers who may also find it difficult emotionally to care for individuals with a dementing disease who may be close to them in age.

MANAGEMENT

Since there is no cure for frontal lobe dementia, management must focus on the prevention of intercurrent illness and the management of problematic behaviours. The 'apathetic' type may, in many ways, be managed as an Alzheimer's disease patient and indeed some of the non-pharmacological and practical management techniques described below will be familiar to those working with Alzheimer's disease. These management techniques, however, can be applied even more successfully to the frontal lobe patient because of their relatively retained cognitive skills, especially in the area of praxis, gnosis and perhaps memory. The management of the 'disinhibited' type is considerably more problematic and it is the management techniques for this sub-type to which this chapter is largely devoted.

Table 6.2 Characteristics of frontal lobe dementia versus Alzheimer's disease

	Frontal lobe dementia	Alzheimer's disease
History	Early personality change Social breakdown Multiple psychiatric diagnoses	Early memory dysfunction Spatial dysfunction Dyspraxia
Conduct and Affect	Apathy, 'depression', emotional unconcern, disinhibition, grandiosity, jocularity, loss of social graces, ritualistic behaviours, gluttony, obsessiveness	Preserved social awareness and propriety, depression, anxiety
Language	Economical output, concrete stereotypic, mutism in middle stages	Impaired repetition, nominal aphasia, mute in end stages
Spatial ability	Preserved	Impaired in early stage
Memory	Variable, some preservation likely	Consistent memory problems early in disease course
Physical signs	Pout, snout, grasp reflexes appear early	Normal until middle stages

A major difficulty in the assessment and management of the frontal lobe dementias continues to be the lack of appropriately constructed and validated assessment instruments. The literature is replete with instruments for the assessment of the Alzheimer's disease patient – especially in the pre-institutional stages of the disease. Such instruments, however, have not been validated on frontal lobe patients and, indeed, may specifically exclude the behaviours so commonly found in frontal lobe dementia.

PHARMACOLOGICAL MANAGEMENT

The mainstay of pharmacotherapy for problem behaviours in dementia has for years been the use of neuroleptic agents. This approach has been limited by the low efficacy and adverse side effect profile associated with these agents. Whilst the neuroleptics may be helpful in ameliorating overt psychotic symptoms, their use in the control of agitation in the absence of psychosis is essentially that of chemical restraint – using the sedative, as opposed to the anti-psychotic properties of the drug. Indeed it has been demonstrated in a meta-analysis of controlled trials of neuroleptic treatment in dementia (Schneider *et al.*, 1990) that neuroleptics have only minimal efficacy and that no one drug is better than another. Thapa *et al.* (1994) noted no escalation of index behavioural problems when anti-psychotics were discontinued, but a marked improvement in affective state and no deterioration in functional status.

Many other medications have been proposed for this use, including Proprananol, Lithium, Benzodiazepines, sedating anti-depressants such as Trazedone, and anti-convulsants such as Carbomazepine and Sodium Valcroate. Controlled data for the efficacy of these agents is essentially non-existent.

Essentially in all studies of pharmacotherapy for behaviour problems in dementia, the populations studied have either been defined Alzheimer's disease subjects, or no attempt has been made to exclude non-Alzheimer's subjects. There exist, then, essentially no data to suggest that any psychoactive agents are effective in controlling behavioural symptoms in the frontal lobe dementia patient. Indeed, our own clinical experience suggests that all the agents described above are ineffective at a wide range of doses in controlling problematic behaviour, except when the dosage level has been raised to the point where it is clear that the effect has been one of chemical restraint, and where the patient has clearly been sedated.

Cloripramine, which is indicated for the treatment of obsessive-compulsive disorder (Anafranil Product monograph, 1991; Cloripramine Study Group, 1991), has been used in an unblinded study of three of our patients who exhibited ritualistic, 'obsessive-compulsive' behaviours that interfered with management and therapy. Normal therapeutic doses were used. Although this was an unblinded study, and no objective measurements of change were made, it was remarked that all three showed considerable diminution of troublesome behaviours and became easier to care for and were able to be involved more fully in recreation therapy.

NON-PHARMACOLOGICAL MANAGEMENT

Environmental design and safety issues

As opposed to the Alzheimer's disease patient who tends to neglect his/her environment, the frontal lobe patient will frequently demonstrate intense utilization behaviour (unrestrained exploration of objects in the environment – Lund and Manchester Groups, 1994), and hyperoral behaviour. Attention must be paid therefore to creating a safe environment without sharp objects or toxic substances. Attention must be paid in particular to storage of cleaning fluids, medication carts and plants. Exposure to the external environment must be judicious since those with hyperoral behaviours may eat anything in sight. Clothing should be without buttons or other detachable parts and recreational materials, such as crayons, should be non-toxic. Where the presence of toxic substances is unavoidable, the staff member or therapist may offer acceptable food treats to serve as a counter-attraction.

Lighting and other electrical fixtures should be out of reach since these are attractive to the stimulus-bound, and all other electrical fixtures should be covered or otherwise secured. Eating utensils should be metal or china, since plastic and styrofoam become objects for consumption.

Staff and patients may become irritated by constantly disturbed bedrooms and utility rooms – one patient (apparently) methodically stripped each of thirty beds on a daily basis. Hiding and hoarding behaviours often elicit complaints from other residents and families. Garbage cans, especially, may become a repository for other patients' valuables – including dentures!

We find it helpful to assess the pattern of these behaviours – such as the type of behaviour, the time of day it occurs, the frequency with which it occurs and the predictability of hiding places – and to adjust ward routines accordingly. Locking bedroom doors as a first and only response to these behaviours infringes upon the freedom and rights of other patients and residents.

The patient with frontal lobe dementia often retains considerable agnosia and praxis and can pose a safety hazard to other residents or patients by untying lap belts or other safety devices. We have also observed a perfectly retained skill in memorizing and reproducing the code for secured exits, with ensuing absconding. Since this population tends to be younger and fitter than the typical Alzheimer's-type dementia sufferer, the absconding can be 'high speed' and present a challenge.

ACTIVITIES OF DAILY LIVING

As with all dementias, it is important to encourage independence and retention of skills. As opposed to the Alzheimer's disease patients, frontal lobe patients may have relatively little difficulty with the mechanisms of handling cutlery and foodstuffs, but because of problems with attention and concentration, they cannot be presented with an entire meal on a tray at one time. Distraction at mealtimes is therefore to be avoided and the patient should be served one course at a time and given his/her meals either individually or with a single other patient or resident. Sometimes, as a last resort, the patient must be restrained to prevent interference with other residents – they will remove food from other patients' trays – but also to ensure that they themselves get enough to eat.

Assisting with such tasks as toileting and dressing can be frustrating for staff because of the extreme distractibility and short attention span of the patient, but this frustration can be lessened if care-givers appreciate the extent to which Activities of Daily Living (ADL) skills may be preserved relative to the Alzheimer patient. It is not clear whether the duration of continence is different from the patient with Alzheimer's disease. Reduced attention span, however, makes successful toileting difficult and may lead to incontinence.

Nurses must be educated that stereotypic speech is not a deliberate irritant but a behaviour due to a dementing illness. The content of stereotypic speech can be complex and may be unpleasant (of a violent or sexual nature) but is delivered in a bland and 'automatic' manner that should allow the clinician to deduce that, whatever the content of the speech, it is not the product of negative emotion directed at the care-giver.

LIFE SKILLS

Whilst all disciplines should promote the preservation of skills in activities of daily living, recreation therapists can show leadership in the preservation of Independent ADL skills through using knowledge of the patient's pre-morbid activity and occupation to design a programme of activities. The ex-nurse, for example, can be directed towards 'assisting' nurses with such tasks as bed-making, and housewives can assist the housekeeping staff with minor cleaning chores.

FAMILIES AND FRIENDS

Families are often angry and confused at the time of presentation to our Unit, not only because of the disease pathology itself, but because of prior mislabelling and multiple, ineffective treatments. They may even have been involved in an Alzheimer's support group because they have been told the patient has Alzheimer's and been unable to understand why their relative is so different from the common experience. Since the average age in frontal lobe dementia tends to be lower, Alzheimer's support groups and respite programmes may be unsuitable.

We prefer to involve the families in assessment and diagnosis issues and, having provided them with as accurate a diagnosis as possible, to involve them in planning therapy and life-enrichment programming and to introduce them to families with similarly affected family members. In our experience, families are too overwhelmed by the nature and extent of the behavioural and cognitive pathologies to consider the sometimes understandably high risk associated with home visits. Contact, therefore, must be maintained by the treatment team in a manner that is in the best interest not only of the patient, but also of family and friends. Frequently, because of the relative youth of the patient and the extent of the behaviour disruption, families have extreme difficulty coping with regular contact, and this distancing must be respected.

LIFE-ENRICHMENT THERAPY

Again, it must be recognized that the frontal lobe patient differs from the Alzheimer's patient in that there may be some retention of learning ability, and retained praxis and memory. However, attention and concentration are severely diminished except when presented with a strong stimulus. In addition, communication skills are relatively severely affected. The frontal lobe patient tends to be younger and therefore fitter than the Alzheimer's patient and, importantly, tends to come from a different generation from the Alzheimer patient and therefore has different tastes and interests.

It is therefore important to capitalize on previous personality and interests, and to ensure that therapy is age-appropriate. In our experience, appropriately structured recreation therapy can improve such cognitive attributes as attention span (in one case increasing attention span from two to twenty minutes), thus ultimately making care and management easier.

Art therapy

In common with the Alzheimer patient, the use of bright, primary colours can be an aid to maintaining attention. The less impaired can work at assembling simple models such as cars (for men) or working with historical or ethnic costume dolls (for women). Working with edible 'play dough' to create simple shapes can be satisfying, as can finger-painting. Our patients have also coloured in age-appropriate picture outlines. On occasion, we have used some of the resulting art to mount small displays of patient art on the walls.

Communication therapy

We have found that reading ability is relatively preserved, as is repetition, and have therefore found the use of cue cards, using word and picture signs for key living areas such as toilets, to be successful. Because of new learning ability and some evidence of retained memory, a patient may be able to identify staff, adding to a sense of security and lowered anxiety. We use music that is culturally and age-appropriate (in our population, Neil Diamond and Elvis Presley are favourites) to enhance communication. These patients tend to have very well preserved motor coordination and praxis, and dancing is a useful aid to physical fitness, as well as being one of the few activities that is overtly enjoyable to a population that is partly characterized by emotional blunting.

Outdoor activities

These require close supervision often on a one-to-one basis. Family members can often be of assistance where staff shortages make a one-to-one staff/patient ratio impossible. A simple walk can be used to promote visual, auditory and tactile stimulation by touching tree bark, smelling pine trees and even taking patients' shoes off and letting them walk on grass with bare feet. Motor vehicle outings can be useful to provide a change in the environment and may stimulate memories and communication by visiting or passing familiar settings. In many cases, where patients must remain on a mini-van or bus, the therapist can point out schools, shops or other familiar settings. Where it is planned to visit restaurants or scenic attractions, enough staff must be available to provide adequate supervision. It has been noted by our staff that even severely disruptive patients will 'act normally' when they are in a familiar environment outside the institutional setting, although this 'normality' cannot be maintained for long periods – for more than two hours at a time.

PHYSICAL ACTIVITY

This should be 'fitness and fun'. Dancing is a favourite activity. Our patients tend to have very well preserved eye/hand coordination and games such as table tennis and badminton and floor hockey are useful. It is important that the therapist keep the ball in sight and in play at all times and encourage continuous play to maintain attention span. In the earlier stages of the disease, staff and patients have gone on short bicycle rides together, but in later stages stationary bicycles inside are more practical.

Fun and games

These must allow active participation at all times. Video games can be excellent stimulation since they capitalize on relatively well preserved fine motor and eye/hand coordination. Large jigsaw puzzles, draughts or checkers with large pieces, and dominoes are surprisingly well played and the success of these games exemplifies the relative preservation of visual spatial function in these patients. As the dementia increases in severity, functional similarities to Alzheimer's increase, but the frontal lobe patient seems to become more overtly childlike, and play stimulation with soft toys and coloured building blocks can be enjoyable.

CONCLUSION

Care and management of the frontal lobe patient can be rewarding because it is possible to see some improvement in some aspects of function and because the patient can recognize and attach to staff cognitively in a way that the Alzheimer patient can rarely achieve. *Per contra*, the patient's less well preserved personality and diminished range of affect can discourage staff. It is essential that care-givers recognize that the frontal lobe patient can be very different from the Alzheimer patient, and that traditional care and management strategies designed for the Alzheimer patient must be considerably adjusted in order to provide an optimal care-giving environment for the patient with frontal lobe dementia. It is essential for care-givers to remember that the frontal lobe patient, despite emotional blunting and often bewildering behaviours, can have retained cognitive strengths upon which a therapeutic programme may be built. It is, overall, vital to manage disturbed behaviours in a proactive and appropriate manner because the alternatives are behaviours that are unacceptable and unmanageable, leading to undesirable chemical restraint, and frustrated and ultimately burnt-out staff.

REFERENCES

Anafranil Product Monograph (1991) August 22.

Blumer, D. and Benson, D. F. (1975) 'Personality changes with frontal and temporal lesions'. In D. F. Benson and D. Blumer (eds) *Psychiatric Aspects of Neurological Disease*. New York: Grune and Stratton.

Brun, A. (1987) 'Frontal lobe degeneration of non-Alzheimer type I. Neuropathology', *Archives of Gerontology and Geriatrics* 6: 193–208.

Burns, A., Jacoby, R. and Levy, R. (1990) 'Psychiatric phenomena in Alzheimer's disease. IV: Disorders of behaviour', *British Journal of Psychiatry* 157: 86–94.

Cloripramine Study Group (1991) 'Cloripramine in the treatment of patients with obsessive compulsive disorder', *Archives of General Psychiatry* 48: 730–738.

Cummings, J. L. and Duchen, L. W. (1981) 'Kluver-Bucy Syndrome in Pick Disease: Clinical and pathologic correlations', *Neurology* 31: 1415–1422.

Gustafson, L. (1987) 'Frontal lobe degeneration of non-Alzheimer type: II. Clinical picture and differential diagnosis', *Archives of Gerontology and Geriatrics* 6: 209–223.

——, Brun, A. and Risberg, J. (1990) 'Frontal lobe dementia of the non-Alzheimer type'. In R. J. Wurtman (ed.) *Advances in Neurology*, vol. 51: *Alzheimer's Disease*. New York: Raven Press.

Heston, L. L., White, J. A. and Mastri, A. R. (1987) 'Pick's Disease', *Archives of General Psychiatry* 44: (May): 409–411.

Lishman, W. A. (1987) *Organic Psychiatry*, Oxford: Blackwell.

Lund and Manchester Groups (1994) 'Clinical and neuropathological criteria for frontotemporal dementia', *Journal of Neurology, Neurosurgery, and Psychiatry* 57(4) (April): 416–418.

Miller, B. L., Cummings, J. L., Villaneuve-Meyer, J., Boone, K., Mehringer, C. M., Lesser, I. M. and Mena, I. (1991) 'Frontal lobe degeneration: Clinical neuro-psychological, and SPECT characteristics', *Neurology* 41: 1374–1382.

Neary, D., Snowden, J. S., Northen, B., *et al.* (1988) 'Dementia of frontal lobe type', *Journal of Neurology, Neurosurgery and Psychiatry* 51: 353–361.

Risberg, J. (1987) 'Frontal lobe degeneration of non-Alzheimer type. III. Regional cerebral blood flow', *Archives of Gerontology and Geriatrics* 6: 225–233.

Schneider, L. S., Pollock, V. E. and Lyness, S. A. (1990) 'A meta-analysis of controlled trials of neuroleptic treatment in dementia', *Journal of the American Geriatrics Society* 38: 553–563.

Thapa, Purushottam B., Meador, K. G., Gideon, P., Fought, R. L. and Ray, W. A., (1994) 'Effects of antipsychotic withdrawal in elderly nursing home residents', *Journal of the American Geriatrics Society* 42: 280–286.

Chapter 7

Psychomotor group therapy for demented patients in the nursing home

R. M. Dröes

PSYCHOMOTOR THERAPY IN PSYCHOGERIATRICS

We define psychomotor therapy as the treatment of people who are confronted with psychosocial problems, using movement activities and/or special attention for bodily experiences (Vermeer and Sonius, 1976; Fahrenfort, 1986; van Coppenolle, 1989). Over the past twenty years, psychomotor therapy has developed rapidly in The Netherlands. As part of the psychosocial care offered in psychiatric hospitals, it is now a generally accepted and applied form of treatment.

In the field of psychogeriatrics this development has been much slower. Although some attention has been given to the possible applications of psychomotor therapy in the case of geronto-psychiatric patients in psychiatric institutions in The Netherlands and Belgium (Kouwenhoven, 1977; Rijsdorp, 1977; Faber, 1977; Koevoets, van den Heede and Vervloet, 1979; Probst, 1980; Hungenaert and Schaekers, 1982; Dröes, 1991), this type of therapy has penetrated the psychogeriatric nursing home environment only to a limited degree. Very few papers on the subject have been published in The Netherlands in the past twenty years (Dröes, 1991). Perhaps this is partly due to the deeply rooted notion in the mental health sector that no *real* help can be offered to demented patients (who constitute the majority of the nursing home residents), because a dementia syndrome implies an irreversible process of degeneration. We now know that this therapeutic nihilism is not justified in view of the (frequently positive) results of psychosocial forms of treatment in demented elderly which have been described in international literature (for example Jenkins *et al.*, 1977; Yesavage and Karasu, 1982; Welden and Yesavage, 1982; Gorissen, 1985; Reeve and Ivison, 1985; Olderog-Millard and Smith, 1989; Pinkston and Linsk, 1988; Götestam and Melin, 1990; Dröes, 1991; Jones and Miesen, 1992). Such findings indicate that the performance of these patients is definitely affected not only by the organic degeneration, but also by psychological and social factors, and that favourable psychosocial circumstances can certainly have a positive effect on the well-being of demented patients and on the way they function (Gustafsson, 1976; Melin and Götestam, 1981; Cleary *et al.*, 1988). In this light, it is quite understandable that interest in the possibilities of psychomotor therapy for psychogeriatric patients is growing.

THEORETICAL MODELS

Psychomotor therapy comprises many different methods (see below), based on various theoretical models (cognitive, neurophysiological, holistic, psychodynamic, or based on learning theory) that are used to explain psychosocial problems. The method of psychomotor therapy for demented patients as described later on in this chapter is based on the psychodynamic interactional adaptation-coping model (Dröes, 1991; see Figure 7.1).

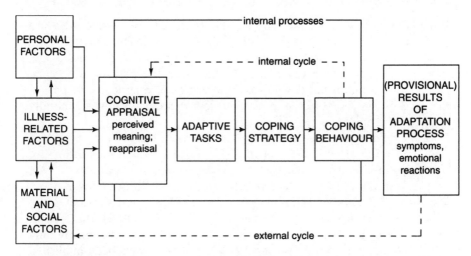

Figure 7.1 The adaptation-coping model (Dröes, 1991): a conceptual model for understanding adaptation and coping in illness and crises in general, based on the crisis model of Moos and Tsu (1977) and the coping theory of Lazarus and Folkman (1984).

The basic supposition in this model is that mental and behavioural problems (symptoms) in institutionalized demented patients are not simply a result of the organic degeneration of the brain, but are partly generated by the way in which the individual patient adapts to, or copes with, the consequences of the dementia and institutionalization – for example, the way in which the patient handles his/her own invalidity, is capable of maintaining an emotional balance and a positive self-image and accepts the uncertain future he/she is confronted with. For patients who are admitted to a nursing home, mental and behavioural problems can also be generated by the way they deal, or get habituated with the nursing home environment and treatment procedures, and are capable of developing an adequate relationship

Table 7.1 Adaptive tasks which can play a role in the adaptation and coping process in persons who are confronted with dementia according to the adaptation-coping model (Dröes, 1991)

Adaptive tasks related to the illness
1 Coping with one's own disability
2 Preserving an emotional balance
3 Preserving a positive self-image
4 Preparing for an uncertain future

Adaptive tasks related to the institutionalization
5 Dealing with nursing home environment and treatment
6 Developing adequate relationship with staff
7 Developing new social relations

with the professional staff and maintaining social relationships. Each change requires adaptation and brings new, so-called *adaptive tasks* (Table 7.1).

The stress and emotional response evoked by the separate adaptive tasks (such as anxiety, grief, shame, anger), as well as the way these are dealt with, are determined by the significance each individual ascribes to the experienced changes. For instance, a dementia patient who used to be a bookkeeper and who owed his status to this profession suffers immensely when he finds out that he is not able to calculate any more, not even simple sums. Or a demented woman, who has always been a good housewife and cook, feels suddenly stressed when she enters the kitchen and does not know what to do any more because of her increasing agnosia. This signification process is called *cognitive appraisal*, and is influenced – obviously – by personal, illness-related, material and social factors.

The generally positive results of psychosocial intervention studies in demented patients support this adaptation-coping model (see, for a review of intervention studies between 1970 and 1990, Dröes, 1991). For example, several *reactivation strategies* have resulted in demented patients making more use of their residual abilities leading to a more adequate coping with their own disability (Greene *et al.*, 1982; Reeve and Ivison, 1985; Karlsson *et al.*, 1985) or with the activities offered in the nursing home (Gustafsson, 1976; Melin and Götestam, 1981; Götestam, 1987). Patients who are activated take a less dependent attitude towards the staff, indicating that these patients are capable of developing a more independent relationship with the staff (see adaptive task 6, Table 7.1). In a number of cases interventions aimed at *resocialization* (interventions which attempt to stimulate patients to develop and maintain social relations within and sometimes also outside the nursing home) turn out to be effective (Gustafsson, 1976; Melin and Götestam, 1981; Williams *et al.*, 1987; Olderog-Millard and Smith, 1989). Finally, positive results are also reported with regard to *affective functioning*, especially with regard to aggression and night-time restlessness

(Welden and Yesavage, 1982; Birchmore and Clague, 1983; Pinkston and Linsk, 1988; Cleary *et al.*, 1988; Dröes, 1991).

MOVEMENT-ORIENTED AND BODY-ORIENTED METHODS

As we have mentioned before, psychomotor therapy utilizes many different methods. If we look at these methods from the perspective of therapeutic intervention, the following remarks are in order. In general, the therapy programmes which are based on a *cognitive* and/or *neurophysiological* perspective and which are perhaps best characterized as types of function training, utilize movement activities from the realm of physical training, sports and games. Movement activation is used to attempt stimulation of the person as an information-processing system and/or to influence the neurophysiological processes that underlie the (impaired) system. In addition to movement exercises aimed at fostering self-expression, self-image and self-esteem, the therapy programmes that are based on a *holistic* perspective, and are thus aimed at restoring the so-called bio-psycho-social system, use music, breathing exercises, informal conversation and nutrition education as therapeutic means. *Behaviour therapy* programmes, which are based on principles from learning theory (learning through the positive consequences of particular behaviour) often use (progressive) relaxation exercises and verbal rewards. *Psychodynamic (interaction-)* oriented therapy programmes, in which behavioural symptoms are partly explained as a result of demented patients' psychological reactions to their cognitive impairments and the changing environment in the case of admission to a nursing home, mainly offer movement activities in which the participants can experience a certain degree of success and confidence in themselves and others. In this way an appeal is made to them to (once again) make contact with their environment. In summary we can say that some methods focus on the use of movement activities, and others use body experience to influence the functioning of the demented person.

As a general categorization of the range of methods used in psycho-motor therapy, Fahrenfort (1986) introduced the terms *movement-oriented* methods and *body-oriented* methods. Movement-oriented methods refer to treatments which consist mainly of offering carefully selected movement arrangements or movement activities, and body-oriented methods emphasize body experience, as for example in the case of relaxation exercises.

WHY USE MOVEMENT AS A THERAPEUTIC MEANS?

Research and practical experience have shown that simple movement activities in the form of games and sporting activities are generally valued positively by demented patients who need assistance and care (Dröes, 1985, 1992). Although this in itself can be sufficient reason to choose movement activities as a therapeutic means, philosophical and theoretical considerations also play a role. For example: the expectation that movement activities can be used for reactivation and resocialization purposes is based partly on a *relational movement concept*. This means that the individual is viewed as an undivided and indivisible whole, who enters into interactions and relations with the environment not only in terms of perception, thinking and speech, but also in terms of movement (Buytendijk, 1972; Gordijn *et al.*, 1975; Rijsdorp, 1977; Tamboer, 1985). When perception, thinking and/or speech are impaired, movement is an alternative form of communication. By having patients participate regularly in movement activities, they are given the opportunity to maintain a relationship with the environment. This possibly will make it easier for patients to accept their own invalidity, to learn to utilize activities in the nursing home, to develop a more independent attitude towards the staff and to develop social contacts.

The expectation that a movement-oriented therapy programme can in addition have a positive effect on the emotional balance and self-image of demented patients, is partly based on knowledge about the *impairments and disabilities* that demented patients are faced with. In general, several aspects in the areas of memory, perception and action are (comparatively) preserved in the early stages of degeneration. We refer to, for example, procedural learning (that is, remembering *how* to use game materials), somato-sensory perception, body scheme, understanding physical expression (motor and procedural) movement, imitating movement actions and social skills. Because these functional aspects are preserved, patients in the early stages of dementia will still be able to participate in simple movement activities in groups without too many problems. Regular use of the undamaged functional abilities, the success and pleasure experienced in this way, can offer some emotional compensation for the disabilities these patients have to deal with. Regulation of emotions in dementia is of the utmost importance for achieving a balance. The regular positive experience of success and pleasure can help these patients maintain an emotional balance and a positive self-image (Goldberg and Fitzpatrick, 1980). Assuming that in the case of invalidity a revised self-image is a precondition for experiencing continuity in the past, present and future, it is conceivable that psychomotor therapy will help some patients accept the present and the (uncertain) future (van der Wulp, 1986) by giving them the opportunity to experience their own abilities.

PSYCHOMOTOR GROUP THERAPY FOR DEMENTED PATIENTS

Level of dementia

Research has shown that each level of dementia requires a specific movement programme (Dröes, 1985). In general, modified sporting movement activities (such as football, hockey and badminton), movement activities in the form of games (such as bowling and boules) and hobby activities (such as dancing to music) are valued positively by the group requiring only partial assistance. The group moderately in need of care appreciates the games and simple hobby activities, while the group requiring total care values only very simple games and senso-motor activities (music in particular has a stimulating effect). Of the different levels, the patients requiring assistance, that is, those who have a score from 0 to 4 on scale 3C (mental invalidity) on the Assessment Scale for Elderly Patients (ASEP; van der Kam, Mol and Wimmers, 1971), are activated most by movement activities in a group setting (Dröes, 1992). However, psychomotor group therapy is also suitable for patients in more severe need of care (up to ASEP score 6), although individual treatment will be chosen more frequently for patients in this category, as well as for patients requiring total care (ASEP score 7 or 8).

The method described in this chapter focuses on the first two groups mentioned above: the group that needs only partial assistance and the group that needs moderate care. In other words, we will focus on psychomotor therapy for patients with mild and moderate dementia. Though the movement activities differ in these groups, as mentioned before, the therapy method is almost the same.

Indication for psychomotor therapy; the general request for assistance

Psychomotor therapy is indicated (see Figure 7.2) when the demented patient:

- is in a crisis due to ineffective coping with the stress generated by particular adaptive tasks;
- is in an unstable balance and threatens to fall into a downward spiral of psychosocial problems (for example problematic behaviour, communication problems, isolation) as a result of inadequate coping with certain adaptive tasks; or
- has fallen into a downward spiral of psychosocial problems due to prolonged inadequate coping with certain adaptive tasks.

Of course it should be checked whether the treatment (movement or body-oriented) appeals to the patient.

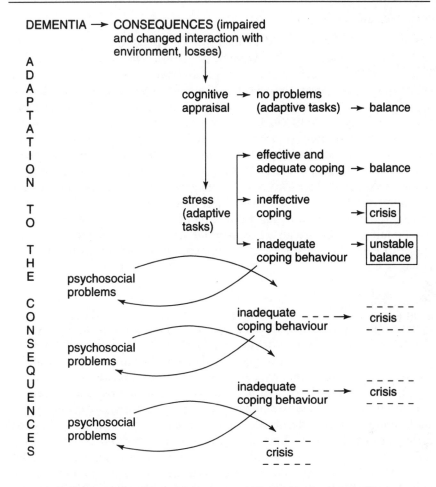

Figure 7.2 The process of adaptation to the consequences of dementia and the three kinds of problem situations in which psychosocial assistance is indicated: crisis (1), unstable balance (2) and downward spiral (3) of psychosocial problems.

Crisis (1)

A crisis, which can be looked upon as a disrupted balance, can be recognized by the relatively *sudden occurrence* of behavioural symptoms. The patient is off-balance and no longer in control of his situation. A crisis is characterized by the temporariness of the problematical situation: in general it will last several days or weeks (Istha and Smit, 1977). A crisis can manifest itself in, among other things, depression, acute anxiety, panic attacks and physiological disorders.

Unstable balance (2)

Patients in a state of unstable balance are characterized by *regular, temporary* – mostly incidental – behavioural problems. Some examples: arguing with co-residents, swearing at the staff, emotional instability, uncooperative behaviour, withdrawal, rebellious behaviour, suspicion, confabulation, accosting passers-by because one wants to go home, and walking away from a group activity in a huff. Such behavioural problems are generally linked with specific situations or events, which, after a period of observation, makes it possible to recognize them as problems the patient has with one or more adaptive tasks. For example: the patient becomes anxious, agitated or sad when confronted with his own invalidity and finding that he is no longer in (complete) control of the situation; or he rebels because of his inability to accept being institutionalized in a nursing home. Or he can be slightly emotionally unstable because he misses his spouse, children and own home and/or because he has not (yet) developed social relations in the nursing home.

Downward spiral (3)

Patients already in a downward spiral of psychosocial problems are characterized by *chronic* behavioural problems, in which there frequently occurs a gradual increase or change of behavioural symptoms. For example: increasing insecurity, anxiety and/or suspicion as a result of protracted regressive coping with their own invalidity; passive and dependent behaviour as a result of regressive coping with the nursing home environment and staff; continuously wandering around the ward to suppress negative feelings or feelings of agitation which emerge in the not very stimulating institutional environment; social isolation as a result of not developing new social relations in the nursing home (it often turns out that these patients have a long history of social withdrawal, which is why other residents have remained strangers to them).

Case

> Mrs Nigel has been living in the nursing home for a year. She is 83 years old. Her dependence is caused not only by her 'dementia', but also by the fact that she is barely able to move around without help and her eyesight is limited. Although she appreciates the help she receives in the nursing home (as shown by the profuse expressions of thanks when she is being helped), she completely rejects the idea that she is no longer able to live independently. She has not (yet) come to terms with her institutionalization in the nursing home. She accosts passers-by to take her home. When reminded by the staff that the move was unavoidable, she is often overcome by emotion and cannot hold back her tears: how

can it be true that she has lost her own home? And what about all her 'nice things', where did they go?

Because she denies her disability and the institutionalization, and because she has now forgotten that she agreed to it, she blames her environment for arranging everything behind her back (termination of the tenancy of her house, the sale of her possessions, etc.). The feelings of powerlessness that accompany this, frequently result in weeping fits and floods of abuse towards staff and fellow patients. Attempts by nurses to involve her in activities on the ward, so that she will begin to feel more at home in her new surroundings, are often met with aggressive and paranoid reactions: 'Piss off! You're only after my money. First my house and now it's my money. You're not getting anything, you hear! Piss off I tell you.'

One of the consequences of this situation is that fellow patients don't want to sit near Mrs N. in the living room and that the nursing staff leave her alone as much as possible.

The story of Mrs Nigel shows how inadequate coping with adaptive tasks in combination with certain types of interaction with the environment can lead to a succession of psychosocial problems. By denying her invalidity and institutionalization, the patient remains in a state of unstable emotional balance (confrontation with the move upsets her every time). The way in which she tries to maintain her self-image and emotional balance (projection and aggressive behaviour respectively), also interferes with the communication with her environment. Partly because of the reactions of the environment to this situation, a type of interaction pattern develops over time that generates a third problem, that is, the problem of social isolation. If this downward spiral is not broken, there is a possibility that the patient will eventually go into a depression (disruption of balance or crisis).

Primary goal of the treatment

The primary goals of psychomotor therapy follow directly from the general request for assistance. For situation 1 (crisis) the primary goal can be described as restoring the balance; for situation 2 (unstable balance) as stabilizing the balance and preventing (additional) psychosocial problems; for situation 3 (downward spiral) as breaking out of the downward spiral. In other words: for patients in an unstable balance, the function of participation in psychomotor therapy, by means of fostering adequate coping with adaptive tasks, is primarily preventive. For patients who are already caught in a downward spiral, a therapeutic effect is striven for in addition to a preventive effect. These primary treatment goals are determined in multi-disciplinary consultation.

In general, patients with incidental psychosocial problems (unstable balance) and patients with protracted psychosocial problems (downward spiral), can participate in the same therapy group. However, we do not recommend including patients who are (still) in a crisis in the group right away – for example, patients who suffer from a major depression or are very anxious. Moreover, patients who clearly indicate at the beginning of therapy, for example through agitated behaviour, that they do not want to participate in the group therapy, should not be persuaded to do so. In both cases there is a high risk that these patients would disrupt the group process which must be developed. In time these patients can be re-invited to participate in the psychomotor therapy, when – as Saul (1988: 200) observes – 'the group has settled into a culture', and it can offer some structure and support to these patients.

Diagnostic examination and psychosocial diagnosis

When the primary goal of the treatment has been established in multi-disciplinary consultation, an observation period of several weeks can start. Based partly on behaviour observation scales, the patient is then observed (and sometimes tested) in therapy situations, with regard to cognitive function (memory, perception, action) on the one hand, and social and affective functions on the other hand. In addition, information about the life-history of the patient is gathered from the case history to get insight into his or her personality, social life and coping strategies used in difficult periods. Based on these data a preliminary psychosocial diagnosis is formulated (see Figure 7.3). This means that conclusions are drawn regarding those aspects of adaptive tasks (see Table 7.1) that generate stress in the patient, and the way in which he or she copes with that. The degree in which ineffective and inadequate coping behaviour in the patient is possibly (partly) induced by the problem-solving capacity of the environment, that is, the way in which the environment deals with the patient, is also indicated. Based on observations within and outside the therapy situation, the psychomotor therapist then lists, if possible, personal, illness-related, social and/or material factors which appear to affect the experience of stress negatively and positively. For example, severe language problems caused by cerebral degeneration can hinder a patient in communicating with fellow patients. On the other hand, respecting a patient's bedside cabinet with special family photographs as his or her property, which will not be touched by the personnel, gives the patient some feeling of privacy. If the preliminary psychosocial diagnosis is supported by the multi-disciplinary consultation, a treatment plan is developed.

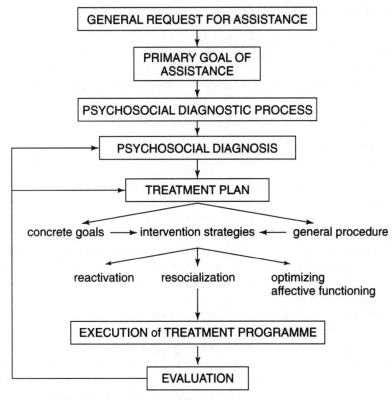

Figure 7.3 General procedure in psychomotor therapy

Treatment plan

The treatment plan is an action plan, in which the primary goal of psychomotor therapy is defined in concrete terms of adaptive tasks that the therapy will focus on, the concrete goals which are set and the appropriate intervention strategies. It also indicates which aspects of the adaptation-coping process the therapy will focus on and which variables are targeted (personal, illness-related, social and/or material environment, coping strategy, coping behaviour; see Figure 7.1). Finally, the treatment plan covers the (tentative) time schedule of the treatment and the methods of evaluation. The entire action plan should be in accord with the general assistance strategy or care programme which has been drawn up for the patient in multi-disciplinary consultation, and it must be consistent with other possible types of assistance. We will address several aspects of the treatment programme in more detail below.

Concrete goals of psychomotor group therapy

After the adaptive tasks on which the therapy will focus have been determined, the goal(s) of the therapy must be defined in more concrete terms. An individual treatment programme will consist of one or more of the following concrete goals depending on which adaptive tasks are judged as problematic:

- (re)activation
- (re)socialization
- stimulation of affective functioning.

Reactivation is aimed at preventing, or reducing in the patient excessively regressive methods of coping with the adaptive tasks 'coping with his or her own invalidity', 'dealing with the nursing home environment', and 'developing an adequate care-relationship with the staff'. This is done by means of stimulating residual cognitive abilities (with regard to memory, perception and action). The final aim is to accomplish a reduction of symptoms that often accompany regressive coping, such as anxiety and suspicion, feelings of unease, excessively dependent behaviour, not participating at all in organized recreational activities, and incontinence.

Resocialization aims at preventing patients from withdrawing socially when they have problems with the adaptive task 'developing and maintaining (new) social relations'. The aim is to prevent or push back socially isolated behaviour, and further social relations by stimulating communication between patients and their environment (fellow residents, therapist). In this way attempts are made to reduce symptoms that may accompany the coping strategy 'social withdrawal', such as social isolation, non-social egocentric or aggressive behaviour, loss of decorum and a decrease of social and verbal skills.

Stimulation of affective functioning aims at supporting patients who have problems with the adaptive tasks 'maintaining an emotional balance' and 'preserving a positive self-image'. By encouraging patients to participate in movement activities, to show initiative and to make choices in various situations, they are stimulated to experience success and pleasure and an increased sense of control and identity. In this way attempts are made to reduce projective and regressive behaviour symptoms, such as paranoid, hostile and sad behaviour, anxiety, restlessness by night and excessive wandering around.

Intervention strategies

Depending on the concrete goals aimed for with the treatment, the psychomotor therapist will utilize certain intervention strategies. Individual differences between patients are naturally taken into account by tuning in to his personality, his interests and personal skills. We will now discuss these general strategies for each of the concrete goals separately.

Reactivation

To prevent, or reduce, an excessively regressive way of coping with the dementing process the patients are encouraged to use their cognitive abilities with regard to memory, perception and action, through movement activities and group discussions during the psychomotor therapy sessions. For those patients also who have difficulties accepting their admittance to the nursing home, movement activities can sometimes be of great help. The movement activities are organized in such a way that patients with various types of cognitive impairment are basically able to participate without any problems. A general assignment is given to the whole group, and limited or expanded in accordance with individual abilities during the execution of the movement activity. For example: the assignment for a bowling game is: 'Try to knock over as many pins with the ball as possible.' During the game this assignment can be limited to 'Try to knock over the pins', or expanded to 'The pins are numbered; try to score as many points as possible.'

Memory To stimulate memory, movement activities are generally evaluated in the group at the end of each session by means of a group discussion and questions and answers. Attention is paid to the patients' personal memories or associations. To this end the therapist attempts to discover during the activity and in the closing discussion/evaluation which aspects of the movement activity (such as movement actions, materials, group arrangement, music) have made an impression on the participant, and he or she records these in a descriptive evaluation after the meeting. If necessary these aspects which have importance for the participants, are mentioned in the introductory discussion of the next session, to help the patients remember the previous therapy session. Another way to stimulate the memory is to show the materials used in the previous session, or let the patients handle them. This proves to be a productive approach: patients often report that they remember the movement activity and are able to then give some details (Faber, 1977; Bourgeois, 1990). This is a pleasant experience for the patients: it puts their being together at that moment in a broader time frame, which helps them to experience continuity and to develop an awareness of the activities done with the group, the materials used and the location (Ernst, 1977).

Perception To stimulate perception, somato-sensory perception as well as orientation with regard to space, time and persons is stimulated. The somato-sensory system is naturally stimulated by the movement itself, but also by introducing variation into the materials used (large, small, heavy, light, rough, smooth, soft, etc.). To exercise *spatial orientation*, various group arrangements are used, for instance small and large circles, two groups opposite each other, participants spread freely across the space, etc. Assignments and materials are also used to introduce some variety in the way the space is structured. In addition, movement assignments that appeal to the ability to distinguish between left/right, front/back and under/over (like passing the ball around the circle counterclockwise, or playing it to the other side across a rope) are frequently used. Finally, to exercise spatial orientation in the nursing home, the therapy sessions are generally held in the same room.

To stimulate *orientation* in terms of *time* (awareness of time), therapy takes place at fixed times (preferably in the morning), and the meetings are generally structured in the same way: introductory discussion (10 minutes), main activity (30 minutes) and closing discussion/evaluation (5 minutes). To enhance the awareness of time, conversation subjects such as duration of the session, the moments of gathering over the week, the time of the next session and the possible activities after the therapy session (coffee, lunch), are brought up during these meetings.

The fact that action is taken to stimulate the awareness of time does not imply that participants who live in their own reality are expected to demonstrate verbally or through their orientation that they are fully aware of reality and concrete relations in the present. The interweaving of past and present, which we frequently see in dementia patients, is not corrected, but attempts are made to find possible explanations for the disoriented behaviour. For according to the adaptation-coping model, denial of the present and withdrawing into the past can be viewed as a way of coping with (certain) events or circumstances in the present. To be able to offer adequate help, tracing these explanations is more important than correcting behaviour, which could also be detrimental to the patient. In that sense this approach deviates from the traditional approach to stimulate orientation used by the Reality Orientation groups (Ingersoll and Silverman, 1978).

To stimulate *orientation* to *people* the composition of the groups is kept constant whenever possible and the participants are offered a fixed place in the group (especially in the starting phase of the therapy), so that they have the opportunity to get to know their neighbours. Everybody is welcomed by the therapist individually (for example with a few words and/or a hand-shake: Unger, 1985; Saul, 1988). In some movement activities name tags are used, providing the patients with the opportunity to call one another by name, and briefly focusing attention on the identity of the participants. In addition, the therapist regularly takes the role of intermediary between the participants, drawing their attention to reactions and/or attempts by others to make contact (Sandel and Kelleher, 1987).

Action To stimulate action, various types of sporting movement activities and movement activities in the form of games are used, with a range of game materials, such as different kinds of balls, pins, balloons, rings, sticks, ropes, rackets and music. In general, the first few meetings are used to practise (parts of) situations or actions (so-called theme exercises) which are important for an activity, in preparation for the more complex movement arrangements (and for the purpose of observing the participants' abilities). The fact that this method yields better results in most patients than immediately offering the more complex activity, is an indication that the procedural learning function has been (to some extent) spared in this patient group.

To encourage the generalization of the performance in the therapy group to everyday performance, activities of a hobby or domestic/ functional nature are offered at set times (for instance, dancing to music or collectively organizing the coffee and cakes, respectively). Simple assignments are used for the purpose of structuring movement arrangements or activities. If the patients' behaviour shows that they are unable to function adequately because they have forgotten the assignment, the therapist regularly repeats the movement assignments during the movement activities.

Resocialization

In connection with the therapy objective of preventing or reducing socially isolated behaviour and stimulating social relations between the participants, a part of each session is spent on group discussions. The task of the therapist is to stimulate the participants into verbal/non-verbal communication; the aim is not only to express emotions and individual opinions, listen to one another and respond to each other, but also to generate understanding (if possible) for the limitations of others, for example when these others communicate inadequately. This procedure aims at fostering a group identity (Sandel, 1978; Schwab et al., 1985). If necessary, the therapist assists patients during these discussions, for instance by explaining remarks and responses of fellow group members. In addition, there are regular movement assignments which focus on verbal/non-verbal communication and co-operation, for example working in pairs or with two groups.

Stimulating affective functioning

To improve the affective functioning of patients, the therapy spends much time and effort on stimulating experiences of success and pleasure, as well as enhancing a sense of control and identity. To increase the possibilities of successful and pleasurable experiences, the therapist creates a relaxed and positive atmosphere during the movement activities, among other things by using flexible movement assignments. The patients are furthermore systematically rewarded for active participation in the movement activities. Games and sporting movement activities, which have a certain element of tension (such as stopping balls in front of a goal, keeping a balloon in the air as long as possible or trying to knock over pins with a small ball) are frequently chosen to stimulate pleasure. Experience shows that these types of activities, partly because they evoke associations with (undamaged) childhood years in the participants, generate much enthusiasm (Sandel, 1978, 1987; Weingarden-Albert, 1987).

During the group discussions and movement activities, the sense of control is enhanced by acting upon the participants' initiatives as much as possible; for instance: pursuing subjects that the patients bring up, modifying movement assignments to the desires of the participants, or agreeing to do the proposed activity at a later date. The therapist rewards all patient initiative verbally (Weingarden-Albert, 1987). Furthermore, the movement activities are regularly organized in such a way that taking the initiative is a precondition for being able to carry out the movement assignment adequately. In addition to initiative, free choice is also stimulated, for instance by letting the patients choose from various activities and materials, or by emphasizing free choice in the movement activity itself (for example, deciding who to throw the ball to, or which pin to hit; see also Crepeau, 1988; Rodin and Langer, 1977).

To stimulate the sense of identity, the patients are greeted individually at each session and attention is paid regularly, both in discussions and during movement activities, to individual characteristics of patients (for example through positive comments about dress, hairstyle and jewellery, a powerful or elegant style of movement, or the patient's sense of humour). In discussions with the therapist and in group discussions the patients are furthermore stimulated to express personal opinions and emotions (an ability that remains intact in these patients for a relatively long time, according to Verwoerdt (1981)). In this way the development of mutual understanding is stimulated in the participants, which in turn enables them to offer each other emotional support. To this end, the therapist tries to create an inviting and safe atmosphere using empathic communication with the patients (see also Rogers, 1967; Sandel, 1978; Verwoerdt, 1981; Sandel and Kelleher, 1987).

General guidelines for the therapy

The optimal therapy *frequency* is two to three times a week – the same frequency we often encounter in other psychosocial assistance activities (Jenkins *et al.*, 1977; Burton, 1980; Welden and Yesavage, 1982; Gorissen, 1985; Sandel and Kelleher, 1987). A duration of 45 minutes per session offers sufficient time for an introductory discussion, a main exercise and a closing discussion. A longer session is generally too much of a burden for these patients, because of their diminished powers of concentration.

Group size should be limited (six to eight patients). This prevents the group becoming disorderly and confusing for the patients. Experience shows that demented patients soon withdraw when they are confronted with too many impressions. Working in small groups furthermore enables the therapist to assist the participants in the therapeutic process on an individual basis.

Group therapy should preferably take place in a *separate space*. This generates an intimate, safe atmosphere. It also prevents the participants being distracted by passers-by. A third reason is that a fixed space stimulates the spatial orientation in the nursing home. The cognitive impairments of the participants must, of course, be taken into account when the movement arrangements, or activities, are developed. Existing games and sports (including the rules that go with them) will therefore have to be adjusted. All kinds of basic actions (for example throwing, catching, playing football, taking penalties, hockey) can be applied in a simplified form (Dröes, 1987). Assignments that are too complex (that is, composite assignments) should be avoided.

The *assignments* are preferably simple and brief and can be repeated several times, if necessary. Individual abilities must take a central place during therapy, not the differences between the participants' performances. Experience shows that introducing a competitive element in particular games and types of sport can definitely motivate the participants to become extra active! The therapist must, however, be alert that this does not enhance possible feelings of insufficiency in the patients (for instance by rewarding patients on the basis of effort). Finally, the movement activities must be offered as much as possible in an atmosphere of communication, pleasure and sociability to motivate the elderly to participate regularly and actively in the meetings.

With regard to the *materials* used: they should be easy to handle, invite movement and must be able to serve as a means to make contact with other participants (Overduin-Swets, 1977; Faber, 1977; Janssen and Giberson, 1988; Dröes, 1991). In other words, light materials in strong (bright) colours are preferred, for example foam balls (red, yellow) in various sizes, beach balls (many colours), plastic footballs (with a colourful design), plastic hockey sticks (different colours), balloons (different colours), plastic rackets, coloured pins, plastic colourful animals, colourful images of fruit. By introducing the material before the movement activity is started, the patients will become familiar with it. This pre-empts patients refusing to participate because the material appears too heavy, too difficult to handle or too dangerous. In addition to materials, music can be used (Hanley and Peele, 1985; Olderog-Millard and Smith, 1989) as well as objects from everyday life, such as scarves, teatowels, ropes and refreshments (Sandel and Kelleher, 1987).

In conclusion, a few remarks about *intervention techniques* are in order. The term intervention techniques refers to the way in which the therapist approaches the individual participants or the group to explain a movement assignment, and the way in which the therapist assists individual patients or the group in the execution of the movement assignments. The therapeutic method contains elements from both analytic and behaviour therapy. It attempts to facilitate discussion of psychosocial problems; rewards are used to motivate patients into taking an active part in the therapy activities. Other intervention techniques are demonstration, verbal explanation, changing of the context and permanent assistance. Following a brief explanation, the therapist will demonstrate the purpose of the assignment with one or several participants. During the activity the patients are then assisted verbally (or non-verbally) in their actions and supported by means of remarks, rewards, intonation, emotional tone, observation and feedback, saying names, asking concrete questions and interpreting behaviour (see also Verwoerdt, 1981; Feil, 1985; Stark and Lohn, 1989). If, for whatever reason, a movement activity does not appeal to patients, the therapist will have to examine – for example by introducing small changes in situations (context variation) – what the participants will respond to or get enthusiastic about. In some cases, permanent assistance will be required, for example when patients are unable to remember the assignment, when they have to ask what it was all the time, or when they have trouble focusing their attention. The therapist must guard against the patient experiencing the contact as an intrusion in his personal space, or territory, which would increase the risk of the patient withdrawing further, becoming aggressive or breaking off all contact with his environment. So the therapist must be alert and show respect for the patients's personal need for distance.

ASPECTS OF EVALUATION

'Standard descriptive evaluation forms' or 'behaviour checklists' or 'observation scales' are often used for evaluation of the treatment. To compare functions at different times, standard observation sessions which offer fixed movement arrangements are used (Dröes, 1991). This procedure provides a systematic check to see if changes have occurred in the coping of the patients with the various adaptive tasks mentioned before. At present a study is being conducted (by the Faculty of Human Movement Sciences of the Free University of Amsterdam in collaboration with the Department of Psychiatry of the Faculty of Medicine of the same university) into the reliability and validity of the Behaviour Observation Scale for Psychomotor Therapy in demented elderly (BPMT-demented elderly). This observation scale, which is based on the Behaviour observation scale for Intramural Psychogeriatrics (BIP; Verstraten and Van Eekelen, 1987), contains the following nine categories: memory, orientation, communication and praxis, contact with others, initiative, depressive behaviour, paranoid behaviour, anxious behaviour, aggressive behaviour and liveliness (see Figure 7.4).

MODIFIED CHECKLIST GPMT – 73

Checklist of the Behaviour observation scale for Psychomotor Therapy
in demented elderly

Name of patient:	Sex:
Date of birth:	Diagnosis at admission:
Mobility:	Screened at:
Institute:	Date of admission:
Name of judge/rater:	Function:
Date on which the checklist is completed:	

Short instruction

Answer every statement by putting a mark in one of the three columns.
Give only one answer for each statement. In case of doubt, for example,
between 'sometimes' and 'often/always', try to make a choice all the same.
The score is as follows
(0) behaviour never occurs
(1) behaviour occurs sometimes
(2) behaviour occurs often or always

Scale scores	*(min.–max.)*	
A Memory	(0–18)	☐
B Orientation	(0–18)	☐
C Communication & praxis	(0–18)	☐
D Contact with others	(0–16)	☐
E Initiative	(0–8)	☐
F Depressive behaviour	(0–14)	☐
G Anxious behaviour	(0–10)	☐
H Paranoid behaviour	(0–8)	☐
I Aggressive behaviour	(0–12)	☐
J Liveliness	(0–24)	☐

GPMT – Demented elderly

	2	1	0	
1. Reacts when he/she is spoken to.				J
2. Reacts nonverbally on remarks of others.				J
3. From the verbal/nonverbal behaviour it can be gathered that he/she believes him or herself to be in a different place.				B
4. Helps somebody when asked to.				C
5. Greets and/or answers greetings of other participants on entering or leaving the therapy room.				D
6. Undertakes self-invented actions in the therapy assignment.				E
7. Knows the therapist by name and/or recognizes the name on a nameplate.				A

(A)

Figure 7.4 The Behaviour observation scale for Psychomotor Therapy in the
demented elderly; the sub-scales and some items.

Apart from evaluation within the therapeutic situation, the psycho-motor therapist participates in the multi-disciplinary treatment evaluation of the team. Here he reports on the cognitive, social and emotional functions of patients during therapy. Based on these reports, advice can also be given about how to handle individual patients.

DISCUSSION

Between 1986 and 1988 the effectiveness of psychomotor therapy for demented patients as described here was studied in three nursing homes in Amsterdam among forty patients diagnosed with mild to moderate demen-tia of the Alzheimer type. The study focused on the question of whether the adaptive problems, as discussed earlier, and more in particular the behavioural symptoms accompanying these problems, are influenced in a positive way if these patients participate in psychomotor group therapy on a regular basis and for a considerable length of time.

To evaluate psychomotor therapy an experimental design was used, that is, a 'pre-test/post-test control group design' with matched pairs. The experimental group received psychomotor therapy three times a week for eleven months, and the control group was offered general activity therapy at the same frequency. Controlling took place for relevant (non-experimental) variables, such as circumstances, autonomous changes, test effects, instrumentation and drop-out due to death or transfer to another nursing home.

Based on the results of this evaluation (Dröes, 1991), we may conclude that psychomotor therapy has a positive effect on emotional symptoms, such as degree of satisfaction, aggression and night-time restlessness. In other words psychomotor therapy seems to have a specific and positive effect on demented patients with respect to the adaptive task of 'maintain-ing an emotional balance'. The effects are, however, dependent on the severity of dementia. In patients with slight functional disabilities this therapy has a positive effect on degree of satisfaction (F $(1, 17) = 2.66$, $p = .03$) and in patients with more severe functional disabilities it has a stabilizing effect on aggression (F $(1, 12) = 7.82$, $p = .008$) and night-time restlessness (F $(1, 12) = 3.46$, $p = .05$). These symptoms became significantly more severe in the control group. The group with more severe functional disabilities furthermore seemed to express feelings of discontent related to the functional disabilities more adequately. Psychomotor therapy proved to be clearly more effective in these aspects than general activity therapy (occupational therapy). In other words, psychomotor group therapy can be employed specifically to prevent or treat emotional behavioural problems in demented patients. This means it could supplement the presently available treatments in nursing homes and homes for the elderly. Because symptoms such as aggression and night-time restlessness frequently cause the family care-givers to have demented patients admitted to a nursing home, psychomotor therapy can also be applied in a preventive way for demented patients who live at home, for example through day care, ambulant geriatric services or geriatric outpatient clinics.

With regard to other psychosocial symptoms in daily life (for example, communication problems, incontinence, bed restraints, unwilling behaviour, apathy and dependent behaviour), clinically small to moderate, but statistically insignificant, positive effects were found. In the context of therapy sessions, however, statistically significant improvements in memory, liveliness and initiative were observed. Although these findings confirm the results of earlier intervention studies carried out in this field (Diesfeldt and Diesfeldt-Groenendijk, 1975; Ernst, 1977; Ernst *et al.*, 1978; Molloy *et al.*, 1988; Molloy, Delaquerriere Richardson, and Grilly, 1988; Jenkins *et al.*, 1977; Götestam and Melin, 1990; Burton, 1980; Sandel, 1987) no definitive statements can be made based on these findings, because no control measures were taken. Future research will have to provide answers about the extent to which these symptoms can be influenced.

REFERENCES

Birchmore, T. and Clague, S. (1983) A behavioral approach to reduce shouting. *Nursing Times* 79 (4): 37–39.

Bourgeois, M.S. (1990) Enhancing conversation skills in patients with Alzheimer's disease using a prosthetic memory aid. *J. of Applied Behavior Analysis* 23 (1): 29–42.

Burton, M.A. (1980) Evaluation and change in a psychogeriatric ward through direct observation and feedback. *Br. J. of Psychiatry* 137 (4): 566–571.

Buytendijk, F.J.J. (1972) *Mens en dier*. Het Spectrum, Utrecht.

Cleary, T.A., Clamon, C., Price, M. and Shullaw, G. (1988) A reduced stimulation unit: effects on patients with Alzheimer's Disease and related disorders. *The Gerontologist* 28 (4): 511–514.

Coppenolle, H. van (1989) Psychomotor therapy and adapted physical activity: defining the concepts. In: *Better by Moving. Proceedings of the 2nd International Symposium on Psychomotor Therapy and Adapted Physical Activity*, Leuven, 1989, Uitgeverij Acco, Leuven/Amersfoort.

Crepeau, E.L. (1988) Activity programming for the elderly. In: Activity programming for the elderly (book review). B. Wade, *Int. J. Nursing Studies* 25 (1): 79–84.

Diesfeldt, H.F.A. and Diesfeldt-Groenendijk, H. (1977) Improving cognitive performance in psychogeriatric patients: the influence of physical exercise. In: *Age and Aging* 6: 58–64.

Dröes, R.M. (1985) Eindrapportage exploratie-onderzoek 'Bewegingsactivering bij demente bejaarden'. Deel 1: Het practijkonderzoek. Intern rapport, Interfaculteit Lichamelijke Opvoeding, Vakgroep Bewegingsagogiek/Werkgroep Inspanningsfysiologie/Gezondheidkunde m.b.t. het bewegen, Vrije Universiteit, Amsterdam, februari.

—— (1987) Een bewegingsactiveringsprogramma voor demente patiënten. Intern rapport, Faculteit der Bewegingswetenschappen, vakgroep Bewegingsagogiek.

—— (1991) *In Beweging; over psychosociale hulpverlening aan demente ouderen*. Intro, Nijkerk.

—— (1992) Beweging als middel in de reactivering en resocialisering van demente ouderen; over de ontwikkeling van bewegingsprogramma's. *Bewegen & Hulpverlening* 9 (2): 118–137.

Ernst, P. (1977) Treatment of the aged mentally ill: further unmasking of the effects of a diagnosis of chronic brain syndrome. *Journal of the American Geriatric Society* 25 (10): 466–469.

——, Badash, D., Beran, B., Kosovsky, R. *et al.* (1978) Sensory stimulation of elderly patients: preliminary report on the treatment of patients with chronic brain syndrome in an old age home. *Israels Annals of Psychiatry and Related Disciplines* 16 (4): 315–326.

Faber, J. (1977) Bewegingstherapie aan demente bejaarden. Interne publicatie, Afdeling Bewegingstherapie, Vogelenzang, Bennebroek.

Fahrenfort, J. (1986) *Psychomotorische therapie; een onderzoek naar het gebruik van bewegings- en lichaamsgeoriënteerde methoden in de psychiatrie.* VU-uitgeverij, Amsterdam.

Feil, N. (1985) Resolution: The final life task. *J. of Humanistic Psychology* 25 (2): 91–105.

Goldberg, W.G. and Fitzpatrick, J.J. (1980) Movement therapy with the aged. *Nurs. Research* 29: 339–346.

Gordijn, C.C.F., Brink, C. van den, Meerdink, P., Tamboer, J.W.I. *et al.* (1975) *Wat beweegt ons.* Bosch and Keuning N.V., Baarn.

Gorissen, J.P. (1985) Een onderzoek naar het effect van realiteitsoriëntatie-training op een groep psychogeriatrische patiënten. *T. Gerontologie and Geriatrie* 16: 235–239.

Götestam, K.G. (1987) Learning versus environmental support for increasing reality orientation in senile demented patients. *European Journal of Psychiatry* 1: 7–12.

—— and Melin, L. (1990) The effect of prompting and reinforcement of activity in elderly demented inpatients. *Scandinavian J. of Psychology* 31: 2–8.

Greene, J.G., Smith, R., Gardiner, M. and Timbury, G.C. (1982) Measuring behavioral disturbance of elderly demented patients in the community and its effects on relatives: a factor analytic study. *Age and Aging* 11: 121–126.

Gustafsson, R. (1976) Miljötherapi pa en avdeling för patienter med senil demenz. *Scandinavian J. of Behavior therapy* 5 (1): 27–37.

Hanley, O. and Peele, K. (1985) An active occupational therapy programme for the severely demented patient in a psychogeriatric day hospital. *Occupational Therapy* 48 (11): 336–338.

Hungenaert, R. and Schaekers, R. (1982) Psychomotorische therapie voor psychogeriatrische patiënten. *Vlaams Tijdschrift voor Psychomotorische Therapie* 9 (4): 190–206.

Ingersoll, B. and Silverman, A. (1978) Comparative group psychotherapy for the aged. *The Gerontologist* 18 (2): 201–206.

Istha, D. and Smit, N.W. de (1977) *Crisisinterventie: therapie of strategie.* Samson Uitg., Alphen a/d Rijn.

Janssen, J.A. and Giberson, D.L. (1988) Remotivation Therapy. *J. of Gerontological Nursing* 14 (6): 31–34.

Jenkins, J., Felce, D., Lunt, B. and Powell, L. (1977) Increasing engagement in activity of residents in old people's homes by providing recreational materials. *Behavior Research and Therapy* 15: 429–434.

Jones, G.M.M. and Miesen, B.M.L. (1992) *Care-Giving in Dementia. Research and Applications*, vol. 1. Routledge, London.

Kam, P. van der, Mol, F., Wimmers, M.F.H.G. (1971) *Beoordelingsschaal voor Oudere Patiënten.* Van Loghum Slaterus, Deventer.

Karlsson, I., Båne, G., Melin, E., Nuth, A.L. *et al.* (1985) Mental activation – brain plasticity. In: *Normal Aging, Alzheimer's Disease and Senile Dementia.* C.G. Gottfries, (ed.), Editions de l'Université de Bruxelles.

Koevoets, G., van den Heede, P. and Vervloet, R. (1979) De psychogeriatrische patiënt in psychomotorische therapie. *Vlaams Tijdschrift voor Psychomotorische Therapie* 6 (1): 23–25.

Kouwenhoven, M. (1977) Meer bewegen voor geronto-psychiatrische patiënten. *T. Psychomotorische Therapie* (4) 151–175.

Lazarus, R.S. and Folkman, S. (1984) *Stress, Appraisal, and Coping.* Springer Publ. Comp., New York.

Melin, L. and Götestam, K.G. (1981) The effects of rearranging ward routines on communication and eating behaviors of psychogeriatric patients. *J. of Applied Behavior Analysis* 14: (1): 47–51.

Molloy, D.W., Beerschoten, D.A., Borrie, M.J. *et al.* (1988) Acute effects of exercise on neuropsychological function in elderly subjects. *Journal of the American Geriatric Society* 36: 29–33.

Molloy, D.W., Delaquerriere Richardson, L. and Grilly, R.G. (1988) The effects of a three-month exercise programme on neuropsychological function in elderly institutionalized women: a randomized controlled trial. *Age and Aging* 17: 303–310.

Moos, R.H. and Tsu, V.D. (1977) The crisis of physical illness: An overview. In: *Coping with Physical Illness.* R.H. Moos (ed.), Plenum Medical Book Company, New York/London.

Olderog-Millard, K.A. and Smith, J.M. (1989) The influence of group singing therapy on the behavior of Alzheimer's Disease patients. *J. of Nursing Therapy* 26 (2): 58–70.

Overduin-Swets, C. (1977) Toen ik oud was ... psychomotorische therapie bij psychisch gestoorde bejaarden. *T. Psychomotorische Therapie* (4): 176–190.

Pinkston, E.M. and Linsk, N.L. (1988) *Care of the Elderly: A Family Approach.* Pergamon Press Inc., New York/Oxford.

Probst, M. (1980) Beschouwingen rond psychomotorische therapie bij psychogeriatrische patiënten. *Vlaams Tijdschrift voor Psychomotorische Therapie* 7 (1–2): 28–39.

Reeve, W. and Ivison, D. (1985) Use of environmental manipulation and classroom and modified informal reality orientation with institutionalized, confused elderly patients. *Age and Aging* 14: 119–121.

Rijsdorp, K. (1977) *Gymnologie.* Het Spectrum, Utrecht/Antwerp.

Rodin, J. and Langer, E.J. (1977) Long-term effects of a control-relevant intervention with the institutionalized aged. *J. of Personality and Social Psychology* 35 (12): 897–902.

Rogers, C.R. (1967) The therapeutic relationship: recent theory and research. In: *The Human Dialogue.* F.E. Matson and A. Montagu (eds), Free Press, New York, pp. 246–259.

Sandel, S.L. (1978) Reminiscence in movement therapy with the aged. *Art Psychotherapy* 5: 217–221.

—— (1987) Expressive group therapy with severely confused patients. *Activities, Adaptation and Aging* 9: 117–128.

—— and Kelleher, M. (1987) A psychosocial approach to dance-movement therapy. *Activities, Adaptation and Aging* 9: 25–39.

Saul, S.R. (1988) Group therapy with confused and disoriented elderly people. In: *Group Psychotherapies for the Elderly,* American Group Psychotherapy Association.

Schwab, M., Rader, J. and Doan, J. (1985) Relieving the anxiety and fear in dementia. *J. Gerontological Nursing* 11: 8–15.

Stark, A. and Lohn, A.F. (1989) The use of verbalization in dance-/movement therapy. *The Arts in Psychotherapy* 16: 105–113.

Tamboer, J.W.I. (1985) Mensbeelden achter bewegingsbeelden; kinanthropologische analyses vanuit het perspectief van de Lichamelijke Opvoeding. Academisch proefschrift, Vrije Universiteit, Amsterdam, Uitgeverij de Vrieseborch, Haarlem.

Unger, A.K. (1985) Movement therapy for the geriatric population. *Clinical Gerontologist* 3 (3): 46–47.

van der Wulp, J.C. (1986) *Verstoring en verwerking in verpleeghuizen.* Uitg. Intro, Nijkerk.

Vermeer, A. en Sonius, Y. (1976) Wat is bewegingstherapie. *T. van de Werkgroep Bewegingsonderwijs* (3): 2–9.

Verstraten, P.F.J. and Eekelen, C.W.J.M. van (1987) *Handleiding voor de GIP; Gedragsobservatieschaal voor de Intramurale psychogeriatrie.* Van Loghum Slaterus, Deventer.

Verwoerdt, A. (1981) Individual psychotherapy in senile dementia. In: *Clinical Aspects of Alzheimer's Disease and Senile Dementia (Aging,* 15). N.E. Miller and G.D. Cohen (eds), Raven Press, New York.

Weingarden-Albert, P. (1987) Dance-movement therapy with the elderly at Baycrest Center for geriatric care. In: *International Perspectives on Adapted Physical Activity.* M.E. Berridge and G.R. Ward (eds), Champaign (IL), Human Kinetics Publ. Inc.

Welden, S. and Yesavage, J.A. (1982) Behavioral improvement with relaxation training in senile dementia. *Clinical Gerontologist* 1 (1): 45–49.

Williams, R., Reeve, W., Ivison, D. and Kavanagh, D. (1987) Use of environmental manipulation and modified informal reality orientation with institutionalized, confused elderly subjects: a replication. *Age and Aging* 16: 315–318.

Yesavage, J.A. and Karasu, T.B. (1982) Psychotherapy with elderly patients. *American Journal of Psychotherapy* 36 (1): 41–55.

Chapter 8

'Snoezelen'

A new way of communicating with the severely demented elderly

Ilse Achterberg, Wilma Kok and Cees Salentijn

INTRODUCTION

About five years ago, action-oriented activities were offered to demented elderly residents in our department: flower arranging, craftwork, collage-making and physical exercise. However, it soon became apparent that these activities made impossible demands on the residents: they walked away or fell asleep. The materials used in the activities were cuddled, touched, smelled and examined, both visually and aurally, independent of the goal of the activity.

We concluded that these activity-oriented approaches no longer had any connection with the inner world of the people to whom they were offered. For these severely demented elderly persons, experience had taken the place of action.

Care-givers also experienced much frustration in providing daily care to severely cognitively impaired demented elderly residents. These people seemed to have withdrawn into a world of their own where they could not be reached.

In our search for solutions to the problem of establishing and maintaining communication with these residents, we made a study of literature from the area of care for the mentally retarded.

It was in this area that 'snoezelen' was created in the 1970s by a remedial educationalist and two recreational therapists at the Larendaal Institute in Laren, Holland. They coined the term 'snoezelen', a combination of two other Dutch words meaning 'doze' and 'sniff', to describe the combination of relaxation and sensory stimulation involved in the new approach. Snoezelen with mentally disabled people occurs in one or more large, dimly lit spaces in which music is playing at low volume; several assistants use a number of apparatuses to stimulate the senses of the group of most severely mentally disabled. A strong appeal is made to the senses, using various materials for touching and tasting, as well as sound and light effects (Bloemendal, 1983a and b, 1987a and b; Glorius, 1990).

The aim of snoezelen with the mentally disabled is to provide an opportunity for development. It is also a means of making contact and of offering distraction and entertainment (Hulsegge and Verheul, 1986).

Like the severely demented elderly, the severely disabled have an extremely limited capacity for verbal communication, a very low intellectual level and often seem to be in a world of their own to which it is very difficult for care-workers to gain access (Cleland *et al.*, 1966).

This perception formed the basis of a combined project in which snoezelen was offered both as a supervised activity and as an integral part of the daily care of demented elderly. For conciseness' sake, we refer to both assistants and nurses as care-givers.

This chapter is about what snoezelen has come to mean to our elderly residents and care-givers. We have drawn on literature and on our own experience. We will also devote attention to organizational and management aspects.

WHAT IS SNOEZELEN?

Snoezelen with the demented elderly is an individually oriented approach that employs active sensory stimulation to share and enter into the experience of the demented elderly in an attempt to increase and maintain their well-being (Achterberg and Kok, 1992).

The main concepts of snoezelen can be expressed in terms of *technique*, *method* and *attitude*. The technique of snoezelen is the use of materials and devices for the stimulation of specific senses. A key aspect of this technique is that one shares in the experience of the material — shared personal experience creates mutual trust and a kind of 'common ground' for communication. The method involves observation, reporting and systematic application in daily care, including evaluation at regular intervals. The attitude of care-workers must be empathic, and oriented to the well-being of individuals.

The place occupied by snoezelen and its effectiveness in comparison with the techniques of reality orientation and validation therapy might best be understood in relation to the degree of severity of dementia: reality orientation is most effective and suitable with mildly demented elderly; validation therapy with moderately demented and snoezelen with the severely cognitively impaired demented elderly (Hitch, 1994).

Reality orientation offers a number of strategies to help the mildly demented elderly person maintain his or her grasp of current 'here and now' reality (signs, pictures, large clocks, orientation to care-giver's identity, place and time by care-workers). However, as dementia increases in severity, these strategies lose their effectiveness and orientation to the 'here and now' loses its relevance. For elderly people in this more advanced stage of dementia, the validation method (Feil, 1992) assumes that intellectual thinking has been replaced by a kind of reminiscing state and focuses on the emotional content of what is being said, attempting to recognize and confirm emotions, restore the person's self-esteem and understand the person in the context of the reality they perceive themselves to be in at the moment. As the dementia progresses, cognitive impairment increases to the degree of making this kind of verbal communication more difficult; verbal validation therapy techniques in turn may lose effectiveness and need to be replaced by non-verbal methods such as 'mirroring', movement, touch and music. This is when snoezelen also becomes beneficial. Like validation therapy, snoezelen is also based on the assumption that all behaviour has an underlying meaning; empathy also plays a central, determining role. Snoezelen might be seen as an extension of these basic insights to the inner world of the severely demented elderly, a world in which intellectual thinking and corresponding action has been replaced by experience. What distinguishes snoezelen, however, is its powerful appeal to the senses as a way of establishing contact (Shapiro, 1995a).

SNOEZELEN: ACTIVITIES AND PROCESS

Snoezelen, first, is a direct and emphatic appeal to specific senses.

As an activity, snoezelen occurs in a cozy, dimly lit space where music is playing at low volume. In daily care, aspects of snoezelen are used in the living room, at the bedside and in the bathroom. Snoezelen is also a way of personally approaching residents in our everyday dealings with them.

In snoezelen, one offers materials to the person and responds to the person's reactions to them. Both verbal and non-verbal expression provide insight into what the person likes. We use light and sound effects, as well as a variety of materials for touching, smelling and tasting. In daily care, the use of dolls, hand puppets and teddy bears is quite common. This creates an atmosphere of warmth and confidence, in which the demented elderly can 'tell' about their inner world through subtle responses such as facial expression and touch. This increases their involvement in their environment (Pinkney, 1993).

New kinds of communication may emerge from this interplay of response and counter-response. For example, when one gives a demented elderly person a feel-bag with rice in it in the snoezelen room, one does not expect the person to tell what is in it. The central thing is the person's experience of the material. It is the nature of the experience that is important, rather than the exactness with which it is comprehended.

This sharing of personal experience creates mutual trust. To find common ground with the demented elderly resident, one must share in the experience of the material. Shared experience and the use of bodily contact can open doors to a demented elderly person's inner world.

Criteria for the use of snoezelen may be:

- If one ceases to be able to make contact in the usual way (a breakdown in communication).
- If the elderly person uses materials in a completely individual way.
- If materials have a positive effect on an elderly resident's behaviour.

The snoezelen plan

There is an absolute need for written documentation of the effects of snoezelen. It is necessary to use a snoezelen observation form. This form is used to document the responses of the residents: which materials they respond to and *how* they respond during snoezelen.

Both positive and negative reactions occurring during snoezelen activities are described and documented. After ten observation hours, a clear pattern emerges and a snoezelen plan is created (Kane and Kane, 1981).

Mrs N. is angry and aggressive. Direct verbal contact does not help. Neither does medication. When I make indirect non-verbal contact through a mirror, Mrs N. establishes eye contact and imitates what I do in the mirror. This communication seems to make her less aggressive. After a while, Mrs N. begins establishing direct contact in this way. We participate; no more medication is given. Mrs N. has become much less anti-social and aggressive.

The observation form and snoezelen plan are kept in a multi-disciplinary individual dossier. They aid in determining which activities can be offered in situations of fear, aggression, disturbance, sadness and pain. They can also offer a basis for establishing everyday contact with a demented elderly person.

Snoezelen in daily care

In our experience, snoezelen has a positive influence on the emotional well-being of severely demented elders. Our aim is for these positive effects to acquire constancy. This is why snoezelen has been integrated into the daily care of clients.

Specific information from the snoezelen plan can be an excellent aid to the integration of snoezelen into daily care. Care-givers often encounter expressions of fear, aggression, pain, unease and sadness among the demented elderly when carrying out basic, necessary duties like washing, getting dressed and eating. Information from the snoezelen plan of a particular client may be of great use in overcoming such difficulties.

Mrs L. spat, scratched, struck out and kicked while being washed. It therefore required the efforts of four people to wash her. Mrs L. reacted well to a doll during snoezelen in the 'snoezel space'; she considers it a child. Taking the doll along to the shower room and using it to demonstrate to Mrs L. what was going to happen during washing caused Mrs L. to calm down and accept what was happening. Step by step, the doll and then Mrs L. were washed.

Because she could see that the doll was not frightened and did not cry, she was reassured and allowed herself to be washed by only one person.

It is important to integrate snoezelen into the nursing home department's activities. The goal is the general integration of facets of snoezelen into daily care. A project group can develop a phase plan and be responsible for the gradual introduction and integration of snoezelen into daily care. This group also motivates co-workers to put snoezelen into action in their daily work with clients.

Mrs R. is sad. She misses her son Karel. He has not been to see her for a while. She wanders through the corridors. I hand her a doll. She smiles, takes the doll and says: 'Karel.' She walks away, contentedly cuddling her 'child'.

Snoezelen has caused more attention to be paid to the individual needs and wishes of the residents within the framework of daily care.

COMPONENTS OF IMPLEMENTING SNOEZELEN

Preconditions

The method of snoezelen is relatively unknown. Many, especially family members, do not understand it and feel a certain aversion to this new approach. In nursing, with the exception of care for the mentally retarded, snoezelen is still the object of much incomprehension. However, it is very important to the ultimate success of the technique that it meets with a high degree of acceptance from all those involved. We have identified the following as pre-requisite conditions for snoezelen activities in an organization.

The organization must be open to this new approach. We keep the nursing home administration informed of the goal and the phases of introduction of snoezelen. The organization must be prepared to make an investment, and, further, it must be prepared to devote a separate space to snoezelen. In our view, a separate space is essential. The attention of the demented elderly tends to wander if other people are present. A separate space also allows for better privacy. Intimacy is an important pre-requisite.

To become well acquainted with a demented elderly person and to establish a relationship, it is essential that supervised activities form a constant component of the activities of the departmental team of care-givers.

The organization must be willing to invest time: to encourage discussion among care-givers, for example, of the development of snoezelen in the department; to arrange family evenings to provide information to family members; to provide other disciplines with information, for example, by scheduling information afternoons or writing a brief study of snoezelen; to collect and compile written information from other sources; and to allocate time for preparation, study and development.

RESIDENT AND CARE-GIVER OUTCOMES

Snoezelen has positive effects for both care-givers and for the demented elderly.

The snoezelen plan helps to preserve continuity in snoezelen activities. Snoezelen occurs at a variety of times and places; this has the effect of removing barriers between care-givers and elderly demented.

Body language, facial expression and sounds are not produced arbitrarily. Snoezelen causes one to realize that the demented elderly are indeed trying to communicate something specific about their own inner world.

Through snoezelen, one obtains information that would otherwise remain unknown. For example, one person had associations with the Second World War in a dark snoezelen space. This explained his fear and unease in a dark bedroom.

A close relationship is created, allowing care-givers to be more open as individuals when dealing with the demented elderly.

Care-givers are afforded an opportunity to empathize with the person's situation and thus to do the maximum possible for him or her. They are stimulated to become involved in the emotions of the demented elderly, and to devote more attention to them.

One sees the elderly with dementia as fully mature persons in their own right, and no longer solely in the context of their limitations.

One may show more of one's self in one's work.

One feels less powerless in dealing with the demented elderly. One knows that a situation can be influenced positively. Care-givers' feelings of frustration and impotence are reduced.

One experiences many valuable moments together with the demented elderly. One shares feelings. One's respect for and appreciation of them is enhanced.

Snoezelen helps to provide a clearer image of the mental and physical condition of the demented elderly to other health care disciplines, allowing them better to attune their treatment to individuals (Kolanowski et al., 1994).

New and different forms of communication may emerge from snoezelen. Increased attention to non-verbal communication leads to better understanding of the demented elderly. Snoezelen can offer ways of removing barriers to contact. In addition, snoezelen reduces the amount of sedation administered, which is beneficial to residents' health and the all-round well-being of the demented individual.

CONCLUSION

Snoezelen has proved an innovative and effective approach in communicating with the severely cognitively impaired demented elderly. It has offered ways of entering into their experience and overcoming obstacles to communication. Such extremely demented elderly persons make up a more or less forgotten group. The use of snoezelen can help to place them in a new light and to be seen once again as people who deserve respect and appreciation; it allows them to become involved in personal, human relationships. We believe this to be fundamental to the approach to working with the demented elderly.

Very few research studies, however, have been conducted on the efficacy of snoezelen both as an activity and in daily care. Shapiro (1995b) was the first to demonstrate significant behavioural and physiological effects of snoezelen in mentally handicapped children. These findings suggest that more research needs to be carried out on the use of snoezelen. The Bernardus Nursing Home in Amsterdam repeated the Shapiro research during the spring of 1996. We used the same cross-over design with a group of thirty severely demented elderly. We wanted to know the effects of snoezelen on the well-being of the demented elderly. The hypothesis was that there would be a significant decrease in the number of disruptive behaviours when the elderly were in the snoezelen-room.

REFERENCES

Achterberg, I. and Kok, W. (1992) 'Snoezelen met psychogeriatrische bewoners: Integratie in de dagelijkse zorg'. *AS: Maandblad Activiteitensector* 11: 16–19.
—— and —— (1993a) 'Voelen, kijken, luisteren, ruiken en proeven'. *Denkbeeld: Tijdschrift voor Psychogeriatrie* 3: 12–13.
—— and —— (1993b) 'Snoezelen met psychogeriatrische bewoners: het snoezel-project in verpleeghuis Bernardus (2)'. *TVZ: Vakblad voor Verpleegkundigen* 4: 131–134.
—— and —— and Salentijn, C. (1994) 'Snoezelen met diep demente bewoners: integratie in de dagelijkse zorg'. *Verpleegkundigen en Gemeenschapszorg* 5: 153–156.
Bloemendal, G. (1983a) 'Snoezelen met dieper gestoorde demente bejaarden (1): gericht op zintuiglijke waarneming en primaire behoeften'. *AS: Maandblad Activiteitensector* 5: 133–138.
—— (1983b) 'Snoezelen met dieper gestoorde demente bejaarden (2): beschrijving van een voorbeeld uit de praktijk'. *AS: Maandblad Activiteitensector*, 6: 150–152.
—— (1987a) 'Snoezelen met demente bejaarden: Deel 1: de begrippen'. *Tijdschrift voor Bejaarden-, Kraam- en Ziekenverzorging* 4: 98–102.
—— (1987b) 'Snoezelen met demente bejaarden: Deel 2: vormen van snoezelen'. *Tijdschrift voor Bejaarden-, Kraam- en Ziekenverzorging* 5: 134–139.

Cleland, C., Clark, J. and Charles, M. (1966) 'Sensory deprivation and aberrant behaviour among idiots'. *American Journal of Mental Deficiency* 5: 213–225.

David, F. and Cella, PhD. (1994) 'Quality of life: concepts and definition'. *The Journal of Pain and Symptom Management* 9: 186–192.

Feil, N. (1992) 'Validation therapy with late onset dementia populations', in G.M.M. Jones and B.M.L. Miesen (eds), *Care-Giving in Dementia: Research and Applications*. London/New York: Tavistock/ Routledge, pp. 199–218.

Glorius, J. (1990) 'Snoezelen in Haarendael: een oude gewoonte: Geen activering, maar een vrijblijvende ontspanningsactiviteit'. *AS: Maandblad Activiteitensector* 9: 4–8.

Hitch, S. (1994) 'Cognitive therapy as a tool for caring for the elderly confused person'. *Journal of Clinical Nursing* 3: 49–56.

Hulsegge, J. and Verheul, A. (1986) *Snoezelen: Een andere wereld*, Nijkerk: Intro.

Jones, G.M.M. and Miesen, B.M.L. (1992) *Care-Giving in Dementia: Research and Applications*, vol. 1. London/New York: Tavistock/Routledge.

Kane, R.A. and Kane, R.L. (1981) *Assessing the Elderly, a Practical Guide to Measurement*. Massachusetts: DC Heath.

Kempen, G.I.J.M. and Ormel, J. (1992) 'Het meten van psychologisch welbevinden bij ouderen'. *Tijdschrift voor Gerontologie en Geriatrie* 23: 225–235.

Kolanowski, A., Hurwits, S., Taylor, L.A., Evans, L. and Strumpf, N. (1994) 'Contextual factors associated with disturbing behaviors in institutionalized elders'. *Nursing Research* 2: 73–79.

Lankveld, J.J.D.M. van (1990) 'Onderzoek naar de beleving van diepzwakzinnigen is nodig. Snoezelen in de praktijk van de zorg voor diepzwakzinnigen'. *AS: Maandblad Aktiviteitensektor* 5: 121–125.

Miesen, B. (1992) 'Dement: zo gek nog niet'. Houten: Bohn Stafleu van Loghum.

Nationale Raad voor de Volksgezondheid (1994) *Psychogeriatrie: Zorg voor dementerenden 2; Een kwalitatieve analyse van de ontwikkelingen in de zorg voor dementerenden*. Zoetermeer: NRV.

Pieterse, M. and Geelen, R. (1990) 'Snoezelen met demente bejaarden: een aanzet tot een systematische aanpak'. *AS: Maandblad Activiteitensector* 6: 1–5.

Pinkney, L. (1993) 'Snoezelen – an evaluation of a sensory environment used by people who are elderly and confused'. Bournemouth: Kings Park Community Hospital.

Schneider, L.S. (1993) 'Efficacy of treatment for geropsychiatric patients with severe mental illness'. *Psychopharmacology Bulletin* 29: 501–524.

Shapiro, M. (1995a) 'Progress report of the "Snoezelen"'. Beit Issie Shapiro, Ra'anana, Israel.

—— (1995b) 'The efficacy of the 'Snoezelen' in inhibiting maladaptive behaviors and facilitating adaptive behaviors in children who are mentally retarded'. Hebrew University of Jerusalem.

Testa, M.A. and Nackley, J.F. (1994) 'Methods for quality of life studies'. *Journal of Public Health* 15: 535–559.

Whally, L.J. (1989) 'Drug treatments of dementia'. *British Journal of Psychiatry* 8: 595–611.

Chapter 9

Psychosocial treatment for demented patients
Overview of methods and effects

R. M. Dröes

INTRODUCTION

In this chapter an overview is presented of the various types of psychosocial treatment used for demented patients during the last twenty years: psychotherapy, psychomotor therapy, behaviour modification, remotivation and resocialization therapy, reminiscence therapy, reality orientation training, activity groups, validation, and normalization of living patterns and living environment. We will address the theoretical backgrounds, the most common methods in psychogeriatric practice and the results achieved with these types of treatment. The term 'psychosocial treatment' is limited here to include only those types of treatment that focus explicitly on psychical and social problems that demented patients can experience during the dementing process, or the prevention of those problems. Only treatments that utilize interactive methods are described – psychopharmaco therapy is not discussed here.

This overview clearly shows that attention to the experiences of the demented elderly patient has increased over the past twenty years. Whereas in the 1970s behaviour therapeutic interventions were emphasized, in recent years we have seen more and more forms of treatment based on psychodynamic and interactional theories. There is a growing understanding of the often bizarre behaviour of the demented elderly, and this opens up perspectives for the treatment of this group of patients.

PSYCHOTHERAPY

Since the 1940s different kinds of psychotherapy have been used in the treatment of geriatric patients. An overview can be found in several works (Ingebretsen, 1977; Sparacino, 1978–79; Götestam, 1980; Yesavage and Karasu, 1982; Mosher-Ashley, 1986–87). Although the first publications on group psychotherapy for elderly patients started to appear some forty years ago (e.g. Linden, 1953), research in this area proves to have been limited (see Zwanikken and Janssens, 1977; Petzold, 1985; Gilewski,

1986; Tross and Blum, 1988; Lazarus and Sadavoy, 1988; Radebold, 1989b). Three approaches can be distinguished in both individual treatment and group therapies: a supporting approach, an analytical approach and a cognitive approach.

Supportive psychotherapy

A form of individual psychotherapy reputed to have favourable effects on elderly patients with brain damage is Goldfarb's 'brief therapy' (Goldfarb and Turner, 1953). In this method the therapist regularly has short talks (fifteen minutes) with the patient, in which the emphasis is on concrete subjects (Sadavoy and Robinson, 1989). He makes therapeutic use of the dependent position of the patient by taking on the role of protective parent who is capable of fostering a sense of safety and control in the patient (see Maletta, 1988). Although Goldfarb got positive results in large numbers of geriatric patients with his 'brief therapy' (Sparacino, 1978–79; Götestam, 1980), we know of no studies that prove the effectiveness of his method for patients with a dementia syndrome. Verwoerdt (1981), who focuses specifically on elderly patients suffering from senile dementia, feels that psychotherapy for these elderly patients should be used especially as a form of therapeutic communication. By analysing verbal expressions the psychotherapist will have to find out what the patient is feeling/experiencing, so that an empathic understanding for the patient's current emotional life can develop. In a therapeutic relationship, the therapist can try to enhance adaptive coping strategies and eliminate ineffective coping strategies (see Lewis, 1987; Norberg and Athlin, 1989; Kihlgren et al., 1990; Dröes, 1991). The ultimate goal of the therapy is to restore a psychological balance. Up to the present day no studies have been undertaken to assess the effect of this 'dynamic' approach.

The supportive *group* psychotherapies are best described as discussion groups that compensate for the curtailment of the social network, exercise social skills and serve as a source of consensus and empathy with regard to problems that are specific to old age and ways of coping with them (Krebs-Roubicek, 1989). The final goal of the therapy is acceptance of and adjustment to the changing circumstances and improvement of practical functioning (Tross and Blum, 1988; Cox, 1985). In general, clinical experiences with supportive group psychotherapies for the elderly are positive (Burnside, 1978; Williams et al., 1980; Johnson et al., 1982; Bircher-Beck, 1983). However, these publications are mostly of an anecdotal nature and as a rule contain only very general information about the patient group and the evaluation methods used. The reports, based on clinical observations, indicate that an increase of social relations, initiative and attention is observed in demented patients who participate in supportive group therapy, and that restlessness and wandering around decreased (e.g.

Åkerlund and Norberg, 1986). One of the few experimental studies we encountered in this field was the study of Dye and Erber (1981). They studied nursing home patients who participated in a discussion group during the three and a half weeks immediately after admittance (pre-test/post-test control group design). They concluded that the discussion groups had had a positive effect on the adjustment (especially emotionally): the participants in the experiment displayed significantly less 'trait anxiety' and more 'internal locus of control' than the people from the control group.

Insight-oriented psychotherapy

This type of psychotherapy is believed to be especially suitable for elderly people who have problems with the general changes that accompany the ageing process, such as: change in appearance, loneliness, changes in relationships with family and friends, and approaching death (Yesavage and Karasu, 1982; Myers, 1984; Joraschky, 1986; Lazarus and Sadavoy, 1988). According to Maletta (1988), the insight-oriented approach can be used with demented patients, only when there is a mild form of dementia. The therapist must also take care not to mobilize unresolved conflicts from the past that the patient is perhaps no longer able to cope with. According to some authors a (modified) analytical approach is *particularly* useful in the treatment of elderly patients, because people often look back (unconsciously) on their own life in this final phase of life. This can trigger the emergence of conflicts from the past which demand resolution. An example of such a modified analytical approach is the 'Life Review' method (Butler, 1963; Lewis and Butler, 1974).

Insight-oriented *group* psychotherapies for elderly patients often use, apart from the 'Life Review' method (Leszcz *et al.*, 1985; Tross and Blum, 1988), the analytical method. Central in this method are the inter-pretation of resistance, actions and transference (to therapists, group and individuals), and it uses free association and expression, interpretation and structured methods (Radebold, 1983, 1989b; Wächtler, 1983; Bolk-Weischedel, 1985). So far the effectiveness of this group psychotherapy with regard to elderly patients with senile dementia has not been studied.

Cognitive-behavioural psychotherapies

These types of psychotherapy have also been used for a few years on a limited scale with mildly demented patients. They focus on countering cognitive deterioration, in so far as it appears to be influenced by mental and social factors, by teaching specific (control) techniques (Arenberg and Robertson-Tchabo, 1977; Lazarus and Sadavoy, 1988). Cognitive perfor-mance can be affected by, among other things, a negative thinking pattern (the so-called negative cognitive sets), memory problems and concentration problems. In the case of negative cognitive sets one can teach thinking stops; supporting organization techniques for memory problems; and for concentration problems relaxation exercises can be taught (Rimm and Masters, 1974; Yesavage, 1984; Nouws, 1988; de Ronde and Kamm, 1989; Warmelink, 1990; Vink, 1991). In recent years the cognitive-behavioural approach has also been applied in group therapies for elderly patients with cognitive impairments. Zarit (1982) conducted a study among cognitively impaired elderly patients (diagnoses are not listed), who participated in memory training (for three and a half weeks). The cognitive functioning (recall) of the experimental group improved. However, this improvement was accompanied by a deterioration of the affective function: after participating in the training group, the patients scored higher on the Zung-depression list.

PSYCHOMOTOR THERAPY

Psychomotor therapy is defined as the treatment of people who have to contend with psychosocial problems with the aid of movement activities and/or special attention to body experience (Fahrenfort, 1986; van Coppenolle, 1990). In the past twenty years psychomotor therapy has developed rapidly in the Netherlands. In the psychiatric discipline it has become a generally accepted and applied type of treatment. The development is much slower in the psychogeriatric field. Although in the past decades there has been increasing attention to the possibilities of psychomotor therapy in psychogeriatric patients in Dutch and Belgian psychiatric institutions (see Kouwenhoven, 1977; Rijsdorp, 1977; Koevoets et al., 1979; Probst, 1980; Hungenaert and Schaekers, 1982; Dröes, 1991, van Dasler, 1995), this form of therapy has penetrated the world of the psychogeriatric nursing home only to a limited extent.

Many different methods are used in psychomotor therapy because of the various theoretical models that are used to explain psychosocial problems, for example: models based on cognitive, neurophysiological, holistic, psychodynamic and learning theory principles. To make a general classification of the range of methods, Fahrenfort introduced the terms *movement-oriented methods* and *body-oriented methods*. The first term applies when the treatment consists mainly of offering carefully selected movement arrangements or movement activities, the second when the emphasis is on body experience, as for example in the case of relaxation exercises. Based on research and practical experience we may conclude that simple *movement activities in the form of games* and *sporting movement activities* are generally appreciated as positive by demented patients requiring assistance and those requiring care (Dröes, 1991). There have also been publications in the past, however, that have reported the positive effects of body-oriented methods (including Welden and Yesavage, 1982; Haber, 1988).

Looking at the methods used in psychomotor therapy from a therapeutic means perspective, the following remarks are in order. The therapy programmes based on a *cognitive and/or neurophysiological perspective*, generally appear to utilize movement activities from the fields of physical education, sports and games. By means of these movement activities the therapist attempts to stimulate the person in his/her capacity as information-processing system and/or influence the neurophysiological processes that underlie the (impaired) system (Diesfeldt and Diesfeldt-Groenendijk, 1977; Menks *et al.*, 1977; Molloy *et al.*, 1988; Molloy, Delaquerriere Richardson and Grilly, 1988). The general goal of these programmes is twofold. In the first place they want to offer some compensation for the understimulation of elderly patients that frequently occurs in the intramural (or home) setting; second, they hope to counter the cognitive deterioration that is caused in part by understimulation (see Kouwenhoven, 1977; Koevoets *et al.*, 1979; Levy, 1987). There has been some research on the effects of these methods in psychogeriatric nursing home patients (Diesfeldt and Diesfeldt-Groenendijk, 1977; Ernst, 1977; Molloy, Delaquerriere Richardson and Grilly, 1988; Dröes, 1991) and in elderly patients with memory impairments who live at home (Molloy *et al.*, 1988). The programmes consisted of movement activation and sensory stimulation. In these (controlled) studies activation proved to have a positive influence on several aspects of cognitive functioning such as: immediate memory, recognition, word fluency, logical memory and mental state. However, these effects were observed only immediately after the activity (so-called acute effects). Later measurements (three to seven days after the activity) showed no changes, except with regard to word fluency (Molloy, Delaquerriere Richardson and Grilly, 1988). The therapy programmes based on a *holistic perspective*, and therefore aimed at the recovery of the so-called bio-psycho-social system, use – in addition to movement exercises to stimulate self-expression, self-image and self-esteem – music, breathing exercises, informal conversation and nutrition education as therapeutic means (Goldberg and Fitzpatrick, 1980; Karl, 1982; Allen and Steinkohl, 1987; Stetter and Stuhlman, 1987; Haber, 1988). Up to now no research on the effect of this method has been done. The *behaviour therapeutic* programmes, which are based on principles from learning theory (which will be discussed later) often use (progressive) relaxation exercises and verbal rewards. Welden and Yesavage (1982) studied the effect of intensive relaxation training on behavioural problems. The training consisted of exercises for progressive muscle relaxation, body-oriented attention, imagination and self-hypnosis. Using a pre-test/post-test control group design, with pairs that were matched in advance on cognitive impairments, they were able to show that relaxation training has a positive effect on every behavioural aspect that was being assessed (psychiatric symptoms, eating, bathing, dressing and toilet problems, responsibility, communication, social interaction and independence). In addition, 42 per cent of the participants needed no further sleep medication after the training.

The *psychodynamically oriented (interactional)* therapy programmes, that explain behavioural symptoms in part as a result of psychological reactions of demented patients to their cognitive impairments and changing environment, mainly offer movement activities in which the participants can experience a certain measure of success and confidence in themselves and in others. It can involve elements from sports and games, but also hobby activities and dancing to music, in combination with a social group activity, such as drinking coffee afterwards. The aim is to reduce feelings of anxiety, stimulate feelings of well-being and positively influence everyday functioning. Reported therapeutic effects are: increased interpersonal contact during the therapy sessions and in daily life, reduced need for psychopharmacological drugs and less disruptive behaviour like aggression and night-time restlessness (Schwab *et al.*, 1985; Sandel, 1987; Dröes, 1991; Namazi *et al.*, 1995).

BEHAVIOUR MODIFICATION

The aim of behaviour modification is to change the patient's behaviour with the aid of techniques based on learning theory. The behaviour modification methods used with demented patients are generally based on operant conditioning. This means that stimuli of which it is known (or suspected) that they are strongly desired by the elderly individual, are used as rewards in order to stimulate the desired behaviour (positive reinforcement). These stimuli can be of a social or material nature (a conversation, attention, a compliment or a drink), but they can also concern specific activities, such as a walk outside or listening to music. In some cases attempts are made to influence behaviour solely by introducing changes in the immediate environment (environment manipulation). Over the years several reviews have been published in which behaviour therapeutic methods that are frequently used successfully with elderly patients are described (e.g. Woods and Britton, 1985; Mosher-Ashley, 1986–87; Holden and Woods, 1988; Dröes, 1991). The goals of behaviour modification turn out to vary from increasing the activity level and stimulating self-care and continence on the one hand to the reduction of all kinds of behavioural problems on the other.

Increasing the activity level

Strategies in this category have been studied in different groups of psychogeriatric patients in institutional settings. In general they are aimed at stimulating the elderly patients to use and maintain their cognitive and social residual abilities in the process of adjusting to the own invalidity and institutionalization. By activating the patients to activities and social interaction, it is hoped that adjustment will be stimulated, degenerative processes which can be induced by inactivity countered, and so-called excess disabilities, where the patient shows more disabilities than expected in view of his functional possibilities, prevented or undone (see, *inter alia*, Powell *et al.*, 1979; Held *et al.*, 1984; Reifler *et al.*, 1986; Yates, 1987; Rovner *et al.*, 1990). Most of the time these strategies prove to be effective. Recently Teri (1994) showed on the basis of a controlled clinical trial with patients suffering from Alzheimer's disease that activation can also be effective in reducing depression.

Stimulating self-care and continence

In the past two decades several studies have been conducted in the field of self-care and continence in patients with organic brain impairments (Rinke *et al.*, 1978; Schnelle *et al.*, 1983; Pinkston and Linsk, 1988). These studies showed that operant conditioning had a positive effect on autonomous bathing and incontinence. The latter was reduced by 45 per cent if patients were checked regularly for continence, were stimulated to ask to be taken to the bathroom if they felt the need, and were rewarded with attention if the check-ups showed them to be dry, and/or they had asked for the help mentioned (see Burgio *et al.*, 1990).

Reduction of behavioural problems

Some examples from the range of behavioural problems in (psycho)-geriatric patients that behaviour modification therapy has (frequently successfully) tried to influence are: stereotype movements (Hussian, 1988), expressing accusations and outbursts of anger (Wisner and Green, 1986), eating non-edible things (Nash *et al.*, 1987), aggressive behaviour (Vaccaro, 1988) and yelling (Blackman *et al.*, 1979; Hussian, 1988). The behaviour modification techniques used are verbal encouragement and praise, and if necessary (as in the case of inappropriate eating behaviour) interruption and practical assistance.

Birchmore and Clague (1983), for example, report on behaviour modification in a 70-year-old blind woman with senile dementia, who was treated to reduce frequent yelling. The strategy consisted of rewarding the patient (by rubbing her back) when she was quiet. The treatment was carried out systematically for one hour a day for twenty-seven days. Compared to the baseline measurements the screaming clearly diminished during the treatment sessions, and even one hour after the sessions the effect could still be measured. Pinkston and Linsk (1988) report on the treatment of a 73-year-old patient with senile dementia of the Alzheimer type, who lived at home, and who frequently made paranoid remarks to his wife if she did not give him attention, or left him alone temporarily. The treatment, which consisted of ignoring these remarks and praising or giving attention to positive remarks, proved to be successful.

REMOTIVATION AND RESOCIALIZATION THERAPY

The first publications about remotivation and resocialization groups for institutionalized elderly patients date from the 1960s. The goals and methods of these types of group therapy follow from each other.

Remotivation therapy

This treatment, originally developed by Smith to treat chronic schizophrenic patients (Thralow and Watson, 1974), has been used frequently with institutionalized (psycho)geriatric patients over the past two decades (e.g. Storandt, 1978; Abrahams et al., 1979; Levy, 1987). In the United States the groups are generally supervised by nursing staff who have been trained as remotivation therapists (Tolbert, 1984). In other countries comparable groups are supervised by, for example, activity therapists. The therapy aims to get patients who have withdrawn into themselves interested again in their environment. They are stimulated, either individually or as a group, to focus their attention on simple, everyday subjects and events (history, holidays, vacation, food, money). Unlike group psychotherapy, subjects that might be related to emotional problems, such as family relations, illness, institutionalization, religion and sex, are avoided as much as possible (Toepfer et al., 1974; Levy, 1987). The method used during the remotivation group sessions is highly structured and usually consists of five steps. First of all an atmosphere of acceptance is created. Then the therapist attempts to make a connection with reality by introducing a subject (for example by reading a poem). Subsequently the subject will be discussed, after which the patients are stimulated to talk about activities they have carried out during their own active life period. Finally, the session is summarized by the therapist and concluded in an atmosphere of appreciation. Janssen and Giberson (1988) showed that elderly patients suffering from mild to serious cognitive impairments (70 per cent primary degenerative dementia) had more interest in group activities after a period of remotivation therapy and their verbal communication and emotional expression increased. The social contacts also continued outside the therapy sessions.

Resocialization therapy

This type of therapy aims, in addition to renewing attention for the environment (the main goal of remotivation therapy), to improve social skills and initiate interpersonal relationships between participants (Barns *et al.*, 1973). Resocialization therapy is less structured than remotivation therapy, and the subjects brought up for discussion frequently concern the immediate environment or general social themes. The expression of individual thoughts and opinions is emphasized during the discussions. A good example of a resocialization group is Chien's 'beer and social therapy group' (1971), in which a group of elderly patients (some of them suffering from functional psychoses and the others from organic brain syndrome) came together for one hour five days a week in the hospital 'pub' to have a beer (see Carroll, 1978). Shoham and Neuschatz (1985) conclude that social interaction increases by participation in a resocialization group. They even speak of closer relationships.

REMINISCENCE THERAPY

The literature distinguishes three types of reminiscence: simple or informative reminiscence, evaluative reminiscence, and obsessive-defensive reminiscence (LoGerfo, 1980; Thornton and Brotchie, 1987; Rossaert, 1989). These different forms are similar in essence, however, in the sense that their importance appears not to be located in a realistic rendering of the life history, but rather in a cognitive reconstruction of this history (Lieberman and Falk, 1971; Revere and Tobin, 1980–81). The motives are shown to be *intra*-personal as well as *inter*-personal (Romaniuk and Romaniuk, 1981; Kaminsky, 1984; Tarman, 1988).

The point of *simple reminiscence*, a non-conflictive and informal type of reminiscing, is the joy one gets from reminiscing itself on the one hand, and the increase of self-esteem and sense of identity it involves on the other (Merriam, 1980; Coleman, 1986). In this context some authors point out the coping function of reminiscing in times of stress and/or mourning (Atkins, 1980). Frequent reminiscing is believed to reduce injury to the self-image and diminish the occurrence of depression. Finally, reminiscing can also create a feeling of intimacy in communication with others.

Evaluative reminiscence, a second type which has, among other things, a conflict-resolving function, is initiated in elderly people by the confrontation with approaching death, biological deterioration and the 'life-review' process (Butler, 1963, 1974). Research results confirm this hypothesis (Romaniuk and Romaniuk, 1981). By actively evaluating and reconstructing the personal past, the patient is taking stock of what he has achieved in his life and also attempting to resolve intra-psychical conflicts. That there is indeed a positive correlation between the 'life-review' type of reminiscence and ego-integrity has been established by Boylin *et al.* (1976), and more recently by Taft and Nehrke (1990).

Obsessive-defensive reminiscence, a pathological type of reminiscing, occurs when the feelings of guilt and despair about the past or present are so overwhelming that the patient is unable to accept them. It can also occur when the patient is not given the opportunity to resolve conflicts from the past, for example if the patient is in an institutional environment that generally ignores such autonomous processes (Molinari and Reichlin, 1985; Poulton and Strassberg, 1986). Obsessive-defensive reminiscence can be accompanied by agitation, depression or suicidal tendencies (LoGerfo, 1980). By concentrating on the problematic past experiences and by expressing pent-up thoughts and feelings that emerge, the elderly patient might still find some peace in this final phase of life.

Taking the aforementioned functions of reminiscence as a starting point, reminiscence therapy attempts 'to improve intra-personal and inter-personal functioning by means of reliving, structuring, integrating and exchanging memories' (Bremers and Engel, 1985: 130). Aids used include autobiographies, trips to locations from the past, photo albums, cuttings, scrapbooks, materials/objects from old times and drama/role play. The research results in elderly patients with cognitive impairments vary considerably and the research is often anecdotal. Berghorn and Schäfer (1987) found that the therapy most common changed the attitude of the elderly patients, especially those who had not adjusted their values and standards to those of the home. From this they concluded that reminiscence groups were apparently a compensation for these patients, because talking about the past means that much attention is paid to their values and standards. This, they feel, is experienced by the patient as the nursing home making an effort, which would result in a milder attitude in the patient towards himself and others. Elderly patients who adjust to the values of the institution (community spirit, dependency) of their own accord, will benefit little from reminiscence groups. A comparable difference in effect is also mentioned by Head *et al.* (1990), who found that reminiscence groups produced a dramatic change in interaction between professional staff and patients who previously did not interact that much, while in an initially 'richer' environment reminiscence did not effect a change in either staff or patients (Head *et al.*, 1990).

REALITY ORIENTATION TRAINING

Reality orientation training (ROT) was originally developed by Folsom in the late 1950s as a rehabilitation technique for elderly (chronic) psychiatric patients, to encourage nursing staff to spend more time on personal contact with the patients and to stimulate the patients into activity (Folsom, 1983). ROT was viewed especially as a means to compensate for sensory and emotional deprivation in the case of long-term institutionalization. When in the 1960s ROT began to be used also with demented patients, emphasis shifted to stimulation of undamaged cognitive functions in order to counter the disorientation and confusion caused by sensory deprivation and social isolation. ROT takes place in groups and in a twenty-four-hour approach.

The latter means that all staff members are instructed to involve the patient in reality all through the day. Furthermore, supporting measures are taken in the material environment (signposts, signs on toilet and bedroom doors, etc.). In the past two decades ROT has been applied and studied extensively in different treatment institutions (Eysma, 1982; Folsom, 1983; Holden and Woods, 1988). However, in quite a few studies the research population is only described in very general terms ('psychogeriatric patients', 'institutionalized elderly', 'disoriented elderly') so that it is not immediately clear for which diagnostic group(s) results can be expected. The programmes that were studied have durations varying from three to fourteen weeks and most concern the RO-class method (e.g. Baldelli *et al.*, 1993); in some cases this was combined with 24-hour RO (Gorissen, 1985; Reeve and Ivison, 1985) or a spatial orientation training on the ward (Hanley *et al.*, 1981). In other cases programmes were limited to 24-hour RO and environment manipulation (Williams *et al.*, 1987). In almost every study the RO-classes scored positive results on orientation questionnaires or cognitive tests, such as the Mini Mental State Examination (Folstein *et al.*, 1975). As some of these studies used a controlled experimental design, we may assume that reality orientation training has an effect on cognitive functioning that is more than a non-specific result of a random intervention. However, the effects are limited, and only seldom are the learned skills observed *outside* the training situation (e.g. Reeve and Ivison, 1985; Baldelli *et al.*, 1993). In the past years ROT is therefore rarely offered in the form of the original classes. Follow-ups of spatial orientation training on the ward do show measurable effects two weeks after the training (Hanley, 1981): some patients are better able to find their way. The combination of 24-hour RO and environment manipulation has a stabilizing effect on behavioural symptoms, while cognitive functioning is also stimulated (Williams *et al.*, 1987). So far the effect of ROT on the patients' mood has barely been studied. In recent years ROT has been increasingly propagated only when it could enhance the demented patient's sense of control. If the patient has withdrawn into the past, a validating approach (to be discussed later) would be more appropriate.

ACTIVITY GROUPS

The goals of therapeutic group activities can be summarized as follows (Woods and Britton, 1977; Kartman, 1979): *motivate* (getting patients interested in their environment), *stimulate* (appeal to cognitive, social and physical abilities), *socialize* (offering patients the opportunity to enter into contact with contemporaries, express themselves and develop meaningful social roles), and *learn to recreate* (teaching patients that they can spend their leisure time in an enjoyable way by offering different recreational activities).

Various activity programmes from demented elderly patients are described in the literature (see Bloemendal, 1983; Zachary, 1984; Zgola, 1988; Dröes, 1991). Recommendations are also made with regard to adjusting the activities to individual needs and abilities of patients with different degrees of dementia (Pierrehumbert *et al.*, 1978; Charatan, 1984; McCrum Griffin and Matthews, 1986). Examples of therapeutic group activities are: art groups (painting and drawing), sewing and handicraft clubs, gymnastic groups, movement groups, cooking clubs, music groups, singing groups and sensory stimulation groups. So far, relatively little research has been done into the effectiveness of these group activities for patients with senile dementia (Panella *et al.*, 1984; Karlsson *et al.*, 1985; Olderog-Millard and Smith, 1989; Bach *et al.*, 1993) although they constitute the largest part of psychosocial aid to elderly patients. Hanley and Peele (1985) evaluated an activity programme, consisting of warming-up exercises, RO activities, music and family games, for severely demented patients who visited a day clinic twice a week. They concluded that music activities were probably the most successful for these patients, because they release emotional reactions (see also, Gerdner and Swanson, 1993). These activities give the patients, who are often no longer able to express themselves well verbally, a different means of expression. They found a reduction in wandering behaviour and an increase in awareness of the social environment and joy, improved communication, orientation and participation, a more caring attitude towards other group members, more self-confidence and higher self-esteem in the participants in this programme.

McGrowder-Lin and Bhatt (1988) experimented with an activity programme for demented patients (mostly SDAT) that took up one and a half hours a day and consisted of music, physical exercise, sensory stimulation, dancing, and a snack and a drink to stimulate the patients to participate. They observed in individual patients, among other things, improved appetite, an increase in communicative skills and the ability to participate in simple everyday activities, and a reduction of night-time restlessness and incontinence.

VALIDATION

Validation is a supportive stage-specific communication method for disoriented elderly patients (Feil, 1982, 1989, 1992). It is recommended especially for those who show both verbally and in their actions that they have withdrawn (temporarily) into the past and experience emotions that concern unresolved conflicts or losses from the past. The method has similarities with the psychodynamic *coping perspective* (see Verwoerdt, 1981). The process of withdrawing is viewed both as a result of progressive brain damage, and as an (unconscious) strategy of the demented patient to escape the painful reality of the present. By exploring the patient's experiences, by showing understanding and empathy and directly validating these experiences (without further analysis or interpretation), the aim is to make the patient feel understood and accepted. This validating support is thought to reduce stress and restore self-esteem (Babins, 1988; Morton and Bleathman, 1988; Meulmeester *et al.*, 1989; Kihlgren *et al.*, 1990).

Apart from this coping perspective a *developmental perspective* is used. The starting point is Erikson's (1963) theory, which considers finding ego-integrity the final developmental task in the life cycle. Patients would engage in evaluative reminiscence to resolve conflicts from the past (see above). According to Feil the dementing patient, partly because of his or her cognitive impairments, will not always be able to carry out this developmental task well. By being offered the opportunity, through empathic communication and stimulating the expression of the conflicting as well as positive feelings, the patient might experience, perhaps not insight, but (at least temporarily) relief or 'resolution'. This can enhance feelings of integrity. In Feil's (1985) opinion, *resolution* is the final developmental task for the disoriented elderly before death. If they are not understood and supported in this, then the chances of a further breakdown of contact with persons and the environment are high. This increases the risk of vegetation.

Validation contains a number of well-described verbal and non-verbal empathic communication techniques to be applied with different behavioural patterns (which Feil calls 'stages of confusion'). In addition the method provides instructions for setting up and supervising so-called validation groups. These groups function in a structured manner (a standard opening song, a conversation about a subject that evokes universal emotions, a movement game, and a closing song accompanied by refreshments. The results of a few (controlled) effect studies have shown that participating in a validation group for ten to eleven weeks can lead to an improvement of the ADL-functions and an increase in verbal and non-verbal expression during the group sessions (Babins, 1988; Fritz, 1986; Morton and Bleathman, 1988). Not much is known about the generalization effect so far, although experiences in practice are positive (see Dröes, 1991).

NORMALIZATION OF LIVING PATTERNS AND LIVING ENVIRONMENT

The adjustment of the social and material environment to the needs of demented patients concerns two types of measures. On the one hand manipulation of the environment (signs, lighting, colours, information boards, arrangement of tables and chairs, activities, etc.) is used to respond to the (permanent) physical, social, and cognitive disabilities of the patient, in such a way that these are counterbalanced, and so-called excess disabilities are prevented. Around the patients a 'prosthetic' environment is created, which enables them and activates them to keep functioning as independently as possible, despite their disabilities. On the other hand all kinds of measures are taken to make the institutional setting as substitute living situation as normal as possible, so that it can be experienced as a home by the demented resident. Prevention of hospitalization symptoms and improving the quality of life are important goals here (Beerthuizen, 1981). Examples of such measures taken over the past decades are: normalization of the meal, coffee and tea provision; supervised shopping and cooking; searching for ways to interact with the individual patient which are experienced by the patient as familiar (by studying patient life-histories etc.); adjusting furnishings to the wishes of the patient; creating privacy for the resident; creating a familiar environment (photographs, personal belongings); providing several (small) living rooms on one ward; organizing the space into sub-spaces, each with their own function (reading, television, dining area), so that patients will move around more and will not stay in the same chair all day long; pets and single-family-accommodation projects, group living (Woods and Britton, 1977; Sjoers, 1978; Peters and Spätjens, 1983; Wattis and Church, 1986; Peters and Duine, 1987; Annerstedt, 1993).

Reviews of effect studies concerning normalization initiatives for institutionalized psychogeriatric patients were written by, among others, Gottesman and Brody (1975), Lawton (1981), Mosher-Ashley (1986-87), Levy (1987), Holden and Woods (1988) and Dröes (1991). In general the observed effects can be summarized as: increased activity, social involvement, contentment, happiness and sense of control, improved mood and offering volunteer aid to other residents. A few studies also found a reduction of incontinence and behavioural problems. Cognitive changes (for example in memory or orientation) or changes in ADL-functioning were not found. These studies were all conducted among mixed samples of elderly patients, so it is not clear which effects are achieved in the different diagnostic groups.

CONCLUSIONS

This overview of types of psychosocial treatment shows that over the past twenty years attention to the experiences of the demented elderly patient has increased. Whereas in the 1970s emphasis was on behaviour-therapeutic interventions, in the past few years we increasingly see types of treatment that are based on psychodynamic and interactional theories. Understanding of the often bizarre behaviour of the demented elderly is growing. This opens up perspectives for the psychosocial treatment of this group of patients. In spite of the large amount of research conducted in the past twenty years in the field of psychogeriatric aid, there has been remarkably little focus on specific diagnostic groups. The majority of the researchers studied mixed populations of (psycho)geriatric patients, whose diagnoses are indicated only in very general terms (or not at all). Because only a few effect studies use an experimental design (pre-test/post-test control group design) and the variables studied show considerable variation, we must be cautious when drawing conclusions about the effectiveness of individual intervention methods for the treatment of specific psychosocial problems. Thoroughly organized research, including control measures with regard to the diagnosis as well as more general psychological and social factors, is needed to get definitive answers in the future. On the whole we may conclude that most types of psychosocial treatment show positive results in terms of cognitive, social, or emotional effects. This seems to be sufficient to disprove the therapeutic nihilism which so dominated psychogeriatric care in the past.

REFERENCES

Abrahams, J.P., H.F. Wallach and S. Divens (1979) 'Behavioral improvement in long-term geriatric patients during an age-integrated psychosocial rehabilitation program', *Journal of the American Geriatric Society* 27: 218–221.

Åkerlund, B.M. and A. Norberg (1986) 'Group psychotherapy with demented patients', *Geriatric Nursing* 7: 83–84.

Allen, K.S. and R.P. Steinkohl (1987) 'Yoga in a geriatric mental clinic', *Activities, Adaptation and Aging* 9: 61–68.

Annerstedt, L. (1993) 'Development and consequences of group living in Sweden; a new mode of care for the demented elderly', *Soc. Sci. Med.* 37 (12): 1529–1538.

Arenberg, D. and E.A. Robertson-Tchabo (1977) 'Learning and aging', in: J.E. Birren and K.W. Schaie (eds), *Handbook of the Psychology of Aging*. Van Nostrand Reinhold, New York, pp. 421–449.

Atkins, A.L. (1980) 'Research finds distortions in diagnosis of elderly', *Psychiatric News* 15: 7–32.

Babins, L. (1988) 'Conceptual analysis of Validation therapy', *International Journal of Aging and Human Development* 26: 161–168.

Bach, D., F. Böhmer, F. Frühwald and B. Grilc (1993) 'Aktivierende Ergotherapie; ein Methode zur Steigerung der kognitiven Leistungsfähigkeit bei geriatrischen Patienten', *Z. Gerontologie* 26: 476–481.

Baldelli, M.V., A. Pirani, M. Motta, E. Abati, E. Mariani and V. Manzi (1993) 'Effects of reality orientation therapy on elderly patients in the community', *Archives of Gerontology and Geriatrics* 17: 211–218.

Barns, E.K., A. Sack and H. Shore (1973) 'Guidelines to treatment approaches', *The Gerontologist* 14: 513–527.

Beerthuizen, J. (1981) 'Het leefbare verpleeghuis', *Intermediair*, 17e jrg., 1/2–9 Jan.

Berghorn, F.J. and D.E. Schäfer (1987) 'Reminiscence intervention in nursing homes: What and who changes?', *International Journal of Aging and Human Development* 25: 113–127.

Bircher-Beck, L.M. (1983) 'Kurzpsychotherapie mit psychogeriatrischen Patientengruppen', in: H. Radebold (ed.), *Gruppenpsychotherapie im Alter*. Verlag VandenHoeck and Ruprecht, Göttingen, 86–90.

Birchmore, T. and S. Clague (1983) 'A behavioral approach to reduce shouting', *Nursing Times* 79 (4): 37–39.

Blackman, D.K., C. Gehle, and E.M. Pinkston (1979) 'Modifying eating habits of the institutionalized elderly', *Social Work Research and Abstracts* 18: 18–24.

Bloemendal, G. (1983) *'Demente bejaarden, activiteiten en omgang'*, Intro, Nijkerk.

Bolk-Weischedel, D. (1985) 'Analytische psychotherapie im höheren Lebensalter', *Münchener Medizinische Wochenzeitschrift* 127: 54–58.

Boylin, W., S.K. Gordon and M.F. Nehrke (1976) 'Reminiscing and ego integrity in institutionalized elderly males', *The Gerontologist* 16: 118–124.

Bremers, P.G.V.M. and M. Engel (1985) *'In de ban van de herinnering'*, *Een literatuuronderzoek naar reminiscentie bij ouderen*, Doctoraalscriptie, Rijksuniversiteit Utrecht.

Burgio, L.D., K.L. Burgio, B.T. Engel *et al.* (1986) 'Increasing distance and independence of ambulation in elderly nursing home residents', *Journal of Applied Behavior Analysis* 19: 357–366.

Burgio, L.D., B.T. Engel, A. Hawkins *et al.* (1990) 'A staff management system for maintaining improvements in continence with elderly nursing home residents', *Journal of Applied Behavior Analysis* 23: 111–118.

Burnside, I.M. (1978) *'Working with the Elderly: Group Processes and Techniques'*, North Scituate, Duxbury.

Butler, R.N. (1963) 'The life review: an interpretation of reminiscence in the aged', *Psychiatry* 26: 65–76.

—— (1974) 'Successful aging and the role of the life review', *Journal of the American Geriatric Society* 22: 529–535.

Carroll, P.J. (1978) 'The social hour for geropsychiatric patients', *Journal of the American Geriatric Society* 26: 32–35.

Charatan, F.B. (1984) 'Mental stimulation and deprivation as risk factors in senility', in: A. Rothschild (ed.), *Risk Factors for Senility*. Oxford University Press.

Chien, C.P. (1971) 'Psychiatric treatment for geriatric patients: "Pub" or drug', *American Journal of Psychiatry* 127: 110–115.

Clark, B.A., M.G. Wade, B.H. Massey *et al.* (1975) 'Response of institutionalized geriatric mental patients to a twelve-week program of regular physical activity', *Journal of Gerontology* 30: 565–573.

Coleman, P. (1986) 'Issues in the therapeutic use of reminiscence with elderly people', in: I. Hanley and M. Gilhooly (eds), *Psychological Therapies for the Elderly*, Croom Helm, London.

Coppenolle, H. van (1990) 'Psychomotor therapy and adapted physical activity: defining the concepts', in: *Better by Moving. Proceedings of the 2nd International Symposium on Psychomotor Therapy and Adapted Physical Activity*. Leuven 1989. Uitg. Acco, Leuven/Amersfoort.

Cox, K.G. (1985) 'Milieu therapy', *Geriatric Nursing* 6: 152–154.

Dasler, J. van (1995) 'Bewogen door beweging', Intro, Nijkerk.

Diesfeldt, H.F.A. and H. Diesfeldt-Groenendijk (1977) 'Improving cognitive performance in psychogeriatric patients: the influence of physical exercise', *Age and Aging* 6: 58–64.

Dröes, R.M. (1991) *In Beweging; over psychosociale hulpverlening aan demente ouderen*, Intro, Nijkerk.

Dye, C.J. and J.T. Erber (1981) 'Two group procedure for the treatment of nursing home patients', *The Gerontologist* 21: 539–544.

Erikson, E.H. (1963) *Childhood and Society*, W.W. Norton and Company, New York.

Ernst, P. (1977) 'Treatment of the aged mentally ill: further unmasking of the effects of a diagnosis of chronic brain syndrome', *Journal of the American Geriatric Society* 25: 466–469.

Eysma, I.D. (1982) 'Realiteitsoriëntatietraining: een voorlopige evaluatie', *Tijdschrift Gerontologie and Geriatrie* 13: 107–113.

Fahrenfort, J. (1986) *Psychomotorische therapie; een onderzoek naar het gebruik van bewegings- en lichaamsgeoriënteerde methoden in de psychiatrie*, VU-uitgeverij, Amsterdam.

Feil, N. (1967) 'Group therapy in a home for the aged', The Gerontologist 7: 192–195.

—— (1982) '*V/F Validation: The Feil Method*', Feil Productions, Cleveland, Ohio.

—— (1985) 'Resolution: The final life task', *Journal of Humanistic Psychology* 25: 91–105.

—— (1989) *Validation, Een nieuwe benadering in de omgang met demente bejaarden*, Versluys, Almere.

Feil, N. (1992) Validation therapy with late-onset dementia, in G.M.M. Jones and B.M.L. Miesen (eds), *Care-Giving in Dementia: Research and Applications*, vol. 1. London/New York: Tavistock/Routledge.

Folsom, J.C. (1983) 'Reality orientation', in: B. Reisberg (ed.), *Alzheimer's Disease*. The Free Press, New York/London.

Folstein, M.F., S.E. Folstein and P.R. McHugh (1975) 'Mini-Mental State', a practical method for grading the cognitive state of patients for the clinician', *Journal of Psychiatric Research* 12: 189–198.

Fritz, P.A. (1986) '*The Language of Resolution among the Old-Old*', Speech Communication Association Convention, Chicago, Illinois.

Gerdner, L.A. and E.A. Swanson (1993) 'Effects of individualized music on confused and agitated elderly patients', *Archives of Psychiatric Nursing* VII (5): 284–291.

Gilewski, M.J. (1986) 'Group therapy with cognitively impaired older adults', *Clinical Gerontologist* 5: 281–296.

Goldberg, W.G. and J.J. Fitzpatrick (1980) 'Movement therapy with the aged', *Nursing Research* 29: 339–346.

Goldfarb, A.I. and H. Turner (1953) 'Psychotherapy of aged persons; II Utilization and effectiveness of brief therapy', *American Journal of Psychiatry* 109: 916–921.

Gorissen, J.P. (1985) 'Een onderzoek naar het effect van realiteitsoriëntatie-training op een groep psychogeriatrische patiënten', *Tijdschrift Gerontologie and Geriatrie* 16: 235–239.

Götestam, K.G. (1980) 'Behavioral and psychodynamic psychotherapy with the elderly', in: J. Birren and B. Sloane (eds), *Handbook of Mental Health and Aging*. Englewood Cliffs, NJ, Prentice Hall, pp. 775–805.

—— and L. Melin (1990) 'The effect of prompting and reinforcement of activity in elderly demented inpatients', *Scandinavian Journal of Psychology* 31: 2–8.

Gottesman, L. and E. Brody (1975) 'Psychosocial intervention programs within the institutional setting', in: S. Sherwood (ed.), *Long-Term Care*. Spectrum Publ. Inc., New York.

Haber, D. (1988) 'A health promotion program in ten nursing homes', *Activities, Adaptation and Aging* 11: 75–84.

Hanley, I.G. (1981) 'The use of signposts and active training to modify ward dis-orientation in elderly patients', *Journal Behavior Therapy and Experimental Psychiatry* 12: 241–247.

——, R.J. McGuire and W.D. Boyd (1981) 'Reality orientation and dementia: A controlled trial of two approaches', *British Journal of Psychiatry* 138: 10–14.

Hanley, O. and K. Peele (1985) 'An active occupational therapy programme for the severely demented patient in a psychogeriatric day hospital', *Occupational Therapy* 48 (11): 336–338.

Head, D.M., S. Portnoy, R.T. Woods (1990) 'The impact of reminiscence groups in two different settings', *International Journal of Geriatric Psychiatry* 5: 295–302.

Held, M., P.M. Rasohoff and P. Goehner (1984) 'A comprehensive treatment program for severely impaired geriatric patients', *Hospital and Community Psychiatry* 35: 156–160.

Holden, U.P. and R.T. Woods (1988) *'Reality Orientation; Psychological Approaches to the "Confused" Elderly'*, Churchill Livingstone, Edinburgh.

Hungenaert, R. and R. Schaekers (1982) 'Psychomotorische therapie voor psychogeriatrische patiënten', *Vlaams Tijdschrift voor Psychomotorische Therapie* 9 (4): 190–206.

Hussian, R.A. (1988) 'Modification of behaviors in dementia via stimulus manipulation', *Clinical Gerontologist* 8: 37–43.

Ingebretsen, R. (1977) 'Psychotherapy with the elderly', *Psychotherapy: Theory, Research and Practice* 14: 319–332.

Janssen, J.A. and D.L. Giberson (1988) 'Remotivation Therapy', *Journal of Gerontological Nursing* 14 (6): 31–34.

Johnson, D.R., S.L. Sandel and M.B. Margolis (1982) 'Principles of group treatment in a nursing home', *The Journal of Long-term Care Administration*, 19–24.

Joraschky, P. (1986) 'Psychotherapie im höheren Lebensalter', *Nervenheilkunde* 5: 186–189.

Kaminsky, M. (1984) 'The uses of reminiscence: a discussion of the formative literature', *Journal of Gerontological Social Work* 7: 137–156.

Karl, C.A. (1982) 'The effect of an exercise program on self-care activities for the institutionalised elderly', *Journal of Gerontological Nursing* 8: 282–285.

Karlsson, I., G. Båne, E. Melin, A.L. Nuth, *et al.* (1985) 'Mental activation – brain plasticity', in C.G. Gottfries (ed.), *Normal Aging, Alzheimer's Disease and Senile Dementia'*, Editions de l'Université de Bruxelles.

Kartman, L.L. (1979) 'Therapeutic group activities in nursing homes', *Health and Social Work* 4: 135–144.

Kihlgren, M., A. Hallgren, A. Norberg *et al.* (1990) 'Effects of the training of integrity-promoting care on the interaction at a long-term ward', *Scandinavian Journal of Caring Science* 4: 21–28.

Koevoets, G., P. van den Heede and R. Vervloet (1979) 'De psychogeriatrische patiënt in psychomotorische therapie', *Vlaams Tijdschrift voor Psychomotorische Therapie* 6 (1): 23–25.

Kouwenhoven, M. (1977) 'Meer bewegen voor geronto-psychiatrische patiënten. *Tijdschrift Psychomotorische Therapie* 4: 151–175.

Krebs-Roubicek, E.M. (1989) 'Group therapy with demented elderly', *Progressive Clinical Biological Research* 317: 1261–1272.

Lawton, M.P. (1981) 'Sensory deprivation and the effect of the environment on management of the patient with senile dementia', in N.E. Miller and G.D. Cohen (eds), *Clinical Aspects of Alzheimer's Disease and Senile Dementia (Aging*, 15), Raven Press, New York.

Lazarus, L.W. and J. Sadavoy (1988) 'Psychotherapy with the elderly', in L.W. Lazarus (ed.), *Essentials of Geriatric Psychiatrie*. Springer Publ. Comp., New York, pp. 147–173.

Leszcz, M., E. Feigenbaum, J. Sadavoy *et al.* (1985) 'A men's group: psychotherapy of elderly men', *International Journal of Group Psychotherapy* 35: 177–196.

Levy, L.L. (1987) 'Psychosocial intervention and dementia, Part 1: State of the art, future directions', *Occupational Therapy in Mental Health* 7: 69–107.

Lewis, P. (1987) 'Therapeutic change in groups; an interactional perspective', *Small Group Behavior* 18: 548–556.

Lewis, M.I. and R.N. Butler (1974) 'Life review therapy', *Geriatrics* 29: 165–173.

Lieberman, M.A. and J.M. Falk (1971) 'The remembered past as a source of data for research on the life cycle', *Human Development* 14: 132–141.

Linden, M.E. (1953) 'Group psychotherapy with institutionalized senile women: a study in gerontologic human relations', *International Journal of Group Psychotherapy* 3: 150–170.

LoGerfo, M. (1980) 'Three ways of reminiscence in theory and practice', *International Journal of Aging and Human Development* 12: 39–48.

McCrum Griffin, R. and M.H. Matthews (1986) 'The selection of activities: a dual responsibility', *Physical and Occupational Therapy in Geriatrics* 4: 105–112.

McGrowder-Lin, R. and A. Bhatt (1988) 'A wanderer's lounge program for nursing home residents with Alzheimer's Disease', *The Gerontologist* 28: 607–609.

Maletta, G.J. (1988) 'Management of behavior problems in elderly patients with Alzheimer's disease and other dementias', *Clinics in Geriatric Medicine* 4: 719–747.

Menks, F., S. Sittler, D. Weaver *et al.* (1977) 'A psychogeriatric activity group in a rural community', *The American Journal of Occupational Therapy* 31: 381–384.

Merriam, S. (1980) 'The concept and function of Reminiscence: a review of the research', *The Gerontologist* 20: 604–609.

Meulmeester, F., D. Moes and A. Bijlsma (1989) 'Validation, een andere benadering van dementie', *Tijdschrift voor Ziekenverpleging* 43: 673–677.

Molinari, V. and R.E. Reichlin (1985) 'Life review reminiscence in the elderly: a review of the literature', *International Journal of Aging and Human Development* 20: 81–92.

Molloy, D.W., D.A. Beerschoten, M.J. Borrie *et al.* (1988) 'Acute effects of exercise on neuropsychological function in elderly subjects', *Journal of the American Geriatric Society* 36: 29–33.

Molloy, D.W., L. Delaquerriere Richardson and R.G. Grilly (1988) 'The effects of a three-month exercise programme on neuropsychological function in elderly institutionalized women: a randomised controlled trial', *Age and Aging* 17: 303–310.

Morton, I. and C. Bleathman (1988) 'Reality Orientation: Does it matter whether it's Tuesday or Friday? *Nursing Times* 84: 25–27.

—— and —— (1991) 'The effectiveness of Validation therapy in dementia; a pilot study', *International Journal of Geriatric Psychiatry* 6: 327–330.

Mosher-Ashley, P.M. (1986–87) 'Procedural and methodological parameters in behavioral-gerontological research: a review', *International Journal of Aging and Human Development* 24: 189–229.

Myers, W.A. (1984) *Dynamic Therapy of the Older Patient.* Jason Aronson Inc., New York.

Namazi, K.H., N.D. Zadorozny, and P.B. Gwinnup (1995) 'The influences of physical activity on patterns of sleep behaviour of patients with Alzheimer's disease', *International Journal of Aging and Human Development* 40 (2): 145–153.

Nash, D.L., J. Broome and S. Stone (1987) 'Behavior modification of pica in a geriatric patient', *Journal of the American Geriatric Society* 35: 79–80.

Norberg, A. and E. Athlin (1989) 'Eating problems in severely demented patients', *Nursing Clinics of North America* 24: 781–789.

Nouws, A. (1988) 'Een cursus geheugentraining voor ouderen; een eerste beschrijving van opzet, organisatie en mogelijke effecten', *Tijdschrift Gerontologie and Geriatrie* 19: 211–214.

Olderog-Millard, K.A. and J.M. Smith (1989) 'The influence of group singing therapy on the behavior of Alzheimer's Disease patients', *Journal of Nursing Therapy* 26 (2): 58–70.

Panella, J.J., B.A. Lilliston, D. Brush and F.H. McDowell (1984) 'Day care for dementia patients: an analysis of a four-year program', *Journal of the American Gerontological Society* 32 (12): 883–886.

Peters, H.J.M. and T.J. Duine (1987) 'Het project "Genormaliseerd Wonen" van verpleeghuis "De Landrijt" te Eindhoven; Enkele uitkomsten van een experiment in de psychogeriatrische zorg', *Tijdschrift Gerontologie en Geriatrie* 18: 187–191.

Peters, H.J.M. and J.G.A. Spätjens (1983) '"Normaal" wonen en leven ook mogelijk voor psychogeriatrische patiënten', *Het Ziekenhuis* 13: 738–742.

Petzold, H. (1985) *'Mit alten Menschen arbeiten; Bildungsarbeit, Psychotherapie, Soziotherapie'*, Verlag J. Pfeiffer, München.

Pierrehumbert, B., J.G. Boula, A. Mouflin *et al.* (1978) 'Ergothérapie intrahospitalière et démence sénile', *Journal of Social Psychiatry* 13: 85–92.

Pinkston, E.M. and N.L. Linsk (1988) *Care of the Elderly: A Family Approach*, Pergamon Press Inc., New York/Oxford.

Poulton, J.L. and D.S. Strassberg (1986) 'The therapeutic use of reminiscence', *International Journal of Group Psychotherapy* 36: 381–398.

Powell, L., D. Felce, J. Jenkins *et al.* (1979) 'Increasing engagement in a home for the elderly by providing an indoor gardening activity', *Behavior Research and Therapy* 17: 127–135.

Probst, M. (1980) 'Beschouwingen rond psychomotorische therapie bij psychogeriatrische patiënten', *Vlaams Tijdschrift voor Psychomotorische Therapie* 7 (1–2): 28–39.

Radebold, H. (1983) *Gruppenpsychotherapie im Alter*. Verlag VandenHoeck and Ruprecht, Göttingen, 64–74.

—— (1989a) 'Psycho- und soziotherapeutische Behandlungsverfahren', in: D. Platt (ed.), *Handbuch de Gerontologie*, Band V: *Neurologie, Psychiatrie*, Gustaf Fischer Verlag, Stuttgart/New York, pp. 418–444.

—— (1989b) 'Psychotherapie', in: K. Kisker, H. Lauter, J. Meijer, C. Müller and E. Strömgren (eds), *Alterpsychiatrie 8: Psychiatrie der Gegenwart'*, Springer Verlag, Berlin, pp. 313–347.

Reeve, W. and D. Ivison (1985) 'Use of environmental manipulation and classroom and modified informal reality orientation with institutionalized, confused elderly patients', *Age and Aging* 14: 119–121.

Reifler, B.V., E. Larson, L. Teri *et al.* (1986) 'Dementia of the Alzheimer's type and depression', *Journal of the American Geriatric Society* 34: 855–859.

Revere, V. and S.S. Tobin (1980–81) 'Myth and reality: the older persons' relationship to his past', *International Journal of Aging and Human Development* 12: 15–26.

Rijsdorp, K. (1977) *Gymnologie*, Het Spectrum, Utrecht/Antwerp.

Rimm, D.C. and J.C. Masters (1974) *Behavior Therapy: Techniques and Empirical Findings*, Academic Press, New York.

Rinke, C.L., J.J. Williams and K.E. Lloyd (1978) 'The effects of prompting and reinforcement on self-bathing by elderly residents of a nursing home', *Behavior Therapy* 9: 873–881.

Romaniuk, M. and J.G. Romaniuk (1981) 'Looking back: an analysis of reminiscence functions and triggers', *Experimental Aging Research* 7: 477–489.

Ronde, C. de and J. Kamm (1989) *Over geheugen gesproken; een cursus voor ouderen*, Intervakgroep Sociale Gerontologie, Katholieke Universiteit Nijmegen, Intro, Nijkerk.

Rossaert, I. (1989) 'Reminiscentie: leven en werken met herinneringen', *Tijdschrift Gerontologie en Geriatrie* 20: 167–168.

Rovner, B.W., J. Lucas-Blaustein, M.F. Folstein *et al.* (1990) 'Stability over one year in patients admitted to a nursing home dementia unit', *International Journal of Geriatric Psychiatry* 5: 77–82.

Sadavoy, J. and A. Robinson (1989) 'Psychotherapy and the cognitively impaired elderly', in: D.K. Conn, A. Grek, J. Sadavoy (eds), *Psychiatric Consequences of Brain Disease in the Elderly*', Plenum Press, New York, pp. 101–135.

Sandel, S.L. (1987) 'Expressive group therapy with severely confused patients', *Activities, Adaptation and Aging* 9: 117–128.

Schnelle, J.F., B. Traughber, D.B. Morgan *et al.* (1983) 'Management of geriatric incontinence in nursing homes', *Journal of Applied Behavior Analysis* 16: 235–241.

Schwab, M., J. Rader, and J. Doan (1985) 'Relieving the anxiety and fear in dementia', *Journal of Gerontological Nursing* 11: 8–15.

Shoham, H. and S. Neuschatz (1985) 'Group therapy with senile patients', *Social Work* 69–72.

Sjoers, J. (1978) 'Vakantiehuisjes en zelf koken; experimenten in een psychogeriatrisch verpleeghuis', *Tijdschrift voor bejaarden-, kraam-, en ziekenverzorging* 11: 427–430.

Sparacino, J. (1978–79) 'Individual psychotherapy with the aged: A selective review', *International Journal of Aging and Human Development* 9: 197–220.

Stetter, F. and W. Stuhlman (1987) 'Autogenes Training bei gerontopsychiatrischen Patienten', *Zeitschrift für Gerontologie* 20: 236–241.

Storandt, M. (1978) 'Introduction to section 3: Therapy with the aged', in: M. Storandt, I.C. Siegler and M.F. Elias (eds), *The Clinical Psychology of Aging*. Plenum Press, New York, pp. 197–198.

Taft, L.B. and M.F. Nehrke (1990) 'Reminiscence, life review and ego integrity in nursing home residents', *International Journal of Aging and Human Development* 30: 189–196.

Tarman, V.I. (1988) 'Autobiography: the negotiation of a lifetime', *International Journal of Aging and Human Development* 27: 171–191.

Teri, L. (1994) 'Behavioral treatment of depression in patients with dementia', *Alzheimer's Disease and Associated Disorders* 8, suppl. 3: 66–74.

Thornton, S. and J. Brotchie (1987) 'Reminiscence: A critical review of the empirical literature', *British Journal of Clinical Psychology* 26: 93–11.

Thralow, J.U. and C.G. Watson (1974) 'Using elementary school students', *The American Journal of Occupational Therapy* 28: 469–473.

Toepfer, C.T., A.T. Bichnell and D.D. Shaw (1974) 'Remotivation as behavior therapy', *The Gerontologist* 14: 451–453.

Tolbert, B.M. (1984) 'Reality Orientation and remotivation in a long-term-care facility', *Nursing and Health Care* 5: 40–44.

Tross, S. and J.E. Blum (1988) 'A review of group therapy with the older adult: practice and research', in: B.W. MacLennan, S. Saul, M.B. Weiner *et al.* (eds), *Group Psychotherapies For the Elderly*. American Group Psychotherapy Ass., Monograph Series (5) International Universities Press, Madison, Conn.

Vaccaro, F. (1988) 'Successful operant conditioning procedures with an institutionalized aggressive geriatric patient', *International Journal of Aging and Human Development* 26: 71–79.

Verwoerdt, A. (1981) 'Individual psychotherapy in senile dementia', in: N.E. Miller and G.D. Cohen (eds), *Clinical Aspects of Alzheimer's Disease and Senile Dementia* (*Aging* 15). Raven Press, New York.

Vink, M.T. (1991) '*Geheugentraining voor ouderen*', Geriatrie Informatorium, Samson/Stafleu, Alphen a/d Rijn-Brussel, 23, D1130, 1–13.

Wächtler, C. (1983) 'Analytisch orïentierte Gruppentherapie in einer psychogeriatrischen Tagesklinik', in: H. Radebold (ed.), *Gruppenpsychotherapie im Alter*. Verlag VandenHoeck and Ruprecht, Göttingen, 64–74.

Warmelink, C. (1990) 'Leren anders met het geheugen om te gaan', *Leeftijd* 2: 28–30.

Wattis, J.P. and M. Church (1986) 'Neuropsychological assessment and the environment', in: J.P. Wattis and M. Church (eds), *Practical Psychiatry of Old Age*, Croom Helm, London, pp. 141–167.

Welden, S. and J.A. Yesavage (1982) 'Behavioral improvement with relaxation training in senile dementia', *Clinical Gerontologist* 1 (1): 45–49.

Williams, M., H. Robach and J. Pro (1980) 'A geriatrics' growth group', *Group* 4: 43–49.

Williams, R., W. Reeve, D. Ivison and D. Kavanagh (1987) 'Use of environmental manipulation and modified informal reality orientation with institutionalized, confused elderly subjects: a replication', *Age and Aging* 16: 315–318.

Wisner, E. and M. Green (1986) 'Treatment of a demented patients' anger with cognitive-behavioral strategies', *Psychological Reports* 59: 447–450.

Woods, R.T. and P.G. Britton (1977) 'Psychological approaches to the treatment of the elderly', *Age and Aging* 6: 104–112.

—— and —— (1985) *Clinical Psychology with the Elderly*. Croom Helm, London/Australia.

Yates, J. (1987) 'Project pup: the perceived benefits to nursing home residents', *Anthrozoös* 1: 188–192.

Yesavage, J.A. (1984) 'Relaxation and memory training in 39 elderly patients', *American Journal of Psychiatry* 141: 778–781.

—— and T.B. Karasu (1982) 'Psychotherapy with elderly patients', *American Journal of Psychotherapy* 36 (1): 41–55.

Zachary, R.A. (1984) 'Day care within an institution', *Physical and Occupational Therapy in Geriatrics* 3: 61–67.

Zarit, S.H. (1982) 'Families under stress: Interventions for care-givers of senile dementia patients', *Psychotherapy, Theory, Research and Practice* 19: 461–471.

Zgola, J.M. (1988) *Doing Things; A Guide to Programming Activities for Persons with Alzheimer's Disease and Related Disorders*. The Johns Hopkins University Press, Baltimore/London.

Zwanikken, W. and M. Janssens (1977) 'Psychotherapie voor ouderen; een literatuur overzicht', *Nederlands Tijdschrift Gerontologie* 8: 124–133.

Part III

Interventions in the community

Chapter 10

The homeostasis model and dementia
A new perspective on care-giving
Anneke van der Plaats

INTRODUCTION

In this chapter I describe what can happen to an elderly person who becomes permanently infirm. Insight into their behaviour will be provided by specific examples. A key issue in managing the situation of the chronically ill elderly person is their 'Understanding of the Situation' (US). This means the idea and assessment of what is going on by the elderly person himself or herself. This US is usually conceived of negatively, based on feelings of loss of control. Behaviour thereafter will largely be determined by this US. Often, the behaviour can be characterized as acts of despair. People becoming demented realize that they are ill and are losing touch with the outside world. It may be assumed that the experiences and feelings of the non-demented elderly also apply to those who are becoming demented. These experiences will be described in this chapter, and on the basis of these, fundamental assumptions for care can be deduced. These will be introduced and illustrated with practical examples at the end of this chapter.

Care is supposed to offer security and should try to facilitate the fulfilment of human needs. The point is that often care is initially not directly aimed at the patient, but on improving the (material and immaterial) environment. The carer tries to lead the dementing person to a more positive US, and from there, to acting in a more calm and competent manner.

DOES OUR CARE HELP?

During the 1980s I participated in several studies within the field of geriatrics and psychogeriatrics (e.g. Nuy *et al.*, 1984; Bouwhuis, 1990). The primary goal was to make an inventory of and do descriptive research on the effects of both nursing-home and day-centre types of care. Chronically ill elderly people still living at home were included as part of this last study. The results of these studies were surprising in the following ways.

Signs of not feeling well

Most of the chronically ill elderly showed many signs of not feeling well, in spite of the help and care they received. In terms of 'well-being' the Elderly Mentally Infirm (EMI) patients felt worse than the somatic patients. The results should be understood in the light of the fact that at the beginning of the 1980s care for the elderly was provided according to a traditional 'medical model' rather than a holistic, psychosocial model. A brief summary of the data follows.

- Of all patients, 54 per cent expressed having more than five physical complaints.
- Bad temper was found more often with completely institutionalized people; 26 per cent compared to 12 per cent of the patients who were in daycare.
- 'Sad and dejected' described 60 per cent of the patients; 40 per cent were apathetic.
- 'Changing moods' were common to 46 per cent of the completely institutionalized, and to 29 per cent of daycare patients.
- Of the institutionalized 39 per cent 'often cry'; 27 per cent of daycare patients did.
- Pain is a regular companion in both categories; 59 per cent and 40 per cent respectively.
- Fatigue was reported by 63 per cent and 57 per cent of the patients respectively.

(Nuy *et al.* 1984, part 1: 37–38)

- 'Little contact possible' with 85 per cent of EMI patients compared with 42 per cent of the somatic patients.
- 'Does not take initiative' described 66 per cent of the EMI patients, and 50 per cent of the somatic patients.
- 'Character more difficult' described over 40 per cent of the EMI versus 33 per cent of the somatic patients.

(Nuy *et al.* 1984, part 1: 28–29)

Nuijens *et al.* (1987: 11) reported on the chronically ill elderly at home.

- 'Frequent rebellious behaviour' was found in 30 per cent of the patients.
- 'Moderate degree of depression' was found in 40 per cent of them.
- Fifty per cent of the patients had a clear 'negative attitude to life'.
- Where their 'perception of the future' was concerned, 30 per cent had a somewhat negative attitude and 20 per cent had a markedly pessimistic view. Half the patients displayed a serious degree of feeling socially aggrieved.

In the nursing home, mood-disturbances of depression and apathy occurred at a high frequency. Behavioural categories that stand out in a negative sense are:

- being withdrawn, which occurs with many of the residents of a nursing home;
- not interested in anything, also a common feature;
- many residents of nursing homes need significant help or encouragement with dressing;
- finally, many residents are quickly shaken by little things going wrong

(van Eekelen, 1981: 95)

43 per cent of the nursing home residents were never active, they were never seen occupied with anything.

(Kochen and Roelofs, 1983: 151)

59 per cent of the chronically ill at home do not have any means of passing the time.

(Nuy *et al.*, 1984, part 2: 124–140)

Many of the residents of a nursing home have too few contacts and daily pursuits. . . .

(Bouwhuis, 1990: 60)

Having a friend among fellow residents proves to be a rare occurrence.

(van Eekelen, 1981: 28)

During the research in daycare and nursing homes it was observed that, besides the care, the help offered was of a medical and paramedical nature. Pastoral care, social work, psychological counselling, groupwork and counselling are almost not on offer.

(Nuy *et al.*, 1984, part 1: 47–48)

Yet, this 'mostly medical' care often does not result in greater feelings of well-being or autonomy for the disabled elderly. On the contrary, feelings of helplessness, somatic complaints and disturbing behaviour increase. It appears that the care provided does not always further well-being and health, but seems to evoke more signs of illness.

Dementing elderly have an 'Understanding of the Situation' (US)

We asked all the elderly people in the nursing home and daycare centre if they had come into this service with their own full consent and co-operation, or against their will. The directors had some reservations about this line of questioning, because we were also asking the demented patients. (One couldn't expect to get reliable answers from them, was the general expectation.) About 30 per cent of the dementing patients could not answer, but most actually gave a clear answer and opinion.

At least 65 per cent of the elderly people in the nursing home reported being admitted against their will; in the day-hospital, 20 per cent of the patients stated that they had not approved of going there.

Covert attempts to be in control

During the same years (1982/1983) I supervised a research project on the toilet patterns of chronically ill patients admitted to the nursing home. Elderly Mentally Infirm (EMI) patients were also included. They did not differ from somatic patients in their toileting behaviour. Again, it should be said that the EMI wards were derivations of somatic wards and that, in both, the same strictly medically oriented approach to care prevailed. The most widespread problems regarding 'going to the toilet' were:

- Is worried or embarrassed about being incontinent.
- Has problems with excretion when others are present.
- Constantly wants to go to the toilet (with results).
- Is afraid of being 'ordered to urinate'.
- Gets angry when not helped immediately.
- Has problems with sanitary regulations imposed by the nursing staff.

Of the overall population 89 per cent displayed one or more problems (on average, four or five) in their behaviour related to toileting. Nine or more behavioural problems were shown by 25 per cent of the population. Emotional conflicts, somatic changes and social changes were the chief cause of these behavioural problems (Kochen and Roelofs, 1983: 147–148).

A medical investigation of the patients was carried out, and practically no abnormalities were found that could have explained the strange toileting behaviour.

> The need for autonomy and control can however take a compulsive shape, so that toileting behaviour no longer primarily serves to maintain control over excretion. Instead, it serves as a defence against uncertainty, feelings of insecurity and unpredictability.
>
> (Kochen and Roelofs, 1983: 54)

There were many signs from the patients that could be interpreted as being expressions of fear, helplessness and as attempts to gain control over the environmental living situation.

Difficult diagnostics

Another noteworthy result was that many of the neurologically disturbed patients had not been properly medically examined. It became clear that with the CVA and dementia patients in 30 and 32 per cent respectively of the cases, no additional diagnosis was known to the charge nurse. With 'internal medicine' and 'orthopaedic' patients it would be common for several additional diagnoses to be known to the charge nurse (Nuy *et al.*, 1984, part 1: 72).

Dröes (1991) came up with the same data in her research. A possible reason for the inadequate diagnoses could be the poor treatability of such abnormalities. Moreover, a large number of the abnormalities cannot be explained from pathological anatomy, for example brain-lesions. Likewise, in the case of dementia, some of the symptoms of the disease cannot be directly explained from observable abnormalities in the brain. The medical model does not apply here. Miesen introduced the concept of 'awareness-context' (see Chapter 5). In his research (Miesen, 1990, 1993) points towards the primary and secondary effects of disease. The primary effects are explicable directly from the anatomical and physiological abnormalities found in the body; the secondary effects are individual reactions to the knowledge of their physical/mental condition or its treatment. Hence, the secondary effects document how an individual deals with knowing/ having the disease. The individual thoughts and behaviour that result from the 'awareness-context', are thus often perceived as symptoms of the disease. Naturally they cannot be directly explained from anatomical or physio-logical abnormalities (van der Plaats 1994). Interest in these secondary symptoms of the disease has recently been growing.

THE HOMEOSTASIS EXPLANATION MODEL (HEM). A SYNTHESIS OF THE LITERATURE

The above-mentioned studies led me to do research into the care provided for long-term ill and disabled elderly people. My goal was to find a scien-tific foundation for care. I suspected that the care aimed at medical and nursing needs only, would not lead to sufficiently high levels of well-being. Many types of inter-personal and psychosocial care are already available (Jones and Miesen, 1992). This study tries to give them a place in 'care' as a whole; a place in relation to each other through a theoretical framework and foundation. The ultimate goal was to develop a single-explanation model. The literature reviewed was selected for the criteria for such a model. The model had to:

• have existed for a number of years;
• fit in with the theories of biological ageing;
• apply to several levels of the human existence, not just the biological;
• be acceptable to various disciplines.

A theoretical Homeostasis Explanation Model

The Homeostasis Explanation Model was derived from studies on the physical ageing process. The way in which, through time, the empirical data had been explained was examined. The concept of homeostasis was selected to serve as a theoretical framework for further research. Homeostasis has not been unequivocally defined in the literature. For the purpose of this study, homeostasis was defined as the continuous striving towards a condition of balance of the body, its goal being to preserve life in varying circumstances.

Becoming ill can be considered as unstable homeostasis. Ageing, illness and chronic disease can all be described as modes of homeostasis; respectively as vulnerable, disturbed and permanently disturbed homeostasis with shifting balances. In the description of symptoms of a given disease there were shortcomings in the physiological concept of homeostasis. Once again, there are primary and secondary symptoms of a disease. The primary symptoms can be explained by looking at the physical abnormalities that occur with a disease. The secondary symptoms can be explained by means of physical stress reactions to threatening circumstances or may have physical or psychological origins. Cannon (1941), probably the first one to use the term 'homeostasis', referred to physical reactions and to emotions as the 'wisdom of the body'.

A closer look at the concept of homeostasis

Homeostasis in a technical sense includes the maintenance of balance within a system. But within that system there are sub-systems in which there is homeostasis too. Outside the system there are larger systems in which homeostasis also works. The concept of homeostasis therefore possesses the theoretical potential to be extended to several systems and levels. In this way it explains how changes in one system outside the body, can lead to changes in sub-systems inside the body. This means that the source of 'not being well' could be traced, and that more specific care-measurements could be devised. In the system theory it is assumed that homeostasis is a mechanism that can run partly automatically and partly consciously. People influence their environment and therefore contribute to maintaining their own physical homeostasis. By affecting certain circumstances they can further their own health. Whenever they can no longer do that, for example because of their need for help, others will have to do it for them.

Homeostasis in its theoretical meaning refers to the intensive, combined action of human activities on a physical, psychic and social field. The redefinition of homeostasis is: harmonizing different processes of human life in such a way that the health of the individual is promoted. Health is defined as functional autonomy – an individual's assessment of his or her own physical performance, feelings, self-caring activities and other actions in relation to the (social) environment. Care is now defined as a balanced set of measures that aim to further the functional autonomy of the individual by means of homeostasis.

After this extension of the concept of homeostasis, it becomes possible to elaborate on the subject of this research. Psychological and social human structures can now be included in the description of disease. Further research could therefore be focused on the psychosocial consequence of becoming ill and needing help. This study shows that the way in which the victim assesses his own 'ill-being' is of crucial importance to the course of the disease.

DEMENTIA: KNOWING OR NOT KNOWING?

In this book several chapters have considered dementia patients' perception of their environment. It turns out that the demented are definitely afraid and feel uncertain. But it is only just recently that scientific research has paid any attention to these feelings.

The 'not-knowing' patient

The days in which one seriously considered not telling someone he had cancer are not far behind us. People were often not told. A result of this was that usually everybody, except the person concerned, knew he had the dreaded disease. This led to a strained relationship between patients and their relatives. Outsiders had the impression that the patient 'went along with the game' for the sake of the relatives. He could sometimes come out with a telling remark such as: 'Next summer I'll have a nice holiday somewhere far away.' Then several 'expressed emotions' could be observed in the relatives: desperate looks, soothing gestures, intense shaking of the head behind the patient's back. When the relatives had fled after making numerous excuses, the patient confided to a nurse that he thought he wouldn't live to enjoy this holiday. 'Denial' was a word much used at that time to typify the behaviour of cancer patients. In this context, van der Bom (1984) describes several (alleged) psychiatric symptoms with haemodialysis patients. Care-takers were convinced that these symptoms were the result of the kidney disease and that this disease occurs especially with people with certain characteristics. Van der Bom showed in his study that these psychiatric symptoms are elicited by the care itself. He too saw a shortage of real information and the creation of false expectations. But, most importantly, care-givers themselves were so enthusiastic about the way they provided care that they couldn't acknowledge that living with haemodialysis is certainly no picnic. Because of this, patients were more or less forced not to complain about the downside of a life with haemodialysis. The negative feelings of the patient then of course found other outlets, such as compulsive and risky behaviour.

Keeping silent about dementia

At present many are still convinced that demented patients had better not know that they are demented. What is more, such is our reasoning, they wouldn't understand. So it is of no use to inform them. Silence is legitimized by an 'alleged' symptom of the disease: lack of understanding. Yet here and there the idea that dementing people have a clear understanding of their decline is beginning to take shape. Because of their thinking disorders, however, they are not able adequately and consistently to put into words the limitations they notice. In his doctoral research Miesen (1990) concluded that dementing people are actually confronted with experiences of loss. They experience their own situation as being very threatening. This manifests itself in, among other things, their parent-orientation and parent-fixation.

Dröes (1991) draws the same conclusions in her doctoral research. She explained that much of the so-called abnormal behaviour developed from a threatening situation, and was the individual's response to it. For example, she considers regressive behaviour to be a way of coping with one's own decline. Obsessive, compulsive behaviour and denial can be looked upon in the same way. Aggression, agitation, aimless wandering, and repeated asking for help can be explained as attempts to maintain an emotional balance. To maintain a positive self-image dementing people use denial, avoidance and projection as defence-mechanisms. Paranoid, delusional thinking and avoidance of test-situations can be the results of this. Such behaviour cannot be the direct expression of anatomical or physiological abnormalities. It consists of individual reactions to becoming disabled, experiences of loss, and not being able to control the environment. Apparently, then, dementing people go through the same experience as people who have been affected by other kinds of disability, although maybe not as consciously.

BECOMING DISABLED AS A 'THREATENING SITUATION'

The majority of studies about becoming chronically infirm go back to the 1970s. These studies indicate that disability is an existential problem and affects *all* levels of human functioning (see van der Pas, 1964). The psychological and social implications of disability are often not taken into account with the medical treatment. It is true that the physical damage is the basis of disability, but the consequences become evident mainly in the way in which the body is part of the self-image (Metz, 1970; Dechesne, 1978). Leering (1968) studied frailty, in particular with elderly people. He showed that disability and being chronically ill are closely related. He stresses however that self-knowledge and understanding about one's own disease can decrease because of the nature and the location of the disability. He therefore pointed to a special form of disability, caused by brain disorders.

The significance of disability to one's life

The literature study conducted by van den Bos and Danse (1986) provides a good analysis of the difficult existence of a person who has become disabled. They say that the social status of the disabled person requires adaption to a new life and to not being able to fulfil tasks and roles. Disability affects all levels of life so profoundly, that making life controllable again in the new situation seems an impossible task. A fear of discomfort, dependence and being cast out develops. Attempts to reduce this fear result in withdrawal, denial of the impairments, being over-concerned about further discomfort, refusal to co-operate with rehabilitation and the refusal of help. Other reactions such as depression, aggression, death wishes and psychotic reactions are not uncommon.

Self-image – the image of one's own body, mind and one's social activities – can be seriously damaged by disability. People who grow old, as well as those who become infirm, no longer meet the prevailing 'standards' of society. These standards include youthfulness, physical soundness, dexterity, independence, and verbal and social skills. In the light of these standards, disabled people feel they fall short, and are ashamed of themselves. This also happens to people who are becoming demented. For example, a person will try to hide his deficiencies for as long as possible. In dementia this is called 'social facade'.

Well persons and care-givers sometimes feel an aversion towards people who do not meet the societal standards of normality. To neutralize these feelings, counter-measures are taken with regard to the disabled or infirm, which leads, for them, to control, pressure towards normality, punishment, being treated as a child and social isolation. Van der Bom (1973) indicates that certain chronically ill and infirm elderly are the worst off. Harmful effects result from damaged self-image and feelings of powerlessness. Cognitive disorders can intensify the negative aspects mentioned above, according to van der Bom.

The damaged self-image

The dementing person is confronted with a changing self-image. What is more, the change is unexpected and negative. Both of these make the confrontation all the more painful. The unexpected occurs because the dementing person is not well prepared in the early stages of his illness. The surroundings keep it from him or her. The negative aspect is enhanced by the stigma of the disease itself, but also by the attitude of denial of the surroundings. At the same time these surroundings radiate shame, blame, anger and grief without it being made explicit.

Munnichs (1990) indicates that continuity of the self-image is necessary for the well-being of a human being. This continuity has in the case of a

demented elderly person been rudely interrupted and he or she will
initially employ behaviour to enable them to look upon themselves as
'still the same old me'. Nell (1988) calls this behaviour 'tactics'. One tactic,
for example, is to boss the care-givers in order to pretend to a sense of
independence. The tactics lead to (counter)measures by those around the
elderly person, as a result of which the discrepancy between the former,
more accepted, self-image and the present unacceptable one, grows bigger
and bigger. The individual can now either employ all sorts of tactics or try
to accept a changed self-image. According to Nell, the latter is a strategy.
One example of a positive coping strategy would be to participate in a
counselling group to work on acceptance of certain disorders. Tactics are
the often failed attempts at attention seeking, referred to as annoying
behaviour. Strategies would imply more successful forms of behaviour. In
the first case, those people who might help the victim to find a new self-
image, would turn away. In the latter case, the positive coping strategy
could lead to acceptance of the new self. The damage is still there, and
life becomes yet more limited, yet one can still reach a certain degree of
fulfilment of needs.

Sources of annoying behaviour

The tragedy of the dementing person is that because of cognitive limitations he or she is no longer capable of using strategies consciously. The
care-giver cannot expect any acceptance that comes about rationally. What
they can do is bring about an instinctive acceptance. The conditions for this
are to be created by the care-givers. These conditions lie embedded in a
kind of care in which the dementing person can have the feeling of being
able to live a 'normal' life. The normality includes providing for common
human needs such as belonging, receiving attention, avoiding feelings of
failure, and finding a significant pastime.

Care rarely meets the fulfilment of these needs. In this context, Kochen
and Roelofs (1983: 54) write: 'When needs can't be fulfilled in one's own
way, inadequate actions, desperate attempts of behaviour can be the result.
Also expressive utterances with no goal can develop, purely as an expression of some emotional condition.' She describes the problem behaviour
of residents of nursing homes concerning toilet visits. She encounters a
lot of annoying behaviour. She finds that the chronically ill elderly have low
self-esteem and a great deal of shame and grief. This seems also the case
with the demented elderly.

Annoying behaviour is often called 'inadequate'. This is a misleading
term because, in view of the awkward situation, this behaviour might be
very appropriate. The source of this behaviour is a negative self-image.
It is prompted by the loss of the feeling of control; specifically, the
irreversible need for help and the loss of insight and overview lead to a

marked sense of powerlessness. Much incomprehensible behaviour of chronically ill people within geriatric care could probably be traced to the loss of control. Generally this behaviour is described as dependent and apathetic and as having a kind of resistance to it. This is coupled with feelings of depression. Heightened stress leads to ineffective actions such as restlessness or aggression (Kahana *et al.*, 1987; Wheaton, 1980; Shupe, 1985; Willis, 1991).

THE NEED FOR HELP CONJURES UP POWERLESSNESS

Thomae (1984) did a longitudinal study with a large group of elderly people. He saw that they often reacted to health problems with feelings of powerlessness. The result is that all consequences that follow the disease are experienced by them as beyond their control. The elderly take a very dependent attitude because they think that there is nothing that can be done now. They do not take their fate into their own hands and they let themselves be governed by the disease, the complaints and disorders. With dementing people the same reactions can be expected. Because of their cognitive disorders, they cannot fully realize what is going on. None the less, according to Miesen (1990, 1993), they still experience the situation they are in as threatening.

Personal thoughts of the disabled elderly people

The thoughts and motives that influence the actions of the chronically ill elderly have been described. These descriptions come from non-demented elderly people but it can be assumed that demented people experience the same threats. The perception of their situation can lead to the following thoughts (Kruse, 1987; Lehr, 1980):

- assuming that the situation cannot be changed
- having the feeling that life has been severely restricted
- thinking that everything, oneself included, has been damaged
- the idea that one doesn't have a solution to the problems
- foreseeing no future
- feeling lonely and abandoned
- the illness controls one's whole life
- feeling strongly linked to the pleasant things of the past

Reactions and behaviours that derive from these ideas are:

- withdrawal
- apathy
- complaining

- blaming others
- denigrating others
- actively resisting care
- deathwishes

All in all it is clear that being chronically ill or disabled in itself can mean a constant source of stress (see also Ben-Sira, 1984; Knussen and Cunningham, 1988). Added to that, additional events such as admission to a hospital or nursing home, treatment, moving to a home for the elderly, and becoming dependent on others can considerably enhance this stress (Kessler and McLeod, 1984; Thomae, 1989). So in spite of the care, additional symptoms of disease can develop. The care that was meant to help the person, can in fact work to the contrary because it reinforces a sense of powerlessness. Next, the disabled person, who wants to hold on to his or her self-image, can become very annoying. How can this behaviour of elderly people who have become infirm be influenced?

A central concept: one's own estimation

The image individuals form of themselves about their new situation, is crucial for the way they act. Lazarus *et al.* (1986) calls it 'appraisal', and in the case of dementing elderly persons Miesen (1990) calls it 'awareness-context'. This 'own estimation' is a key-concept in the search for balance with which every human being is occupied.

Stimuli from the environment affect the individual and his or her body; for example think of turning red from anger, becoming white when frightened, and shaking with fear. So when individuals experience a situation as threatening, it will have repercussions on their physical and mental balance. People with a shaky physical balance, such as the elderly and chronically ill, are extra-sensitive to threats and they develop symptoms of disease in a short time.

Reker (1985) too considers the Personal Estimation a key concept within the general maintenance of balance. If there is no homeostasis then that will reveal itself with the chronically ill elderly in an increase of physical complaints, need for physical help and annoying behaviour. In the case of chronically ill elderly people, medically trained care-givers tend to interpret these symptoms as an increase of the disease from which the person is suffering, for example a dementia. Van der Plaats (1994) reveals that this conclusion is premature. The increase of symptoms of disease can also be attributed to the distressing situation in which dementing elderly people find themselves. They feel fear, powerlessness and grief. It is therefore essential to know what image a person with symptoms of disease has of his or her own situation. So as a care-giver one should try and discover the cognitive and emotional appraisal of the individual. This appraisal determines his or her actions. Moreover, Lazarus *et al.* (1984) found that the personal appraisal of the situation was more significant for subsequent behaviour than the actual situation as it was perceived by outsiders.

The environment

If the concept of homeostasis is taken as a basis, then research about the environment will be important – particularly the question of whether the environment is appraised as being threatening for the person concerned. Care-givers are a part of it. It is important that we notice processes in it which the dementing person experiences as threatening. Our own behaviour can be frightening for him or her. An example would be appropriate:

> *In a group home for demented elderly people much of the residents' health is failing rapidly in a very short period of time. There is considerable agitation and annoying behaviour. A student on work-placement is asked to observe the daily business carefully. This outsider notices a great many things: care-givers are very busy with instrumental duties. They talk to each other as if the residents are not there. They openly argue with residents. The behaviour of some of the residents is discussed in public. Residents sometimes just sit doing nothing for an hour, wearing big bibs, and waiting for dinner. These things are discussed with the care-givers. They manage to change their behaviour significantly. The result was that the residents started behaving more 'normally' again.*

If the threats present in the situation are not noticed and removed, the annoying behaviour will continue and it is possible that tranquillizers or neuroleptics will be administered to the residents.

BASIC ASSUMPTIONS IN CARE-GIVING ABOUT ILLNESS AND HEALTH

Homeostasis creates conditions for health. Homeostasis deals with the balance between numerous processes – physical, mental and social. These can also compensate for each other's effects. If a demented person is overstimulated or ignored, he or she will increasingly behave inadequately. If this person, however, is helped and comforted, he or she will act almost 'normally'. The environment can therefore compensate for the physical and mental limitations by offering supporting care.

In the case of demented elderly people the environment can offer much protection. The homeostasis of the demented elderly person has diminished in such a way that environmental care or situational care is of crucial importance. It is possibly even more important than other kinds of care such as medical, paramedical and nursing care.

Several kinds of care; curative, situational and transforming

Here a short summary of types of care will be given. All care concentrates on homeostasis, but most of ordinary care often concentrates on the physical part only.

1 Most care practised, therefore, is cursive. Homeostasis is, in the physical area, supported by measures that directly affect the anatomical or physiological structures of the body. These measures often have the disadvantage that they – simultaneously with their curative effects – cause damage to homeostasis. This damage can also affect other levels (mental and social). Curative care should really only be used when a disease is evident and when it appears to be threatening the life of the patient. With the chronically ill these measures are appropriate only in the early stages of the disease. When curative possibilities have been exhausted, the switch is made to palliative care or 'non-invasive' curative care. In the light of the concept of homeostasis, however, there are additional kinds of care that could be of interest for the chronically ill.

2 Situational care can be given. Homeostasis as a whole can be protected and reinforced by creating certain conditions through which the chronically ill elderly person can feel more comfortable, safer or more satisfied. It mainly concerns itself with the approach of the care-givers, with an institution that is small and open and that has a layout that is cosy and stimulates communication. Situational care has the highest priority with the chronically ill elderly. The other forms of care cannot be effective when the care environment (in both a material and non-material sense) is not optimal.

3 Transformative care can be given. In the physical area this kind of care is well-known: the state of the body can be changed or strengthened by using, for example, vaccination, vitamin-diets, physiotherapy, plastic surgery, etc. In the psychosocial area, transformative care could involve psychotherapy, counselling, rediscovering a person's identity, cognitive training, and improving relations with and within the social network. Re-establishing balance on the psychosocial level has a beneficial effect on the physiology of the body.

At present, too much curative and palliative care is given. Too little attention is given to situational and transformative care. An expansion of these two kinds of care follows.

Transformative and situational care

These new kinds of care begin and end with the image of the patient as a fellow human being, who has the same wishes and needs as everybody else; the care-giver in this instance only has to consider his or her own needs to understand the logic of that. So she has to be able to be 'just a fellow human being'. Care-givers use their professionalism to give the patient and relatives insight into the situation. The professional, the patient and the family will together look for meaningful ways to fulfil the human needs of the patient. Such care leads to a more comfortable life for the patient (Cousins 1979, 1983). Professional care-givers realize that their attitude towards the patient and the way in which they give care, are essential elements of care (see also Thung, 1990).

Buijssen and Mertens (1990) refer to four conditions that should be met by this care so that it is not stress-provoking, and consequently disease-promoting. These conditions are:

- The care should be clear and transparent. The elderly person should know what to expect.
- The care should be surveyable. The elderly must have the feeling that they can have some influence on the care they are receiving and that their wishes are respected.
- The care should provide for the making or maintaining of social contacts.
- Activities within the care plan should provide an optimal stress-level for the patient. They should be challenging and satisfying, neither too stressful nor below a person's abilities.

SUMMARY AND CONCLUSION

In this chapter it has been argued that dementing people feel and realize that they are ill and losing their skills. Research on becoming chronically ill and being in need of help has described what the chronically ill experience and go through themselves. A key issue in these descriptions is patients' understanding of their situation, an image that they form for themselves of themselves and about the situation they are in. For people who are ill the situation is often negative and frightening – which derives mainly from a negative self-image and feelings of losing control.

The care being provided often turns out to be a source of this negative self-image. Such an 'awareness-context' forms the foundation for the coping that ensues. Panic or desperation can follow. A further result could be that symptoms of disease increase, such as incontinence, annoying behaviour, crying, asking for too much help, and physical complaints. The cause does not lie in the disease itself but in the circumstances. Care should therefore be aimed at creating favourable circumstances. This type of care is specific and concentrates on experiencing the situation more positively. The behaviour of the sufferer becomes more competent as a result.

NOTE

In my research I define health as an individual's assessment of his or her own physical performance, feelings, self-caring activities and other actions in relation to the social environment. The central point here is the individual estimation of his or her own performance. Furthermore, environmental factors weigh as heavily as individual abilities. Care is now defined as a balanced set of interventions with the aim of furthering the health of an individual by means of stabilizing homeostasis.

REFERENCES

Ben-Sira, Z.V. (1984) Chronic illness, stress and coping. In: *Social Science and Medicine* 18 (9): 725–736.

Bom, J.A. van der (1973) Langdurige invaliditeit. Rapport Gerontologisch Centrum, 28.

—— (1984) Patienten met nierlijden. Dissertatie Nijmegen.

Bos, G.A.M. van den and Danse, J.A.C. (1986) De betekenis van het chronisch-ziek-zijn: enkele benaderingswijzen en hun implicaties voor de zorgverlening. In: *Metamedica* 65: 406–420.

Bouwhuis, H. (1990) Wachten op verpleeghuiszorg in Oost-Gelderland. In: H. Bouwhuis (ed.), *Deelonderzoek 2, kwalitatief*. Arnhem: Gelderse Raad voor de Volksgezondheid.

Buijssen H. and Mertens, F. (1990) Preventie doordacht. In: H. Nies *et al.* (eds), *Contouren van het ouder worden*. Deventer: Van Loghum Slaterus.

Cannon, W.B. (1941) *Bodily Changes in Pain, Hunger, Fear and Rage*. New York: Macmillan.

Cousins, N. (1979) *Anatomy of an Illness: As Perceived by the Patients*. New York: W.W. Norton and Co.

—— (1983) *The healing heart*. New York: Aron Books.

Dechesne, B.H.H. (1978) Jeugdige gehandicapten. Dissertatie Nijmegen. Meppel: Krip Repro bv.

Dröes, R.M. (1991) *In Beweging*. Dissertatie. Nijkerk: Intro.

Eekelen, C.W.J.M. van (1981) *De validiteit van de verpleeghuisbewoner: eindrapport*. Nijmegen: KU, Intervakgr Sociale Gerontologie.

Gallé, E. (1986) Leefstijldifferentiatie in verpleeghuis 'Mariahoeve'. In: J. Groen (ed.), *Patiëntendifferentiatie op basis van leefstijl in verpleeghuizen*. Reeks Moderne Gerontologie. Lochem: De Tijdstroom.

Jones, G.M.M. and Miesen, B.M.L. (eds) (1992) *Care-Giving in Dementia: Research and Applications*, vol. 1. London/New York: Tavistock/Routledge.

Kahana, E. and Kiyak, H.A. (1984) Attitudes and behaviour of staff in facilities for the aged. In: *Research on Aging* 6 (3): 395–416.

——, Kahana B. and Young R. (1987) Strategies of coping and post-institutional outcomes. In: *Research on Aging* 9 (2): 182–199.

Kessler, R.C. and McLeod, J. (1984) Social support and psychological distress in community surveys. In: S. Cohen and L. Syme (eds), *Social Support and Health*. New York: Academic Press.

Knussen, C. and Cunningham, C.C. (1988) Stress, disability and handicap. In: S. Fisher and J. Reason (eds), *Handbook of Lifestress, Cognition and Health*. New York: John Wiley and Sons.

Kochen, J.A.W. and Roelofs, J. (1983) Het excretie-syndroom, probleemgedrag rond mictie en defaecatie bij oudere verpleeghuisbewoners. Doctoraal scriptie Sociale Gerontologie en Geneeskunde. Nijmegen: KU.

Kruse, A. (1987) Coping with chronic disease, dying and death. A contribution to competence in old age. In: Compr Gerontol, C, 1: 1–11.

Lazarus, R.S. and Folkman S. (1984) *Stress, Appraisal and Coping.* New York: Springer Pub. Co.

Leering, C. (1968) Gestoord menselijk functioneren. Dissertatie. Nijmegen: Dekker en Van der Vegt.

Lehr, U. (1980) Alterszustand und Altersprozesse. Biografische determinanten. In: *Zeitschrift für Gerontol.* 13: 442–457.

Metz, W. (1970) *Het dorp.* Nijkerk: Intro.

Miesen, B. (1990) Gehechtheid en dementie/Attachment and dementia. Thesis. Nijkerk: Intro.

—— (1993) Alzheimer's disease, the phenomenon of parent fixation and Bowlby's attachment theory. *International Journal of Geriatric Psychiatry* 8: 147–153.

Munnichs, J.M.A. (1990) *Gerontologie, levensloop en biografie.* Afscheidscollege KU Nijmegen. Deventer: Van Loghum Slaterus.

Nell, H.W. (1988) De draad vasthouden, de eigen identiteit na opname in het somatisch verpleeghuis. Dissertatie. Leiden: Spruyt, Van Mandegem en De Does bv.

Nuijens, M.J.M., Plaats, J.J. van der, Nies, H.L.G.R. and Bom, J.A. van de (1987) *Sociale dagopvang voor ouderen in Arnhem.* Nijmegen: KU Intervakgr Soc. Gerontol.

Nuy, M.H.R., Plaats, J.J. van der and Vernooij, M. (1984) *Dagbehandeling in verpleeghuizen.* Nijmegen: Inst. voor Sociale Geneeskunde.

Pas, J.H.R. van der (1964) Validiteitsschattingen. Dissertatie Utrecht. Assen: Van Gorcum.

Plaats, J.J. van der (1994) Geriatrie een spel van evenwicht. Dissertatie Nijmegen. Assen: Van Gorcum.

Reker, G.T. (1985) Toward a holistic model of health, behaviour and aging. In: J.E. Birren and J. Livingston (eds), *Cognition, Stress and Aging.* Englewood Cliffs, NJ: Prentice Hall.

Shupe, T.R. (1985) Perceived control, helplessness and choice. In: J.E. Birren and J. Livingston (eds), *Cognition, Stress and Aging.* Englewood Cliffs, NJ: Prentice Hall.

Thomae, H. (1984) Reaktionen auf gesundheidliche Belastung im mittleren und höheren Erwachsen-alter. In: *Zeitschrift für Gerontol.* 17: 186–197.

—— (1989) Persoonlijksheids dynamiek en patronen in ouder worden. In: J. Munnichs and G. Uildriks (eds), *Psychogerontology* Deventer: Van Loghum Slaterus.

Thung, P.J. (1990) Morgen brengen, een terugblik op wat ons toekomt. In: *Scripta Medische Philosophie* 7: 61–72. Zeist: Kerckebosch bv.

Wheaton, B. (1980) The socio-genesis of psychological disorder. In: *Journal of Health and Social Behaviour* 21 (2): 100–124.

Willis, S.L. (1991) Cognition and everyday competence. In: K.W. Schaie and M. Powell Lawton (eds), *Annual Review of Gerontology and Geriatrics*, 11. New York: Springer Pub. Co.

Chapter 11

Supporting informal care-givers of demented elderly people

Psychosocial interventions and their outcomes

Pim Cuijpers and Henk Nies

SUMMARY

In recent years various types of psychosocial interventions have been developed to support the informal care-givers of demented elderly people. The present chapter presents an overview of the research into the outcomes of these interventions. The relatively few studies that meet scientific standards are confined to support groups, respite care and individual psychosocial interventions. It appears that the more cure-oriented interventions may have positive outcomes with regard to severe emotional problems of care-givers. Preventive measures that are unselectively applied only have limited effects or no effects at all. The absence of significant effects may be caused by methodological shortcomings and the limited scope of the studies.

INTRODUCTION

Approximately two thirds of all modestly to severely demented patients are taken care of at home by their next of kin. Usually, it is one person who takes responsibility: the partner or a daughter (Duijnstee, 1992). These key supporters face a wide variety of (possible) behavioural problems related to the mental deterioration of their demented relative, e.g. aggression, nightly unrest, wandering around and loss of decorum. At the same time – while envisaging the gradual disintegration of the patient's personality – they experience a premature mourning process (van de Ven and Hectors, 1983) and their social contacts decrease and deteriorate. There is, therefore, a high risk of emotional problems among informal care-givers. They frequently suffer from depression, ill health, chronic tiredness and social isolation (Peute, 1988).

First, this chapter adresses the objectives and the various types of psychosocial interventions. Then, the (quasi-)experimental research into the outcomes of support groups, respite care and individual counselling is reviewed. Finally, closing remarks will be made on the validity of the findings and on future research.

OBJECTIVES

In many cases, the objectives of these types of interventions are barely articulated (Cuijpers, 1993). It is simply assumed that the burden of the family provides sufficient reasons for interventions and services. Family members of demented elderly people seem to have become a new target group of (mental) health care. However, therapeutic or supportive measures are only sufficiently legitimized when a relationship between burden and (mental) health can be established or reasonably assumed. From a health care point of view, the measures to support informal care-givers of demented elderly people serve four objectives (see Peute, 1988).

First, the heightened risk of severe emotional problems legitimizes interventions aimed at prevention. Second, some care-givers actually suffer from severe mental problems which are – at least partially – caused by the burden of care-giving. In these cases curative objectives prevail. Third, the burden of some care-givers has exceeded (or is likely to exceed) their capacities and resources. As a consequence, the elderly person concerned has to be admitted into an institution, or else needs a vast amount of community care. These situations call for preventive interventions to restore the faltering balance at home and to avert long-term admissions. The latter is often also a secondary objective of both preventive and curative interventions. The fourth objective is directly related to the previous one. It aims at the improvement of the quality of care and, thereby, the quality of life of the demented person. This also happens to be a secondary aim of preventive and curative interventions.

TYPES OF INTERVENTIONS

Three main categories of interventions can be distinguished: the provision of information, consultation and emotional support to key care-givers, respite care and individual psychosocial interventions.

Information, consultation and emotional support

Within this category the main types of interventions are:

1 Support groups for next of kin: these groups aim at the prevention of severe emotional problems, caused by the continuous burden of care-giving. Sometimes these groups also strive towards better quality of care for the demented relative. In many of these cases care-givers are not too severely affected by the burden of caring for their relatives, while in some cases they are (see Cuijpers, 1993; see also chapter 15 below, on carers' support groups).
2 Information meetings on dementia and alternatives in care: these meetings tend to address quite large groups of informal care-givers. Usually

information is provided on the disease and its consequences, participants can make inquiries and obtain material with additional information.

3 Written educational material: many care-providing organizations issue leaflets specifically designed for informal care-givers of demented patients.

4 Support by telephone: some organizations (often in the voluntary sector, such as the Alzheimer Society) provide support by telephone for inquiries, advice and emotional support.

Respite care

The various forms of respite care strive towards a temporary and partial relief of the key care-givers by taking over a part of the care. Usually, respite care serves preventive objectives: to relieve the burden of the family and to prevent or postpone admission into residential care. Further, it may provide opportunities for (para)medical and psychosocial treatment of the demented person.

Two types of respite care can be distinguished (Visser and Cornel 1993):

1 Respite care elsewhere than in the client's home: the client is admitted or taken care of for at least a continuous number of hours during the day, evening or night. Further planned or unplanned admissions for longer, but limited periods of time make up this category: relief admissions, intermittent admissions and admissions in case of acute crises. In addition, some holiday resorts and guest houses exist for next of kin. Many types of external respite care exist. Sometimes they are specifically designed for (informal care-givers of) demented clients, sometimes they are also intended for other target groups.

2 Respite care in the clients' own home: professional care-givers or – more often – volunteers attend the demented at home. This allows the informal care-givers to spend some time on their own and to find some relief and relaxation. Sometimes, these sitting services operate independently, sometimes they are affiliated with larger organizations of volunteers or professional care-providers.

Individual psychosocial interventions

Individual psychosocial interventions may be specifically designed for informal care-givers, but usually they are part of regular care provision to the population at large. In general, the objectives of these interventions are curative for cases in which the continuous burden has caused an escalation of the situation. The interventions in this category may be directed towards the individual or to the entire client-system.

RESEARCH INTO THE OUTCOMES

Much has been published about supportive interventions and services, especially on support groups, respite care, and – to a lesser extent – individual interventions. Most of these publications are descriptive. Often they touch only lightly upon the evaluation of these interventions. In most cases no standardized instruments are used nor (quasi-)experimental designs.

Many of these evaluations suggest that the informal care-givers and to some degree the demented clients are positive about the particular supportive measures. However, the few available (quasi-)experimental studies give rise to a more critical appraisal of the effects of these types of support.

For the present chapter an extensive search was carried out in the international literature of the last five years to find (quasi-)experimental studies into the above types of interventions. Only publications using standardized instruments, applying control and experimental groups and/ or pre–post measurements were taken into consideration. The studies that met these criteria are summed up in Table 11.1.

The results of the various studies are difficult to compare. Some interventions, for instance, aim at care-givers of frail elderly people in general, others at those who suffer from severe stress. There are also differences between the interventions with respect to their design and contents. There

Table 11.1 Types of (quasi-)experimental studies into psychosocial supportive interventions

Type of intervention	Type of study	
	Experimental[1]	Quasi-experimental[2]
Support groups	Haley *et al.*, 1987 Montgomery and Borgatta, 1989 Zarit *et al.*, 1987 Toseland *et al.*, 1989 a and b, 1990; Lovett and Gallagher, 1988	Kahan *et al.*, 1985 Dellasega, 1990 Greene and Monahan, 1987
Respite care	Lawton *et al.*, 1989, 1991 Montgomery and Borgatta, 1989	Koloski and Montgomery, 1993 Milne *et al.*, 1993 Wimo *et al.*, 1993
Individual interventions	Zarit *et al.*, 1987 Sutcliffe and Larner, 1988 Toseland and Smith, 1990 Toseland *et al.*, 1990	

Notes: 1 Control group + random assignment
2 Control group, no random assignment

is little uniformity of the instruments that are used. Further, it appears to be a problem to establish control groups. In many cases the key concepts of the studies (such as burden, health, well-being) are ill-defined and theoretical frameworks tend to be virtually absent. Nevertheless, some conclusions can be drawn.

RESULTS

Support groups

The research into support groups has demonstrated only limited evidence of positive effects (for a more detailed review see chapter 15 below). Three studies showed major, statistically significant effects on well-being, depression and stress. On all other health and well-being variables no or only minor changes between pre- and post-measurement were observed in the studies under consideration. This holds for both the experimental and the control groups. However, according to a reanalysis of one of the studies (Whitlach *et al.*, 1991) it is likely that many participants of support groups do not feel themselves severely burdened or depressed. They merely participate to enhance their skills in caring tasks. Therefore, one cannot reasonably expect a reduction of feelings of burden and depression among these care-givers. On the other hand, participants who feel burdened and depressive appeared to benefit from participation. These findings are confirmed by three studies in which the participants were selected beforehand with regard to severe stress. In these cases positive effects on well-being and feelings of burden could be established (Toseland *et al.*, 1989a; 1989b; Lovett and Gallagher, 1988; Greene and Monahan, 1987).

Further, the research points at positive effects on the behaviour of participating care-givers, the problems they encounter, the social support they receive and actual coping behaviour. Haley *et al.* (1987) found an increase of behaviours that were previously labelled as positive outcomes, such as information-gathering, logical analysis and active problem solving. Another study demonstrated a marked decrease of problems experienced in relation to caring tasks and an increase of social networks (Toseland *et al.*, 1989a, 1989b). In two studies short-term effects proved to last over a longer period, although to a lesser degree (Greene and Monahan 1987; Toseland *et al.*, 1989a, 1989b).

Three studies have investigated the effects of support groups on admission into residential care (Brodaty and Gresham, 1989; Greene and Monahan, 1987; Montgomery and Borgatta, 1989). Two studies indicated a limited postponement of admission. The relationship between the informal care-giver and the patient seems to be a relevant variable. For instance, the third study addressing admission effects, shows a tendency towards earlier admissions in cases where the spouse is the informal care-giver. Post-ponement can often be observed when (one of) the children take(s) responsibility for the main caring tasks. In this context one could argue whether postponement is always a desirable objective. A late admission may be too great a burden and threat to the informal care-giver's health and well-being. Both the client's and the care-giver's health may benefit from residential care.

Respite care

The studies into respite care also show only limited effects. No significant effects on the burden of care-givers were found in the experimental studies of Lawton and colleagues (1989, 1991) and of Montgomery and Borgatta (1989). In one of the quasi-experimental studies a limited but statistically significant effect was found on feelings of burden and on well-being (Koloski and Montgomery, 1993).

The study of Lawton and colleagues (1989, 1991) indicates that respite care hardly affects the time of admission into a nursing home (an average delay of twenty-two days). Wimo et al. (1993) found that after one year 24 per cent of the experimental group was admitted into residential care compared to 44 per cent of the control group.

Some studies show that many care-givers refrain from respite care (Lawton et al., 1989; 1991; Montgomery and Borgatta, 1989). This might cause a bias in the findings. However, it also raises the question whether respite care reaches those who might benefit most. According to Gonyea et al. (1988) informal care-givers are often reluctant to call for external assistance. They tend to feel guilty about their incapacity to sustain their caring tasks. Some regard themselves as the only persons who can offer what the demented patient really needs. It is also observed that resistance from clients themselves may obstruct respite care (Stolker and Nies, 1993). All this may cause severe emotional problems in the informal care-givers, especially in the case of a longstanding poor relationship with the demented person. On the other hand, among many care-givers there is no need for respite care because they can provide the care without too many problems themselves. A great number of them also receive informal respite care from their kin and acquaintances (Brody et al., 1989). Finally, respite care is a new and therefore unknown phenomenon to a number of care-givers (Stolker and Nies, 1993). In sum, the barriers to respite care – especially outside the users' homes – are high.

The study of Brody et al. (1989) shows that the majority (67 per cent) of the users of respite care prefer to receive this type of care in their own homes. It might be questioned whether external respite care adequately meets the needs of care-givers (see also Tester, 1989). Berry and colleagues (1991) found that informal care-givers spend an equal amount of time on caring tasks on days on which they receive respite care as on other days. On 'respite-days' most of the tasks (such as washing and dressing their relative) remain, as contrasted with respite care in the clients' own homes. In that case many tasks are taken over.

Further, there are some indications that characteristics of both the client and the care-giver affect the observed outcomes. The relationship of the care-giver to the client, his or her perception and tolerance with respect to the client's behaviour, and the sex of the care-giver (female/male) may influence the experience of burden and other outcomes. However, in the currently available research they are hardly taken into consideration (Nuijens, 1988, 1989).

Individual interventions

Although there is extensive literature on the various types of individual interventions, only a few describe findings of (quasi-)experimental studies (see Table 11.1). The few studies that do exist, however, are quite clear in their outcomes: significant positive effects are apparent with respect to feelings of burden, mental health (psychiatric symptoms), the quality of the relationship with the demented person and well-being. The only exception to these outcomes was the study by Zarit and others (1987). At first, they found no effects, but re-analysis of the data – taking previous levels of burden (i.e. before the intervention) into consideration – showed individual interventions to be effective with respect to burden of care and mental health.

Two studies (Zarit et al., 1987; Toseland et al., 1990) compared the effects of individual interventions with the effects of support groups. Indications were found that individual interventions have more positive outcomes with respect to mental problems than support groups. On the other hand, the latter provide more social support and improve the participants' perceptions of their roles as care-givers. Toseland and Smith (1990) compared the effects of individual counselling by professionals with the effects of the same amount of counselling by (trained) volunteers and with participation in a control group. No differences were found between counselling by professionals or by volunteers. Sutcliffe and Larner (1988) compared two types of counselling with a control group. One type of counselling focused on emotional support, the other on the provision of information. Emotional counselling appeared to be far more effective in reducing the burden of care and in improving mental health.

CLOSING REMARKS

It can be concluded from the present findings that cure-oriented interventions may be effective with respect to severe mental problems of informal care-givers of demented elderly people. When support groups are specifically targeted they also may be suitable for treating severe mental problems. The research is quite unambiguous about the effects of the various types of interventions on the demand for institutionalization. Both support groups and respite care hardly postpone admission into residential care. However, they lead to a better use of existing services. This may imply that heavily burdened spouses whose health is threatened by their continuous tasks are more prone to have their demented partner institutionalized. In cases where adult children are responsible for the caring tasks, postponement of admission is a realistic option. The various interventions appear to be only marginally effective in averting severe mental problems among next of kin.

These findings should be regarded with some caution. First, the outcomes are biased by numerous methodological shortcomings. Second, the many non-experimental evaluations of the various types of interventions should not be neglected. They tend to be positive in their conclusions. Because these evaluations are usually very concrete, and because the most frequently described effects are very similar, their outcomes can also be valid (Cuijpers, 1993). Therefore, the absence of parallel effects in (quasi)-experimental research may be due more to the design of the studies and the instruments than to the interventions as such. Third, it may be reasonable to assume that only certain categories of care-givers benefit from certain types of interventions (see also Brodaty and Gresham, 1992). According to Brodaty and Gresham, many informal care-givers make too late an appeal to respite care. In those cases institutionalization cannot be averted and effects on the burden of care are very limited.

More refined research is required before a final judgement about the outcomes of the various types of interventions is justified. This research should address issues such as for whom, at what moment, and how much each intervention is effective on which aspects of individual and social functioning. It is also important that further research is more process-oriented (at what moment in the process of the demented patient's illness which type of intervention should be applied), that it addresses the segmentation of the target group (which care-givers benefit from which type of intervention), that the effects are tested against earlier defined objectives and that the research is embedded in more sophisticated theoretical frameworks. From this point of view the research into the outcomes of psychosocial interventions to support informal care-givers of demented elderly people is only at its pioneering stage. The potential contribution of this type of care to the well-being of both patients and their care-givers justifies further efforts of researchers and practitioners.

REFERENCES

Berry, G.L., S.H. Zarit and V.X. Rabatin (1991) Caregiver activity on respite and nonrespite days: a comparison of two service approaches. *The Gerontologist* 31: 830–835.

Brodaty H. and M. Gresham (1989) Effect of a training programme to reduce stress in carers of patients with dementia. *British Medical Journal* 299: 1375–1379.

—— and —— (1992) Prescribing residential respite care for dementia – effects, side-effects, indications and dosage. *International Journal of Geriatric Psychiatry* 7: 357–362.

Brody, E.M., A.R. Saperstein and M. Powell Lawton (1989) A multi-service respite program for caregivers of Alzheimer's patients. *Journal of Gerontological Social Work* 14: 41–73.

Cuijpers, P. (1993) *De werking van ondersteuningsgroepen voor centrale verzorgers van dementerende ouderen.* Department of Social Gerontology, University of Nijmegen.

Dellasega, C. (1990) Coping with caregiving; stress management for caregivers of the elderly. *Journal of Psychosocial Nursing* 28 (1): 15–22.

Duijnstee, M. (1992) De belasting van familieleden van dementerenden. dissertation introduction, Nijkerk.

Gonyea, J.G., G.B. Seltzer, C. Gerstein and M. Young (1988) Acceptance of hospital-based respite care by families and elders. *Health and Social Work* 13: 201–208.

Greene, V.L. and D.J. Monahan (1987) The effect of a professionally guided caregiver support and education group on institutionalization of care receivers. *The Gerontologist* 27(6): 716–721.

Haley, W.E., S.L. Brown and E.G. Levine (1987) Experimental evaluation of the effectiveness of group intervention for dementia caregivers. *The Gerontologist* 27(3): 376–382.

Kahan, J., B. Kemp and F.R. Staples *et al.* (1985) Decreasing the burden in families caring for a relative with a dementing illness; a controlled study. *Journal of the American Geriatrics Society* 33(10): 664–670.

Kosloski, K. and R.J.V. Montgomery (1993) The effects of respite on caregivers of Alzheimer's patients: one-year evaluation of the Michigan Respite. *Journal of Applied Gerontology* 12: 4–17.

Lawton M.P., E.M. Brody and A.R. Saperstein (1989) A controlled study of respite service for caregivers of Alzheimer's patients. *The Gerontologist* 29: 8–16.

——, —— and —— (1991) *Respite for Caregivers of Alzheimer Patients.* Springer Publishing Company, New York.

Lovett, S. and D. Gallagher (1988) Psychoeducational interventions for family caregivers: Preliminary efficacy data. *Behavior Therapy* 19: 321–330.

Milne, D., I. Pitt and N. Sabin (1993) Evaluation of a carer support scheme for elderly people; the importance of coping. *British Journal of Social Work* 23: 157–168.

Montgomery, R.J.V. and E.F. Borgatta (1989) The effects of alternative support strategies on family caregiving. *The Gerontologist* 29(4): 457–464.

Nuijens, M.J.M. (1988) *Evaluatie-onderzoek sociale dagopvang voor ouderen in Arnhem.* Nijmegen: Katholieke Universiteit, Intervakgroep Sociale Gerontologie.

—— (1989) Well-being of primary caregivers of the frail elderly: the significance of semi-institutional care facilities. In: J.M.A. Munnichs and N.L. Stevens (eds), *Evaluation and Intervention. Research on Ageing.* Nijmegen/Berlin: Dpt. of Social Gerontology, University of Nijmegen/German Centre of Gerontology, pp. 97–111.

Peute, L.J.M. (1988) Dementie als belasting voor de familie: onderzoek en hulpverlening. *Tijdschrift voor Psychiatrie* 30: 82–93.

Stolker, D.H.C.M. and H.L.G.R. Nies (1993) *Intervalopnamen in verpleeghuizen. Een verkenning van mogelijkheden.* Nationaal Ziekenhuisinstituut, Utrecht.

Sutcliffe, C. and S. Larner (1988) Counselling carers of the elderly at home: A preliminary study. *British Journal of Clinical Psychology* 27: 177–178.

Tester, S. (1989) *Caring by Day: A Study of Day Care Services for Older People.* Centre for Policy on Ageing, London.

Toseland, R.W. and G.C. Smith (1990) Effectiveness of individual counselling by professional and peer helpers for family caregivers. *Psychology and Aging* 5: 256–263.

Toseland, R.W., C.M. Rossiter and M.S. Labrecque (1989a) The effectiveness of peer-led and professionally led groups to support family. *The Gerontologist* 29: 465–471.

——, —— and —— (1989b) The effectiveness of two kinds of support groups for caregivers. *Social Service Review* 63: 415–432.

Toseland, R.W., C.M. Rossiter, T. Peak and G.C. Smith (1990) Comparative effectiveness of individual group interventions to support caregivers. *Social Work* 35: 209–217.

Ven, L. van de and R. Hectors (1983) Reflekties over de begeleiding van familieleden van dementerende bejaarden. *Tijdschrift voor Gerontologie en Geriatrie* 14: 149–156.

Visser, E.J. and A. Cornel (1993) *Respite-care voor mantelzorgers van mensen met dementie; een presentatie van mogelijkheden.* NIZW, Utrecht.

Whitlach, C.J., S.H. Zarit and A. von Eye (1991) Efficacy of interventions with caregivers: a reanalysis. *The Gerontologist* 31(1): 9–14.

Wimo, A., B. Mattson, R. Adolfson and T. Erikson (1993) Dementia day care and its effects on symptoms and institutionalization – a controlled Swedish study. *Scandinavian Journal of Primary Health Care* 11: 117–123.

Zarit S.H., C.R. Anthony and M. Boutselis (1987) Interventions with caregivers of dementia patients: Comparison of two approaches. *Psychology and Aging* 2(3): 225–232.

Chapter 12

Activation of care-giver coping processes through professional support

Myrra Vernooij-Dassen and Carolien Lamers

INTRODUCTION

The dementing process affects the interaction between the person suffering from a dementia syndrome and his or her social network. Because of organic brain changes, the sufferer begins to perceive the world differently from his/her care-giver. Based on this altered understanding of the world, the behaviour of the dementia sufferer will start to change. These changes in behaviour can affect the relationship with their primary care-givers whose ability to continue the care might be affected.

In recent years a growing number of studies have been published in which professional interventions have been developed with the aim of improving care-givers' perceived ability to care for their demented relatives. The results of these studies are inconsistent (Vernooij-Dassen *et al.*, 1995). One of the reasons for the often disappointing results of intervention studies can be that most intervention studies did not use a theoretical intervention model.

Vernooij-Dassen studied the effect of a theoretically based professional intervention on primary care-givers of persons suffering from dementia. The intervention used was the family-support model of Bengtson and Kuypers (1981, 1985). The family-support model offers a flexible framework for intervention, and describes how a professional can help a family to recognize, utilize and appreciate their own skills and limitations as care-givers. The intervention did not improve the perceived ability of the whole group of care-givers to provide care, but was effective for a sub-group of female care-givers sharing a household with the person suffering from dementia (Vernooij-Dassen *et al.*, 1995).

How is it that some people are able to utilize the help and support offered and others do not seem to benefit? Our understanding of how interventions work may be enhanced by considering intervention as a technique that activates psychological processes. An intervention can only be effective when the recipient makes use of the information or suggestions offered. We are not aware of any study in dementia care that explores the ways that interventions are being used by the carers, but there are results on psychological processes which determine the perceived ability to care for a demented person. Duijnstee (1992a, 1992b) found three psychological processes which intervene positively between objective burden (facts) and subjective burden (the perception of these facts), that is, coping, acceptance and motivation.

The purpose of this chapter is to compare the findings of the studies by Vernooij-Dassen and Duijnstee in terms of (i) their contribution to theoretical knowledge in understanding how interventions work and (ii) in terms of practical suggestions for practitioners. We develop hypotheses on which psychological processes can be activated in care-givers of dementia sufferers by using a professional intervention. These hypotheses will be derived from combining the theoretical intervention guidelines of the Family Support Model of Bengtson and Kuypers and the intervening factors found in the Duijnstee study.

THE TWO STUDIES

This chapter is based on two Dutch studies. They both used the same general theoretical underpinning: a Symbolic Interactionistic Perspective (SIP) and focus on the perception of (care-giving) situations. The SIP operates on the assumption that people have the capacity to create and alter meaning in the process of interacting. According to the SIP, the perception of a situation is open to change and consequently open to intervention. A brief description of both studies will be presented. (A schematic summary of the two studies can be found in Table 12.1.)

The Duijnstee study

Duijnstee (1992a; 1992b) studied the processes which intervene between objective and subjective burden. These so called 'intervening' factors are considered as personal factors because they explain why a care-giver attaches a different significance to the components of objective burden from that expected.

Respondents were recruited via general practitioners, home helps, district nurses, community mental health teams and day-hospitals. The respondents were forty care-givers of people suffering from a dementia syndrome and were living in the community. Following a qualitative method, Duijnstee continued to select respondents until no new information was obtained. Qualitative research deals with the description of quality (Wester, 1987) and seeks to describe a phenomenon in depth and in context (Bromley, 1986; Patton, 1987).

In the Duijnstee study, subjective burden was used to denote the perception of objective burden. From every aspect of objective burden

Table 12.1 Theoretical and methodological comparison of the Duijnstee and the Vernooij-Dassen studies

Subject	Duijnstee	Vernooij-Dassen
General theoretical background	symbolic, interactionistic perspective	symbolic, interactionistic perspective and systems theory
Number of respondents	40 pairs of dementia patients and care-givers living in the community	141 pairs of dementia patients and care-givers living in the community
Intervening factors	ways care-givers themselves intervene between objective and subjective burden	theoretical guided ways offered by professionals aimed at improving care-giver sense of competence
Design	two interviews to enhance validity and reliability	randomized controlled trial
Analysis	qualitative analysis	analysis of co-variance

(facts) mentioned by the care-giver, the subjective burden (perception) was identified. The characteristics of the patient considered to be objective burden were functional disturbances: level of assistance needed to fulfil the activities of daily living; required supervision; disturbing behaviour in the interaction with other persons; limitations in social contact; and deviating behaviour. These characteristics are regarded as objective burden which increases in relation to the severity and number of exhibited behaviours.

Duijnstee found that some psychological processes reduced subjective burden. Coping, acceptance and motivation were common factors that intervened positively between objective and subjective burden. Coping is used to refer to care-givers' active adjustment to the situation confronting them, with the result that they are better able to resist or reduce problems. Acceptance comprises the process by which the care-giver takes objective circumstances for what they are. Motivation refers to subject-related motives which strengthen the subjective capacity of the care-giver.

With each intervening factor, there were variations on the same basic theme. The coping variations were adaptation, distance and anticipation.

- Adaptation: the care-giver correctly deals with the specific demands made by the disease and the care for the demented person.
- Distancing: a method of coping which enables the care-giver to maintain a distance from aspects of the objective burden.

- Anticipation: A proactive variant of coping aimed at preventing problems by weighing profits and losses.

The acceptance variations were conformity, extinction and consideration.

- Conformity: problems are recognized but no attention is paid to them; people take things as they come.
- Extinction: a method of acceptance indicating that growing accustomed to and being absorbed by the circumstances has diminished the problematic aspects. One is not able to live with the situation, one simply lives in it.
- Consideration: care-givers are able to be more understanding of undesirable behaviour. Care-givers are usually quite specific as to why and for whom they show consideration.

The motivation variations were equalization, compensation, and congruency.

- Equalization: the care-giver gives something back to the demented person. Give and take are in balance.
- Compensation: a type of motivation geared at getting something back, for example money, or being proud and satisfied about the way one executes the care-giving task.
- Congruency: a motivational variant related to social network or professional help. One receives more than expected or has been accustomed to, that is, the care-giver regards the home help as being more than exceptional: 'a lucky draw in the lottery'.

The distinction Duijnstee used between objective and subjective burden is a relative one, when the information about objective and subjective factors is given by the same primary care-giver. Even the observation of behavioural problems might be coloured by the perception of the primary care-giver. And so, yet another discrepancy has been found between the objective observation of behaviourial problems and the subjective perception of these problems.

The Vernooij-Dassen study

Vernooij-Dassen studied the effects of an intervention based on the Family Support Model by Kuypers and Bengtson on care-givers' perceived ability to be able to care. This is denoted as a sense of competence. The Family Support Model was adapted for practical implementation with primary care-givers (Vernooij-Dassen *et al.*, 1992) and formulates ten guidelines to help the professionals in the process of supporting care-givers. The intervention was carried out by home helps at the home of the dementia sufferer, four hours a week for ten months. These home helps were specially trained to use the model and they provided both emotional and practical support.

Vernooij-Dassen (1993) recruited the respondents via general practitioners in both urban and rural regions in the eastern part of the Netherlands. Agreeing to take part in the study were 141 pairs of respondents, that is, people suffering from dementia syndrome, living in the community, and their care-givers. Of the care-givers 43 per cent were women sharing a household with the dementia sufferer, 32 per cent were women not sharing a household with the dementia sufferer and 25 per cent were men.

Vernooij-Dassen designed a questionnaire based on issues identified in the Family Support Model (Bengtson and Kuypers, 1981), and the 'Burden scale' developed by Zarit *et al.* (1980), and used this to measure the sense of competence. The sense of competence is the perceived ability of the care-giver to carry the burden of care-giving. The following three domains of sense of competence were identified: 'satisfaction with the demented person as a recipient of care', 'satisfaction with one's own performance as a care-giver', and 'consequences of involvement in care for the personal life of the care-giver' (Vernooij-Dassen *et al.*, forthcoming).

The effect of the intervention was determined in a randomized controlled experiment, by analysis of covariance (Vernooij-Dassen *et al.*, 1995). In the analysis used to determine the effect of the intervention on care-givers' sense of competence, the effect of the intervention was controlled for the severity of the dementia (BCRS) (Reisberg *et al.*, 1986), the initial sense of competence, professional assistance from regular home helps and district nurses, and the interaction with the care-givers' categories – female care-givers living with the sufferer, female care-givers not living with the sufferer, and male care-givers. The intervention had no overall effect on the care-givers' sense of competence. The sub-group female care-givers who shared the household with the dementia sufferer showed a significant favourable change in a sense of competence in the experimental group compared with the control group (β =.42, .p =.04). Process evaluation through analysis of the diaries of the home helps revealed that practical support was accepted by the whole experimental group, whereas only women sharing a household with the dementia sufferer accepted emotional support.

HOW IS THE FAMILY SUPPORT MODEL MEANT TO SUPPORT CARE-GIVERS OF DEMENTIA SUFFERERS?

The underlying assumption of the Family Support Model is that these guidelines activate certain psychological processes within the care-giver, which will improve his/her sense of competence. We have attempted to establish which processes as described by Duijnstee can be involved in the ten guidelines described in Kuypers' and Bengtson's Family Support Model (see Table 12.2). The following case-study will illustrate some of the practical implementations of the guidelines and possible psychological processes activated.

> *Mrs Thornton lives in a flat near her daughter. She is becoming increasingly more forgetful. She is still self-caring but requires help with cleaning and shopping. Her behaviour can be erratic and disinhibited. She uses inappropriate language and is verbally abusive towards her daughter. The daughter is finding it more difficult to care for her mother. She cannot understand why her mother has changed from a caring, compassionate woman into a selfish and demanding patient.*

Clarification versus crisis

Most family members operate in an information vacuum and might even not be aware of the underlying reason for their relative's unfamiliar behaviour. We hypothesize that clarifying the reasons for the changes in behaviour will have a positive effect on a care-giver's sense of competence through the mechanisms of adaptation and/or consideration.

The professional can offer information regarding the underlying disease, perhaps a diagnosis, explain the behaviour to the carer in terms of organic brain damage suffered by the relative, and subsequent behaviour patterns typical of the disease. This might help care-givers to respond more appropriately to their relatives' behaviour and difficulties. This knowledge can also help them to become more considerate towards the relative.

Table 12.2 Hypothesized processes operating within care-givers that change their sense of competence

Family Support Model	Coping	Acceptance	Motivation
clarify the event	adaptation	consideration	
limited roles of involvement	distancing		
information, professional support			congruency
dialogue regarding expectations and conflicts	anticipation		
reasonable obligations	distancing		
feasible goals	distancing		
honest appraisal of future	anticipation, adaptation	conformity	
focus on strength			compensation
quick success			compensation
activated social network			congruency

*The General Practitioner refers Mrs Thornton to the memory clinic,
in order to find an explanation (diagnosis) for her mother's behaviour.
The assessment at the clinic indicates that Mrs Thornton suffers from a
dementia syndrome, probably of the Alzheimer type. The daughter is
upset about this diagnosis, but at the same time relieved to have found an
explanation for her mother's behaviour. The psychologist explains the
likely progression of this illness and the difficulties that might arise from
her mother's failing cognitive function.*

Limited roles and involvement

The professional should recognize the personal anxieties concerning
overtaxed resources of time and effort. The professional can help the carer
by limiting the duties and tasks carried out for the relative. This will also
encourage the care-giver to maintain a certain distance from an otherwise
burdensome situation.

*The community psychiatric nurse, who has been visiting Mrs Thornton
since she was diagnosed at the memory clinic, notices that the daughter
looks tired and appears tearful. It transpires that the daughter has started
visiting her mother every day to prepare a meal and that she takes her
mother to her house every Sunday. The daughter finds this commitment
a burden: she has no time left for herself and her family.*

Information regarding professional support

The care-giver should be made aware of services and help that are
available from social and health care services. Care for the relative can be
shared with others. The experience of being able to share the care can
be an unexpected relief.

*The nurse points out that there are services such as 'meals on wheels' or
day centres that her mother could attend, to ensure that she receives a
proper diet. The daughter is surprised at the range of options available
to her and her mother. She is not sure whether her mother would want to
accept this kind of help.*

Dialogue regarding expectations and conflict

Initiating an open dialogue regarding expectations and conflicts that can
arise in a situation where people care for a person with dementia, can
release guilt and can reduce fears of being unable to meet (un)reasonable
expectations. Such help works on the premise that problems can be prevented if care-givers realize that they impose unreasonable obligations
upon themselves.

Reasonable obligations

Entering a care-giving relationship can alter previously established tasks and duties considerably. The demands the sufferer puts on the care-giver can be unreasonable and can cause great stress. The professional can help the care-giver to decide what are acceptable duties and enable her to disentangle herself from the care-giving situation and achieve more distance.

As the daughter expected, Mrs Thornton is reluctant to go anywhere and insists that the daughter provides the best care possible. The daughter continues to explain that in order for her to continue the care for her mother she will need to accept help. The mother grumbles but agrees to 'try the place out'.

Feasible goals

Setting feasible goals tries to activate adaptation, distancing and/or anticipation of future developments. Adaptation means that the care-giver no longer tries to fulfil all the duties that should be performed, but selects those which can be fulfilled. It is often necessary that the care-giver distances him/herself from goals which cannot be achieved. Setting feasible goals will be easier once the care-giver has recognized that it is necessary to save energy now, in order to continue the care in the future.

Honest appraisal of the future

It might be very difficult and frightening for the care-giver to recognize actual and future problems. However, fostering an honest appraisal of the future can help lead a care-giver to adaptation, anticipation and/or conformity. Conformity is reached when problems occur but the care-giver can accommodate them.

The nurse takes Mrs Thornton to Sevenfields day centre. Mrs Thornton likes the staff there and is happy to visit them again. The daughter feels she will be able to continue to look after her mother for some time longer, but she is also beginning to realize that her mother might require more help in the future. She discusses this with the nurse who confirms her fears, but also points out that Sevenfields provides residential care.

Focus on strength

Focusing on what care-givers *can* do, rather than on what might or should be done, can make them feel more satisfied about themselves as care-givers. These feelings can compensate for having to deal with difficult situations. Emphasizing the strength of the care-giver enhances the care-giver's sense of self-worth.

Quick successes

Programming some quick, demonstrable and successful outcome measures focuses the care-giver on aspects of the care that are successful. These will need to be carefully planned so that success is ensured. This success can have a positive effect on the care-giving situation: it can motivate the care-giver to continue the care. This can compensate for the disappointments which occur in the care-giving situation.

Activating the social network

Sharing care with a family member or friend may help to prevent the 'shared loneliness' of the care-giver and care-receiver and can lead to congruency. The care-giver will receive the help he/she expected or perhaps even more.

The nurse suggests that the daughter asks her sister to help in some domestic tasks as these take up a long time in the care for her mother as well as being the cause of several arguments. The sister is happy to give a hand and share in the practical care for her mother.

Most of the ways care-givers dealt with the care-giving situation in the Duijnstee study, seemed to be in general accordance with some of the implicit aims of the Family Support Model. However, two variants – extinction and equalisation (see p. 181) were incompatible with the theoretical model used by Vernooij-Dassen.

DISCUSSION

Hypotheses on psychological processes which influence the sense of competence of care-givers positively have been derived from combining the theoretical intervention guidelines of the Family Support Model of Bengtson and Kuypers and the empirical findings of the Duijnstee study.

The theoretical relevance of these hypotheses is that they offer an opportunity to refine interventions by focusing on the processes that are meant to be activated in the care-givers. These hypotheses make explicit the ways interventions can be used. Studying the ways interventions are used can contribute to an understanding of why certain interventions can be effective for some care-givers and not for others.

The hypotheses also have practical relevance: not only have researchers neglected the ways care-givers use an intervention, but *practitioners* also have ignored this aspect. By paying attention to the way an intervention is used, practitioners can adapt their interventions to individuals' needs and utilize their existing coping styles and therefore make the interventions more successful. For instance, if information is given, it might be useful to formulate what one hopes to achieve by providing it. The aim might be that the care-giver will adapt better to the situation. In order to assess whether adaptation is taking place, it is important that continuity of care to the care-giver is provided by the practitioner. If the information provided does not lead to better adaptation, the obstacles which hinder this process might require further exploration. Based on this, the intervention might need to be changed in order to trigger a different psychological process.

The Family Support Model of Bengtson and Kuypers refers to active adjustment to the situation. However, the qualitative analysis of Duijnstee revealed some passive 'intervening' factors, which led to a situation where the care-giver was able to bear the distress by either growing accustomed to and/or being overwhelmed by the circumstances. Both mechanisms are not considered within the Family Support Model.

Practitioners should also be attentive to the fact that some care-givers manage the care-giving situation by becoming absorbed by it. However, monitoring the care-giver who has adopted this passive process might be required as the long-term effects of this type of care-giving are not clear yet.

Despite (or because of) differences in conceptualization, operationalization, interventions and analysing methods, combining both studies has contributed to formulating hypotheses on the ways that care-givers utilize interventions and these hypotheses are theoretically and practically relevant. These hypotheses need to be tested, and appropriate tools should be developed to measure the psychological processes at work.

The findings of the studies by Duijnstee and Vernooij-Dassen and of this chapter agree that an individualized approach is to be recommended. They advocate careful clarification of the care-givers' perception of the problems in the care-giving situation and that consideration should be given to the solutions that care-givers have themselves found for their problems. This reflects the 'inter-professional philosophy statement', that professionals should value the individuality, dignity and independence of care-givers and their need to play an active role in decision-making (Jones and Miesen, 1992).

These findings support the statement of Murphy and Mattson (1992) that quantitative and qualitative methods each have their own specific value and can be used as complementary methods.

REFERENCES

Bengtson, V.L. and Kuypers, J. (1981) 'Change, competence, crises and intervention: a systems model of aging and family relations'. Paper presented at the

International Pre-Congress Workshop on 'Life-span and Change in Geronto-logical Perspective', Nijmegen.

—— (1985) 'The family support cycle: psychosocial issues in the aging family', in J.M.A. Munnichs, E. Olbrich, P. Mussen and P.G. Coleman (eds), *Life-span and Change in a Gerontological Perspective*, New York: Academic Press.

Bromley, D.B. (1986) *The Case-study Method in Psychology and Related Disciplines*, London: J. Wiley and Sons.

Duijnstee, M. (1992a) De belasting van familieleden van dementerenden, Dissertation, Nijkerk: Intro.

—— (1992b) 'Caring for a demented family member at home: objective and subjective evaluation of the burden', in G.M.M. Jones and B.M.L. Miesen (eds) *Care-Giving in Dementia: Research and Applications*, vol. I, London: Routledge.

Jones, G. and Miesen B. (1992) 'The need for an interdisciplinary core curriculum for professionals working with dementia', in G.M.M. Jones and B.M.L. Miesen (eds) *Caregiving in Dementia: Research and Applications*, London: Routledge.

Murphy, E. and Mattson, B. (1992) 'Qualitative research and family practice: a marriage made in heaven?' *Family Practice* 9: 85–90.

Patton, M.Q. (1987) *How to Use Qualitative Methods in Evaluation*, Newbury Park: Sage Publications.

Reisberg, B., Borenstein, J., Franssen, E., Shulman, E., Steinberg, G. and Femis, S.H. (1986) 'Remediable behavioral symptomatology in Alzheimer's disease', *Hospital Community Psychiatry* 37: 1199–1201.

Vernooij-Dassen, M.J.F.J. (1993) *Dementie en Thuiszorg: Een Onderzoek naar Determinanten van het Competentiegevoel van Centrale Verzorgers en het Effect van Professionele Interventie*, Lisse: Swets and Zeitlinger.

—— Felling, A. and Persoon, J. (forthcoming) 'Predictors of sense of competence in primary caregivers of demented persons', *Social Science and Medicine*.

—— Huygen, F., Felling, A. and Persoon, J. (1995) 'Home care for dementia patients: a controlled study of professional support for caregivers', *Journal of the American Geriatrics Society* 43: 456–57.

—— Plaats, J. van der and Hogeling, J. (1992) *Zorgen voor dementerende ouderen thuis; een handleiding voor de verzorgende beroepen*, Nijkerk: Intro.

Wester, F. (1987) *Strategieën voor Kwalitatief Onderzoek*, Muiderberg: Coutinho.

Zarit, S.H., Reever, K.E. and Bach-Peterson, J. (1980) 'Relatives of the impaired elderly: correlates of feelings of burden', *The Gerontologist* 20: 649–55.

Part IV

Interventions for the family

Chapter 13

Attachment, loss and coping in caring for a dementing spouse

Reidun Ingebretsen and Per Erik Solem

SUMMARY

The burden of caring for a dementing spouse is well documented. Changes in the marital relationship, such as loss of the dementing person as he or she used to be, are part of the burden. The history of the relationship and the attachment between spouses are crucial in understanding the individual burden and adaptation to changes. John Bowlby describes three kinds of insecure attachment, which tend to increase proneness to loss: (i) anxious attachment, (ii) compulsive care-giving and (iii) strenuous attempts to claim emotional self-sufficiency and independence. Insecure attachment is seen in relationships between care-givers and dementing spouses, reflecting problems of dependency and of regulating the relational dynamics of closeness and distance. Attachment behaviour is often overtly expressed by the dementing person. For spouses insecure attachment may cause reluctance to accept that changes are in conflict with their basic needs of stability and security.

The discussion in this chapter is illustrated with case material from a study of support groups for elderly persons caring for a dementing spouse. Such groups often focus on training in problem-focused coping to find better ways of doing practical work and managing everyday life. They also focus on emotion-focused coping, such as accepting the deterioration as an inevitable illness. A third kind of coping, which is relationship-focused, requires identification with the other in order to understand, and at the same time recognize one's own separateness from the other. Training in communication may help establish empathy and balance identification and separateness.

When dealing with married couples, former and actual role distribution, tacit understandings, collusions, patterns of complementation, and attachment between spouses, are keys to understanding their losses and strivings during the dementing process. Training in care-giving skills and coping strategies may prove futile unless actual and former qualities of the relationship, and the care-giver's own needs, are taken into consideration.

Even when looking for ways of offering practical help that the carer can accept, understanding the relationship may be of the utmost importance. Further development of differentiated psychological intervention methods in this field is called for.

INTRODUCTION

Caring for a dementing spouse is a demanding task. The care situation is ambiguous and constantly changing. When dementia is emerging, a number of unanswered questions and uncertainties arise. What is really happening to my spouse? Why doesn't he remember? What can I do? Where will this end? The process of dementia creates new and hitherto unfamiliar situations for both of the spouses. Care-giving spouses must take over more and more practical and personal care for the dementing spouse, decision-making, and tasks they used to do together. They have to relate to a changing person, and cope with a changing marital relationship.

A great number of studies have investigated the nature of burden associated with care-giving, and how coping strategies, social support, and professional interventions may ease the burden. However, research does not reveal any clear and simple general conclusions. Individuals differ in the way they experience burdens, how they cope, and what kind of interventions they profit from. As Zarit *et al.* (1986) state, variability in care-givers' responses to care-giving demands is an important research issue. Different results from studies on burden may partly be due to different conceptualizations and measurements (Vitalino *et al.*, 1991). A distinction is made between objective and subjective burden (Duijnstee, 1992a; Morris and Morris, 1993). The objective burden, often measured by severity of dementia symptoms, is not strongly associated with subjective burden as experienced by the care-giver (George and Gwyther, 1986, Zarit *et al.*, 1986). Findings by Stommel *et al.* (1990) suggest 'that it is the interpretation and evaluation of the objective processes that add to differing amounts of burden among different care-givers' (p. 97). Thus objective burden, or elements of objective burden, may even be evaluated in positive terms by the care-giver (Collins *et al.*, 1993; Farran *et al.*, 1991; Grafström, 1994; Harris, 1993; Motenko, 1989). However, there is substantial agreement that care-giving for a demented person increases the risk of depression (Morris and Morris, 1993). Feelings of loss seem to be a common denominator for family care-givers (Nordhus, 1994; Miesen, 1995).

Several researchers categorize determinants of burden in three broad variables; characteristics of the patient, the care-giver, and the situation (Duijnstee, 1992b; Stommel *et al.*, 1990). Such characteristics can be described in both objective (severity of dementia, care-givers' health status, and housing conditions) and subjective terms (for example, the experienced burden of the dementia sufferer's symptoms, of own health problems, and of poor housing conditions). Several factors are described as intervening between objective and subjective burden; the care-giving relationship, coping strategies of the care-giver, and the degree of formal social support (Morris and Morris, 1993). According to Duijnstee (1992a), intervening factors are variants in coping; actions taken to adjust the situation in as favourable a manner as possible, in acceptance, taking objective adverse circumstances for what they are, and in motivation to render care.

In this chapter we shall discuss the marital relationship, losses and coping strategies, and consequences for therapeutic interventions. Our main focus is the marital relationship from the care-giver's perspective, and the care-giver's attachment behaviour. This attention on relationship is supported by the conclusion of Grafström (1994) that the complex pattern of reactions in family care-giving calls for a relational perspective where the quality of the past relationship and the care-giver's ability to find gratification in the present relationship is taken into account. In our experience coping with a changing relationship seems to be more of a challenge to several spousal care-givers than coping with burdens of practical care, even if practical burdens may be extremely heavy. Even from the other side the relationship is important. The dementia sufferer 'needs the Other for personhood to be sustained' (Kitwood and Bredin, 1992: 285).

THE MARITAL RELATIONSHIP

All aspects of a relationship seem to be affected by dementia (Wright, 1991). Due to the gradual loss of meaningful mutual contact, shared meaning is lost. This tends to expand the distance between the spouses, as it gets hard to maintain a dialogue and to cope with care-giving demands. A good relationship may ease coping. Gilleard et al. (1984) found that care-givers who rated the quality of their past relationship as low had a higher incidence of poor mental health, and Morris et al. (1988) found lower levels of past marital intimacy in care-givers reporting higher levels of strain and depression. However, the association between quality of the past relationship and present coping is hardly simple and one-dimensional. As Duijnstee (1992a) finds, a good past relationship may strengthen the motivation to care, but may also interfere with successful coping. The care-giver may ignore his own needs, and become enmeshed in a symbiotic relationship, where the dementing process is hard to accept.

The dimension of distance versus closeness is important in relationships in general, and it is challenged by the dependency of one of the partners. Johnson and Catalano (1983) describe how family care-givers of elderly individuals discharged from hospital, cope with distancing techniques or with enmeshing techniques. There seems to be no easy way to find a balance between separation and distance on the one hand, and closeness and the continuation of a 'we'-relation, on the other. When one of the spouses is dementing, the loss is gradual, and completing grief work to the extent of finishing the relationship may be impossible. Letting go, or what is described as a separation–individuation conflict (Gwyther, 1990; Rose and DelMaestro, 1990) is hard to resolve when the mutuality of the relationship is fading away at the same time as the dementing spouse is increasingly dependent upon the care-giver's attention. There is a risk of rushing to extreme reactions like either enmeshing or distancing. We may get some help in understanding this risk by considering more carefully the history of the relationship, and the attachment behaviour of both partners.

LOSS AND ATTACHMENT

For care-giving spouses the process of mental deterioration implies a gradual loss of meaningful interaction; a loss of the marital relationship as adapted to over decades. Some of the reactions connected to care-giver burden may be seen as grief reactions to the gradual loss of their dementing spouses. Since marital relationships are many-sided, losses are equally so. Common themes in a dementia process are loss of predictability, continuity and meaningful interaction. But relationships differ in those aspects also before the onset of a dementia; accordingly the degree of loss differs. Because of the gradualness of the process not everything is lost at once, and behaviour may fluctuate, with occasional glimpses of intact mental functioning. This may stimulate fantasies about recovery, and denial of the reality of the disease. One wife told how happy she was when her demented husband asked her how she was doing, only to be disappointed when he immediately lost the thread and did not expect any answer from her. Gradually such painful experiences of hope, with immediate backlash, may help a stepwise working-through of losses. However, complete resolution is hindered by the contradictory tasks of, on the one hand, accepting the separation and, on the other, remaining close in order to care. Often daily practical hassles consume major parts of the care-giver's energy, and little is left to be invested in grief work.

As the dementia process is gradual, so is the grief process. The two processes are not necessarily synchronized. The disease may be accepted as hopeless and the person abandoned, while he or she is still able to communicate. Or the care-giver may remain in a protest stage of grieving, and may argue with the dementing person far beyond the point at which he is able to understand arguments. Through all shifts in hopes and back-lashes, synchronism between the dementia process and the grief work of the care-giving spouse would be hard to obtain.

Distress at being separated unwillingly from an attachment figure is seen as an indissoluble part of being attached to someone (Bowlby, 1973). Distress may be eased by attachment behaviour intending to regain the figure or to compensate the loss.

Attachment behaviour is defined as all behaviour which has the goal of obtaining and/or maintaining a desired proximity with another person (Bowlby, 1969). The seeking of proximity is released when safety needs are threatened. The main focus of attachment theory and research on infant/mother attachment has been extended to different kind of family dyads and is now concerned with all phases of the life course (Bretherton, 1992). In the process of dementia, feelings of uncertainty and lack of safety are fostered. The demented person's clinging and crying may be understood as attachment behaviour (Miesen, 1992). In addition, spouses and families are subject to uncertainties and fragmentation in their interaction with the dementing person. Some of their reactions also may be understood as efforts to maintain a desired proximity to their dementing spouse. Their attachment to the dementing spouse is challenged. According to Bowlby (1980) three kinds of insecure attachment promote vulnerability to loss in general; anxious attachment (clinging), compulsive care-giving, and strenuous attempts to claim emotional self-sufficiency and independence.

In insecure attachment the clinging, compulsive or self-sufficient behaviour of the care-giver may be in conflict with the needs of the dementia sufferer and may interfere with successful coping. Flexible use of various coping strategies is hampered by insecurity, which makes it hard for the care-giver to attend adequately both to his own needs and to the needs of the dementia sufferer.

COPING STRATEGIES

In a broad classification, coping strategies could be described in an active–passive dimension. This is conceptualized in different ways, for example as two primary coping functions: (i) active management of the situation (problem-focused or instrumental coping) and (ii) emotion regulation (emotion-focused coping) (Lazarus and Folkman, 1984). Action directed at altering the stressful situation is problem-focused, while coping directed at regulating negative emotions resulting from the situation is referred to as emotion-focused. Denial and wishful thinking are examples of emotion-focused coping, directed at altering the appraisal of the situation rather than the situation itself.

Even if, in general, active problem-focused coping is more likely to result in improvements of the situation, thus being more adaptive (Morris and Morris, 1993), and passive mechanisms are more frail and in the long run less protective against breakdowns, no single mode of coping is the ideal. The complex and changing situation of dementia care calls for flexible coping strategies.

When the situation is uncontrollable, regulation of emotional distress may be more successful than attempts to solve the problem (Pruchno and Resch, 1989). The term 'emotion-focused coping' is part of a cognitive model of stress and coping, where it implies a rather passive orientation of adapting to a situation out of control. However, emotions play a main role in the process of coping with losses. There is a challenge, as a part of the grief process, to work through negative emotions emerging from losses themselves, by restructuring the meaning and understanding of the harmful situation. This requires emotional and cognitive effort. Running away from core emotions of loss, or cutting them off, will hardly promote acceptance of the gradual separation. Such acceptance may be crucial to the ability to keep a balanced relation of both closeness to and distance from the demented spouse. Since the demented person is constantly changing, the balance of the relation also has to be changing. This requires active emotional work.

De Longis and O'Brien (1990) have introduced a third category of coping – relationship-focused coping – which is of special relevance to coping with a changing marital relationship. Relationship-focused coping is directed at regulating and maintaining social relationships of importance in coping with the stressful situation. This includes both relationships as sources of external support and relationships that are part of the stressful situation. Negotiating and compromising with involved others, and being empathic, are examples of relationship-focused coping. Empathic coping seems to be a special challenge to spouses of demented elderly, as the demented persons' behaviour often is very difficult to understand. Empathy is characterized not only by identification with the other in order to understand and experience the situation in the way the other does, but also by recognition of one's own separateness from the other, that is, not to merge with the other.

Empathy is not easily achieved. The mental deterioration of the demented spouse constitutes a barrier to understanding, and a strong motivation to assist the deteriorating spouse involves a risk of merging with the demented spouse in a symbiotic relationship where the carer's own needs are neglected. When attachment is insecure, own attachment needs are likely to overshadow the needs of the other, and to interfere with empathy. In this situation, working on communication skills to clarify the needs of both spouses and promote empathy, is a great challenge.

THE STUDY

In this exploratory case-study we had 15–20 hours' interaction with each care-giving spouse, group interaction and individual contact taken together. The material consists of six female and four male spouses aged 63 to 82 years. The cases reported are taken from two spousal care-giver support groups conducted by the authors. Each group met eight times for one and a half hours. Two of the group members also had individual therapy sessions. One spouse who only came for individual sessions is included in the material. All the subjects lived at home with their spouses, who had been dementing for an average of six years. Interviews were carried out before and after the group intervention and again six months later. The members of one of the groups were re-interviewed two years later. The interviews were semi-structured and included scales measuring burden and coping. Because of the small number of cases and incomplete answers, the scales are not processed quantitatively. Some of the subjects were reluctant to answer scale questions; they wanted to tell their story. To avoid endangering rapport they were not pushed. We have no systematic observation on interaction between the spouses. Thus the relationship is described as seen from the care-givers' point of view.

CASES ILLUSTRATING KINDS OF ATTACHMENT

To illustrate kinds of attachment we shall report on four cases, characterized by anxious atttachment, compulsive care-giving, self-sufficiency and independence, and secure attachment. The cases are summarized in Table 13.1, describing how main losses as experienced by the person, coping behaviour, and utilization of intervention are different. The material is too scanty to justify any generalization about how kinds of attachment are connected to kinds of loss or coping behaviour. We want to underline that the individual pattern of attachment, loss and coping have to be the basis for intervention.

Mrs R: Anxious attachment

Mrs R was emotionally disturbed by the emerging cognitive deterioration of her husband. She attended to him diligently to keep him active and oriented. She took him to physical training and reminded him on matters he ought to remember, and got desperate and angry when he nevertheless forgot. This was a constant source of frustration and conflict. Obviously Mrs R did not respond to the needs of her spouse, but to her own need to see him as a secure and solid husband. She continued in this pattern at severe cost to her own resources and harmony in the relationship. Her husband got angry and defended himself, and she was almost over-whelmed by anxiety. When this woman came to individual consultations, she reflected back on her life. Her own dependency needs and her child-hood longings for a lost father became apparent. The relation to her husband had filled this gap, and his deterioration aroused in her anxiety about a new loss. In the process of realizing this connection, she clung to the husband and searched for closeness and contact without being on at him to remember and to stay fit. The husband responded more positively to this than to criticism and commands. Gradually she was able to accept her earlier loss and appreciate the memory problems of her husband more realistically. She accepted some assistance in caring for her husband, and made use of her own opportunities for contact and comfort. Shortly after the last consultation her own health problems became aggravated and she died after a short terminal phase. Her husband was able to stay with her all through the terminal phase, and his presence was good for her. She had stopped clinging to him and died calmly.

Loss

For Mrs R the memory problems of her husband were experienced as a loss of a solid husband and a threat to her security. It activated her anxiety about being left alone without a trustworthy partner to lean on.

Coping

From the beginning her coping stategies seemed instrumental in the way that she worked hard to activate her husband and remind him of what to do. In this process she became exhausted. She neither attained her goal of better functioning for her husband nor the longed-for security for herself. As a couple they had been inseparable. In the process of fighting back the dementia, her close relationship with him was threatened by anger and fuss. She panicked, and physically clung to her husband.

Intervention

The feeling of proximity to him and a therapeutic relation helped her in the process of working through her childhood traumas of losing her father

Table 13.1 Summary of four cases

	Mrs R Anxious attachment	Mrs O Compulsive care-giving	Mr T Self- sufficiency	Mrs Q Secure attachment
Main loss	security and support	confirmation and belonging	a stable structure	mutuality
Typical coping behaviour	fighting, clinging	compensation, sensitive attention	resisting, arguing, searching for meaning	gradually letting go
Utilization of intervention	working through and reflection on past/present attachments	taking support, ventilating feelings of rejection and guilt	sharing protest and seeking confirmation	learning and discussing

and not being able to grieve for the loss. In this process she showed enormous strength and was able to sort out her own needs from the needs of her husband, which resulted in a better balance between closeness and distance and more empathy in her relation to him. Before she died she managed to loosen the bonds, to go and let go.

Mrs O: Compulsive care-giving

Mrs O described her marriage as happy. The couple had enjoyed each other's close company, but not to the exclusion of wide social contacts with family and friends, though usually as a couple. 'Most of the time we stuck to each other's tail', she said. When Mrs O discovered the first symptoms of forgetfulness in her husband, she felt insecure, but gradually accepted his decreasing mental capacity. She tried to maintain a spirit of marital community. She tried to compensate for her husband's deficits by almost imperceptibly taking over tasks he was no longer able to perform. She was very sensitive to his needs and reactions, and everything apparently ran smoothly in an increasingly close relationship. It was literally close, as she stood by his side and assisted him, for instance in setting the breakfast table, and he stuck to her and followed her, even when she used the bathroom. Only when her husband started to ask her to take him 'home' (to his mother), could she not manage any more. She felt rejected and started to grieve for the heavy relational loss. Since she had invested so much of herself in efforts to maintain a mutual relationship she was overly vulnerable to what was experienced as a rejection of her as the most important person in his life. She felt desperate and helpless in her efforts to convince him that he already was at home, and she reacted alternately with crying spells and outbursts of anger.

In this period she shared her emotions and felt acknowledged in the support group; 'Here in the group I can relax, here I don't feel rejected.' The group gave her room to express emotions without having to consider whether her husband would be upset by her reactions, and she managed to reconsider the situation both from her own and her husband's perspective. After a long period of hesitation, resistance, crying and feelings of guilt, Mrs O finally agreed to send her husband to a nursing home. She assured the group that she still loved him. Mr O came home on visits every weekend. She looked forward to having him with her, and felt relief when he left. When he was at home the relationship had to be exclusively on his terms. In this way she could maintain her role as a care-giver, keep in contact with her husband and at the same time attend to her own needs and take care of her own health problems. Reluctantly, with the help of her family and the group, she had become able to listen to herself and started to accept her own limits.

When she was interviewed two years later her husband was in constant need of physical care and surveillance. During the daytime he mostly rested in a chair and slept a lot. Mrs O had herself been seriously ill, and her husband's visits to their home were rare. She still felt close to him, visited him in the institution and liked to hug and caress him. It was no longer threatening to her that he did not recognize her as his wife, as long as he related to her as someone he felt close to. He no longer expressed wishes to go to his mother. The relationship was more as if both of them had accepted her in the role of the 'good mother'. She called him 'my boy', but was at the same time eager to support his dignity.

Obviously Mrs O wanted to maintain as much of her close relationship to her husband as possible. When leaving him after visits at the nursing home she told him she had to go out to do some shopping. This was a way to prevent him protesting, but it also fitted her own wish of belonging together and assuring him that she would not leave him. It is difficult to ascertain if her husband could understand her message. From her perspective, however, it served to confirm their everlasting relationship and her fidelity. The increasing deterioration and passivity of her husband made it easier for Mrs O to sustain her definition of the relationship. She could connect his vague responses to their former reality and to her longings for closeness, and this was a basis for her continuous caring.

Loss

Mrs O only reluctantly accepted the piecemeal losses of the marital relation: 'I have to run my head against the brick wall to realize.' The most critical phases were when her husband seemed to prefer his mother to her, and when she had to accept putting him in a nursing home. In the first instance she felt rejected, and in the second she felt guilt about rejecting him. Both situations constituted loss of confirmation and were a threat to her need to belong together.

Coping

During the whole process Mrs O strove to maintain as much of their earlier relationship as possible. It seemed as if her care-giving served to confirm a lifelong happy marriage. She had a strong wish to support her husband's self-image and his position as the 'man of the house'. She tried to compensate for his deficiencies and watched over him with sensitive attention. In the last interview she expressed satisfaction with her coping: 'I have managed without becoming bitter, but it hurts. We had looked forward to a happy old age together.' Mrs O rated her coping as good in the early and late phases, and as poor in the critical phase in between. Her coping strategies were varied, with elements of both emotion-, problem-, and relationship-focused coping, all adapted to the primary intention of maintaining, under changing circumstances, as much of the relationship as possible. On a deeper level her clever and sensitive adaptation to his deterioration may be seen as attachment behaviour searching for as much closeness as possible. Such clever, but compulsive, care-giving is in danger of wearing the care-giver out physically, and even mentally – by the almost fatal hurt inflicted by the rejection felt when the husband fails to confirm her as the woman of his life, and even fails to recognize her as his wife.

Intervention

Mrs O was the one who used the group most actively in her emotional work. She brought the central topics of feeling rejected and of rejecting directly into focus. She appreciated the interest and empathy she met in the group and felt she got space to ventilate her feelings and to analyse her situation. The process she passed through demonstrated the emotional costs, while still retaining the ability to cope with imperative life transitions. The group was available and responsive at the time she needed it most in her strivings to let her husband go (away from her 'to his mother' and later to an institution). She received support when she cried and talked about her feelings of guilt.

Mr T: Independence and self-sufficiency

Mr T's wife had been mentally deteriorating over a period of ten years. It started with negligent cooking. When coming to the group he described her as wandering, restless, and asking repetitive questions. He had to help her in personal care. Mr T was primarily burdened by her inability to do housework. She had kept the house clean, mended his clothes and made plans for their daily living, but now he had to do everything himself. Additional strain came from the fact that he had no time for his own activities, such as maintaining the house, reading, and other interests. Even when his wife was away at the day-care centre, he was unable to concentrate on his own matters. Reluctantly, but dutifully, he did the necessary housework and care-work, not without guilt over unfinished tasks and insufficient care. His resentment at the situation was directed towards the authorities who gave him insufficient help and at the same time claimed fees and taxes. Even though he knew his spouse could do nothing about the situation, he got very aggressive when she failed to be adequate and realistic. He argued and argued and refused to give in. This reaction may be understood as a protest at her reduction, as if he could argue her back to normal, to a stable position in his life. His deep concern about the cause of the illness may be seen as a search for meaning and an implicit hope for cure. All the suggestions made for recreation, to get more help, or to change his pattern of communication with his wife, were refused. He seemed to be 'waiting for' the stable pattern of the past to return, and resisted the necessary transition. Even though he cognitively realized her deterioration, his behaviour seemed to keep alive a hope of recovery.

Two years later the dementia had progressed. Mr T had to help his wife with intimate care, but she was more indulgent when he corrected her disorientations. He described her as a 'spiritually dead person', and as a 'non-person'. He was still focused on his duty to care 'until death do us part', but was more open to considering a possible placement in a nursing home. He resisted taking such an initiative himself, but would probably accept an offer from the public care system. He would not 'betray' his wife by his own initiative.

Loss

The main loss to Mr T. was the loss of a housekeeper who could do her share of the necessary activities of daily living. His wife's infirmity, irrationality, and unrest disturbed the order, peace and quiet he needed to concentrate on his own interests and his inner world. He was moderately depressed and irritable. In the late phase he was still protesting against the situation and was resentful, but gradually he had come to realize the fact that his wife was not going to improve. He hoped someone or something would help him out of the situation.

Coping

Mr T was dissatisfied with his coping. He called himself a perfectionist and rated his performance as far from good enough. His coping was passive, and he described himself as 'lazy'. He did what was required out of duty and felt obliged to stay the course. He was reluctant to work on his emotional reactions. The relationship with his wife was 'written off' and he was not relationship-focused in the sense of seeking social support. Regarding the history of attachment in the relationship, Mr T was reluctant to talk about his past. However, we can see the outline of a traditional division of work where the couple performed their separate tasks. Their emotional relationship was probably not very close. The marriage represented a stable structure in his life, a structure which was now threatened. During the dementia process Mr T disengaged emotionally, but stayed with his care duties.

Intervention

In the group Mr T expressed his search for meaning and his protest in his preoccupation with questions related to the causes of dementia. 'Why should this happen to her [and me]?' He described her functioning badly, mostly from the perspective of showing how miserable life was. He was reluctant to try new ways of communicating and of helping his wife. He was given support from the other group members to seek more help and take some time off. He profited somewhat from the container function and social aspect of the group. He sometimes regretted his own appearance and grooming and reflected upon possible changes, but he was not in a position to challenge his coping style.

Mrs Q: Secure attachment

At the beginning of the support group Mrs Q was caring for her dementing husband at home. She received a couple of hours home help per week. Mr Q was anxious, clung to her most of the day, and repetitively asked the same questions. For the most part he could manage the activities of daily living, but needed assistance and surveillance. Mrs Q was distressed at not having a moment for herself. Being physically weak herself she felt the burden of work and of being constantly attentive. She was concerned by the changes taking place in the relationship since they could no longer share common interests and discuss current matters. She was in a process of adjusting to her husband's deterioration and increasing dependency, and she described this process as painful and emotionally demanding. Two years later her husband moved to a nursing home. She was glad the public care system advised her that this was necessary. In that way she did not need to take full responsibility herself for sending him away. When he moved she felt both grief and relief. In the beginning she visited him every day, but six months later she was going there once or twice a week. She was now re-establishing contact with friends and was taking up old interests.

Loss

Mrs Q saw the dementia process as a great loss. She stressed the loss of a partner with whom to discuss current concerns. She missed having somebody to understand and care for her. She had felt anger and despair during the process, but gradually she had become resigned and felt she had grown more patient.

Coping

She was proud to have been able to manage the heavy tasks of care-giving at home. In doing this she had used a mixture of different coping styles. In the later phase she did not try to understand his thinking and did not strive to be empathic. She liked to be with him without necessarily sharing any common understanding. It was comforting to see that he had settled, and was calm and content at the nursing home. Mrs Q had been able to let go, without abandoning her husband. She was dedicated to ensuring that her husband got as good care as possible. Their earlier relationship seemed to have been fairly close without being emotionally very intimate. It was characterized by a secure attachment with a space for individual interests and independence. Mrs Q was confident that her husband would have given her the same care if she had suffered from dementia. When the balance of the relationship was threatened by her husband's dementia, Mrs Q adapted to the changes, not smoothly, but with pain and distress. She accepted an increasing emotional and intellectual distance, without being destroyed herself. On the contrary, she felt more whole as a person, more patient, more tolerant and more reflective.

Intervention

In the support group Mrs Q was broadly interested in different topics related to dementia, care-giving, loss and coping. She was supportive and listened carefully to the other group members. She was eager to learn how to take care of her husband. Typical questions she raised were: 'How much shall I explain to him?' 'How can I stimulate him?' Retrospectively she appreciated that the group atmosphere had made it possible for her to take part in an open discussion without feeling disloyal toward her husband. She had the benefit of joining the group at a relatively early stage of her husband's dementia, before she was 'worn out'. She felt sad and uncertain about what to do. She was, however, open and receptive and did not have to defend a given definition of the relationship or of her husband. When her husband later moved to an institution she felt strengthened by having been able to reflect about the decision and to 'go through' the process together with another group member.

ATTACHMENT AND IMPLICATIONS FOR INTERVENTION

The cases reported illustrate four individual patterns in caring for a dementing spouse. They are examples of various kinds of attachment, loss, coping behaviour and ways of profiting from intervention.

The woman demonstrating secure attachement (Mrs Q) was able to let go without abandoning her husband. Their former relationship had been secure, giving space for independence. Through an emotionally demanding process she accepted the gradual loss of a mutual relationship, but wanted to stand by her husband during his deterioration. Mrs Q was the one in the group who showed the broadest interest in different topics related to dementia, care-giving, loss and coping. She was highly motivated to learn how to take care of her husband, and was able to redefine the relationship.

She profited both from cognitive, emotional and social aspects of the group.

Secure attachment seems to facilitate flexible coping, while insecure attachment may cause reluctance to accept changes that are in conflict with the care-giver's basic needs of stability and security. A good earlier relationship is found to be an advantage in coping with emerging dementia (Gilleard et al., 1984; Morris et al., 1988). In some cases, however, losses are harder to accept when there is more of a 'good' relationship to loose (Duijnstee, 1992a). Good or bad relationships are not to be confused with secure versus insecure attachment. Both apparently good and apparently bad relationships may reveal patterns of attachment that represent great challenges to coping with changes.

Mrs O described her marriage as happy and their relationship as close. In spite of a realistic appraisal of the deterioration of her husband, she was still holding on and searching for hints from him in confirmation of an everlasting bond. She demonstrated the forceful drive of compulsive care-giving, as if she was saying: 'I know that you are slipping away from me, but I will never ever stop confirming you and our exclusive lifelong relationship.' Mrs O made active use of the group in her emotional work related to her feelings of belonging and rejection. She profited from the interest and empathy in the group and felt safe both to ventilate her feelings and to analyse her situation.

Even Mr T tried to fulfil his duties of care-giving, but complained about his own frustrated needs and longed for independence and self-sufficiency. He seemed to blame his wife, as if he was saying: 'You have frustrated my needs and you cannot take care any more; at least I want you to leave me alone.' His rather passive coping style was reflected in the way he used the group. He told them about his misfortune and search for meaning, but was unable to profit from learning new ways of helping his wife. However, the opportunity to complain about his situation and the feeling of social support seemed to mean something to him.

Support groups for family care-givers may have different objectives (Toseland and Rossiter, 1989). The aim of our groups was to help spousal care-givers to find successful ways of coping. The group setting was organized to allow expression and working through of feelings, and to stimulate the process of clarifying and modifying cognitions about dementia, the care-giver role, the relationship and communication with the spouse. However, a group intervention method has certain limits in the follow up of individual attachment history. Even if old conflicts resurface in the group, a group context is not always appropriate for a direct focus on such matters. Mrs R (anxious attachment) did not attend a group, but came for individual sessions. With close follow up in a therapeutic relationship she was able to reflect on her own life-history, earlier attachments and how she was threatened by her husband's mental deterioration. She worked it through emotionally, and to do that she needed to depend on the therapist for a period, before she was able to let the idealized strong husband go. His dependency had evoked her own dependency needs, which was an incentive to work through traumas both in the relationship to her husband and to her late parents. This had an effect on her relationship with her children. In the beginning she felt bitter for not getting more help from them. Later she was able to talk about her feelings and need for support, without leaning too strongly on them. This case reminds us that life transitions may uncover deep personal conflicts and give the incentive to work through problems of attachment to the benefit of the individual, the couple and the family in the next generation as well.

Cognitive and emotional acceptance of loss seems to require the recollection and neutralization of memories about the past. This connection is illustrated by Mrs O who repeatedly expressed her sadness about not being able to visualize her husband the way he used to be 'before all this happened'. She tried to look at pictures from the good old days, but she did not manage to 'vitalize' the memories. She commented that this would probably be easier after his death. In this way she pointed directly to the link between grief work and the availability of memories. She longed for the picture of her proud and strong husband from previous years. However, her bond to him and feeling of responsibility did not allow her to contrast the frail old man with the man of the past. She rather continued to search for him 'behind the mask of dementia'.

The cases reported here illustrate that the spouses have different needs and different bases for profiting from interventions, depending on their experiences of loss, attachment and coping. This demands flexible and individualized methods of intervention. Even when groups are meant to be mainly informative or educational, individual and relationship-oriented factors are to be considered. Otherwise teaching about principles of communication, available community service, and care facilities may fall short in meeting the actual needs of the spouses. Well-intended advice from group leaders or fellow group members will hardly be of any help unless the needs of the care-giver are taken into consideration.

Thus, information about dementia and educational approaches are probably not enough to help the care-giving spouses. The internal working models, developed by the care-givers to forecast and interpret the partner's behaviour, are threatened by changes in the behaviour. According to Bretherton (1992), working models of insecure attachment are more inflexible and difficult to change. Intervention strategies have to take into account and respect the attachment behaviour, emotional needs and cognitive style of each individual care-giver.

Our case material indicates that to improve coping and adaptation it is sometimes necessary to address the marital relation, the grief and individuation process of the care-giving spouse directly. This process is painful, and care-givers willing to see the numerous challenges in the situation often have a feeling of unresolved tasks and cope less than perfectly according to measurements of care-giver burden and emotional distress. Such, less than perfect, coping may be part of a process towards acceptance of inevitable changes in the relationship. For some care-givers individual intervention is needed to reach such acceptance. In any case, assessment of subjective, and not objective burden only, is basic to all intervention.

Care-giving spouses react in different ways to changes in the relationship with the dementing partner. Some protest strongly and engage in activities to help the demented to 'keep going' as an expression of their need to have a stable and fit partner to rely on. Some tend to merge with the other in a kind of symbiosis. Their sensitive attention to the needs of the dementing spouse and their own need of belonging together may result in physical and mental overload. Other care-giving spouses react to changes by discounting any possibility of meaningful contact, and by claiming emotional independence.

It is a challenge to help care-giving spouses find their best balance between closeness and distance in the caring relationship. Training in communication skills may be helpful in the process of differentiating the viewpoints and needs of the couple. This may be a start in the direction of individuation and greater distance (Rose and DelMaestro, 1990), and improvement of empathic coping. In empathy, identification with the other in order to understand is one part of the story, and recognition of one's own separateness from the other and own needs is the other part. When the care-giver has a strong need to have their partner in a fixed, stable position in their own life, it may be too much to ask them to see the world from the point of view of their dementing spouse. On the other hand, extreme sensitivity and eagerness to tune in to the spouse may be based on anxiety about rejection, and over-identification. These care-giving spouses have the double burden, in spite of their considerable efforts, of being hurt by rejection from a spouse who is less and less able to give confirmation and even recognition. Professional care-givers should be aware of the risk of self-effacement in these spouses, rather than just applauding their care-giving and communication skills.

In some relationships the partners are already so distant before dementia emerges, that grief and working through of losses seem less relevant. For better or worse, however, the relationship to the demented spouse will be influenced by the history of the relationship. Old conflicts, bitterness and resignation can close the door to the other person. The motivation to keep going, and to maintain daily interaction as smoothly as possible, may nevertheless be strong.

The strivings of different care-giving spouses to cope with relational, attachment and practical problems create on the one hand a firm basis of respect for the individual's efforts, and, on the other hand, a call for further development of differentiated psychological intervention.

REFERENCES

Bowlby, J. (1969) *Attachment*, vol. 1 of *Attachment and Loss*, London: The Hogarth Press.
—— (1973) *Separation: Anxiety and Anger*, vol. 2 of *Attachment and Loss*, London: The Hogarth Press.
—— (1980) *Loss, Sadness, and Depression*, vol. 3 of *Attachment and Loss*, London: The Hogarth Press.
Bretherton, I. (1992) 'Attachment and bonding', in V.B. van Hasselt and M. Hersen (eds) *Handbook of Social Development. A Lifelong Perspective*, New York: Plenum Press, pp. 133–155.
Collins, C., Liken, M., King, S. and Kokinakis, C. (1993) 'Loss and grief among family caregivers of relatives with dementia', *Qualitative Health Research* 3(2): 236–253.
De Longis, A. and O'Brien, T. (1990) 'An interpersonal framework for stress and coping: An application to the families of Alzheimer's patients', in M.A.P. Stephens, J.H. Growther, S.E. Hobfoll and D.L. Tennenbaum (eds) *Stress and Coping in Later Life Families*, New York: Hemisphere, pp. 221–239.
Duijnstee, M. (1992a) 'De belasting van familileden van dementerenden', doctoral dissertation (English summary: pp. 341–353), Nijkerk: Intro.
—— (1992b) 'Caring for a demented family member at home: objective observation and subjective evaluation of the burden', in G.M.M. Jones and B.M.L. Miesen (eds) *Care-Giving in Dementia: Research and Applications*, vol. 1, London/New York: Tavistock/Routledge, pp. 359–379.
Farran, C.J., Keane-Hagerty, E., Salloway, S., Kupferer, S. and Wilken, C.S. (1991) 'Finding meaning: An alternative paradigm for Alzheimer's disease family caregivers', *The Gerontologist* 31: 483–489.
George, L.K. and Gwyther, L.P. (1986) 'Caregiver well-being: A multidimensional examination of family caregivers of demented adults', *The Gerontologist* 26: 253–259.
Gilleard, C.J., Belford, H., Gilleard, E. *et al.* (1984) 'Emotional distress among the supporters of the elderly mentally infirm', *British Journal of Psychiatry* 145: 172–177.
Grafström, M. (1994) 'The experience of burden in the care of elderly persons with dementia', doctoral dissertation, Karolinska Institute, Stockholm, Stockholm Gerontology Research Center, and Umeå University, Sweden.
Gwyther, L.P. (1990) 'Letting go: Separation-individuation in a wife of an Alzheimer's patient', *The Gerontologist* 30: 698–702.
Harris, P.B. (1993) 'The misunderstood caregiver? A qualitative study of the male caregiver of Alzheimer's disease victims', *The Gerontologist* 33: 551–556.
Johnson, C.L. and Catalano, D.J. (1983) 'A longitudinal study of family supports to impaired elderly', *The Gerontologist* 23: 612–618.
Kitwood, T. and Bredin, K. (1992) 'Toward a theory of dementia care: Personhood and well-being', *Aging and Society* 12: 269–287.
Lazarus, R.S. and Folkman, S. (1984) *Stress, Appraisal and Coping*, New York: Springer.
Miesen, B.M.L. (1992) 'Attachment theory and dementia', in G.M.M. Jones and B.M.L. Miesen (eds) *Care-Giving in Dementia: Research and Applications*, vol. 1, London/New York: Tavistock/Routledge, pp. 38–56.

—— (1995) 'Family care-giving in Alzheimer's disease: Coping with a beloved, missing person', paper presented at the Third European Congress of Gerontology, Amsterdam, August/September.

Morris, L.W., Morris, R.G. and Britton, P.G. (1988) 'The relationship between marital intimacy, perceived strain and depression in spouse carers of dementia sufferers', *British Journal of Medical Psychology* 61: 231–236.

Morris, R.G. and Morris, L.W. (1993) 'Psychosocial aspects of caring for people with dementia: Conceptual and methodological issues', in A. Burns (ed.) *Aging and Dementia: A Methodological Approach*, London: Edward Arnold, pp. 251–274.

Motenko, A.K. (1989) 'The frustrations, gratifications and well-being of dementia care-givers', *The Gerontologist* 29: 166–172.

Nordhus, I.H. (1994) 'Parter i samspill – pårørende i demensprosessen', in P.E. Solem, R. Ingebretsen, K. Lyng and Aa-M. Nygård (eds) *Psykologiske perspektiver på aldersdemens*, Oslo: Universitetsforlaget, pp. 170–181.

Pruchno, R.A. and Resch, N.L. (1989) 'Husbands and wives as caregivers: Antecedents of depression and burden', *The Gerontologist* 29: 159–165.

Rose, J.M. and DelMaestro, S.G. (1990) 'Separation–individuation conflict as a model for understanding distressed caregivers: Psychodynamic and cognitive case studies', *The Gerontologist* 30: 693–697.

Stommel, M., Given, C.W. and Given, B. (1990) 'Depression as an overriding variable explaining caregiver burdens', *Journal of Aging and Health* 2: 81–102.

Toseland, R.W., and Rossiter, C.M. (1989) 'Group interventions to support family caregivers. A review and analysis', *The Gerontologist* 29: 438–448.

Vitalino, P.P., Young, H.M. and Russo, J. (1991) 'Burden: A review of measures used among caregivers of individuals with dementia', *The Gerontologist* 31: 67–75.

Wright, L.K. (1991) 'The impact of Alzheimer's disease on the marital relationship', *The Gerontologist* 31: 224–237.

Zarit, S.H., Todd, P.A. and Zarit, J. (1986) 'Subjective burdens of husbands and wives as caregivers: A longitudinal study', *The Gerontologist* 26: 260–266.

Chapter 14

Understanding the social context of families experiencing dementia

A qualitative approach

Caroline LeNavenec

SUMMARY

Enhancing personhood well-being is one major goal for effective health care and social service delivery systems for families experiencing dementia (Kitwood and Bredin, 1992). Central to this goal, and the implementation of programmes that include reminiscence, music therapy and related treatment modes, is the need for those in the helping role more fully to understand the unique social context of the patients and their families. In order to facilitate this shift from a focus on the individual's 'presenting problem' to the family's 'presenting situation', several methods for gathering and presenting qualitative family contextual data are described. It is hoped that this approach will lead to more empathic caring relationships, more effective methods of documentation or charting by professionals, and the development of a contextualized model of care based on concepts derived from attachment theory, career theory (Barley, 1989), and a family systems perspective (Boss, 1988; Tomm, 1988; Wright and Leahey, 1994).

INTRODUCTION

One central assumption expressed in this chapter is that we all have our own way of understanding and creating meaning in our lives, and that these perceptions, definitions of the situation, and/or constructions of reality can be understood 'correctly' only if the social context is also understood (Dey, 1993). Context is conceptualized here, following Boss (1988) and Wright and Leahey (1994), as encompassing not only the family's physical setting, but also their interpersonal context – both within the family (their internal context) and their outside contacts or connections (their external context). It also includes both the objective and subjective dimensions (Hughes, 1958). A major component of the subjective dimension is the family's 'situation', that is, 'the [significant] concerns, issues, information, constraints, and resources at a given time or place as experienced by the particular person[s]' (Benner and Wrubel, 1989: 412).

The purpose of this chapter is to describe several qualitative approaches for obtaining and recording data about the social context of families experiencing dementia. It is expected that this contextualized approach will assist practitioners to 'individualize', care plans, as opposed to issuing a 'standard' care plan with patients with dementia and their families. In addition, this approach should facilitate researchers investigating the care-giving burden to articulate more clearly the contexts in which those caring relationships are embedded (Gubrium and Sankar, 1990). A final advantage of a contextualized approach that this author has identified is its utility in facilitating both patients and family 'to tell their story' (LeNavenec, 1993; LeNavenec and Vonhof, 1996). If the latter does not occur, staff in hospitals or community agencies will have inadequate knowledge about the social context of the patients and their families, resulting in interpretive and/or communication errors on the part of the care-givers 'because a "wrong" context is assumed or incomplete contextual information exists' (Dey, 1993).

This chapter begins with a discussion of five types of visual gestalts, which are diagrams that have been developed as assessment, planning and intervention devices, and which convey a great deal of information about the family context. Next, the advantages of including an illustrative life history in the medical file are outlined. The third section focuses on journal writing or compilation of daily logs by staff or family members as a source of contextual data. The final section contains practical suggestions about documenting or charting that includes 'thick' description in order to develop a holistic approach and the creation of accurate 'interpretive biographies' (Denzin, 1989b) about, and a contextualized model of care for, families experiencing dementia.

FIVE TYPES OF VISUAL AIDS/GESTALTS

Genograms

As noted previously, the term 'family context' refers to the nature of their internal context, for which the genogram can be used, and its external context, for which the ecomap (see following section of this chapter) can be used. The genogram, which is sometimes described as the helper's roadmap of the family's emotional process (Bowen, 1980), is a short-hand technique to derive a picture of three generations of the family. This family constellation data base includes: a rank-ordering of their membership structure by age and sex, major life events, including both positive (e.g., marriage) and negative ones (e.g., losses of various types), relationships, life-style practices, occupational and geographical mobility, health status and naming practices. The illustrative genogram that this author compiled (see Figure 14.1) includes some of these data, as well as the 'definitions of

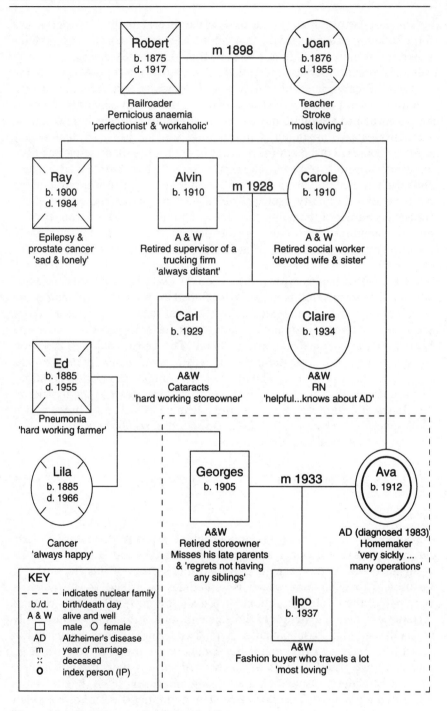

Figure 14.1 Genogram – the Adam family

self' that the participants gave for each of the members of the family based on the question 'how would you describe that person/yourself in ten words or less'.

One major purpose of using a genogram in initial interviews with families is to obtain contextual data regarding the family's definition of the situation – past, present, and their anticipated future – as well as their definitions of self, particularly the identity accorded the elders. Furthermore, the use of a genogram by the interviewer has been found to be a useful rapport-building tool, both during the initial assessment and during subsequent ones (Wright and Leahey, 1994). Similarly, because of the semi-structured nature of these interviews, it should help the families to 'tell their story', which this author has identified as a difficulty for many families who are experiencing dementia (LeNavenec, 1993). Although the genogram is started during the initial interview with the family, it should be an ongoing construction and should be placed near the front of the elder's chart along with a case history (which I will discuss shortly) on a page that is entitled 'meet . . . ' (give name and title by which the elder prefers to be addressed). Some illustrative case study examples of the ways this author has found genogram data to be useful for understanding the behaviours of the elders in a nursing home setting include:

1 *Reinterpreting 'bizarre' behaviour*: Mr Jones would often pull the fire alarm and was sometimes seen bringing women down the hall. The staff were able to understand his behaviour only after they discovered from the genogram that his previous occupation was with the Fire Department.

2 *Understanding 'wandering' behaviour*: Mrs Smith would become depressed whenever the slightest change in routine occurred, at which time she also displayed episodes of 'wandering' behaviour. Staff were later able to identify from her genogram that she had a long pattern of depression whenever there were changes, such as geographical moves, job changes, spouse's health changes, etc. During such times, she derived comfort from her husband's presence. However, Mr Smith was recently hospitalized, and because he could not visit his wife regularly, she would 'look for him' – or what staff referred to before as wandering behaviour.

3 *Recognizing attachment needs*: Mrs White, who was orphaned at a young age, and who became widowed a decade after her marriage, was described by her sons as very 'domineering' with them because of fear of losing them. Following admission to the nursing home, she continued to be the same with the private-duty nursing assistant that the family hired on a part-time basis to serve as an attachment figure. (Parenthetically, Mrs White just recently died at the age of 104, which appears to lend some support for Bowlby's work (1977) on the importance for one to have a securely based attachment with at least one other person).

4 *Affording knowledge to enhance self-esteem*: Mr Lajoie was sitting slouched in his chair and appeared to be very withdrawn while waiting to see his doctor. This doctor, after reviewing Mr Lajoie's genogram and discovering that he was previously an Army Captain, addressed him by saying 'Good morning, Sir'. Mr Lajoie immediately sat up in his chair, greeted the doctor with a big smile and shook hands, and appeared to be ready to salute.

Contextual information in a well-completed genogram may afford a sound framework of life-history data on which to build a treatment approach that is family-centred. Similarly, genograms can be used at many different settings – institutional, community agency, or home-settings – as a basis for planning new or additional interventions. Moreover, it permits not only an orderly and relatively unintrusive way of obtaining information about the family's historical and present context, and their anticipated future context, but also involves the family during the construction of it, and later in studying it together with the helper. So in a way, you are helping the family to become, in effect, qualitative researchers while creating their 'partnership' with the treatment team in ways described previously by this author (LeNavenec, 1991).

Ecomaps

Whereas the genogram provides contextual data regarding the internal context of the family, the ecomap (see Figure 14.2) is a diagram of the qualitative nature and types of connections/attachments between the family system and its external context. One useful type of contextual data it provides includes the family's perceived demand–resource balance, or as Antonovsky (1987) might put it, the ratio of generalized resistance resources (GRRs) and resistance deficits (RDs), and the interplay of that balance or imbalance with the family's 'sense of coherence'. In the words of Hartman, who utilized an ecological model to develop this visual gestalt, the ecomap

> portrays an overview of the individual or family in their situation; it pictures the important nurturant or conflict-laden connections between the family and the world. It demonstrates the flow of resources, or the lacks and deprivations. This mapping procedure highlights the nature of the interfaces and points to conflicts to be mediated, bridges to be built, and resources to be sought and mobilized.
>
> (1978: 467)

Hartman emphasizes how sharing the eco-mapping process with the family may lead to their increased understanding and acceptance of other family members and to evaluate outcomes and measure change (1978:

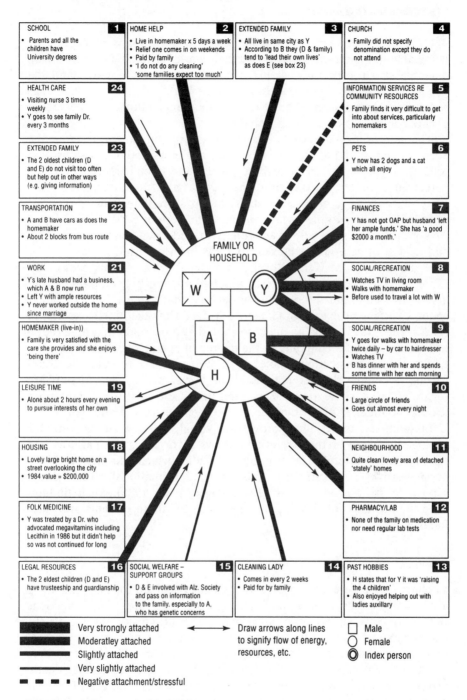

SCHOOL 1
• Parents and all the children have University degrees

HOME HELP 2
• Live in homemaker x 5 days a week
• Relief one comes in on weekends
• Paid by family
• 'I do not do any cleaning' 'some families expect too much'

EXTENDED FAMILY 3
• All live in same city as Y
• According to B they (D & family) tend to 'lead their own lives' as does E (see box 23)

CHURCH 4
• Family did not specify denomination except they do not attend

HEALTH CARE 24
• Visiting nurse 3 times weekly
• Y goes to see family Dr. every 3 months

INFORMATION SERVICES RE COMMUNITY RESOURCES 5
• Family finds it very difficult to get into about services, particularly homemakers

EXTENDED FAMILY 23
• The 2 oldest children (D and E) do not visit too often but help out in other ways (e.g. giving information)

PETS 6
• Y now has 2 dogs and a cat which all enjoy

TRANSPORTATION 22
• A and B have cars as does the homemaker
• About 2 blocks from bus route

FINANCES 7
• Y has not got OAP but husband 'left her ample funds.' She has 'a good $2000 a month.'

WORK 21
• Y's late husband had a business, which A now run
• Left Y with ample resources
• Y never worked outside the home since marriage

SOCIAL/RECREATION 8
• Watches TV in living room
• Walks with homemaker
• Before used to travel a lot with W

HOMEMAKER (live-in)) 20
• Family is very satisfied with the care she provides and she enjoys 'being there'

SOCIAL/RECREATION 9
• Y goes for walks with homemaker twice daily – by car to hairdresser
• Watches TV
• B has dinner with her and spends some time with her each morning

LEISURE TIME 19
• Alone about 2 hours every evening to pursue interests of her own

FRIENDS 10
• Large circle of friends
• Goes out almost every night

HOUSING 18
• Lovely large bright home on a street overlooking the city
• 1984 value = $200,000

NEIGHBOURHOOD 11
• Quite clean lovely area of detached 'stately' homes

FOLK MEDICINE 17
• Y was treated by a Dr. who advocated megavitamins including Lecithin in 1986 but it didn't help so was not continued for long

PHARMACY/LAB 12
• None of the family on medication nor need regular lab tests

LEGAL RESOURCES 16
• The 2 eldest children (D and E) have trusteeship and guardianship

SOCIAL WELFARE – SUPPORT GROUPS 15
• D & E involved with Alz. Society and pass on information to the family. especially to A, who has genetic concerns

CLEANING LADY 14
• Comes in every 2 weeks
• Paid by family

PAST HOBBIES 13
• H states that for Y it was 'raising the 4 children'
• Also enjoyed helping out with ladies auxillary

FAMILY OR HOUSEHOLD
W Y
A B
H

Very strongly attached
Moderatley attached
Slightly attached
Very slightly attached
Negative attachment/stressful

Draw arrows along lines to signify flow of energy, resources, etc.

□ Male
○ Female
◎ Index person

Figure 14.2 Ecomap – the Quiz family

Note: This Ecomap is a modified version of those developed by Hartman, 1978
© Le Navenec 1988

471–472). In other words, it enables them to 'gain a new perception by being able to look at themselves and their world' (ibid.: 471). The ecomap data may also be especially useful for nursing home staff to understand 'the goings on' of family visits; that is, as Gubrium (1991: 121) notes, 'what has been played out in domestic life outside the nursing home is repeated in, or lurks in the background of, visitation'.

The author has found that family participation in constructing the ecomap and studying the finished diagram enhanced discussions that followed regarding planning how they might draw upon resources that they perceived as required for desired changes in family functioning. Further-more, insights were gained about the family's pre-illness phase patterns in regard to leisure-time use, including both 'serious' and 'casual' types. This information may help practitioners to understand better the nature and degree of care-giving burden that has been reported in past studies (see summary in McKee, Whittick, Ballinger *et al.*, forthcoming). For example, several family care-givers who had previously been music teach-ers, mentioned to the author many of the ways that music helped both their spouses and themselves with managing stress during the illness experience (LeNavenec, 1995). Finally, mention should also be made that in addition to affording an understanding of the degree of openness of the family sys-tem to outside connections, the ecomap data were also found to be useful for understanding the perceptions of the family during the illness phase regarding what some researchers refer to as the confusing and rather 'closed' boundaries of various community agencies (e.g., Land, 1991).

In summary, the ecomap provides a visual overview of the complex ecological system of the family and shows its organization patterns and the qualitative nature of relationships, including which ones are perceived as supportive in an affective, affirmative, informational and/or direct service sense (Norbeck *et al.*, 1983; Pagel *et al.*, 1987). Such findings have implications for developing care plans for these patients and their families.

Lifelines

Lifelines (see Figure 14.3) are another useful visual aid for mapping along a chronological axis the family's perceptions regarding the connections they make between the onset of various behavioural manifestations ('signs and symptoms') in both the elder *and* the significant other and the occur-rence of significant life events. The latter may include a range of positive events or negative happenings such as those involving losses through death, divorce, occupational, geographical, or health status changes of one or more of the family members. In addition, other periods of the family's life-cycle when changes or upheavals occurred can be identified (Burgess, 1985, 1990).

These behaviour–event lifelines, which draw on some of the notions of the research on family constellation and its effects on personality and social behaviour (see summary of the latter work in Wright and Leahey, 1994: 41–42), can be constructed on the basis of data obtained during the genogram interviews, and more fully explored during other family sessions. One potential value of lifeline data for professionals planning or providing care for patients with dementia and their significant others is the information it may provide regarding the nature of the attributions (e.g., internal or external) or 'causes' of the elder's current and past behaviour patterns that are made by families. Illustrative examples of the latter from the author's clinical experiences include:

- Mrs Shaw interpreted some of her husband's current behaviour (e.g., teasing some of the older ladies in the nursing home, and the particular way he sometimes treated her) to be the result of being the youngest in the family and the only boy.
- Mrs Lee perceived an increase in sexually ineffective behaviour on the part of her husband since he became ill with dementia, to be the result of a shunt procedure.
- Adult children perceived the development of 'strong alliances' between themselves and their mothers (the patients) to be the result of their father's death while they were still adolescents.

Other researchers have derived lifeline data based on self-reports, followed by an interview that involves obtaining a verbatim report that is analysed accordingly. For example, Schroots and Ten Kate (1989) have developed the Lifeline Interview Method (LIM) on the basis of metaphors (e.g., peaks and valleys) that people commonly use to describe their life-histories and future expectations. They conclude that the LIM

> can serve as a diagnostic and process-facilitating tool, especially with the elderly, not only because of the quality of self-structuring, but also – and maybe even more important – because of the self-pacing quality, which allows the older person to set his or her own pace in giving biographical information.
>
> (Schroots and Ten Kate 1989: 296)

In this writer's opinion, the LIM may be useful in overcoming some of the difficulties she had in obtaining from the significant others contextual data pertaining to the affective meanings of personal life events in and through time (LeNavenec, 1993). In addition to the contextual data afforded, a recent study by Merriam and Clark (1991) points to the therapeutic value of lifeline construction for individuals. In many ways, these benefits appear to resemble the value accrued from reminiscence therapy (Gerfo, 1980; Gillies and James, 1994).

Significant Other, L.

Age/Year	Behavioral Manifestations / Life Events
1930	L. born as the youngest in a sibline of 4
18 (1948)	– completes high school – father dies – L's 3 siblings have by now left home, 2 of whom moved to a Western U.S. State
18–35 (1948–1965)	– Farms and lives with mother
35–47 (1965–1977)	– L. and Mom move to Western U.S. – worked with Inner City children x 12 yrs.

Index Person, K.

Age/Year	Behavioral Manifestations / Life Events
(11 Nov. 1896)	– K. born in U.S., 3rd in a sibline of 6
4 (early 1900s)	– moves with family to Canada to present farm setting – developed eczema
20 (1916)	– K.'s Dad dies of chronic digestive problem
21 (1917)	– K. marries a man 11 years her senior
22 (1918)	– gives birth to son, 2 daughters & son respectively
24 (1920)	
29 (1925)	
34 (1930)	
46 (1943)	– K.'s mom dies of circulatory problem, at age of 75
52 (1948)	– K.'s husband dies of coronary, at age 63 – around this time 'her eczema disappeared'
70 (1966)	– K.'s daughter, B. gets a divorce – K. diagnosed with cardiac problem
69–81 (1965–1971)	– moves to U.S. with L.
79 (1975)	– develops hyperventilation and has a heart attack and disorientation noted

Lifeline guide – the Snow family

Significant Other, L. (Life Events / Behavioral Manifestations)

Age/Year	Content
47 (1977)	– L. & K. have moved North and L. 'full-time' at home, helping K.
47–57 (1977–1987)	– L. & K. maintain regular phone contact with the family members in Western U.S. – L. finds that his sister 'is really good getting mother to talk and laugh on the phone' but his brother does not attempt to do the same – L. gets involved in the last year in community groups and church groups and some formal agencies provide home making services – However, once K. was hospitalized he would visit her each afternoon and stay until bed time

Index Person, K. (Life Events / Behavioral Manifestations)

Age/Year	Content
79 (1975)	– This disorientation was found to be to time and place and 'was better at times' – Physician suspected K. may be having small strokes in the brain (multiple infarct dementia) – The Digitalis and Diazide that she was prescribed earlier was now
81 (1977)	– K. & L. return to their previous Canadian home – K.'s spells of disorientation ↑ and ↓ memory
85 (1981)	– K. is now unable to perform most I-ADL & P-ADL
87 (1983)	– K.'s daughter dies but K seems to 'block it out'
88 (1984)	– K develops speech problems – ↑ swelling in ankles – AD is suspected Dx
89 (Oct. 1985)	– K. falls and breaks her hip – hospitalized and treated with ++++ minor tranquillizers
90 (Nov. '85)	– Coma x 2 days
90 (1986)	– 'Has really rallied' – still in chronic care hospital

Figure 14.3 Lifeline guide – the Snow family

Circular (Communication) Pattern Diagrams (CPDs)

Circular (Communication) Pattern Diagrams (see Figures 14.4a, b and c) are another type of visual aid that professionals might consider constructing to gain insights about the effects of communication patterns on the behaviours of each of the interactants. Developed by University of Calgary family researcher, Tomm (1988), this tool has been extensively used by Wright and Leahey (1994), who have found that it enables one to 'concretize and simplify the repetitive circular sequences noted in a relationship'. The purpose of constructing the CPDs is not so much to identify whose perception of the situation is 'correct', as it is to help families and/or staff members identify how each interactant is mutually affecting the other. They maintain that 'affect or cognition, or both, propel the behaviour' (p. 84) of the interactants and they use inferences about the former to 'illustrate the relationship between these elements' (p. 84), which are depicted in the CPD.

Key: Data in the squares pertain to the types of inferences – cognitive or affective, or both – made
       by the researcher regarding the definitions of the interactions. Data along the arrows represents
       the behavioural responses of the interactants. The mutuality of effects of the interactants on each
       other is indicated by showing how the behavioural output of one set of interactants becomes the
       perceptual input for the other in a circular way.
       IP = Index person: Nanette
       IP's family = (specify type of subsystem) Parent – Child

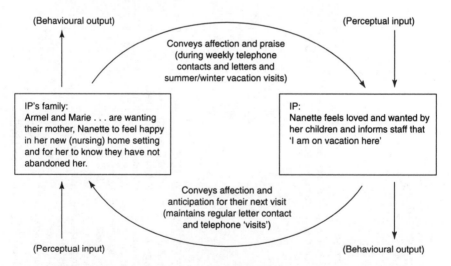

Figure 14.4a Illustrative Circular Pattern Diagram (CPD) – the Le Blanc family

Note: For description of the development and use of CPDs see Tomm (1988) and Wright and Leahey (1994)

Figure 14.4b CPD for a family with a closed style of managing

Figure 14.4c CPD for a family with a closed style of managing

Key: Data in the squares pertain to the types of inferences – cognitive or affective, or both – made
       by the interviewer regarding the definitions of the interactants. Data along the arrows represents
       the behavioural responses of the interactants. The mutuality of effects of the interactants on
       each other is indicated by showing how the behavioural output of one set of interactants becomes
       the perceptual input for the other in a circular way.
       IP = Index person: Mr Dean
       IP's family = a Marital subsystem (MS).

1.

(Behavioural output)   (Perceptual input)

1. Involves Spouse
e.g., shows him bank book as he worries
about investments; involves him in garden work
& light tasks in house, and social activities (e.g., cards)

Mrs Dean:	Mr Dean:
'I feel pleased that he wants to help'	'I think she knows that I want to keep this large home'
'He still likes to think he is in charge of things'.	'I feel proud of my wife and love our home'

2. Praises spouse
e.g., 'She works like hell';
'She's the best cook in the world'.

(Perceptual input)   (Behavioural output)

2.   b

Key: Data in the squares pertain to the types of inferences – cognitive or affective, or both – made by
       the interviewer regarding the definitions of the interactants. Data along the arrows represents the
       behavioural responses of the interactants. The mutuality of effects of the interactants on each
       other is indicated by showing how the behavioural output of one set of interactants becomes the
       perceptual input for the other in a circular way.
       IP = Index person: Mrs Nose
       IP's family = a Parent-Extended family subsystem (P/EFS).

1.

(Behavioural output)   (Perceptual input)

1. Implements 'a Curriculum'
They make available an 'above average stimulating
environment' as outlined in 'the curriculum'
(e.g., four-mile walks, theatre, planned cruises)

IP's family:	IP:
'We feel confident that she'll have not only a much longer life, but quality as well.'	They want me to be like I used to be.
'The agencies available for her care, both hospitals and institutions are not ????'	I feel pleased that they think I can change and 'become fit'.

2. Participates in the 'Curriculum'
'She now likes rock music, poker, coloured outfits, displays
a more youthful and modern attitude devoid of critical
remarks and excuses (based on age/illnesses).'

(Perceptual input)   (Behavioural output)

2.   c

The author has found CPDs useful for students to use in analysing their process recordings of a series of interactions with families of older clients in acute care hospital units and nursing home settings. She also found that by using specific types of questions, which are discussed below, one can more effectively identify the definitions of self that the care-givers (i.e., the significant others) made about themselves and the elder (LeNavenec, 1993). Examples of supportive and non-supportive relationship can be depicted in ways outlined by Wright and Leahey (1994: 83–87).

While constructing the CPD, a variety of 'circular questions' (Tomm, 1988; LeNavenec, 1991) can be used to identify the cognitions, affect and behaviour of each interactant. Some of these might include 'difference' questions (e.g., 'What information did the doctor give you that was most helpful?'); 'behavioural effect' questions (e.g., 'How do you feel when your husband says he must return home and no longer needs nursing home care?"'); 'future-orientated/hypothetical' questions (e.g., 'If the doctor suggests that your husband must go into a nursing home next week, what do you think your spouse will think/feel/do?'); or 'triadic' questions (e.g., 'What do you think your daughter needs to do to help dad [the elder] consent to having the tests done?'). These types of questions have been found to help the respondents 'to discover' how each one is affecting the other and ways of changing an 'unwanted' pattern of communication (Shulman and Mandel, 1988; Wright and Leahey, 1994: 103–104).

Attachment Pattern Diagrams (APDs)

Attachment Pattern Diagrams (APDs) are the final type of visual gestalt that will be mentioned here (see Figure 14.5). Attachment or emotional bonds (Bowlby, 1977) refers to 'a relatively enduring, unique emotional tie between two specific persons' (Wright and Leahey; 1994: 60). Furthermore, as Parkes, Stevenson-Hinde and Morris (1991) note, 'in attachments as in other affectional bonds there is a need to maintain proximity, distress upon inexplicable separation, pleasure or joy upon reunion, and grief at loss' (p. 38). They add, however, that one criterion of attachment that is not necessarily present in other affectional bonds is the desire 'to obtain an experience of security and comfort in the relationship with the [other]' (p. 38).

The attachment pattern diagrams that this author has constructed in both her research and clinical practice were based on the method developed by Wright and Leahey (1994) and involved interviewing the significant others who had a relative who had been diagnosed as having dementia. Information was obtained from the family members about the nature of the attachment pattern (positive or negative, strong or weak) and the changes in those patterns in, and through time (that is, during the pre- and post-illness phase; see LeNavenec, 1993 and Figure 14.5). The

Family's Name or Reference #:   The Camps

Symbols used in attachment diagrams:

Male: ☐

Female: ○

Attachments: ▬▬▬ strongly attached

▬▬ moderately attached

▬ slightly attached

___ very slightly attached

∿∿ negatively attached

◎ Index person

⚬ Deceased

⇌ Direction of energy

⌒ Members of the household/
whole family subsystem

Comments to support inferences:

- The Camps have very limited contact with their extended family. Mrs. A. left home at a young age because of problems with her stepfather and did not keep in touch with her siblings.
- B & C describe their relationships with each other and with their mother as very close.
- B & C are closely attached to friends from work and in the church.
- They involve their mother in household activities (e.g., cooking and gardening), as well as in social activities.

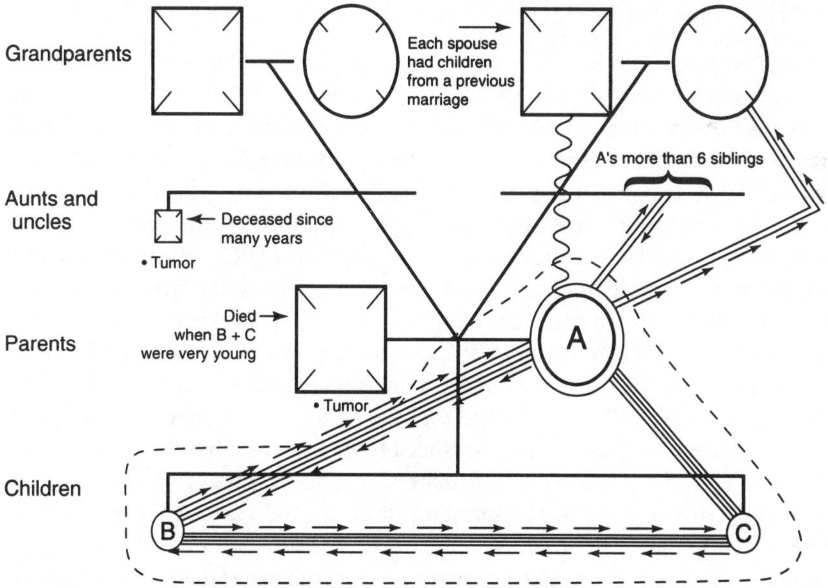

Grandparents

Each spouse had children from a previous marriage

A's more than 6 siblings

Aunts and uncles

← Deceased since many years

• Tumor

Parents

Died → when B + C were very young

• Tumor

A

Children

B

C

Figure 14.5 Attachment Pattern Diagram

Note: The format used for these diagrams is based on the work of Wright and Leahey (1994) information obtained from the informants enabled the author to understand better the nature of their losses and their salient concerns about the present and future that they perceived as areas in which they needed assistance.

Although Bowlby (1977) described attachment behaviour as characterizing human beings from the cradle to the grave, there has been limited research about, and assessment of, the relatively enduring ties between an older person and a significant other in the elderly population (Lipson-Parra, 1990; Miesen, 1993; West and Shelden-Keller, 1994). APDs might be a particularly useful way for staff to develop a broader awareness of the attachment needs of older persons with dementia, as well as their families, and to assess if such needs are being met. In addition, staff may gain an understanding of the problems of disrupted attachment, such as the anxiety and fear caused when these people are unwillingly separated from their significant others (for example, admitted to a nursing home). Finally, it may enable nursing home staff to identify ways to alleviate attachment deprivation such as affording opportunities for the clients to interact with one another, ensuring that photos and other family mementos are displayed, and for those clients who have few visitors, the staff may become the providers of warmth and personal interaction (Parkes, Stevenson-Hinde, and Morris, 1991).

USING LIFE HISTORIES TO CONTEXTUALIZE CARE

Another way to contextualize care of nursing home residents is to include a one-page case study near the front of their charts. Two University of Kentucky researchers, Pietruckowicz and Johnston (1991), used this approach to assess the impact of such data on nursing home staff attitudes. They found that controlling for individual differences such as prior work experience and knowledge about ageing, staff reviewing the chart with the life-history rated that resident as more instrumental, autonomous and personally acceptable than staff who reviewed the chart without the life history (p. 102). This author concurs with their two major conclusions: (i) this is an economically feasible (i.e., low-cost) intervention, which could serve to improve the quality of life of residents (p. 105), and (ii) 'aides who perceive the elderly they serve as vital and unique may also increase their own self-esteem as health care personnel whose work has been routinely devalued' (p.105). Although Pietruckowicz and Johnston's study used a positive life-history, they recommend that future research look at the impact of negative life histories.

Unlike Pietruckowicz and Johnston, who constructed the case history on the basis of the accounts of the clients, this writer would recommend that the family also be asked to prepare one. It may be that this would be therapeutic for the families, given LeNavenec's (1993) finding of the considerable interest expressed by many of those experiencing dementia or a related chronic illness in 'telling their story' (see also Koch, 1990). Indeed, she found that many of the significant others whose relative with dementia had gone to a nursing home or had died, were taking courses such as 'being fully alive' and/or effective writing courses similar to the life-stories described by Ledoux (1993).

DOING JOURNAL-KEEPING/CONSTRUCTION OF DAILY LOGS TO IDENTIFY LEARNING AND SUPPORT NEEDS OF THOSE INVOLVED IN HELPING RELATIONSHIPS

Although often used as a clinical teaching tool for students, journal-keeping could be done by families and/or staff in nursing homes in order to identify their learning and support needs. This interactive journal, log or diary is a daily record of the helper's ideas, feelings and actions, that relate to the caring experience/the caring relationship (Qureshi and Walker, 1989). The journal reviewer – or teacher – responds to these entries, creating a journal that is an interaction between helper and teacher. A notebook, in which pages can easily be added and removed, is used. Thus, the journal often becomes a vehicle for exchanging articles, poetry (such as responses to McCormack's (1976) 'Crabbit old woman'), quotes, and stories about their day's experiences (Landeen, Byrne and Brown, 1992; Sedlak, 1992; Wagenaar, 1984). As used by this author, the journal exercise is focused on having the helper record the following on a daily basis:

1 a point-form outline of today's most important interactions and/or happenings and one's thoughts, feelings and behavioural responses;
2 things that went well today and possible reasons for same;
3 things that I/we wished happened differently and some ways that difference might be achieved for 'next time' (e.g., the next day/week/ or time that I/we are faced with a similar challenge/stress or/task or opportunity;
4 optional: a process recording of a five- or ten-minute segment of your interaction with the elder/staff/family members. Try to use a format that includes analysis of your personal responses to the interaction as well as the themes and symbolism of the encounter (see excellent format provided by Burgess, 1985, 511–519).

Some of the advantages of journal-keeping for helpers that have been identified in studies on this practice include the following:

1 It assists one to understand the 'lived experience' of these families (Cotrell and Schulz, 1993; van Manen, 1990; see also Neimeyer, 1993: 212).

2 It may assist helpers to perceive their role as more valued and as an important contribution to the identified patient's/index person's well-being.

3 It provides an opportunity for helpers to reflect on their learning and/or support needs such as the three types of social support outlined in Norbeck *et al.*'s (1983) typology, that is, emotional support, affirmative support, and support that involves aid-information or aid-direct services (see also the needs outlined by Knight, Lutzky and Macofsky-Urban, 1993).

4 It may facilitate the creation of healthy partnerships between the helpers and the others in the situation because, although the responsibility is placed with the helpers for actively engaging in self-directed learning, the 'teacher', in consultation with others, facilitates that learning through the ongoing, informational feedback by way of written comments.

5 It can facilitate identification of the repertoire of skills or growth that the helper has displayed over a period of time such as:

- recognition of learning from negative experiences (Reiss, 1981; Reiss *et al.* 1986);
- increased awareness of a range of contextual influences aside from the index person–helper relationship (see, for example, the variables outlined by Karr, 1991; Radley, 1988);
- awareness of one's own emotions, including instances of high 'expressed emotion' (Vitaliano *et al.*, 1988–1989), as well as empathy (Rogers, 1980);
- recognition of the need for client advocacy;
- improvement in goal-setting skills (Egan, 1994).

Although Neimeyer (1993) has identified some limitations to journal work, he maintains that if threats and related factors can be managed, 'the diary can be a powerful means of coming to know the client's fundamental concerns and fostering greater self-knowledge, mastery, and coherence even in severely distressed individuals' (pp. 212–213).

THICK DESCRIPTION: WHAT IS IT AND WHY USE IT?

What is 'thick' description, and why, in an age of computer use, structured questionnaires and checklists commonly used in health care delivery systems for older people, would one suggest this approach to contextualizing care? As depicted by Denzin and his associates (Denzin, 1989a and 1989b; Denzin and Guba 1993), thick description includes deep, dense, detailed accounts of problematic experiences of people, including the intentions and meanings that organize their actions. These are often written up in the form of case studies (Bell, 1990; Conrad, 1990; Hanson, 1989; LeNavenec and Vonhof, 1996; Orona, 1990; Sacks, 1985). In contrast to thin descriptions (or 'glosses'), which lack detail and simply report facts, thick descriptions help bring the 'lived experience' of individuals with dementia and their families before the listener/helper in a way that the voices, feelings, actions and meanings of their interactions with others are 'heard' and 'seen' (Denzin, 1989a).

In institutional settings, thick descriptions could be the approach that staff use to conduct the regular patient care conferences, or in the way they do their charting, or a case history containing thick (as opposed to the current thin) descriptions could be included as part of each person's social history section of the medical chart. The latter could be a joint staff–family project and would, we hope, facilitate, as Denzin notes, a better under-standing of 'the relational structures that the persons observed may or may not understand yet are acting in terms of at the moment' (1983: 44).

These thick descriptions, used in conjunction with the previously mentioned visual gestalts, use of life history, and journal-keeping, all represent ways 'to bring the social context back in', which is the plea that other researchers have voiced to balance the current biomedicalization of dementia (e.g., Bond, 1992; Lyman, 1988). This contextualized approach includes all aspects that Denzin (1989a) considers important for 'doing interpretive interactionism', as well as interpretive biography (1989b), and which this author considers important for understanding caring as a relationship and for the development of a holistic contextualized model of care for persons with dementia and their families.

Central to this envisioned contextualized model of care would be numerous programmes that enhance the personhood of both older people with dementia and their significant others (Chesla *et al.*, 1994; Farran *et al.*, 1991; Hagerman and Tobin, 1988; Kitwood and Bredin, 1991, 1992; Knight *et al.*, 1993; Rader and Tornquist, 1995). Many of these programmes would include alternative/complementary treatment modalities such as reminis-cence and music therapies (Butler, 1980; Gerfo, 1980; Gillies and James, 1994; LeNavenec, 1995), as well as new ones being developed in the areas of speech therapy and memory retraining (personal communication with Dr Colin Lane, Bridgwater, Somerset, and Dr Leon Earle, University of South Australia, May 1995).

CONCLUDING STATEMENTS

The discussion presented in this chapter emphasized the importance of understanding the context, both internal and external, of families experi-encing dementia. This understanding can be greatly enhanced through the use of five types of visual gestalts described here, namely, *genograms, life-lines, ecomaps, circular pattern diagrams*, and *attachment pattern diagrams*. Other useful tools that may enhance the understanding by health care staff of the context of the elders and their families are a life-history of the elder and a journal or daily log of interactions with the elder, the latter's family, and/or other staff. Thick descriptions, which are often written up in the form of case-studies, illustrate the day-to-day 'lived experience' of these elders and their families. Taken together, this qualitative approach permits the development of a holistic approach and a contextualized model of care for families experiencing dementia in ways similar to the approach developed by Boss (1988; Boss *et al.*, 1988). Central to the model of care as envisioned here would be the enhancement of personal well-being of older persons with dementia and their significant others (Cotrell and Schulz, 1993; Farran *et al.*, 1991; Hagerman and Tobin, 1988).

From a theoretical and methodological point of view, it is expected that this qualitative approach will assist researchers to understand better, as opposed to measure, the interdependence of context and the nature of the illness career (Barley, 1989; Denzin and Guba, 1993; Gilgun, Daly and Handel, 1992) of families experiencing dementia. One major challenge for this decade is how to increase research-based caring practices based on concepts derived not only from a medical model, but also from theoretical assumptions derived from career theory, attachment theory, and from a family systems perspective (see References for specific works).

REFERENCES

Antonovsky, A. (1987) *Unravelling the Mystery of Health: How People Manage Stress and Stay Well*. San Francisco: Jossey-Bass.

Barley, S.R. (1989) Careers, identities, and institutions: The legacy of the Chicago school of sociology. In M. Arthur, D. Hall, B. Lawrence (eds), *Handbook of Career Theory* (pp. 41–65). New York: Cambridge University Press.

Bell, N.W. (1990) The family's experience of Alzheimer's disease. Paper presented at the First Polish/Second International Conference on Family Therapy, Krakow, Poland, (September).

Benner, P. and Wrubel, J. (1989) *The Primacy of Caring: Stress and Coping in Health and Illness*. Menlo Park, CA: Addison-Wesley.

Blumer, H. (1969) *Symbolic Interactionism*. Englewood Cliffs, NJ: Prentice-Hall.

Bond, J. (1992) The medicalization of dementia. *Journal of Aging Studies* 6(4): 397–403.

Boss, P. (1988) *Family Stress Management*. Beverly Hills: Sage.

——, Caron, W. and Horbal, J. (1988) Alzheimer's disease and ambiguous loss. In C. Chilman, E. Nunnally and F. Cox (eds), *Chronic Illness and Disability* (pp. 123–140). Newbury Park, CA: Sage.

Bowen, M. (1980) Key to the use of the genogram. In E.A. Carter and M. McGoldrick (eds), *The Family Life Cycle*. New York: Gardner Press.

Bowlby, J. (1977) The making and breaking of affectional bonds. *British Journal of Psychiatry* 130: 201–210.

Burgess, A.W. (1985; 1990) *Psychiatric Nursing in the Hospital and the Community* (4th and 5th edns). Englewood Cliffs, NJ: Prentice-Hall.

Butler, R. (1980) The life review: An unrecognized bonanza. *International Journal of Aging and Human Development* 12(1): 35–38.

Chesla, C., Martinson, I. and Muwa Swes, M. (1994) Continuities and discontinuities in family members' relationships with Alzheimer's patients. *Family Relations* 43: 3–9.

Conrad, P. (1990) Qualitative research on chronic illness: A commentary on method and conceptual development. *Social Science and Medicine* 30(11): 1257–1263.

Cotrell, V. and Schulz, R. (1993) The perspective of the patient with Alzheimer's disease: A neglected dimension of dementia research. *The Gerontologist* 33(2): 205–211.

Denzin, N. (1983) Interpretive interactionism. In G. Morgan (ed.), *Beyond Methods* (pp. 129–146). Beverly Hills: Sage.

—— (1989a) *Interpretive Interactionism*. Newbury Park, CA: Sage.

—— (1989b) *Interpretive Biography*. Newbury Park, CA: Sage.

—— and Guba, Y.S. (1993) *Handbook of Qualitative Research*. Thousand Oaks, CA: Sage.

Dey, I. (1993) *Qualitative Data Analysis: A User Friendly Guide*. London and New York: Routledge.

Egan, G. (1994) *The Skilled Helper* (5th edn). Pacific Grove, CA: Brooks/Cole.

Ehrhart, P.M. (1987) Attachment theory. In J. Norris, M. Kunes-Connell, S. Stockard, P.M. Ehrhart and G.R. Newton (eds), *Mental Health – Psychiatric Nursing* (pp. 289–316). New York: John Wiley and Sons.

Farran, C., Keane-Hagerty, E., Salloway, S., Kupfere, S. and Wilken, C. (1991) Finding meaning: An alternate paradigm for Alzheimer's disease family caregivers. *The Gerontologist* 31(4): 483–489.

Geertz, C. (1973) 'Thick' description: Toward an interpretive theory of culture. In C. Geertz (ed.), *The Interpretation of Culture* (pp. 3–30). New York: Basic Books.

Gerfo, M. (1980) Three ways of reminiscence in theory and practice. *International Journal of Aging and Human Development* 12(1): 39–45.

Gilgun, J.F., Daly, K. and Handel, G. (eds) (1992) *Qualitative Methods in Family Research*. Newbury Park, CA: Sage.

Gillies, C., and James, A. (1994) *Reminiscence Work with Older Families*. London: Chapman and Hall.

Gubrium, J.F. (1991) *The Mosaic of Care: Frail Elderly and their Families in the Real World*. New York: Springer.

—— and Sankar, A. (1990) *The Home Care Experience: Ethnography and Policy*. Newbury Park, CA: Sage.

Hagerman, C. and Tobin, S. (1988) Enhancing the autonomy of mentally impaired nursing home residents. *The Gerontologist* 28: 71–75.

Hanson, B. (1989) Definitional deficit: A model of senile dementia in context. *Family Process* 28: 281–289.

Hartman, A. (1978) Diagrammatic assessment of family relationships. *Social Casework* 59: 465–476.

Hughes, E. (1958) *Men and Their Work*. New York: Free Press.

Kahn, R. and Antonucci, T. (1980) Convoys over the life course: Attachment, roles and social support. In P.B. Baltes and O.C. Brim, Jr. (eds), *Life-span Development and Behavior* 3 (pp. 253–286). New York: Academic Press.

Kantor, D. and Lehr, W. (1975) *Inside the Family*. New York: Harper and Row.

Karr, K.L. (1991). *Promises to Keep: The Family's Role in Nursing Home Care*. Buffalo: Prometheus Books.

Kitwood, T. and Bredin, K. (1991) *Person to Person: A Guide to the Care of Those with Failing Mental Powers*. Bradford: University of Bradford Dementia Research Group.

—— and —— (1992) Toward a theory of dementia care: Personhood and well-being. *Aging and Society* 12: 269–287.

Knight, B.G., Lutzky, S.M. and Macofsky-Urban, F. (1993) A meta-analytic review of interventions for caregiver distress: Recommendations for future research. *The Gerontologist* 33(2): 240–248.

Koch, T. (1990) *Mirrored Lives; Aging Children and Elderly Parents*. New York: Praeger.

Land, H. (1991) The confused boundaries of community care. In G. Gabe, M. Colman and M. Bury (eds), *The Sociology of the Health Services* (pp. 203–221). London: Routledge.

Landeen, J., Byrne, C. and Brown, B. (1992) Journal-keeping as an educational strategy in teaching psychiatric nursing. *Journal of Advanced Nursing* 17(3): 347–355.

Ledoux, D. (1993) *Turning Memories into Memoirs: A Handbook for Writing Life Stories*. Lisbon Falls, MA: Soleil Press.

LeNavenec, C. (1988) *The Care Process with Dementia Patients*. Calgary, AB: University of Calgary, Department of Communications Media.

—— (1991) Creating healthy partnerships, mental health professionals and families: The use of 'circular questions' as an interviewing strategy. Paper presented at the British Sociological Association Conference on 'Health and Society', University of Manchester (March).

—— (1993) The illness career of families experiencing dementia: Predominate phases and styles of managing. Unpublished doctoral dissertation, Graduate Department of Sociology, University of Toronto, Toronto, Canada.

—— (1995) The effectiveness of music programs/therapy for people with dementia and their families: A research update. Paper presented at the Eleventh International Conference of Alzheimer's Disease and Related Disorders, Buenos Aires, Argentina (September).

—— and Vonhof, T. (1996) *One Day at a Time: How Families Manage the Experience of Dementia*. New York: Greenwood Publishing Group (Auburn).

Lipson-Parra, H. (1990) Development and validation of the Adult Attachment Scale: Assessing attachment in elderly adults. *Issues in Mental Health Nursing* 11: 79–92.

Lyman, K. (1988) Bringing the social back in: A critique of the biomedicalization of dementia. *The Gerontologist* 29(5): 597–605.

McCormack, P.M. (1976) Look closer (Crabbit old woman). *Journal of Gerontological Nursing* 2: 9.

McGoldrick, M. and Gerson, R. (1985) *Genograms in Family Assessment*. New York: W.W. Norton.

McKee, K.J., Whittick, J.E., Ballinger, B.B., Gilhooly, M.M., Gordon, D.S., Mutch, W.J. and Philp, I. (forthcoming) Coping in family supporters of elderly people with dementia. *British Journal of Clinical Psychology*.

Manen, M. van (1990) *Researching Lived Experience*. London, ONT: Althouse.

Merriam, S.B. and Clark, M.C. (1991) *Lifelines: Patterns of Work, Love, and Learning in Adulthood*. San Francisco: Jossey-Bass.

Miesen, B.M. (1993) Alzheimer's disease, the phenomenon of parent fixation, and Bowlby's attachment theory. *International Journal of Geriatric Psychiatry* 8: 147–153.

Mishel, M. and Braden, C. (1988) Finding meaning. *Nursing Research* 37(2): 98–103, 127.

Neimeyer, G.J. (ed.) (1993) *Constructivist Assessment: A Casebook*. Newbury Park, CA: Sage.

Norbeck, J., Lindsey, A. and Carrieri, V. (1983) Further development of the Norbeck social support questionnaire. *Nursing Research* 32(1): 4–9.

Orona, C.J. (1990) Temporality and identity loss due to Alzheimer's disease. *Social Science and Medicine* 30(11): 1247–1256.

Pagel, M., Erdly, W. and Becker, J. (1987) Social networks: We get by with (and in spite of) a little help from our friends. *Journal of Personality and Social Psychology* 53(4): 793–804.

Parkes, C.M., Stevenson-Hinde, J., and Morris, P. (eds) (1991) *Attachment Across the Life Cycle*. London: Routledge.

Pietruckowicz, M.E. and Johnston, M.M. (1991) Using life histories to individualize nursing home staff attitudes toward residents. *The Gerontologist* 31(1): 102–106.

Qureshi, M. and Walker, A. (1989) *The Caring Relationship: Elderly People and Their Families*. New York: Macmillan.

Rader, J. and Tornquist, E.M. (eds) (1995) *Individualized Dementia Care: Creative, Compassionate Approaches*. New York: Springer.

Radley, A. (1988) Social context and illness experience. In G. Duru, R. Engelbrecht, C. Flagle and W. Van Eimeren (eds), *System Science in Health Care* (vol. 3, pp. 167–169). Paris: Masson.

Reiss, D. (1981) *The Family's Construction of Reality*. Cambridge, MA: Harvard University Press.

—— Gonzales, Z. and Kramer, N. (1986) Family process, chronic illness, and death: On the weakness of strong bonds. *Archives of General Psychiatry* 43: 795–804.

Rogers, C.R. (1980) *A Way of Being*. Boston: Houghton Mifflin.

Rolland, J.S. (1987) Chronic illness and the life cycle: A conceptual framework. *Family Process* 26: 203–221.

Sacks, O. (1985) *The Man Who Mistook his Wife for a Hat and Other Clinical Tales*. New York: Summit Books.

Schroots, J.J. and Ten Kate, C.A. (1989) Metaphors, aging, and the lifeline interview method. *Current Perspectives on Aging and the Life Cycle* 3: 281–289.

Sedlak, C.A. (1992) Use of clinical logs by beginning nursing students and faculty to identify learning needs. *Journal of Nursing Education* 31(1): 24–28.

Shulman, M.D. and Mandel, E. (1988) Communication training of relatives and friends of institutionalized elderly persons. *The Gerontologist* 28(6): 797–799.

Stainton, C. (1985) Origins of attachment: Culture and cue sensitivity. Unpublished doctoral dissertation, Dept. of Family Health Care Nursing, University of California, San Francisco.

Tomm, K. (1988) Interventive interviewing: Part III. Intending to ask lineal, circular, strategic, or reflexive questions. *Family Process* 27(1): 1–15.

Vitaliano, P., Becker, J., Ruso, J., Magona-Amato, A. and Maiuro, R. (1988–1989) Expressed emotion in spouse care-givers of patients with Alzheimer's disease. *The Journal of Applied Social Sciences* 13(1): 215–250.

Wagenaar, T.C. (1984) Using student journals in sociology courses. *Teaching Sociology* 11: 419–437.

West, M.L. and Sheldon-Keller, A.E. (1994) *Patterns of Relating: An Adult Attachment Perspective*. New York: Guilford.

Woog, P. (ed.) (1991) *The Chronic Illness Trajectory Framework: The Corbin and Strauss Nursing Model*. New York: Springer.

Wright, L. and Leahey, M. (1987) *Families and Chronic Illness*. Springhouse, PE: Springhouse.

—— and —— (1994) *Nurses and Families* (2nd edn). Philadelphia: F.A. Davis.
Yin, R.K. (1990) *Case Study Research* (2nd edn). Beverly Hills: Sage.

Chapter 15

Carer support groups
Change mechanisms and preventive effects

Pim Cuijpers, Clemens Hosman and Joep Munnichs

SUMMARY

One of the most important forms of aid and support for care-givers of dementia patients is the support group. Since their first introduction in the late 1970s these groups have become one of the main instruments of health care to support care-givers, to relieve their burden and to prevent the development of psychological problems. Although the support group is a widely spread method of supporting care-givers, little is known about its effects. The aim of this chapter is to discuss what is presently known about the effects and the way these effects are accomplished (change mechanisms). First, the method of the support group is discussed, what it is, what its aims are, the contents of the meetings and the themes that are discussed. Second, a review of the international literature about the effects of the group is presented. The third part of this chapter contains the report of a research project among participants of Dutch support groups in which the change mechanisms of the groups were examined.

INTRODUCTION

Caring for a dementia patient at home can become a heavy burden for the care-giver. Usually there is one person who bears responsibility for the care. This primary care-giver, usually the partner or a daughter, is confronted with many possible behavioural problems which result from the mental deterioration of the elderly, such as aggression, sleeping problems, wandering and mistrust. At the same time they are experiencing a grieving process for the deterioration of the personality of their partner or parent and the change in their relationship. Furthermore, the caring takes a lot of time and social contacts diminish substantially. Therefore it is not surprising that care-givers have an increased risk of developing serious mental problems. Depression, deteriorating health, chronic fatigue and isolation are common problems among care-givers (Pratt *et al.*, 1985; Ory *et al.*, 1985; Silliman and Sternberg, 1988; Duijnstee, 1992).

Because of the expected large increase in the number of dementia patients in the Western world in the next decades, it is of great importance to develop methods to assist these care-givers. One of the most important forms of aid and support for care-givers is the support group.

SUPPORT GROUPS: THEIR AIMS AND THE METHODS USED

Interventions aimed at care-givers generally have three objectives:

1 To relieve the burden of care-givers, to prevent deterioration of the burden and the development of psychological problems, or to improve health and well-being.
2 To improve the quality of care for the dementia patient.
3 To prevent institutionalization of the dementia patient in a nursing home.

In support groups the first objective is usually the most central. The groups are based on the idea that care-givers run an increased risk of developing psychosocial problems, and they are aimed at preventing these problems. Often organizers hope that by decreasing carer burden through running the support group the quality of care will be improved and that any move may be delayed. But these are always secondary goals. Interestingly, some research has examined the effects of the support group on institutionalization and these studies have shown that support groups result in no or only minimal delay. This research is examined in detail below.

Sometimes the first objective can be contradictory to the other ones. It often happens, for example, that a partner who is caring for a demented patient for years is very determined to go on caring even though he or she is at great risk of becoming severely overburdened. In such a situation plans for institutionalization are sometimes stimulated in the support group and the care-giver is helped to accept the loss. Clearly, in such a case, institutionalization is not prevented but stimulated.

Toseland and Rossiter did an extensive literature search in several computerized data bases to review the literature of support groups of care-givers of the frail elderly (1989). In a recent study (Cuijpers, 1993) we added to this review the evaluative publications about support groups that have appeared since then. This review will be discussed in detail later, in the section about the effects of the support groups. Here only the format and design of the groups in the publications are discussed.

We found that most support groups consist of several components, which are all meant to relieve the burden of the participating care-givers:

• care-givers receive information about dementia and professional help they can call on;

- they can exchange personal experiences and emotions;
- they receive understanding, support and confirmation;
- they receive advice (from each other and from the group leaders) on how to handle the problematic situations they encounter.

Most support groups are very similar as far as design, target group, and method are concerned. A typical support group consists of six to ten weekly sessions. Sometimes a booster-session is organized after two months. In each group six to twelve partners, children and other care-givers participate. Sometimes separate groups for partners or children are organized. Participants have read about the group in one of the local papers or are referred by their family doctors or another professional. Sometimes groups are organized by day-care centres or nursing homes and are only meant for family members of their own patients. Often the programme is not fixed, and participants can decide which subjects are and which are not discussed. In many groups each session consists of three parts. First, the participants talk about events that have happened since the last session. Second, the subject of that session is considered, usually in a lecture by one of the group leaders. And third, the personal experiences of the participants, relevant to the subject, are discussed.

Participants are not viewed as 'patients', or as people who need professional help for themselves, in support groups. This is an important difference from group psychotherapy. Care-givers, who join a support group are 'normal' people, but who may have an increased risk of becoming overburdened and developing serious psychological or psychiatric problems.

CENTRAL THEMES

Toseland and Rossiter (1989) in their review found seven central themes that form the basis of the interaction in most support groups.

1 *Information about dementia.* In the groups care-givers receive information about the stages of the dementia process, the effects of the disease, the behaviour of the patient during each phase, and what the care-giver might expect to happen as the disease progresses.
2 *Development of the group as a support system.* Participants are encouraged to use the group as a source of support. Participants are stimulated to exchange experiences and emotions, to empathize with each other's situations, and to maintain contact outside the group.
3 *The emotional impact of care-giving.* Expressing and learning to cope with the emotions that accompany care-giving is the third major theme of the support group. Emotions that are talked about include anger at the situation, at other family members, at professional helpers, feelings of guilt, loneliness and isolation, and anxiety.

4 *Self-care.* Participants are encouraged by the group leaders to schedule time for themselves to relax and to socialize. Difficulties like a lack of support from other family members, or objections to professional help, and ways to solve these problems are discussed.

5 *Improving interpersonal relations and communications.* In the groups participants are helped to cope with and reduce interpersonal conflicts with the patient and with other family members. The groups also help care-givers to consider ways to balance care-giving and other family roles.

6 *The development of a support system outside the group.* Group members receive information about the community agencies they can turn to for concrete assistance. In addition they are stimulated to develop informal supports, by trying to increase the involvement of other family members and friends.

7 *The improvement of home care skills.* This theme, which is a less frequent one, is about topics such as lifting, transferring, bathing, and administering medication.

A REVIEW OF THE LITERATURE ON SUPPORT GROUPS

From the literature review of Toseland and Rossiter (1989) and Cuijpers (1993) we can conclude that in general the evaluative literature about support groups consists of two parts. First, there are many reports of groups in practice, which are evaluated but which have not used an experimental or quasi-experimental design. Second, there are studies with a quasi-experimental or experimental design. These two parts of the literature parallel a historical development. The practice reports came out especially in the first years after the appearance of support groups in the late 1970s in the United States. Mostly they describe the first experiences of groups in practice. The (quasi-)experimental studies mostly appeared in the second half of the 1980s when the method of the support group had become more or less established and questions were being asked about the 'objective' effects of the groups.

Practice reports

In most practice reports it is concluded that participants evaluate the groups very positively (Clark and Rakowski, 1983; Gallagher, 1985). They see the groups as informative, useful and meaningful, and several reports mention active participation, a low drop-out rate, spontaneous positive remarks about the groups and a need to continue meeting other group members after the end of the group (Glosser and Wexler, 1985; Silverman *et al.*, 1977).

Several components of the groups are described as helpful elements. Steuer and Clark (1982) report that first of all the chance to express experiences and emotions is an important support for the participants. Glosser and Wexler (1985) report that because of the sharing of experiences participants learn to deal better with the problems they encounter. Information about dementia increases the understanding of the behaviour of the patient and enables carers to find practical solutions for all kinds of everyday problems (Lazarus et al., 1981; Simank and Strickland, 1986). Other authors report that the support groups often develop into a new network of social support (Reever, 1984; Kapust and Weintraub, 1984).

Because people who receive help are usually inclined to evaluate this help positively, the relation between these positive evaluations and objective effects are doubtful. Perhaps these results can better be seen as a sign of enthusiasm for a new area of assistance to care-givers.

Controlled studies

Three quasi-experimental studies which examined the effects of support groups were found (Kahan et al., 1985; Dellasega, 1990; Greene and Monahan, 1989). In these studies a control group was used, but participants were not divided at random between the experimental and the control group. In the five experimental studies that were carried out, both a control group and a random division were used (Haley et al., 1987; Montgomery and Borgatta, 1989; Zarit et al., 1987; Toseland et al., 1989, 1990; and Lovett and Gallagher, 1988). It is difficult to compare the results of these studies for several reasons. In some groups participants were care-givers of dementia patients, in others care-givers of the frail elderly in general. In some groups participants were screened for the presence of serious stress, in others all care-givers could join. Besides, there were important differences in content and working method among the support groups and there was little correspondence between the instruments used to measure improvement. Despite these problems some general conclusions can be drawn.

It was striking that in only one study was an explicit theoretical framework used. Gallagher and her colleagues (1989; Lovett and Gallagher, 1988) based their interventions on Bandura's self-efficacy theory (Bandura, 1977, 1982).

Only three out of eight studies showed significant improvements (in levels of depression, well-being and stress). No improvement was found in all other characteristics in the eight studies. A re-analysis of the data of one of the studies (Zarit et al., 1987; Whitlach et al., 1991), showed that many participants do not feel seriously burdened or depressed and that they only participate in groups to improve their care-giving skills. Extensive effects should not be expected in these care-givers. This study also showed that positive effects are experienced by participants who do feel burdened and depressed. This is confirmed by three studies in which the care-givers have to have experienced a serious amount of stress before they can participate in the support group (Toseland *et al.*, 1989; Toseland and Labrecque, 1989; Lovett and Gallagher, 1988; Greene and Monahan, 1989); these three studies are also the ones in which some effects on depression, well-being and burden are found.

Besides the effects on seriously burdened and depressed participants, the studies also show positive effects on more specific changes in the behaviour of the care-givers, the problems experienced by participants, the received social support and the coping behaviour. In one study for example (Haley *et al.*, 1987) an increase in behaviours that were labelled in advance as adequate, was found. Another study showed that the number of problems experienced with caring considerably decreased in participants compared with care-givers in the control group (Toseland *et al.*, 1989; Toseland and Labrecque, 1989). The same study showed that participants widened their social network. Gallagher and her collegues found that the self-efficacy of participants increased (Gallagher *et al.*, 1989; Lovett and Gallagher, 1988).

Only in two studies were long-term measurements carried out (Greene and Monahan, 1989; Toseland *et al.*, 1989; Toseland and Labrecque, 1989). It appeared that the short-term effects that were found, continued to exist in the long term, although their strength had decreased.

Effects on institutionalization

Although support groups are not in the first place aimed at dementia patients, in three (quasi-)experimental studies the effects of support groups on institutionalization of the dementia patient are examined. In two studies (Brodaty and Gresham, 1989; Greene and Monahan, 1987) a small delay in hospitalization was found. In the third study (Montgomery and Borgatta, 1989) a small delay was found when the carer was a child of the patient, but when the carer was the partner of the patient hospitalization took place sooner.

From these studies no definite conclusions can be drawn about the ability of support groups to delay institutionalization. One could wonder however, as both Brodaty and Gresham, and Montgomery and colleagues do, if delay of institutionalization should always be aimed at. As we mentioned before, caring for too long can mean a serious threat to the health of the care-giver, and early institutionalization, especially when the care-givers were partners, can often be seen as an adequate use of available community resources.

A STUDY ON CHANGE MECHANISMS AND EFFECTS OF SUPPORT GROUPS

Introduction

All nine experimental and quasi-experimental studies mentioned above concentrated on the question of whether the groups have any effect at all on felt burden, health and well-being of the participants. How the effects are realized, and what circumstances have any influence, has hardly been investigated. Recently we carried out research among 110 participants of 21 support groups in The Netherlands. In this research we investigated the change mechanisms of support groups and the circumstances that determine whether participation has a positive effect on the burden of carers or no effect at all (Cuijpers, 1993).

Theoretical framework

Lazarus' stress and coping theory is taken as a theoretical model (Lazarus and Folkman, 1984; Lazarus, 1981). Several authors emphasize that this theory is very useful in understanding the way support groups work (Gallagher, 1985; Zarit, 1990; Gottlieb, 1987). The theory states that people are continually appraising the events that happen around them, to see what effects they have on their own well-being. When an event is appraised as threatening for his or her well-being, the individual appraises what sources of help or support are available that can help to ward off the threat. If he or she thinks the sources of help are not sufficient, there is stress or burden. The attempts that are taken to handle the threatening event are in this theory the coping actions. The support group is in this theoretical model one of the sources of help that are available to the care-giver. The change mechanisms of the support group influence the appraisal, the coping and the resulting stress. The model is represented in Figure 15.1.

Methods

The research consisted of a quantitative and a qualitative part. In the quantitative part, 110 participants (of 21 support groups from the south and middle of The Netherlands), filled in a questionnaire before the groups started, immediately after the end of the group and six months later. Eighteen participants dropped out. In the questionnaire the most important parts of the theoretical model were measured – the level of stress (an adaptation of the Burden Interview from Zarit *et al.*, 1980); health (General Health Questionnaire, Goldberg, 1978); social support (developed by van Sonderen, 1991, in The Netherlands); the stage of dementia (FAST,

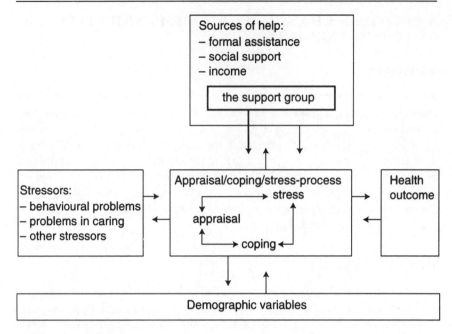

Figure 15.1 Support groups in the stress and coping theory from Lazarus, 1981

Reisberg, 1988); behavioural problems (developed by Lamers *et al.*, 1990); the expectations of participants and change mechanisms (adapted from Haley *et al.*, 1987). Most instruments had been validated in The Netherlands and were sufficiently reliable.

Three clusters of participants

A cluster analysis showed that there were three sub-groups of participants:

1 Participants who feel little or no burden, who are healthy mentally and who mainly participate to receive information. Most participants from this cluster are adult children and some are partners.
2 Participants (mostly daughters of dementia patients) who do feel burdened and who participate mainly to learn how to handle problems in caring.
3 Partners of dementia patients who feel severely burdened, who have to cope with the most serious behavioural problems and who often already receive professional help (counselling).

The mental health of carers

The General Health Questionnaire (GHQ) (Goldberg, 1978; Koeter and Ormel, 1991) made it possible to compare the mental health of participants with the mental health of the 'average' Dutch population. The number of potential 'psychiatric cases' among participants (57 per cent with men and 58 per cent with women) is considerably higher than in the average population (36 per cent with men and 41 per cent with women) and are comparable to the patients visiting a general practitioner.

Perceived burden

The scores on the burden questionnaire, the GHQ and the scores on the social support questionnaire, were compared at baseline and after the end of the group. Although, ideally, an improvement would have been expected, none was found. T-tests showed that the scores on the GHQ even got somewhat worse ($p < .05$). One explanation could be that the support groups prevented a deterioration rather than facilitated an improvement in the health of the participants. This possible preventive effect could only be tested with an experimental research design in which participants could be compared with care-givers who did not participate. This was not possible in our design. But there were indications that normally the burden increases as the duration and phase of the dementia increase.

Another possible explanation for not finding any general improvement is that improvements only occur in certain categories of participants. Table 15.1 shows the percentage of participants who improve or remain equal on the three important scales (two sub-scales are derived from the Dutch burden/stress interview). It can be seen that a considerable number of participants do improve or seem able to stabilize their well-being.

Who benefits most

In order to find out whether there were any categories of participants who benefited by participation more than others, a criterion for successful outcome was developed. It was decided that a care-giver had successfully participated if his score improved on at least two of the three scales

Table 15.1 The number of participants who improved on two of three scales (two sub-scales of the Dutch burden/stress interview and the GHQ) in the short term or in the long term

	M1–M2	M1–M3
– Consequences of the care for the personal life of the care-giver (burden/stress interview)	57.3%	49.3%
– Contentment with one's own role as care-giver (burden/stress interview)	57.5%	60.3%
– GHQ–28	52.7%	61.3%

mentioned in Table 15.1, between the first measurement (before the group started) and the second (immediately after the end) or the third (six months later). Of the care-givers 41 per cent participated successfully in the short term as well as in the long term, whereas 29 per cent participated unsuccessfully, neither improving in the short nor in the long term. Hence it can be estimated roughly that in more than two thirds of the participants improvements can be observed (in important determinants of health) in the short term, in the long term, or in both.

With T-tests and χ^2-analyses it was examined whether significant relations could be found between successful participation and the most important elements of the theoretical model. Five categories of care-givers were found among whom the number of successful participants was significantly higher. In Table 15.2 the division of these categories over successful/unsuccessful participation are described. The five categories are:

1 Care-givers who are *severely burdened* (they are less content with their role as care-giver; one of the sub-scales of the Dutch burden/stress interview). This finding corresponds with the findings of Whitlach *et al.* (1991).
2 Care-givers who have a *paid job*. Possibly the support group takes away or diminishes a feeling of guilt that results from the idea that the care-giver does not spend enough time and attention on the elderly because of the job.
3 Care-givers who care for a *demented patient who lives in an old people's home* (the number of care-givers is small: N=11).
4 Care-givers who care for elderly who are *more apathetic* (measured by the behavioural problems list; Lamers *et al.*, 1990).
5 Participants in support groups which *charge small fees* (between $5 and $20). Close examination showed that support groups for which a contribution has to be paid attract a different population of care-givers than groups which are free. In groups for which a fee is paid, more 'partners' and people who care for elderly in the later stages of dementia participate. They feel more burdened (the consequences of care for the personal life of the care-giver; one of the subscales of the Dutch burden/stress interview), and they are more depressed.

Next it was examined whether differences in successful group participation could be found between the three categories resulting from the cluster analysis. It was found that, long term, the percentage of successful participants was the lowest in the category of care-givers who did not feel heavily burdened, and were mentally healthy (47 per cent). The highest successful participation was found in the categories of moderately and heavily burdened care-givers (respectively 65 per cent and 62 per cent) though these differences did not quite reach significance.

Table 15.2 Successful outcome of support groups in five sub-categories of participants

	N	Success In short term	In long term	Short + long term
Job				
no job	66	45%	49%	33%
job	18	72%	82%	65%
		p < .04	p < .01	p < .056
Accommodation of the elderly				
at home	73	45%	51%	35%
residential home	11	82%	71%	71%
		p < .02	p < .01	(N too small)
Costs				
free	43	44%	33%	25%
participation fee	43	51%	66%	49%
		n.s.	p < .005	p < .02
Apathetic behaviour of the elderly*				
	43	31.1	33.6	33.1
	(39)	(32.5)	(28.8)	(31.3)
		n.s.	p < .004	p < .02
Dissatisfaction about care-givers' role*				
	43	23.9	24.5	24.9
	(43)	(21.4)	(21.6)	(21.0)
		p < .04	p < .03	n.s.

Note:* The means of care-givers for whom participation was not successful are in brackets

QUALITATIVE RESULTS AND DISCUSSION

Extensive semi-structured interviews were held, with eleven participants of three support groups before the start of the group, immediately after the end, and six months later. The interviews were tape-recorded and transcribed verbatim. The interviews concentrated on the problems of the care-giver and the influences they felt the support group had had on these problems. For each participant a survey was carried out about the problems experienced by them; the content of the support group; and the effects of the support group on their appraisal and coping processes and the stress/burden experienced. On the basis of these overviews, four helpful elements of the groups were identified.

1 *Informative support*: participants receive information about dementia and community agencies they can turn to for practical assistance. Furthermore they can broaden their view of their own situation by comparing it with the situation of other care-givers.
2 *Counselling support*: participants are advised about how to handle problematic situations they have to deal with.
3 *Normative support*: in the support group the participants are 'morally' supported by confirmation of the rightness of choices made and acts performed;
4 *Emotional support*: in the groups participants can talk about their problems and emotions and they are listened to by people who know what caring means. Furthermore the group affords the opportunity to build up new social contacts.

It was striking that these components were mentioned by practically all respondents.

Next, the effects on coping which the participants experienced as a result of these four components were examined. It was found in practically all participants that the four helpful elements changed the way they appraised and coped with their situation. First, participants got a better understanding of their own situation which reduced their feelings of uncertainty. This reassurance increased their self-confidence and they were more prepared for the changes which could be expected in the future. Second, coping methods were discussed; those which are useful and efficient, those which are not, and those which are worthwhile trying. This resulted in a decrease of conflicts and irritations, and an increase in solutions for practical problems. Furthermore participants got a better view of the available professional help. In the third place participants reported that they could bear the caring better emotionally; they could face and accept the changes more readily. They also felt that they were not the only ones with these problems. They were listened to with compassion and were not alone any more; they could talk freely about their situation.

The participants described the four components and the experience of being in a group concretely and clearly. Therefore it can be assumed that these helping elements and effects are not just the result of an inclination to evaluate accepted help positively.

CONCLUSION – LESSONS FOR FUTURE RESEARCH INTO SUPPORT GROUPS

Since their first introduction in the late 1970s, support groups for care-givers of dementia patients have acquired a secure place within the professional help available for this population. They can be used as a valuable preventive method for combating stress and deterioration in mental health. With quantitative research the effects of these groups have not yet been firmly established. However, qualitative research convincingly shows that support groups offer care-givers several relevant forms of support. Care-givers experience significant positive effects on coping. Participants gained a better view of their situation, learned to use new and more efficient ways of coping with their situation and to handle the care situation better emotionally. The limited overall effects of the quantitative research results probably arise from the fact that certain categories of participants benefit more from participation than others. Indications can be found, both in the literature and in our own research, that those care-givers in particular who feel heavily burdened find benefit in a support group. But other categories also, such as those who care for dementia patients in residential settings, can also benefit from participation.

For the time being it can be loosely concluded that support groups are probably an effective way of supporting and helping care-givers to cope with their situation. This conclusion should be validated with more quantitative research, on specific sub-groups of participants.

In addition, the evidence stresses the need to develop support group methods further. Several possible improvements which are both suggested by the literature and by our own research, are worth examining – for example, extending the length of the support groups from eight to ten meetings, or longer, possibly even throughout the time that the care-giver provides care. It is unrealistic to suppose that the need for support has been met completely after eight weekly meetings. Several researchers (Haley et al., 1987; Zarit, 1990) suggest that one of the reasons for not finding any 'objective' effects is the limited number of meetings. Research should determine whether long-term groups or monthly 'boosters' would result in an additional increase in these 'objective' effects.

Insight into the different needs of the care-givers and in the preventive mechanisms of support groups, could be used to improve the 'fit' between the support needed and the actual types of support offered. Furthermore, better criteria must be developed to identify those care-givers who are especially at risk of developing emotional problems and who could benefit most from support groups.

Lastly, several possible improvements in the educational programmes of support groups should be considered more extensively. Haley et al. (1987) and Dellasega (1990), for example, have used stress-management techniques in their groups. Gallagher and her colleagues (1989; Lovett and Gallagher, 1988) have developed a 'coping-with-depression' course for depressed care-givers, and a 'coping-with-anger' course for angry ones. These groups are especially interesting because positive effects were shown in experimental research.

These and other variations in the design of the support group make it clear that the definitive and most efficient form of this preventive intervention has not yet been established. This is underscored by the absence of 'objective' effects. Renewal, further development and ongoing evaluation of the method is therefore strongly needed.

REFERENCES

Bandura, A. (1977) Self-efficacy: Toward a unifying theory of behavioral change. *Psychological Review* (2): 191–215.
—— (1982) Self-efficacy mechanism in human agency. *American Psychologist*, February, 37 (2): 122–147.
Brodaty, H. and Gresham, M. (1989) Effect of a training programme to reduce stress in carers of patients with dementia. *British Medical Journal* 299: 1375–1379.
Clark, N.M. and Rakowski, W. (1983) Family caregivers of older adults: Improving helping skills. *The Gerontologist*, 23 (6): 637–642.
Cuijpers, P. (1993) De werking van ondersteuningsgroepen voor centrale verzorgers van dementerende ouderen. Thesis, Nijmegen: Katholieke Universiteit, Vakgroep Psychogerontologie. ('The working of support groups for caregivers of the demented elderly').
Dellasega, C. (1990) Coping with caregiving; stress management for caregivers of the elderly. *Journal of Psychosocial Nursing* 28 (1): 15–22.
Duijnstee, M. (1992) De belasting van familieleden van dementerenden. Nijkerk: Intro.
Gallagher, D.E. (1985) Intervention strategies to assist caregivers of frail elders; current research and future research directions. *Annual Review of Gerontology and Geriatrics* 5: 249–282.
——, Lovett, S. and Zeiss, A. (1989) Interventions with caregivers of frail elderly persons. In: M. Ory and K. Bond (eds), *Aging and Health Care: Social Science and Policy Perspectives*. London: Routledge.
Glosser, G. and Wexler, D. (1985) Participants' evaluation of educational/support groups for families of patients with Alzheimer's disease. *The Gerontologist* 25 (3): 232–236.
Goldberg, D. (1978) *Manual of the General Health Questionnaire*. NFER Publishing Company.
Gottlieb, B.H. (1987) Using social support to protect and promote health. *Journal of Primary Prevention* 8 (1 and 2): 49–70.
Greene, V.L. and Monahan, D.J. (1987) The effect of a professionally guided caregiver support and education group on institutionalization of care receivers. *The Gerontologist* 27 (6) 716–721.
—— and —— (1989) The effect of a support and education program on stress and burden among families. *The Gerontologist* 29 (4): 472–477.
Haley, W.E., Brown, S.L. and Levine, E.G. (1987) Experimental evaluation of the effectiveness of group intervention for dementia caregivers. *The Gerontologist* 27 (3) 376–382.
Kahan, J., Kemp, B., Staples, F.R., et al. (1985) Decreasing the burden in families caring for a relative with a dementing illness; A controlled study. *Journal of the American Geriatrics Society* 33 (10): 664–670.
Kapust, L.R. and Weintraub, S. (1984) Living with a family member suffering from Alzheimer's Disease. In: H.B. Roback (ed.), *Helping Patients and Their Families Cope with Medical Problems*. San Francisco: Jossey-Bass.
Koeter, M.W.J. and Ormel, J. (1991) *General Health Questionnaire; Nederlandse bewerking en handleiding*. Lisse: Swets en Zeitlinger.
Lamers, C., Muskens, J. and Hogeling, J. (1990) De dementerende ouderen. In:

M.J.F.J. Vernooy-Dassen and J.M.G. Persoon, *Het thuismilieu van dementerende ouderen*. Nijmegen: Instituut voor Sociale Geneeskunde, Katholieke Universiteit, Nijmegen.

Lazarus, R.S. (1981) Stress und Stressbewaltigung – Ein Paradigma. In: S.H. Filipp (ed.), *Kritische Lebensereignisse*: Munchen: Urban and Schwarzenberg.

—— and Folkman, S. (1984) *Stress, Appraisal and Coping*. New York: Springer Publishing Company.

——, Stafford, B., Cooper, K., *et al.* (1981) A pilot study of an Alzheimer patients' relatives discussion group. *The Gerontologist* 21 (4): 353–358.

Lovett S. and Gallagher, D. (1988) Psychoeducational interventions for family caregivers: Preliminary efficacy data. *Behaviour Therapy* 19: 321–330.

Montgomery, R.J.V. and Borgatta, E.F. (1989) The effects of alternative support strategies on family caregiving. *The Gerontologist* 29 (4): 457–464.

Ory, M.G., Williams, T.F., Emr, M., *et al.* (1985) Families, informal supports, and Alzheimer's disease; current research and future agendas. *Research on Aging* 7 (4): 623–644.

Pratt, C.C., Schmall, V.L., Wright, S. and Cleland, M. (1985) Burden and coping strategies of caregivers to Alzheimer's patients. *Family Relations* 27–33.

Reever, K.E. (1984) Self-help groups for caregivers coping with Alzheimer's disease: The ACMA model. *Pride Institute Journal of Long-Term Health Care* (3): 23–30.

Reisberg, B. (1988) Functional assessment scale (FAST). *Psychopharmacological Bulletin* 24 (4): 653–659.

Silliman, R.A. and Sternberg, J. (1988) Family caregiving: Impact of patient functioning and underlying causes of dependency. *The Gerontologist* 28 (3): 377–382.

Silverman, A.G., Kahn, B.H. and Anderson, G. (1977) A model for working with multigenerational families. *Social Casework* 131–135.

Simank, M.H. and Strickland, K.J. (1986) Assisting families in coping with Alzheimer's disease and other related dementias. In: R. Dobrof (ed.)., *Social Work and Alzheimer's Disease*, New York: The Haworth Press.

Sonderen, E. van (1991) *Het meten van sociale steun*. Groningen: Rijksuniversiteit, academisch proefschrift.

Steuer, J.L. and Clark, E.O. (1982) Family support groups within a research project on dementia. *Clinical Gerontologist* 1 (1): 87–95.

Toseland, R.W. and Labrecque, M.S. (1989) Evaluating the efficacy of psychosocial interventions for caregivers. New Orleans: Paper presented at the American Psychological Association Meeting.

Toseland R.W. and Rossiter C.M. (1989) Group interventions to support family caregivers: A review and analysis. *The Gerontologist* 29 (4): 438–448.

Toseland, R.W., Rossiter, C.M. and Labrecque, M.S. (1989) The effectiveness of three group intervention strategies to support family caregivers. *American Journal of Orthopsychiatry* 59 (3) (July): 420–429.

Toseland, R.W., Rossiter C.M., Peak, T. and Smith, G.C. (1990) Comparative effectiveness of individual and group interventions to support caregivers. *Social Work* 35 (May): 209–217.

Whitlach, C.J., Zarit, S.H. and Eye, A., von (1991) Efficacy of interventions with caregivers: a reanalysis. *The Gerontologist* 31 (1): 9–14.

Zarit, S.H. (1990) Interventions with frail elders and their families: Are they effective and why? In: M.A.P. Stephens, J.H. Crowther, Hobfoll, *et al.*, *Stress and Coping in Later Life Families*. Washington.

——, Anthony, C.R. and Boutselis, M. (1987) Interventions with caregivers of dementia patients: Comparison of two approaches. *Psychology and Aging* 2 (3): 225–232.

——, Reever, K.E. and Bach-Peterson, J. (1980) Relatives of the impaired elderly: Correlates of feelings of burden. *The Gerontologist* 20 (6): 649–655.

Chapter 16

Behind the facts

An insight into the burden on family carers of dementia patients

Marco Blom and Mia Duijnstee

'No wind favours the ship with no port of destination.'

(Norwegian saying)

INTRODUCTION

Most of the dementing elderly live at home (NRV, 1993). Those no longer able to organize their own affairs are consequently dependent on the care provided by others. It is usually the family, for which read 'partner' or 'daughter', who provides this care – sometimes for many years and seven days a week. Whereas in the past professional help was focused mainly on the patient, now it is essential that the scope of support is widened to include the family, and that this support will have to take account of the dual position of these family members (Duijnstee, 1991): in other words, care professionals will be asked to develop not only a co-operative relationship with a family carer, but also a supportive one (Duijnstee, 1994a).

Dementia has been described as 'the illness of those that are forced to look on' (Buijssen and Razenberg, 1987). Others have referred to the family members of dementia patients as the 'hidden victims' (Zarit *et al.*, 1985) or as the 'prisoners of love' (Barnes *et al.*, 1981), working what Mace and Rabins (1991) called a '36-hour day'. As early as 1969, Golodetz *et al.* had described the problem for caring family members in language that still applies today:

> She is not trained for her job, a priori. She may have little choice about doing the job. She belongs to no union or guild, works no fixed maximum of hours. She lacks formal compensation, job advancement and even the possibility of being fired. She has no job mobility. In her work situation, she has a heavy emotional load, but she has no colleagues or supervisor or education to help her handle this. Her own life and needs compete constantly with her work requirements. She may be limited in her performance by her own ailments. . . .

By likening a family carer's task to a paid job, at least part of the problem is illustrated – irrespective of whether the carer is a man or a woman.

BROAD SPECTRUM

Family carers encounter a broad spectrum of problems. It often appears that the burden of family carers is limited to only part of the problem. Studies have been concerned, for instance, with the functional disabilities and help needs of the dementia patient in particular, or with the social network alone. Thus, not only does much of the problem remain unexamined, but those aspects that *have* been studied continue to exert a disproportionate influence on the debate. Therefore Niederehe and Frugé (1984) have called for an integrated research approach which takes the dementia sufferer, the caring family member and the environmental variables all into account.

In research on the variability of burden on the family carers of dementia patients (Duijnstee, 1992), the design of which is described in volume 1 of this book (Jones and Miesen, 1992) this advice has been adopted. This concerned qualitative research among forty care-providing relatives. The results of this study constitute the basis of this chapter (see also Duijnstee, 1994b). To gain insight into the burden experienced by family carers the personal circumstances of all the respondents were first established according to the following categories (see also Blom and Duijnstee, 1993).

Dementia patient

In the area of disease and infirmity it is about concrete symptoms of illness, behavioural problems, and the degree to which the patient is able to care for him/herself. Questions were asked such as:

- Does the dementia patient allow help in getting washed and dressed?
- Does the dementia patient get up at night, and is there a tendency towards excessive wandering about and compulsive walking?
- Is the dementia patient able to keep him/herself occupied? How is his/her response to family and friends? Does he/she recognize the family carer?
- Is the dementia patient able to go out alone or be left at home alone? Is there a risk of falling, or unsafe behaviour?

Family carer

The physical condition of the family carer has an effect on any problems experienced in carrying out tasks for the patient. A further factor is whether there are any other demands on the carer's time. Some questions were:

- Is the family carer short of breath or less than optimally mobile?
- Does the family carer have a job or family to take care of?

Environment

Neither the dementia patient nor the family carer operate within a vacuum. In fact, there are three important factors which influence the care situation: housing, financial circumstances and help from others. These questions were put to the respondents:

- Does the patient's housing allow for effective care provision?
- To what extent is the family carer financially able to provide domestic adaptations or facilities?
- What is the response on the part of relatives and friends and do they offer assistance?
- Is a professional carer present?

The first step in the study was to carry out an objective assessment of the actual situation, that is, the burden as perceived by a bystander. This provides a first insight into the circumstances of the family carer. But this was just the beginning.

RELATIVES DIFFER

When viewing the situation objectively, we may easily assume, for example, that a family carer is going to be troubled by a situation where money is tight, or worse, if there is not enough money to buy, say, the necessary incontinence materials. Similarly, we may also be inclined to conclude that a carer who has sole responsibility is going to have a harder time than a carer who can rely on the help of others. It also appears a reasonable assumption that the task will be more of a burden to a carer with rheumatism than to one in good health. And from an outsider's viewpoint, a dementia patient who is no longer able to communicate is surely harder to cope with than one with whom some dialogue is possible.

We may sometimes be correct in these assumptions, but we should remember that different people may experience the same situation from different perspectives, and what one family carer regards as a problem may be dealt with quite easily by someone else. To gain insight into the nature of these variables, a qualitative interview method (Kvale, 1983) was used to examine how the respondents experienced their circumstances in relation to the patient, themselves and their environment. The research termed this angle of perception the subjective burden.

In short, the results show that the differences in subjective burdening of family carers is linked to differences in their methods of coping, acceptance and motivation. The positive variants of these factors appear to reduce the subjective burden. Negative forms or absence of effective methods of coping, acceptance and motivation can all increase the burden experienced by the family carer (Duijnstee, 1994b).

Rather than presenting reams of monotonous research results, we relate the story of Mrs Janssen, one of the respondents. Viewed objectively, her circumstances look pretty grim: her husband is doubly incontinent, he no longer recognizes her and he requires constant assistance. Nevertheless she has few problems with the situation. She explains how she copes as well as she does:

> *You learn how to cope. Things go fine now. Like with the incontinence; when I clean him up I put those plastic bags you get from the baker's round my hands and when I've finished, I tie them up and throw them away. You discover ways of doing things to make it easy for yourself.*
>
> *The main reason I've been able to cope is because I came to accept that it's the way it is. At first it was hard to accept things, but once you fit your own life around it, it gets better. I can't go out visiting, because I can't leave him. Of course, I'd like it to be different, but there's no point thinking like that, so I don't.*
>
> *And, of course, I do it because I love my husband, not just because it's my duty. I wouldn't want to have him looked after just so that I could do what I wanted. I'm glad I can do it all for him. I do it for love and it works out fine.*

Mrs Janssen has clearly found a way of handling the care process (coping), she has come to terms with it (acceptance), and she whole-heartedly undertakes it for her husband (motivation). In her case, various background factors are at work. In this interview fragment she refers, for instance, to the length of time she has taken care of her husband and the good relationship she has with him.

Mrs Janssen is not, of course, typical of the entire population of family carers. For every carer who does not feel particularly overburdened there are at least as many who are desperate. As well as objective unfavourable circumstances such as lack of money or chronic behavioural disorders on the part of the dementia patient, the study also shows that the subjective burden can be increased by inadequate coping mechanisms, and problems with acceptance and motivation.

INADEQUATE COPING

Aside from family members who succeed in coping and resolving problems, there are also those who remain passive or, worse still, act in such a way as to aggravate existing problems or give rise to new ones. They may, for example, continually confront the patient with his/her cognitive disorder, making that person even less self-assured and liable to make even more mistakes. Such family members often lack concrete information, or else they simply do not learn from experience.

In other cases, family members may demonstrate an inability to cope. They continually place themselves at the disposal of the patient, pass over their own needs and are unable to be objective about the situation. This often occurs among family members with an extremely caring disposition, as well as among those who are deeply attached to the patient and who 'suffer' along with them. Family carers who feel less affection for the patient find it easier to enjoy the little free time they have for themselves, and to forget, at least temporarily, about the patient. This detachment also allows the carer to act against the wishes of the patient; for example, they may call in home help for their own sake, even if the patient is opposed to the idea.

Finally, coping difficulties also arise when family members fail to anticipate problems; for example, family carers may call on neighbours for help when they know very well that they will criticize their methods, or that the neighbours will then dominate the situation and act as 'saviours'. If it is not realized that the long-term disadvantages may be greater than the initial advantages, such 'help' can create more problems than it solves.

PROBLEMS WITH ACCEPTANCE

The issue here is the degree to which the family carer is able to accept objectively unfavourable and unalterable issues. At the opposite end of the scale from the family members who take things as they come, we have those who nurse and fuel the problems. For example, they may be unable to accept the situation and be constantly angry about the patient's abnormal behaviour. Sometimes this is because they do not understand that this behaviour is part of the disease, so they blame the patient. Some family members may experience severe problems in accepting the situation because the troublesome behaviour of the patient reminds them of problematic aspects in their earlier relationship; for instance, if a dementia patient has always been demanding to start with, extreme dependency may well provoke strong reactions. The family carer is not only reacting to present behaviour but also to past behaviour. Other family carers may not yet have had time to adjust to the new situation and are still in the process of coming to terms with it. Time, for these persons, is not a great healer. And there are those who no longer realize the problems they have so they do not pay any attention any more to the restrictions inherent in the care situation.

Non-acceptance can also arise where family members fail to show consideration towards those around them, a characteristic usually linked to high expectations. For example, the fact that the only daughter currently has a child in hospital and is therefore unable to offer any help is not considered a mitigating factor. Some family carers have high expectations of the help of certain people around them. This may occur in a relationship in which the family carer has invested a great deal in the past. Sometimes these expectations are so high that the family member cannot take mitigating factors into consideration.

LACK OF MOTIVATION

By lack of motivation is meant that family carers are reluctant to carry out the tasks. They may feel that in view of the patient's behaviour in the past there is little justification for demanding care and attention now. They may feel the care they provide is out of all proportion compared to what they had ever received from the patient. Consequently, they regard the care as merely a humane obligation to which they are bound; if someone else were to come along to relieve them they would happily and immediately step aside. Other family members face motivation problems because they resent not receiving a sign of appreciation for their efforts, such as an expression of gratitude or a bunch of flowers; they work against their will and are angry at being taken for granted. These carers do not generally get much satisfaction from their tasks. On the subject of motivation, there is also the question of why care either doesn't help at all or helps less than an objective bystander would expect. This issue is linked to an incongruence between care supply and demand: professional care clashes with the needs of the family member or produces undesirable side-effects. Perhaps the carer doesn't arrive on time, doesn't get on with the patient, or (from the viewpoint of the family member) doesn't treat the patient properly. There are also family members who resent others taking their place, or who feel that there are ulterior motives, such as financial gain, involved.

THE INTERACTION BETWEEN COPING, ACCEPTANCE AND MOTIVATION

Coping, acceptance and motivation are key concepts which allow us to understand individual variation in the subjective burden of family care. They are influenced by an array of background factors such as the carer's personal character, the duration of care, the knowledge of the disease, and the nature of the previous relationship with the dementia patient. The synergy of these factors is a complex and many-sided matter in which both positive and negative effects can simultaneously influence the subjective perception of burden. This partly explains the links between coping, acceptance and motivation; sometimes they support one another, and sometimes one works against another.

Positive influences

Family carers motivated to take care of a dementia patient often find solutions to care problems effortlessly. Here, adequate coping is the result of motivation. 'Where there's a will there's a way.' In another example, a family carer may argue that the advantages conferred by his/her work confirm the choice to stay in work so that the burden of care is easier to bear.

Motivation can also arise from coping. For instance, a family member can be very proud of the success with which he/she manages the care burden. Adequate coping can reduce their subjective perception of the burden of care and indirectly increase their subjective ability to deal with it.

Links can also exist between motivation and acceptance. For instance, the family members of a dementia patient may be so keen to keep the patient at home that they more readily accept whatever situation arises from that choice. In that case they feel they ought to do it and therefore they want to do it. Motivation generates acceptance. The reverse may also be true, for example, where someone sees the care of a dementia patient as a familial duty, acceptance may generate motivation.

Coping and acceptance can also be each other's side-effects. Sometimes acceptance is part of a coping strategy: like the family carer who says 'Far better to accept the situation as it is; turning it into a problem just makes things worse.' Sometimes coping is strengthened by acceptance: for instance, accepting rather than actively resisting difficult behaviour can be a very effective way of dealing with a dementia patient.

Negative influences

Coping, acceptance and motivation can also influence each other in negative ways. Consider the case in which a dementia patient's family is strongly motivated, because of a close and happy relationship in the past, to take care of the patient. However, if this motivation is combined with the tendency not to be able to let things take their course, and if the patient resists help, then motivation can make way for non-acceptance. This non-acceptance can, in turn, lead to ineffective coping strategies; for instance, the family might constantly go against the patient's resisting behaviour, and only make the situation worse.

One factor can also overwhelm another. This can be seen in those families in which the beneficial effect that the passage of time usually has on the acceptance of functional disability is overshadowed by the special relationship which patient and carer have always had; after years of care provision, some carers still have the greatest difficulty in coming to terms with the symptoms of the patient's disability.

Lastly, background factors can have simultaneous positive and negative effects. A close relationship with a patient can encourage carers to keep on caring, but an overly close relationship can also put up a barricade in another area. Family members then want to do everything possible for the patient themselves and end up monopolizing care provision, not because they wish to exclude others, or because they consider them incapable, but simply because the patient shows a preference for being helped by the family. The family, then, may never find out whether options like day care can help. For this reason it is not always true to say that the greater the motivation, the greater the reduction in the subjective burden of care.

FROM THEORY TO PRACTICE

What do these research results mean for care provision in practice? First and foremost, they mean that care professionals cannot tell, on the basis of an objective situation report, what another family member's problems with it actually are. Mapping the subjective experience of the burden of care means carrying out an interview with the family member, in which the problem areas (horizontal burden appraisal) and the reasons why certain situations form a problem (vertical burden appraisal) are fully discussed.

To translate these research results into a useful tool with which care professionals could assess the care burden experienced by the family carers of dementia patients, the Dementia Research Project in Groningen (Hadderingh *et al.*, 1991; Kootte *et al.*, 1994) included an experiment using such an interview. A case-management model was tried out in the care provision for dementia patients living at home and their family carers. The case managers were recruited from district nurses and home help supervisors and were prepared for the work by means of special training and idea-exchanging sessions. An important part of the case managers' work was the assessment of the family carer's demands for assistance.

IDENTIFICATION OF PROBLEMS

We have already shown that the burden shouldered by a family carer can be a varied one. An interview schedule, then, must cover the whole ground. When it has become clear where problems are being perceived, it must then be determined, in conjunction with the family carer, whether (and how) coping strategies, acceptance and motivation play a role.

The interview schedule, broadly speaking, consists of two parts. The first part is mainly concerned with the care of the dementia patient, his or her disorders, and the carer's dealing with them. It covers the following areas:

- medical history
- short biography
- motivation of the family carer

- help needed with activities of daily living
- problems with memory and recognition
- problems in passing the time
- behavioural problems
- supervision required

The second part is concerned with the situation of the family carer, and covers the following areas:

- physical health
- other responsibilities and activities
- finances and housing
- social support
- formal care
- feelings about the care situation
- views on the future.

MEDICAL HISTORY

The experiment showed that care professionals are well advised to look before they leap. Family carers are often reluctant to talk about themselves. On the one hand there is a kind of moral assumption here that the dementia patient is the only sufferer. On the other hand it is also true that carers have to get used not only to the professional care helper but also to the idea that they themselves are being given undivided attention. Experience has frequently taught them that others do not appreciate or understand the situation. They have learnt to be careful, and it may take time to break the ice.

Although the medical history is ascertained by means of fairly neutral questioning, a careful listener can quickly get an idea of the family carer's view of the situation. Much is revealed if the carer readily talks in terms of dementia or prefers to use terms like forgetfulness and confusion. It will also become clear whether the family carer realizes that this illness is not going to go away. This information can enable the care professional to set the right tone and to avoid seeming like a bull in a china shop.

Medical history
When did you first notice that there was something the matter with your ... ? How could you tell?   Could you tell me, in your own words, what the matter is with your ... ?   How long have you been looking after your ... in this way?   Does your ... have any other illnesses or problems which make him/her dependent on your care?

SHORT BIOGRAPHY

Many family carers are eager to describe the dementia sufferer not just as a patient but also as a human being. They want to tell the interviewer how he or she used to be, before the illness. Care professionals usually meet a patient only after the onset of dementia; for family members, the illness is merely the most recent phase in a long relationship.

The first biographical questions are general ones. The next questions are more specifically directed towards the patient's social functioning and character. Besides providing an overview of the patient's life, the interview offers the family carer the opportunity to talk about anything else that might be preying on his or her mind. For some, this is the moment to reveal that the relationship with the patient was a problem even before the onset of dementia. We often find, also, in those cases in which the dementia patient's character has changed markedly or in which the patient displays very problematic behaviour, that relatives wish to mention these matters at an early stage of the interview.

Short biography
What sort of work did your . . . do before? Did he/she have any special hobbies or interests? How did your . . . fit into the family? What kind of a parent was he/she? Did your . . . like having people around? How did he/she get on with other people before? Has anything happened in your . . . 's life that made a deep impression? How did your . . . deal with this? Could you describe your . . . 's character? Has it changed since the illness began?

MOTIVATION OF THE FAMILY CARER

Where the family carer's motivation is low, this is frequently too loaded a subject to be broached early on in the interview. Too many questions at once can also result in never getting the answers and in the interviewee's quickly retreating behind a wall of reticence. Nevertheless, the issue of motivation has to be brought up at this point in the interview, because the answers to these questions provide a reference frame by which the answers to later interview questions may usefully be interpreted. It provides fundamental insight into the carer's relationships with the rest of the family and into the family member's attitudes towards the patient. This sort of information makes the interviewer better prepared for the rest of the interview. Where a family carer has serious difficulties with the care task, the care professional must not be surprised when, in answer to questions about the dementia patient's way of behaving, major problems are suddenly revealed. For this reason, the first part of the interview contains a number of general questions on motivation. These questions offer family carers the room to reveal much more than they are directly being asked, should they wish to do so.

Care motivation
Why are you, in particular, looking after your . . . ? Was there anyone else who might have been able to do it? What is it like to take care of your . . . ?

ASSISTANCE NEEDED WITH DAILY LIVING

Using a short checklist, the family carer is asked to indicate the aspects of personal care actually provided in looking after the dementia patient and performing his/her domestic tasks. The interviewees are asked to indicate the extent of this help with a 'sometimes' or an 'often'. The list covers the following aspects: getting in and out of bed, washing, getting dressed and undressed, grooming, eating and drinking, sitting down and standing up, walking or getting about, going to the toilet, tidying up and cleaning, dealing with money, telephoning, preparing meals and using equipment.

Insight into these matters provides a clear indication of the intensity of the care burden, not just in terms of time spent but also whether tasks are practical ones or also involve personal or intimate care. Following on from this fairly factual checklist, questions are asked to discover how the family carer experiences this care provision, who else is providing help, and how the carer regards this help.

Help with daily living
What is it like to provide this care for your . . . ? Is there anything you find particularly difficult? If so, why? We have already mentioned the care you provide for your. . . . Is there anyone else who helps to look after your . . . ? If so, what do they do? Do you find it easy to accept other people's help in looking after your . . . ?

PROBLEMS WITH MEMORY, RECOGNITION AND FREE TIME

Another checklist generates a catalogue of problems to do with memory and recognition, and this provides a picture of the behaviour which, according to the family carer, the patient frequently displays. The following disturbances are covered: does not know what day it is; does not know what time it is; does not know what season it is; does not know his/her way around the house; does not know his/her way around outside; does not recognize friends; does not recognize immediate family; does not recognize the family carer; lives in the past; asks the same questions repeatedly; forgets what he/she is doing; does not know what is the matter with him/her.

A number of aspects to do with the patient's use of his or her time are also covered. Questions ask whether the dementia patient: can follow conversations; takes part in conversations; is interested in visitors; likes company; reads books or newspapers; listens to the radio; watches television; has contacts with the neighbours; has contacts with family; does nothing all day; has his/her own activities; is difficult to stimulate; can be active only in short bursts.

In addition, attention is given to the subjective perception of the problems. The fact that a given problem exists does not invariably mean that the family carer is troubled by it. To understand this perception, it is important to discover not only the value attached to a given disorder, but the reason this value is given. For instance, why a carer may be happy to gloss over the patient's memory loss and why, in her view, these problems are trivial. In another case, it is important to discover why it is that a family carer returns repeatedly to certain specific problems, for instance the passive behaviour of the patient.

Problems with memory, recognition and free time
Would you say that, all in all, your . . . has few or no problems in this area? Which problems give you the most trouble? Why? How do you deal with these problems? Does your approach work, or do you still get stuck sometimes?

BEHAVIOUR PROBLEMS

A separate checklist in the interview schedule allows family carers to say whether certain behavioural problems come up with any frequency. Carers find it easier to acknowledge problems in this area with the checklist system than with open questions; a problem that the carer assumes is unique to his or her own situation can be legitimized simply by virtue of being included in the list. The following behaviour problems are covered: is suspicious or accusing; is irritable or argumentative; resists help; often hides things; is restless during the day; is restless at night; sees things that aren't there; is violent or abusive; has bad or offensive manners; shouts and screams; shows unwanted sexual behaviour; has alcohol problems.

Behaviour problems
How long have these problems been going on? Which of your ... 's behaviour problems do you have the most difficulty with? Why are these problems the worst? Do they happen a lot? Are these problems related to your ... 's illness, or are they also to do with his/her character? How do you deal with these problems? Does your approach work, or do you still get stuck sometimes?

NECESSARY SUPERVISION

The transition to the second half of the interview is marked by a number of questions which have clearly to do with the degree to which the family carer feels trapped by the situation – not just physically but also emotionally, in the sense that he/she constantly feels anxious about the imminence of danger. Such carers will admit that they never feel free of the care for the patient.

Necessary supervision
Could you leave your ... alone at home for a short length of time, so you could do some shopping, for instance? Could you leave your ... alone at home for an afternoon, or for a whole day? Does your ... ever go out alone? Can he/she still drive a car? Are you afraid that something awful might happen? Are you afraid that an accident might happen at home? Perhaps from a lighted cigarette, the wrong use of equipment, or if he/she fell?

To close the first part of the interview, it is asked whether there are any aspects of the patient's illness and care that have not yet come up and about which the carer would like to say something. The moment has then come to take a short break before turning the cameras squarely on to the family carer. The division of the interview schedule into two parts gives family members the space, literally and figuratively, to shift the perspective from the dementia patient's situation to their own.

In the second part of the interview, the topics are so arranged that attention is first given to matters affecting the family carer directly, later widening the focus to include environmental factors affecting the carer's perception of the care burden. The interview closes with a look at the future, in which the family carer's motivation is explored further.

PHYSICAL HEALTH

Many family carers have the idea that they should not complain or moan about their own health. After all, they're not the patient. For this reason, the discussion of this subject is built up by means of concrete questions. This not only provides the interviewer with insight into the family carer's state of health but it also gives information to the family carer him/ herself, This is true especially for those who want to keep up appearances or who put their patient's health before their own.

Where the family carer turns out to have physical health problems which had never before been given any attention, it is not uncommon for them to decide to consult their GP.

Physical health
If you look back over the last two weeks, would you say that you felt perfectly healthy throughout that time? Do you suffer any sleeplessness, tiredness, depression or lack of appetite?, If so, how often? And how long has it been like this? Do you have any physical complaints that might prevent you from looking after your . . . ? Back pain, for instance? Would you say that your health has suffered because of your caring for your . . . ?

OTHER TASKS AND ACTIVITIES

Some family carers who have additional duties such as a job or small children at home, experience this as a problem; they feel pulled in all directions. Others say their job or family activities provide a distraction, and they welcome the opportunity of being able to talk about things and let off steam if necessary.

Aside from the number of tasks with which the family member has to juggle and the time required to fulfil them, the subjective experience of the family carer needs to be taken into account. People who, from an objective viewpoint, are in a position to create time for themselves are sometimes so immersed in the caring role that they do not feel free of the burden when they are temporarily relieved from their tasks or even when the patient is fast asleep.

Other tasks and activities
Do you have other time-consuming duties and activities such as a job or a family? [If so:] Can you combine caring for your ... with your other duties? Does this cause problems? Do you feel you have enough time to yourself? For relaxing or doing a hobby, for instance?

FINANCES AND HOUSING

Finances and housing are two areas which directly influence the practical side of care provision. When difficulties are experienced in either of these spheres, a cumulative effect sometimes occurs: not only are family carers bothered by the practical consequences, but they are also angry at being expected to cope with limited means. They feel it unjust that they are confronted with these basically avoidable problems while they save the community money by caring for the dementia patient at home.

Difficulties with money and housing are, by their nature, experienced on a daily basis. When the family care-giver experiences these kinds of practical problems, they are often labelled as an area of frustration. The family carer will often refer to the problem early in the interview, perhaps during the inventory of physical and domestic care required by the dementia patient.

Costs and housing
Does the illness and provision of care mean extra expenditure? In what way? Does this cause financial problems? Do you have to economize on other things? Could some of these difficulties be resolved if you had the financial means to pay for, say, taxis or domestic help? Do your domestic facilities allow you to care reasonably for your ... ? What do you feel could be improved upon? [For non-residents:] How long is the journey to your ... 's house? Is this ever a problem, perhaps late at night or for arranging transport?

SOCIAL SUPPORT

The questions concerning social support are general in their formulation. It was decided not to ask first for a rundown of individuals in the network, followed by questions on their behaviour and whether they offer help. General questions avoid relatives giving socially acceptable answers, such as that each child in the family does an equal share of the work. Sometimes, when asked specific questions such as 'who does what?', relatives who have never given the subject much thought suddenly realize that they, alone, are shouldering the burden. Furthermore, a factual inventory may set the interviewer on the wrong course as it is not the quantity of social contacts which is the issue but their subjective quality; this is another reason for opting for neutral questions. Not every offer of help is necessarily a positive contribution.

Support from family and friends

Do you receive enough help from family and friends in domestic tasks and taking care of the patient? Do they help in other ways such as odd jobs, gardening, or taking care of the patient for you?
Do family and friends understand your situation? Do they understand your problems?
Do family and friends appreciate your caring for your . . . ? Are they aware of what the job means for you?
Can you confide in your family and friends?
Would any of your friends or family relieve you of your caring duties for a few hours or a day?
Are any of your friends or family prepared to take over in an emergency for any length of time?
Has contact with family and friends suffered as a result of your caring for your . . . ? In what way?

FORMAL CARE

The family carer is asked to indicate by means of a short checklist which professional carers are available, for example GP, home help, meals-on-wheels, minding service, day treatment, and so on. The family member is then asked for an opinion on the support provided by formal care-givers, to gain insight into the effects on the subjective burden. Further questioning here establishes whether the help provided meets the requirements and experienced difficulties. At this point in the interview one should avoid discussions on adaptations to the care being received, or the possibilities and limitations of the services available. Not until the second visit, once the interviewer has reviewed the information which has emerged from the first interview, can well-founded discussions take place with the family carer as to where the priorities concerning assistance lie.

Social services
Are social services involved in caring for your . . . ? [If so:] Which branch? [If so:] Are you satisfied with the care provided? Do you want a different kind of assistance, more help or actually less help? [If so:] Do you feel appreciated by the professional carers? Do they take you seriously?

FEELINGS ABOUT THE CARE TASK

Earlier in the interview questions were asked concerning motivation. An examination of the family carer's feelings provides greater insight into motivation. These questions are asked later in the interview, by which time it is hoped that the interviewer has succeeded in gaining the trust of the family carer. We are concerned here with those issues which directly refer to the relationship with the dementia patient and, consequently, the personal life of the family carer.

Feelings about the care task
If it had been you who suffered from a disorder, do you think your . . . would have cared for you in the same way? Does the care task dominate your life? Are you always thinking about it? Does looking after your . . . make great demands on you? What would you say has helped you cope until now? Do you feel there are any elements of reward? Are there any positive sides to this situation? Do you ever care for your . . . against your will? Are you sometimes angry? Do you ever feel that you've had enough?

THE FUTURE

The final questions define the extent to which the family carer is able and willing to provide care in the future. Some people prefer not to think about the future, saying things like 'I've never given it any thought' or 'I take each day as it comes', in which case it is preferable to let the matter rest. Others say they have never looked at it in this light and, during the conversation, arrive at new insights. Others take the opportunity to share their fears about an uncertain future.

The future

How do you see the future? What would you see as the biggest problem awaiting you? Have you already thought about it?
Do you ever think about what would happen if you were no longer able to care for your . . . for some reason?
Do you feel that the time may come when you are unable to continue providing care? When do you think this might happen?

INTERVIEW METHOD

An interview is more than a technical procedure whose only objective is to procure answers to questions; the questions are no more than a method of putting a puzzle together. They allow for broader examination, together with the family carer. When difficulties start to become apparent in a particular area, further questions are asked; gradually the pieces of the puzzle fall into place. The questions should, indeed, be regarded as introductory or pointer questions. The experience and skill of the interviewer will largely determine the quality of the information obtained.

The interview develops according to a preconceived plan. It introduces the topics in a certain order, while ensuring that factual questions always precede questions of subjective experience. This does not imply that the interview has to be conducted in the given order. The story related by the family carer is the starting point, and if this starts to focus on a particular topic then it is up to the interviewer to ask the right questions at the most opportune moments, without interrupting the natural flow of informative conversation. The interviewer must, however, be sure to ask all the questions and so obviously has to be familiar with all the items contained in the interview. A further requirement is that the interviewer is able to keep track of information already obtained and can link this to new information. When a family carer answers the question whether he or she helps the dementia patient get in and out of bed, and immediately volunteers that this presents a problem because of back trouble, then this obviates the need to ask later whether any physical disability constitutes an obstacle to the caring process. By listening carefully the family carer will feel he or she is being taken seriously and will be encouraged to continue talking.

At the end of the interview a new appointment is made. The interviewer uses the information to draw up an analysis of the situation. How do the pieces of the puzzle fit together; are there any uncompleted areas? The family carer, too, has been given food for thought; many may never have reviewed their situation in this way; they gain an overview and arrive at new insights.

During the second meeting, the family carer is asked about his or her thoughts about the interview, and the care professional's analysis is discussed, with special focus on the most important problems and their contributing factors. The two then decide on the most suitable form of help or supervision: perhaps the creation of more free time for the family carer by means of domestic help or by placing the patient in a day-care centre; larger contributions towards taxi costs; or structural alterations in the home to reduce the risk of accidents. For family carers who have difficulty in coping, in accepting, or with motivation, these routine forms of assistance are inadequate; they benefit more from individual or group psychosocial support.

Once some form of assistance or supervision has been introduced on the basis of this joint analysis of the problem, we cannot assume that it will invariably have the anticipated effect. It therefore makes sense to build in a number of evaluation points. There are, after all, numerous factors which affect the subjective experience of the care burden. Neither is the burden of care an inert and unchanging matter: the neighbour who always did the shopping can break a leg, the patient's condition can worsen, or a family argument can blow up. Matters can also improve, of course: the patient's dementia can enter a quieter, less restless phase, help can come from an unexpected quarter, and the family carer can become better accustomed to the situation over time.

REFERENCES

Barnes et al. (1981) Problems of families caring for Alzheimer patients: use of a support group', *Journal of the American Geriatrics Society* 24 (2): 80–85.

Blom, M.M. and Duijnstee, M.S.H. (1993) De patient achter de patient, *Patient Care* 4: 53–61.

Buijssen, H.P.J. and Razenberg, T.P.A. (1987) *Dementie. Een praktische handreiking voor de omgang met dementerende ouderen.* Meppel: Boom.

Duijnstee, M.S.H. (1991) De mantel, de spil van de zorg, *Senior* 7/8: 13–15.

—— (1992). *De belasting van familieleden van dementerenden.* Dissertation. Nijkerk: Intro.

—— (1994a) Thuis in familiezorg. Oratie Universiteit Utrecht. Bunnik: LVT.

—— (1994b) Relatives of persons suffering from dementia: differences in the burden, *Ageing and Society* 14: 499–519.

Golodetz, A., Evans, R., Heintitz, G. and Gibson, C.D. (1969) The care of chronic illness. The 'responser' role, *Medical Care* 7 (5): 385–394.

Hadderingh, E., Kootte, M., Velde, B.P. te, Kempen, G.I.J.M. and Bremen, W.M. van den (1991) *De zorg aan thuiswonende dementerende ouderen.* Groningen: Dementie Onderzoek in Groningen.

Jones, G.M.M. and Miesen, B.M.L. (1992) *Care-Giving in Dementia: Research and Applications*, vol. 1. London/New York: Tavistock/Routledge.

Kootte, M., Kammenga, E. and Bremen, W.M. van den (1994) *Een experiment in de hulpverlening aan thuiswonende ouderen en hun naaste omgeving.* Groningen: Dementie Onderzoek in Groningen.

Kvale, S. (1983) The qualitative research interview: a phenomenological and hermeneutical mode of understanding, *Journal of Phenomenological Psychology* 14: 171–196.

Mace, N.L. and Rabins, P.V. (1991) *The 36-hour Day: A Family Guide to Caring for Persons with Alzheimer's Disease, Related Dementing Illnesses, and Memory Loss in Later Life*. Baltimore: Johns Hopkins University Press.

Niederehe, G. and Frugé, E. (1984) Dementia and family dynamics: Clinical research issues, *Journal of Geriatric Psychiatry* 17: 21–56.

NRV (Nationale Raad voor de Volksgezondheid) (1993) *Psychogeriatrie: zorg voor dementerenden. Deel 1: een kwantitatieve analyse van het beleid van de rijksoverheid*. Zoetermeer: NRV.

Zarit, H., Orr, K. and Zarit, M. (1985) *The Hidden Victims of Alzheimer's Disease: Families under Stress*. New York: New York University Press.

Chapter 17

Cultural dimensions of dementia and care-giving

Christopher King

INTRODUCTION

Critical dementia research has covered significant ground over the last decade. Early concerns over the subjectivity of the dementia 'sufferer' were initially displaced by care-giver stress as a research priority but the sufferer seems to have again regained middle field but from a different perspective. Previous Alzheimer's constructs revolved around cognitive function as a central and defining characteristic of the self that is especially vulnerable to attack by the disease. More current models are considering self as distinct from cognitive function. Self is increasingly considered in relational terms, or in terms of social and inter-subjective processes which impact on preservation or dissolution of the self (Herskovits, 1995). Research has come to view demented persons not as a fixed biomedical reality, but as social actors who live with impairment and interact with others in care-giving relationships in part of the sociocultural world of the dementing and their care-givers. Reflecting in this change is an expansion in considerations of subjectivity such as 'incommunicables' (Gubrium, 1986), multiple definitions of self and indeed multiple selves (Young, 1990).

A directing force behind this type of research is a prolonged dissatisfaction with the explanatory power of the biomedical model. Research and critiques have pointed to medical knowledge of dementia as (a) scientifically flawed, and (b) heavily 'tainted' by ageist cultural and social evaluations of old age. It is argued that the dominant role biomedicine plays in the organization of health care has significantly structured the dementing and care-giving experiences. Because dementia is perceived as a progressive and incurable condition, it is not accommodated within the acute medical care system. A paradoxical outcome is the placement of the dementia victim within the family as an appropriate setting for the necessary intimacy of care-giving but sanctioned within a biomedical frame of knowledge which in effect precludes the validity of knowledge arising out of the experience of intimacy. Caregivers continue to accept the biomedical explanation of dementia more out of the need to resolve uncertainty, rather than on the basis of scientific evidence (Kitwood, 1987; Gubrium, 1986). A persisting tension between the 'sociogenic' and 'bio-medical' models as frames of meaning illustrates the ongoing importance of the need to consider dementia in terms of social and cultural processes:

> What is missing from most of the current social and behavioural science research on dementia and caregiver strain is an analysis of the impact of cultural definitions, care settings, and the caregiving relationship on the experience of dementing illness.
>
> (Lyman, 1989: 604)

The subtle yet significant changes in defining subjectivity we have noted are not only indications of shifts in thinking about dementia. They repre-sent paradigm shifts which are responses to social and cultural changes occurring in contemporary societies. These changes include the emerging multicultural and global environment in which local cultures are partici-pating. Not only are local identities in a state of flux, but also the notion of identity itself is undergoing change. These changes will impact on how the care-giving relationship is constructed into the future. From Lyman's exhortation to consider cultures of care-giving, we can study practices and beliefs of 'non-Western' cultures to understand the diversity of care-giving, but also the particular cultural undergirdings of our own practices.

Cross-cultural variations in care-giving generally have been researched under what may be broadly termed the *psychosocial* umbrella which seeks to understand how cultural and social factors concerning *dependency* will determine both the structure of the care-giving arrangement but also the psychological responses of the involved actors (Keith, 1992: Keith, Fry and Ikels, 1990; Draper and Keith, 1992). These studies are particularly valuable in assessing the effects on kin-based support systems of social change in developing countries (Caffrey, 1992; Goldstein and Ku, 1993; Pearson, 1992). What experiences from other cultures may also tell us is how local health and illness belief systems organize the structure of dementia care-giving.

In this chapter I will outline the relationship between care-giving practices in contemporary Japan and traditional values and beliefs particu-lar to the Japanese cosmology. The Japanese case illustrates the proposition that medical systems are essentially cultural systems for organization of medically relevant experiences (Kleinman, 1978). It also demonstrates how the practices, and to a degree the experience, of care-giving reflects spatial and temporal organization of relations between generations. Of particular interest in this model is the role played by the body (Turner, 1984). Japanese people particularly, but not exclusively, express themselves through a 'bodily vocabulary' (Lock, 1987). The body is also increasingly understood as an essential constituent of self, both phenomenologically and in social interactions. In the context of illness, physical loss of the body is linked to loss of self (for example through quadriplegia). In dementia also, the perceived 'loss of self' and the associated loss of communication abilities opens up possibilities for the body. Finally, care-giving, perhaps best symbolized by the hand, represents the practical aspect of caring for the physical body but also as the medium for communication of 'incommunicables'. Care-givers may sense the dementing body is responsive to the caring touch, revealing the possibility that it knows more than we are willing to give it credit for. The quality of the care-giver's interpretations is an overlooked and undervalued aspect which should be considered important and useful in giving meaning and validation to the dementing process.

PHENOMENOLOGY AND DEMENTIA

Interpreting and representing an illness involves consideration of the social and cultural values ascribed to or inscribed in, the body. In this sense, the body becomes a metaphor for the person and by extension, the social body (Sontag, 1978). Studies directed at interpreting the Alzheimer victim's experience have similarly suggested that the victim is trapped within a 'psychic prison' (Garrat and Hamilton-Smith, 1995). Featherstone and Hepworth (1991) refer to the ageing experience *per se* as one of a subjective youthhood trapped behind the 'mask' of a biologically and socially old external body. The exterior ageing body represents a 'betrayal' of the inner self and highlights a problematic disjuncture between the inner self and the external body. In the case of Featherstone's masked identity, the reflexive self continues, but as a 'spoiled identity' (Goffman, 1964). The paralysis victim and the dementia sufferer do share a discontinuity of the somatized self. While the paralysis victim may have the chance to rebuild an identity through rehabilitation (Seymour, 1989), the crucial point of departure between paralysis and dementia, is the factor of memory.

For Seymour, the process of estrangement from self and others results from a declining sense of embodiment in social space and an associated diminishing of communication possibilities. Memory for Seymour is tyrannical because it maintains the image of a past self which is a source of mourning. In the case of dementia, there is a period during which awareness of the loss of memory becomes the cause for reflexivity on the part of the sufferer. Subsequent loss of short-term memory leads, we are told, to loss of awareness of time, place and self. Consistent with the cultural evaluation of the dementing process as a regression, consciousness seems to lose a sense of temporal immediacy. However, long-term memory appears either to remain intact or becomes more vivid for the sufferer. We may infer some logical consistency in this process by suggesting the dementing body is situated temporally and spatially in a known past as opposed to a confusing and incoherent present. From this basis, we can suggest that the not uncommon 'behaviour' of the sufferer who 'wanders' back to the house of their childhood is a motivated attempt to return to the security of a known 'habitus'.

The logic of this argument is derived from the superficially self-evident notion that social and individual identities are tied to the body and its location in time and space. The term *habitus* is used to describe how world views are embodied in members of cultural and social groupings which distinguish them from other groupings (Bourdieu, 1979; Elias, 1978). It is perceived in the myriad ways of using the body which are both a manifestation and reflection of distinguishing dispositions and can be observed in the field of dementia research. For example, highly educated doctors from upper-class social backgrounds often have difficulty diagnosing patients from similar backgrounds because of their shared habitus. Habitus may also be said to be generational, in that cohorts will carry their collective experiences of the body and the meanings attached to the body into old age.

With these thoughts in mind, we might suggest that dementia is a form of nostalgia. The pathological evaluation appears to stem from a reluctance to accept, or give credence to the notion that an old person may seek to return to a habitus which evokes a logical relationship between body and time. Possibly also we are reluctant to accept 'extreme nostalgia' or the yearning for the state of infantile helplessness. Yet I suggest that within Japanese culture such a state is not unacceptable and is actually cultivated.

THE BODY IN SOCIAL AND CULTURAL PROCESSES

This chapter will draw on the impressive ensemble of anthropological literature on health and illness in Japan which consistently reports the centrality of the body in social and cultural processes. It is a broad area of inquiry which involves a need to understand more clearly the interaction between biology and social and cultural processes:

> In order to understand how this is achieved in any given society, it is necessary to examine historical and contemporary cosmologies, ideas about the concept of self and the relationship of self and society, the 'location' of the emotions in the physical body, the language of emotions, forms of expression of pain and discomfort and the meanings that are attributed to them, and ideas about body boundaries. An understanding of the nature of social relationships is also obviously crucial, as is an awareness of the culturally accepted means of expressing dissent and the use of the body as a symbolic medium for this purpose.
>
> (Lock, 1987: 8–9)

A study of care-giving which includes concepts such as nurturance, loss, dependency and responsibility, can show continuities between the physical body, its cultural construction and the larger social context.

Quite a long time ago Marcel Mauss (1935) pointed out that peoples employ a variety of 'techniques of the body' which reflect differences not only between cultures, but also between generations within societies, of ways of conceiving of the body. This phenomenon has been developed into studies of *embodiment*, or the social, cultural and historical processes by which the body is invested with meaning and value. A philosophical anthropology of embodiment attempting to integrate the biological with social and cultural processes proposes the body thus: Lacking an unreflexive biological and genetic certainty which confines most species to specific environmental niches, human beings are born with an unlearned capacity to learn. We construct our cultural environment, which mediates between us and the natural habitat. There are, in this sense, no 'natural men', because humans live in a cultural world. Cultural analysis proposes that the body is deeply invested in social processes of communication, identification and reproduction of socially ascribed meanings (Turner, 1995). That is, the 'body' is socially and culturally constructed, in the first instance, through socialization.

The basic requirements of constructing and maintaining one's abilities and image as an accredited 'human adult' involves rehearsal of three main competencies and controls: (a) cognitive skills – based upon the use of language and communication skills; (b) body controls – control of bodily movements as well as the capacity to become continent and retain bodily fluids; and (c) emotional controls – control of the expression of emotions so that loss of control only takes place on occasions and in forms which are socially sanctioned and acceptable (Featherstone, 1992). It is the visible loss of these competencies which often leads to loss of self and infantilization.

THE SECOND CHILDHOOD AND DEPENDENCY

Care-giving necessarily involves a level of inter-personal intimacy usually associated with the care of infants. To adopt literally such a stance towards an old person would constitute an insult to their dignity as adults. Yet, in western societies, family and professional care-givers tend to see and act towards victims in exactly this way (Lyman, 1988). As competency of the sufferer decreases and their dependency increases, this attitude tends to set up a self-fulfilling process, characteristically culminating in 'loss of self' (Kitwood, 1990; Sabat and Harré, 1992).

By contrast, the way in which dementia sufferers are treated within Japanese culture is in many ways an extension of how old people and children are generally perceived. If broadly interpreted, *regression* carries important meanings attached to the status of both the child and the very old in Japanese thought. Care-givers will often indicate they feel the identity of the sufferer has not undergone any significant change (King, 1993). While this may have been a response to serious illness of pretending it does not exist (Ohnuki-Tierney, 1984), it may equally point to a strategic maintenance of the identity of the old person. The special character of the Japanese care-giving relationship is one which reinforces the ideal of old age as a socially approved return to the blissful state of childish dependency. However it does not entail treating the old person as a 'child', nor does it mean seeing the old person as 'childish'. Whether or not loss of competency in dementia is articulated in this context is irrelevant. In fact, the significance of infantile dependency may be translated into the idealized image of old age.

In western culture, 'infantilization' conveys the full implications of denigration, a valuation which may tell us as much about our attitudes towards children as it does about old people. Paradoxically, while old age in traditional Japanese and Chinese cultures is venerated as attainment of maturity and wisdom, the sixtieth birthday marks a 'return to childhood' and beginning of a new sixty-year cycle. Old age symbolically represents the high point of passage through life and the accumulation of wisdom and experience. The mature soul at the apex of life, stands poised to be reborn at a higher level. This sense of progression is expressed in the Confucian passage, rote-learned by prewar school children:

> The Master said, 'At fifteen, I had my mind bent on learning. At thirty, I stood firm. At forty, I had no doubts. At fifty, I knew the decrees of Heaven. At sixty, my ear was an obedient organ for the reception of truth. At seventy, I could follow what my heart desired, without transgressing what was right.'
>
> (Confucius, 1933)

This passage suggests that old age represents achievement of a high level of cultural maturity. Following the desire of the heart, or spontaneous action, implies that maturity of the soul was in total harmony with the laws of heaven. Despite their 'child-like' lack of inhibition, elders could be respected in the same way as the god-like children who can do no wrong. Dotage in old age was idealized in Japanese literature through the term 'the ecstasy years'. It was resurrected by Ariyoshi (1972) in her popular novel Koukotsu no Hito ('Man in Rapture'). In this text we find a modern interpretation of the ectasy of mindlessness as Akiko, the care-giver of her dementing father-in-law, is drawn to comment: 'I sometimes wonder if I'm having a religious experience, because at times I feel as if I were serving a god' (Ariyoshi, 1972: 192).

For Japanese people at least, the honoured status of dependency in old age is an experience described by the Japanese 'arc of life':

It is a great shallow U-curve with maximum freedom and indulgence allowed to babies and to the old. Restrictions are slowly increased after babyhood till having one's own way reaches a low just before and after marriage. This low line continues many years during the prime of life, but the arc gradually ascends again until after the age of sixty, men and women are almost as unhampered by shame as little children are.

(Benedict, 1946: 253–4)

AMAE

With western patterns of socialization, emphasis is more likely to be placed on early development of independence and individuality and its extension through the life-trajectory in the form of negative sanctions against dependency. The freedom to demand indulgence and assume dependency or to *amaeru* is extended to Japanese children and old people without sanctions. *Amae* represents a key component of Japanese personality and is composed of several characteristics.

Amae is the need to be responded to, taken care of, and cherished; the mutually interactive attitude or behaviour whereby one seeks and (ideally) receives *amayakasu*, the indulgence of another. It is a valued freedom to indulge otherwise suppressed emotions and urges without fear of censure from others and is made accessible, under suitable circumstances, throughout life. The experience of *amae* is perhaps roughly translatable in terms equivalent to the Freudian notion of the undifferentiated mother–child experience of infants (Doi, 1973; Johnson, 1993).

A distinguishing feature of *amae* is the particular meaning attached to the status of dependency. Children and old people have special status because they are both closer to the gods from whom children have just come and to whom old people are in the process of going. Children are valued for their purity and innocence, often characterized as *masshiro*, or 'pure white'. Total indulgence and fostering of passive dependency in a child is regarded as cultivation and protection of this inherent purity (Hendry, 1987: 16). Similarly elders should be cared for and respected as they come increasingly to inhabit the liminal space between the worlds of the living and the dead. *Amae* may in this sense act as an affirmation of identity. The most common form of 'management' reported by care-givers is to engage in *amayakasu* (King, 1993). While care-giving duty may at first be interpreted as one of managing the sufferer's bodily comfort, it becomes management of a 'dying career' towards a satisfactory resolution. Trajectory of the self is not here considered to have been ended by the advent of a dementing condition (Plath, 1973).

The western impulse is to link childlike dependency to the biological realm. Thus the tendency would be to call the dementing person a 'living vegetable'. The Japanese impulse is to link it to the sacred. In traditional

Japanese conceptions, the personal human career does not end with physical death. The 'life-cycle' notion widely used in the social sciences is tinged with a western bias. For a Japanese, to die is to join the departed members or household line of former consociates. Sanctified but not super-potent, they remain 'alive' as significant others to those still in this world (Plath, 1964).

These differences have at least two significant implications for both the experience of dementia and care-giving. First as we concluded in our discussion of infantilization of dementing elders, our views of old age are implicated in processes leading to either loss or maintenance of self. Second, our concepts of health and illness influence not only subjective interpretations of deviance in old age, but also the organizational structure of the societal response to the same condition.

I have suggested that the life-trajectory in Japanese cosmology differs from the western notion of finitude but that it nevertheless makes demands on notions of responsibility for its perpetuation. We could surmise that the notion of an eternal cyclical notion of time introduces an element of certainty into Japanese thinking which is absent from western thought. The Japanese concepts of old age and dementia seem to be institutionalized as a form of nostalgia. That is, nostalgia in the form of *amae* is accessible at crucial times in the life-course. *Amae*, however, does not operate as a free-floating agent. It is situated at the interface of culture and identity. In the Japanese case, the construction of personhood is highly relational, involving membership in a collective identity. It is also structured temporally and spatially.

THE TRADITIONAL STRUCTURE OF CARE-GIVING

Traditionally the Japanese patriarchal household or *ie* was a spatial organization of familial relationships reflecting a concern with perpetuation of a collective identity in which the status of elders plays a crucial role. The *ie* was a 'house' which contained kin and, more often than not, other non-kin members. It was the social unit in prewar Japan and social identity for household members did not exist outside its formal boundaries. The structure of the *ie* defined membership in terms of a shared task which overrode the importance of its constituting members. Identity in this context was defined in terms of the collective 'self'. The *ie* in effect circumscribed its members' existence not only in physical space, but also in social and temporal space. Care-giving was a formalized responsibility within a schema which guaranteed generational succession and perpetuity of the family as a social and temporal identity. Care-giving of elders reflected efforts to maintain this relationship.

The *ie* guaranteed its members physical and psychological security in their lifetime and ontological security in the belief that membership continued in the afterlife in the company of the collective ancestors. In this sense, death of a household member did not represent a break in time and space, but passage into collective memory. For the household member, the knowledge that one was part of a collective entity that preceded them into eternity provided psychological security but also instilled responsibility for its maintenance.

Fulfilling one's filial responsibility was part of this grand scheme (Plath, 1964). A child was assumed to feel and accept absolutely the *on* or obligation to his parents, because his parents gave birth to him and raised him. The parents' *on* should be reciprocated by the child which among other duties included the care of his parents. Traditional arrangements dictated that the first-born son succeeded to the head of the family, and his wife would carry the physical and emotional responsibility of elder care. This arrangement was promulgated in laws of inheritance by primogeniture. The ideological cultural elements of old age and care-giving were therefore interdependently locked together in both the physical and emotional space of the *ie*. While postwar changes have seen the *ie* steadily displaced by the conjugal nuclear family form, the *ie* mentality persists in among other things, notions of the self.

SELF AND BODY

Loss of self has at least two aspects: it may refer to loss of a sense of formal boundaries of the self and the immersion in immediate experience, or it may mean the loss of a self defined by culturally relevant values defining personhood. Draper and Keith (1992) have argued that self is most universally maintained by the value of independence, although our discussion of *amae* suggests the Japanese case contains exceptions to the rule. I would argue that bodily competencies already discussed would feature more strongly as universal measures of selfhood against background social and cultural values. As heirs to the Cartesian dualism of mind and body, western thinking tends to locate 'humanness' in the higher mind/brain and our 'animal' or base side in the body. Yet, paradoxically, we often resort to the body as a metaphor for representing our understanding of the decline of the human in the dementing process.

Conceptually, the dementing process typically involves a 'dismantling' of the socialized adult. Loss of control over bodily processes and emotions, loss of orientation in time and space, and loss of independence and the capacity for reciprocation, all represent a divestment of the qualities which have gone into the construction of a competent social being. We can further see the final dementing stage in terms of regression, as body control is lost and the old person assumes the foetal position. In this position there are no conventional signs affirming self-in-body. At the end of life the dementing body is often seen to have lost most of the socially and culturally inscribed signs by which bodies are recognized as being 'human'. Thus in typical care-giving literature we hear descriptions of the old person as 'just an empty shell from which the soul has escaped', or indeed dementia as 'a total loss of mind, body and soul'.

A central concern in the care-giving process then seems to be dealing with the gradual disappearance of the abstract qualities defining person-hood, while attention becomes focused on the body as a visible display of signs by which to interpret the changing identity of the old person. As the body goes through its behavioural rituals apparently devoid of meaning, it more often than not becomes a self-fulfilling manifestation of dissolution of mind – and by extension, personhood.

HEALTH SYSTEMS AS CULTURAL SYSTEMS

While we may equate loss of autonomy with loss of competency, we are working from a Descartian ontology. Given the centrality of mind in conceptualizing personhood in western culture, it may be an easy jump of logic to equate dementia or *de mentus* literally meaning to be out of one's mind, with loss of self, or at least 'not being oneself'. We should not forget that mind is embodied. Conventional medical knowledge links organic dysfunction of the brain to the loss of personhood. Atrophy of the brain as the seat of the higher human functions leads to a systematic disordering down to the vegetative natural functions.

In Japanese cosmology 'mind' is not equated with consciousness. Mind is a sub-construct of self. Self is usually defined in terms of primary social relationships rather than individual qualities. Because the human spirit is located in the stomach or *hara* rather than the brain, there is a lot of hesitation in Japan in defining brain death as the death of the individual. Essentially the mapping of the self into the body is different for Japanese. Also, as we have noted, the self has temporal dimensions which survive beyond death of the body. Nevertheless, it is no less important, for it is an embodiment of the social relationships and collective identity. Thus, Japanese care-givers continue to pay attention to the physical comfort of the sufferer.

The western biomedical model dominates Japanese *institutional* health care (Steslicke, 1982). Japanese medical science understands brain function in neurological terms. However, it represents only one part of a 'cosmopolitan' health system (Dunn, 1976). In the traditional Japanese cosmology, thought, consciousness and cognition are associated with the heart and stomach. Thought springs from the heart rather than from cognition. The basic tenets of western thought are not compatible with eastern philosophy and religion. McFarland (1967) notes that while ration-ality is the hallmark of western culture, in assessing reality, the Japanese take a phenomenological attitude with experience, influenced by cultural norms, taking precedence over cognition. Reality is conceived as a unity rather than an elimination of opposites. Foreign cultural influences such as neurology which are seemingly in opposition to traditional values can therefore be incorporated into the indigenous cosmology of health and illness. Thus a characteristic of the Japanese health system is the coexistence of multiple, sometimes overlapping and interpenetrating paradigms, which are mobilized according to the requirements of the moment (Ohnuki-Tierney, 1984).

In Japanese medical terminology the term *chihoushou* corresponds to the western biomedical classification of dementia. *Chihoushou* contains two main sub-categories. One is *Arutsuhaima byou* (Alzheimer's disease) with typical atrophy of the brain, the other is *nou kekkan sei* (stroke). These terms are restricted to formal use and otherwise avoided due to the inference of mental illness in the public mind. The word *dementia* (*demensha*) itself conforms to the old German classification of insanity and its use is avoided. To this extent, the implication that *chihoushou* is a form of *mental* disorder is also avoided. While the prevalent attitude that any disorder associated with the brain is a mental disorder, the wide acceptance of brain scan technology in diagnosis is one way of confirming the notion that *chihoushou* is a physical disorder.

While the biomedical category *chihoushou* plays some role in mediating the status of the sufferer, the condition of the old person tends to be interpreted through local paradigms. Thus lay representations of dementia prevail despite considerable public health education efforts and a high diagnosis rate for cases which do come to medical attention. Use of the term *chihoushou* is confined to formal situations. The term commonly used is *boke*, which variously means 'shocking', 'foolish' or 'stupid'. *Boke* nevertheless contains a range of subtle meanings – its use is highly situational locally and also varies from region to region across Japan. In contrast to *chihoushou*, it is not regarded as a disease but as a condition. *Boke* is often considered to be the result of the sufferer's way of life or the way they have been treated by others. Very few care-givers see *chihoushou* in terms of brain pathology, despite apparent awareness of the significance of the results of a brain scan. The overwhelming image of the condition is as an outcome of a disharmony in inter-personal relations between the sufferer and family members or other significant persons (King, 1993). In short, Japanese care-givers tend to see dementia in inter-personal and collective rather than organic and individual terms. From within this frame of reference, the serious consequences of a disruption to highly inter-dependent familial and social relations is a rational basis for seeking the cause in the same context.

The crucial argument here is that medical systems are necessarily cultural systems for dealing with health and illness. They develop from within the social institutions of a culture and represent a total cultural organization of medically relevant experiences. As such, they cannot be considered meaningful outside the context of the local culture (Kleinman, 1978; Leslie, 1978). Socialization instils dependency, but it also inculcates responsibility for self-care and awareness of inter-dependent relationships with others (Hendry, 1987). A period of sickness in this type of medical system severely tests the quality of human and social relationships because often the cause is found in personal irresponsibility and neglect towards others. For Japan where cohesion and harmony of the group and family are supposedly crucial concerns, dementia in this case may be described as a symptom of disrupted relations, not within bodies, but between bodies (Young, 1976).

CONCLUSION

In this chapter I have drawn on material from a non-western culture to illustrate the influence of cultural and social factors in structuring the care-giving experience. In the Japanese example, the care-giving relationship is ordered by an overarching concern with maintenance of a collective identity – a framework which links responsibility for the care of the aged with notions of social solidarity and the continuity of the family in time and social space. Care of a dementing household member involves managing a human–cultural progression through death and into the next life. The 'ecstasy' of mindlessness in dementia may spell regression to the pyscho-pathologist. In Japanese eyes it is evidence of successful 'status passage' and validation of the care-giver's struggle to sustain the sufferer's identity and cultural career path (Plath, 1973).

Much of the Japanese material presented here represents the world-views of the current generation of sufferers and their care-givers, for whom the prewar *ie* was a lived reality. The values of Confucianism explicitly, or implicitly, constitute a significant part of their outlook. In Japan today large numbers of very old people have traditional expectations of family care. There is no guarantee that the aspects of dependency documented here will be relevant to postwar or future generations, particularly in the current climate of rapid social and cultural change in Japan.

At the peak of Japan's remarkable postwar modernization programme, western social gerontologists observed the changes had not affected the status and high levels of social integration of Japanese elders (Palmore, 1980; Palmore and Maeda, 1985), an observation which appeared to dis-prove the theory that the status of old age was inversely proportional to the level of societal modernization (Cowgill, 1972). There certainly has been considerable social and cultural change in the intervening period. Elements intrinsic to the structure of the *ie* household have been seriously under-mined. The principle of *patriarchy* undergirding primogeniture and formal care-giving arrangements, has been challenged by changes to inheritance law (Maeda, 1991), increasing educational levels of women and their movement outside the traditional boundaries of household roles, as well as the emergence of a youth culture (Takada, 1992).

The current situation remains somewhat ambiguous. O'Leary (1993), for example, has linked structural changes in postwar Japan to significant changes in attitudes towards old age. However, at the same time Campbell and Kurokawa (1991) have argued the care-giving relationship is still being formed along the lines of the *ie* with some noted differences. Intergenerational relations have shifted away from obligatory to preferred patterns. Emotive reciprocity has also emerged as a factor in determining inheritance and responsibility in family dynamics (Elliot and Campbell, 1993).

I have argued that medical systems are cultural systems and as such have a strong structuring influence on the organization of medical experiences. Knowledge of dementia in western societies is sociologically seen as an issue in the construction of social problems wherein behaviour which is disruptive to social order is transformed into individualized medical disorders (Conrad and Schneider, 1980). What was heretofore an old-age problem secured in the normal troubles of ageing has become one expressed in pathology. At the societal level, the generic category of senility has been transformed into a medical category through cultural, social and political processes (Fox, 1989; Estes and Binney, 1989). At the social level, medicine fulfils a social control role by constructing confused older persons as 'disease entities' who cause social and personal problems, rather than as social actors who live with impairment and interact with others. It is the disease, not the person, responsible for their 'behaviour' (Lyman, 1989). At the phenomenological level where people construct meaning out of their experiences, cultural values colour our perceptions and limit the possibilities of imagining alternative identities (Crisp, 1993).

I suggest one way around this limitation is to challenge the 'medical' status of dementia through introduction of embodiment to dementia research. There is a need to examine more closely the cultural basis on which we have constructed our knowledge of old age. What seems to be evident about care-giving, particularly in dementia, is that it brings into intimate proximity the bodies of both care-giver and care-receiver. Methodologically the body provides a universal source of understanding and also a basis for action which is not culture-bound. In fact, embodiment has arisen from critiques of cultural bias in the philosophical basis of the western social sciences (Featherstone, 1991; Turner, 1994, 1995) including social gerontology (Swane, 1993; Kirk, 1994). The body has also recently been given attention as a suitable methodology in health care (Seymour, 1989). Importantly, embodiment takes into account the cultural changes affecting identity which have occurred against the background of structural changes in post-industrial societies (Giddens, 1991, 1992; Shilling, 1993; Turner, 1994).

We need to work at defining not only the formal responsibilities of the care-giver, but a responsiveness to the dementing body. An important aspect of this approach is that it is not limited to the Japanese context. A sociology of the body should become relevant to the increasing number of societies in which identity is undergoing a 'crisis'. The diversity of ways of perceiving old age and disordered old age, and the way these perceptions structure the experience, as well as the societal response to old age, demands culture be given greater consideration in care-giving studies and practice. Least of all should we neglect the applicability of this approach to western cultures.

ACKNOWLEDGEMENT

I am most grateful to Christine Swane for her generous comments and suggestions during the preparation of this chapter.

REFERENCES

Ariyoshi, Sawako (1972) *Koukotsu no Hito* ('Man in Rapture'). Tokyo: Kodansha.
Benedict, Ruth (1946) *The Chrysanthemum and the Sword. Patterns of Japanese Culture.* Boston: Houghton Mifflin.
Bourdieu, Pierre (1979) *Distinction: A Social Critique of the Judgement of Taste.* London: Routledge.
Caffrey, Rosalie A. (1992) 'Family care of the elderly in Northeast Thailand: changing patterns', *Journal of Cross-Cultural Gerontology* 7 (2): 105–116.
Campbell, R. and Y. Kurokawa (1991) 'Changing images of caregiving among elderly Japanese and their families'. Paper presented at Fourth Asia/Oceania Regional Congress of Gerontology. Yokohama, 31 Oct.–3 Nov.
Confucius (1933) Confucian Analects (Lun-yu). In J. Legge (trans.), *The Four Books.* Shanghai: Chinese Book Company.
Conrad, P. and J.W. Schneider (1980) *Deviance and Medicalization: from Badness to Sickness,* St Louis: C.V. Mosby.
Cowgill, D. (1972) *A Theory of Aging in Cross-cultural Perspective.* New York: Apple-Century Crofts.
Crisp, Jane (1993) 'Making sense of what people with Alzheimer's say'. Paper presented at Third Annual Conference, Alzheimer's Association (Australia). Melbourne, 2–5 May.
Doi, Takeo (1973) *The Anatomy of Dependence.* Tokyo: Kodansha International.
Draper, Patricia and Jennie Keith (1992) 'Cultural contexts of care: family care-giving for elderly in America and Africa', *Journal of Aging Studies* 6 (2): 113–134.
Dunn, Frederick L. (1976) 'Traditional Asian medicine and cosmopolitan medicine as adaptive systems'. In C. Leslie (ed.), *Asian Medical Systems. a Comparative Study.* Berkeley: University of California Press, pp. 133–158.
Elias, N. (1978), *The Civilising Process: The History of Manners.* Oxford: Blackwell.
Elliott, Kathryn Sabrena and Ruth Campbell (1993) 'Changing ideas about family care for the elderly in Japan', *Journal of Cross-Cultural Gerontology* 8:119–135.
Estes, C.L. and E.A. Binney (1989) 'The biomedicalisation of aging: dangers and dilemmas', *The Gerontologist* 29 (5): 587–596.
Featherstone, M. (1991) *Consumer Culture and Postmodernism.* London: Sage.

—— (1992) 'The life course: body, culture and imagery in the ageing process'. In Shuichi Wada (ed.), *Studies on the Source and Cultural Background of the Image of Ageing*. Tokyo: Waseda University Press.

—— and Mike Hepworth (1991) 'The mask of ageing and the postmodern life course'. In M. Featherstone, M. Hepworth and B.S. Turner (eds), *The Body: Social Process and Cultural Theory*. London: Sage, pp. 371–389.

Fox, Patrick (1989) 'From senility to Alzheimer's disease: the rise of the Alzheimer's disease movement', *The Milbank Memorial Quarterly* 67: 58–102.

Garrat, Sally and Elery Hamilton-Smith (1995) *Rethinking Dementia. An Australian Approach*. Melbourne: Ausmed.

Giddens, Anthony (1991) *Modernity and Self-identity*. Oxford: Polity Press.

—— (1992) *The Transformation of Intimacy. Sexuality, Love and Eroticism in Modern Societies*. Cambridge: Polity.

Goffman, E. (1964) *Stigma, Notes on the Management of the Spoiled Identity*. Englewood Cliffs, NJ: Prentice Hall.

Goldstein, Melvyn C. and Yachun Ku (1993) 'Income and family support among rural elderly in Zhejiang Province, China', *Journal of Cross-Cultural Gerontology* 8: 197–223.

Gubrium, Jaber F. (1986) *Oldtimers and Alzheimer's: The Descriptive Organization of Senility*. London: Jai Press.

—— (1988) 'Incommunicables and poetic documentation in the Alzheimer's disease experience', *Semiotica* 72: 235–253.

Hendry, Joy (1987) *Becoming Japanese: the World of the Pre-school Child*. Honolulu: University of Hawaii.

Herskovits, Elizabeth (1995) 'Struggling over subjectivity: debates about the "Self" and Alzheimer's disease', *Medical Anthropology Quarterly* 9 (2): 146–64.

Johnson, Frank A. (1993) *Dependency and Japanese Socialization*. New York: New York University Press.

Keith, J. (1992) *Care-taking in Cultural Context*. London: Oxford.

——, C. Fry and C. Ikels (1990) *Successful Aging in Cultural Context*. South Hadley, MA: Bergin and Garvey.

King, C. (1993) 'Cultural dimensions of dementia: a Japanese example'. Paper presented at the Fifteenth. Congress of the International Association of Gerontology. Budapest, Hungary, 4–9 July.

Kirk, Henning (1994) 'When old age became a diagnosis'. In Peter Öberg, Pertti Phjolainen and Isto Ruoppila, (eds), *Experiencing Ageing. Kokemuksellinen Vanheneminen Att Uppleva Åldrandet*. Helsingfors: Helsingfors Universitet.

Kitwood, Tom (1987) 'Explaining senile dementia: the limits of neuropathological research', *Free Associations* 10: 117–140.

—— (1990) 'The dialectics of dementia: with particular reference to Alzheimer's disease', *Ageing and Society* 10: 177–196.

Kleinman, Arthur (1978) 'Concepts and a model for the comparison of medical systems as cultural systems', *Social Science and Medicine* 12 (2D): 85–93.

Leslie, Charles (1978) 'Theoretical foundations for the comparative study of medical systems', *Social Science and Medicine* 12 (2B): 65–67.

Lock, Margaret (1987) 'Introduction: Health and medical care as cultural and social phenomena'. In Edward Norbeck and Margaret Lock (eds), *Health, Illness, and Medical Care in Japan. Cultural and Social Dimensions*. Honolulu: University of Hawaii Press.

Lyman, Karen A. (1988) 'Infantilization of elders: day care for Alzheimer's disease victims', *Research in the Sociology of Health Care* 7: 71–103.

—— (1989) 'Bringing the social back in: a critique of the biomedicalisation of dementia', *The Gerontologist* 29 (5): 597–605.

McFarland, H. Neil (1967) *The Rush Hour of the Gods: A Study of New Religious Movements in Japan*. New York: Macmillan.

Maeda, Daisaku (1991) 'Declining family care vs. expanding role of public services: social and legal aspects of Japanese experiences'. Paper presented at the Fourth Asia/Oceania Regional Congress of Gerontology. Yokohama, 31 Oct.–3 Nov.

Mauss, Marcel (1935) 'Techniques of the body', *Economy and Society* 2: 70–88.

Ohnuki-Tierney, Emiko (1984) *Illness and Culture in Contemporary Japan. An Anthropological View*. Cambridge: Cambridge University Press.

O'Leary, James S. (1993) 'A new look at Japan's honorable elders', *Journal of Aging Studies* 7 (1): 1–24.

Palmore, Erdman (1980) 'The status and integration of the aged in Japanese society'. In Jill S. Quadogno (ed.), *Aging, the Individual and Society*. pp. 50–67.

—— and D. Maeda (1985) *The Honorable Elders Revisited*. Durham, NC: Duke University Press.

Pearson, J.D. (1992) 'Attitudes and perceptions concerning elderly Samoans in rural Western Samoa, American Samoa, and urban Honolulu', *Journal of Cross-Cultural Gerontology* 7: 69–88.

Plath, David W. (1964) 'Where the family of God is the family: the role of the dead in Japanese households', *American Anthropologist* 56: 300–317.

—— (1973) 'Japanese psychology through literature: cares of career, and careers of caretaking', *Journal of Nervous and Mental Diseases* 157 (5): 346–357.

Sabat, Steven and Harré, Rom (1992) 'The construction and deconstruction of Alzheimer's disease', *Ageing and Society* 12: 443–461.

Seymour, Wendy (1989) *Bodily Alterations: An Introduction to a Sociology of the Body for Health Workers*. Sydney: Allen and Unwin.

Shilling, Chris (1993) *The Body and Social Theory*. London: Sage.

Sontag, S. (1978) *Illness as Metaphor*. New York: Farrar, Straus and Giroux.

Steslicke, William E. (1982) 'Medical care in Japan: the political context', *Journal of Ambulatory Care Management* 5 (4): 65–77.

Swane, Christine E. (1993) 'Dementia in old age: historical-cultural aspects of concept development, diagnosis, and care'. Paper presented at the fifteenth. Congress of the International Association of Gerontology. Budapest, Hungary, 4–9 July.

Takada, Akihiko (1992) 'Contemporary youth and youth culture in Japan', *International Journal of Japanese Sociology*, 1: 99–114.

Turner, Bryan S. (1984) *The Body and Society. Explorations in Social Theory*. Oxford: Basil Blackwell.

—— (1994) 'The postmodernisation of the life course: towards a new social gerontology', *Australian Journal on Ageing* 13 (3): 109–111.

—— (1995) 'Ageing and identity: some reflections on the somatization of the self'. In Mike Featherstone and Andy Wernick (eds), *The Ageing Body: Cultural Images of the Life Course*. London: Sage.

Young, A. (1976) 'Internalizing and externalizing medical belief systems', *Social Science and Medicine* 10 (3/4): 147–156.

—— (1990) 'Moral conflicts in a psychiatric hospital treating combat-related post-traumatic stress disorder'. In G. Weisz (ed.), *Social Science Perspectives on Medical Ethics*. Dordrecht: Kluwer Academic, pp. 65–82.

Part V

Environment, education and ethics

Chapter 18

In search of the best environment

Results of five experiments in the institutional organization of care for demented people

Mary Fahrenfort

INTRODUCTION

The ever-increasing numbers of demented people encourage us to question the hitherto existing forms of institutional care for the demented. It might well be that the historically developed institutions do not always provide the best answer to the need for care, in terms of quality as well as cost-benefit. At present, there is a widespread conviction that larger changes in the policy of care should not be effected without having tried them out and evaluated the results.

For this reason, during the past years in Holland several types of experiments have been performed to find out the 'best' living situation for taking care of the demented. In this chapter the evaluation of five experiments will be discussed. The five experiments all took place at different sites and in different kinds of (more or less) institutionalized care settings. What the situations have in common is the aim of providing an environment which is as close to a home environment as possible, yet offering the security of control. Although the situations were variable, the method of evaluation has been kept similar in the different situations, in order to enhance the possibility of drawing general conclusions. From the evaluation, a clear picture emerges in all cases of the particular advantages and disadvantages inherent in every type of environment. An analysis of these different situations provides us with guidelines on the best way to deal with care under different circumstances.

Overview of the experiments

In all experiments the aim was innovation by providing a high quality of psychogeriatric care in a less institutionalized environment (i.e. at home, in home-like situations or in 'ordinary' old people's homes).[1] A condition was, that the cost would essentially not be higher. In all situations, medical care was provided by local GPs, with the possibility of consulting the nursing home for geriatric problems. The five different situations can be briefly described as follows:

I A small living group in an old people's home instead of a nursing home. The supervision and added professional care is provided from the nursing home.

At present, this type of situation in The Netherlands has become very common. Because of the limited possibilities of placement in nursing homes, the population of old people's homes, who were initially the 'able' elderly, has become increasingly dependent. The staff and organization of old people's homes are not actually equipped for this kind of care, but several ways of coping with the problem have been devised. Group care for the demented elderly under supervision of a nursing home is one of the most popular measures. The projects vary widely in scope and quality; this particular project is special because it provides a sheltered living environment within the larger organization and much care has been taken to make conditions as ideal as possible.

II A new type of organization combining the living conditions of an old people's home with the provision of nursing home care.

Thus, the process of deterioration does not necessitate transfer. This particular project has the added innovation of being divided into four small-scale annexes, located in different small villages in a rural area. By providing care in this manner, people will not have to be transferred out of the area where they have spent all their lives. Each annexe is meant especially for the population of that particular village, and it provides care for the more able as well as the highly dependent elderly, for psychogeriatric as well as somatic cases. Couples can have an apartment together.

III 'Warm Care' in a non-institutional manner where people live like an ordinary 'family' group of six.

The architecture was new and especially developed for the project to provide an open and yet protected environment: six linked houses around a garden, in a developing area in a town. In both this project and the following, care is provided in the context of helping people to take care of their own living: as far as their condition allows, they take part in ordinary daily activities such as cooking, laying the table, ironing and even shopping.

IV Sheltered housing for demented elderly in an ordinary house in their own neighbourhood. The care is provided by specially trained staff from a nearby old people's home, with possibilities for geriatric consultation from a nursing home.

The location of this project is a city: Amsterdam. This particular neighbourhood in Amsterdam is a cohesive 'blue-collar' community in an area with a lively street-market. These characteristics were used creatively in shaping the experiment; it grew organically from the needs of the elderly living in the neighbourhood and is embedded in community life in the same way as the nearby old people's home.

V Home care by a special project organization closely allied to the nursing home but carried out by home care organizations.

In this project, the people stay in their own houses and daily round-the-clock care is provided by a living-in spouse or relative. Additional care (even daycare) is provided by home help and community nurses.

Experimental shift in degree of institutionalization

As indicated earlier, all experiments were set up with a lesser degree of institutionalization in mind than would in general have been indicated for the individual patient, who would normally have been placed in the institutionalized environment of a nursing home. What are the different characteristics that allow us to provide a 'measure' of the degree of institutionalization of the five? For practical purposes we proposed the following dimensions:

- scale: the bigger, the more institutionalized;
- organizational structure: the more organization-centred as opposed to client-centred, the more institutionalized;
- the degree of possibility for the client to exert independence and autonomy; the less possibility of independence means more institutionalization. This dimension would include the (lack of) freedom in various aspects such as:
  - privacy in having your own living space (room or apartment)
  - being able to come or go as you please (open or closed living space)
  - being able to get up or go to sleep at your own time
  - the possibility of buying and/or preparing your own food

Home care of course is the least institutionalized form – in terms of location as well as preservation of autonomy. Old people's homes, where people have their own apartments and can either use or refrain from using meal services etc., still allows for a great deal of independence, with the added benefit of the security of having help available when needed. Using the above as a 'composite indication', we can visualize the degree of institutionalization in the various experimental projects as in Figure 18.1.

EVALUATION METHODS

In all projects the general aim turned out to be raising the quality of care without increasing the expense involved. For this reason the evaluation

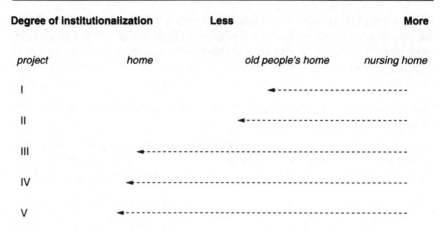

Degree of institutionalization		Less	More
project	*home*	*old people's home*	*nursing home*

Figure 18.1 Levels of diminishing institutionalization in five experimental projects

took the form of a cost–benefit analysis. However, as the experiments had not been set up with the aim of experimental comparison in mind but had widely different origins as well as differing means for achieving the desired goal, they would hardly qualify as a standard 'multiple-site analysis'.[2] Nevertheless, the evaluation in all cases required the following dimensions:

- characteristics of target group (rating scales)
- cost (including costs incurred outside of the budget)
- quality of care
- organizational strengths and weaknesses

The first two are quantitative, the second two mainly qualitative; each with their own problems, which we present below.

Quantitative measures: target group and cost

Target group and cost need quantitative comparison – in rating scales and money, respectively. However, as the evaluation of the different experiments had to be adjusted to the needs of the different situations, partly different measures were used as the case required.

For this particular meta-study comparison is difficult because of the different types of residence. In order to overcome this problem, the figures from different sources were converted into relative percentages. An example of the procedure is given in Table 18.1 below.

In three of our studies, the 'help-index' (a validated selection of SIVIS items, indicating the degree of infirmity) was used. It came out respectively at 8.7, 7.8 and 6.4 in the three experimental populations in that particular year. The comparison figure for the general population in that year[3] was

8.0 (= 100 per cent). Our conclusion is, that in these experiments the degree of infirmity of the target groups was respectively 108.8 per cent, 97.5 per cent and 80 per cent of this norm. These figures can be put in the form of a table, as Table 18.1 below. In the table presenting the results they will be used along with figures from other measures obtained in a similar way.[4]

Table 18.1 Example of converting rating scales for target group to relative percentages

Experiments	Help-index 1992	Relative infirmity
II	8.7	108.8%
III	7.8	97.5%
V	6.4	80%
norm: (nursing home)	8	100%

Qualitative measures of care and organizational process

Evaluation of care was made by client satisfaction as well as by professional standards for quality of (institutional) care. Where possible and applicable, additional data were gathered for comparison with known standards of care in the nursing home.

Because our research in most cases also was concerned with monitoring the innovation process with regard to strengths and weaknesses, we used the data we gathered to give feedback to the organization and in some cases the organizations clearly benefited by this to change course in some regards.

The data for these topics were mainly collected in three ways: by interviews, participant observation and study of relevant written materials (plans, letters, minutes). Interviews were held with clients (if applicable); relatives; professionals, working in the experiments; and with project management. Participant observation occurred at the site of care and at staff and management meetings.

Combining the results on the four evaluation topics outlined above enabled us to give a comprehensive analysis of the results of each experiment and its accompanying strengths and weaknesses. Comparison of the data on the different experiments allowed us to proceed to more general conclusions with policy implications.

RESULTS

Target group and cost

The main purpose of all experiments was, as indicated, to provide better care without increasing the cost. In order to provide a good foundation for a 'fair' comparison as regards quality of care, there are three related aspects to be taken into account:

- the relative severity of the conditions of people in the experiments compared to a nursing home;
- the number of people in the experiments who had to be transferred to a nursing home (for example because the project could not provide the necessary amount of care any more);
- the cost – for purposes of cost comparison, the average cost per day of a nursing home was used.

By using relative percentages indicating the amount of deviation from a norm as explained above, the results from various sources can be fairly easily represented for comparison purposes. The results are given in Table 18.2 below.

Discussion of results on target group

The results show that in most cases the ratings of the experimental population in general did deviate much from the comparison groups. There are two exceptions:

Experiment I – taking place in an old people's home. In this case, the target group had less severe problems, probably due to the fact that they came from a home situation and the evaluation was not continued long enough for further deterioration to develop.

Table 18.2 Severity of condition, percentage of transferrals and cost of five experiments in comparison with the nursing home

	average degree of severity	% transfers	average cost of care
standard norm (nursing home)	100%	0%	100%
I	55.5	12.5	80
II	108.8	0.0	75
III	97.5	8.0	90
IV	109.1	14.0	70
V	80.0	25.0	110

Experiment V – taking place in the home situation. In this case, the cost of round-the-clock care necessary for demented elderly living alone was prohibitive. If there was no living-in partner or relative to provide this care, people were transferred to a nursing home. This accounts for the relatively high percentage of transfers as well as for the relatively high cost. Clearly the conclusion of a cost–benefit analysis in this respect indicates that home care for demented elderly is only feasible for those who do not live alone.

In the other experiments, transfer to a more traditional institution such as a psychogeriatric nursing home mostly turned out to be necessary only in cases which were misplacements from the beginning. In a number of other cases transfer was not necessary, but desirable from the point of view of the client; these cases serve as examples for a more specific demarcation of the target group to benefit most from particular types of care.

We might tentatively conclude in general that the experiments in fact took in the group for which the experiment was designed; the experiments also served to show the limitations in the range of severity which could be handled.

Discussion of cost in relationship to target group

With the notable exception of Experiment V, which has already been discussed above, in all cases the cost of the experimental project turned out to be lower than the cost in traditional nursing homes. As seen from the analysis of the target group above, this cannot in general be attributed to the lower demands on care from the group except in Case I. In Case I the amount of care that has been given would probably be suitable also for a 'heavier' group – we shall return to this topic in the discussion of the quality of care. The reasons for the cost reductions were the following:

1 The housing situation. In all cases the housing situation did not conform to the standards for nursing homes, which take a heavy toll in expenses.
2 Cost reduction in cost of livelihood can be achieved by close monitoring in small-scale situations.
3 Lower personnel cost. Although small-scale situations tend to be more vulnerable in regard to personnel flexibility and overhead tasks, they are more flexible in the use of varied (and sometimes lower-paid) personnel for different tasks. In short, the division of labour is not enforced as rigorously as in larger-scale institutions.
4 Another less tractable factor in cost reduction as regards personnel may be the result of the experimental status itself. In some of the experiments, the motivation of the personnel involved was so great as to reduce absence on account of illness to almost negligible proportions – in itself a cost-reducing factor of no small significance. Under the present

circumstances, it is unclear whether this effect should be looked upon as a 'Hawthorne-effect';[5] namely, the idea that the experimental situation itself lies at the root of this and the effect would vanish after the experimental status ends, or on the other hand whether it is due to the particular organizational form in which small teams have the responsibility for their own unit. Right now, follow-up studies over a longer time are being conducted to determine this.

Before the start of some of the experiments the expectation had been that cost could be reduced as well as quality improved by involving relatives in types of care which in 'ordinary institutions' are performed by personnel. This expectation was mostly disappointed.

The manifest reduction in cost for the care of a group of people in general compared to the nursing home population of course immediately leads us to wonder whether this has been achieved at the expense of quality, or whether the original aim of improving quality has indeed been achieved. We shall turn to this topic now.

Results regarding quality of care

Clients' satisfaction

Quality of care as measured by clients' satisfaction was definitely high as compared to more traditional institutions. The most important factor in this seemed to be that people could stay in an environment which was less institutional and thus continue living in a more or less 'non-institutionalized' way.

This took many forms in the different experiments. People from Experiment V, who received care at home, appreciated being able to remain in a familiar environment. Most important for these clients, as may be inferred from what has been said before, was the possibility for spouses to remain together. This possibility might not in all cases turn out to be a blessing for everyone concerned, as has been documented in The Netherlands.[6] In one of the other projects (III) it was possible for spouses to come and live in a separate apartment on the upper floor of the building. Only a few of the spouses concerned took this up and even then it did not always turn out well. However, the most important factor in these circumstances is to have a choice. The people receiving home care made this choice in order to be together, so the spouses were well motivated and very thankful for an opportunity which they would not otherwise have had.

Similar circumstances prevailed in Experiment II, where spouses could either have an apartment together or two separate apartments near each other. The opportunity to remain together as well as having their own apartment were greatly valued.

Home environment

Three of the five experiments (I, III and IV) involved some kind of small-group situation of a more or less 'family' kind (as opposed to the other two which continued a more independent existence in separate apartments).

In Experiment I, a separate, closed off part of an old people's home was inhabited by twelve elderly women. Experiment III tried to emulate 'normal family' living conditions as much as possible in six 'houses', grouped together. Experiment IV actually used ordinary housing in people's own communities. In all cases this turned out to be highly successful. Staff and 'inmates' became well adjusted to each other, and everyone concerned was enthusiastic about an ordinary 'home' type of environment. In all cases the daily rhythm was to a great extent determined by people themselves; it was clear they took part in the life of a community instead of being part of an institution. During the last decade the importance of attachment theories for interpreting the needs of the demented has been stressed.[7] In particular it is postulated that anxiety arises as the result of being aware of one's cognitive dysfunctioning ('awareness context'),[8] thus enhancing feelings similar to those arising from separation or homelessness. A familiar environment with the continuity of attachment figures 'in loco parentis' seems to have a beneficial effect. In the experiments this was provided for in several ways.

Continuity as a way of improving quality of care was one of the key words in the experiments. Thus, in a number of ways, safety was provided. This provision of safety by continuity took many forms: continuity in the person of the doctor, continuity of contacts with family relations, continuity in the environment and in the daily personnel. Experiment IV scored very high on the provision of safety by continuity in the environment, because it took place in an ordinary house in the neighbourhood where people had lived all their lives. They could continue to visit the market (under guidance of personnel) and the door was not locked – it did not have to be, because the clients felt they belonged where they were, so pre-empting the need to go elsewhere as often happens in these cases.

Continuity of personnel turned out to be a very potent determinant of client satisfaction. This continuity was not established in all cases. In Experiment I (the most 'institutional' one), there was a great turnover; in Experiment III in the early years there was almost no personnel turnover, but this changed over time. In Experiment V the continuity was maintained even after the experiment had been running for five years and could hardly be considered an 'experiment' any more.

However it may have turned out in the various conditions, a safe climate to counteract the anxiety which accompanies the 'awareness context' has been preserved everywhere. The provision of this warm, family type of care had observable beneficial effects. In this respect the experiments were clearly superior to regular institutional care.

Continuity of place

Another goal of the experiments was for the clients to come into a place where they could stay as long as possible without being transferred, in the event of their condition deteriorating. Even in the two experiments (I and IV) where this initially was not formulated as a goal, transfer policy by the end went in this direction. As we saw above in the percentage of transfers, the experiments generally made good this promise. For those with more or less severe disorders this was a great comfort.

However, as regards improving the quality of care, in Experiment II, where the institution cared for a 'mixed' population, there are hidden difficulties. As one of the unforeseen effects in Experiment II, a clear distinction existed between those elderly who were still relatively well-functioning and those with more or less severe (psycho)geriatric disorders, needing most care. Continuity of care in terms of not being transferred as one's condition deteriorates is regarded most favourably by those who are the most dependent on care and have few other options available. On the other hand, many of the relatively 'good' clients in the mixed population resulting from a policy of non-transferral do not wish to be confronted by the deterioration of others – in their view this diminishes the quality of living in their own situation. This view was sometimes mitigated by considerations of compassion for those who were worse off, but surprisingly not by the consideration that the same conditions would allow them to stay if they found themselves in similar circumstances.

Quality of care from a professional viewpoint

Care from a professional viewpoint in these situations has different aspects: from 'hotel' care, pertaining to general living conditions, to nursing and therapeutic activities, and medical care. The general living conditions as we have seen were clearly above standard norms, even though (or maybe even because) in most cases housing conditions did not conform to formal institutional norms. The available living space was in some cases a bit cramped, but in general people thought this was more of an advantage than a disadvantage. In the cases where the general therapeutic ideology was explicitly taken to be 'warm care', derived from Bowlby's attachment theory, no special sessions of activity training, validation or reality training were held. However, the personnel in Experiment IV were educated to have these techniques available and use them whenever the situation called for it. In this way, a therapeutic climate was established that functioned very satisfactorily. In Experiment III, activity training was introduced after some years even though it had not been part of the original set-up. This also turned out well. In general, it might be concluded that for personnel some form of educational background in these techniques is a welcome addition to their training. Quality of geriatric care as measured by professional standards in some experiments initially seemed less satisfactory. However, over time things have been improving and at present guarantees for measuring up to professional geriatric standards are being developed. As most of the problems in this respect were a consequence of the innovation process itself, we shall return to them in the next section.

Special characteristics and organizational strengths and weaknesses

Although much of the data was gathered with the aim of answering questions on the outcome, the innovation process was just as important. From an organizational point of view, the new experimental forms were mainly the following:

1 GPs being responsible for the medical care of people who are usually treated by nursing home specialists. New patterns of relationships for professional consultation between had to be developed to do this properly.
2 Family home helpers and district nurses being employed to help in an old people's home, the group housing experiment or at home, in supplying nursing home care. The organizational form this took varied with the experiments.

In all cases the innovation process was laborious and took a long time; depending on the local and situational conditions and the strength of the management in question these initial difficulties were either overcome or continued to exist. As might be expected, the biggest problem turned out to be that professional organizations (and to a lesser extent the individual professionals) did not look kindly upon what they perceived as infringements upon their own territory. Problems of course are essential to the innovation process. Transferring the location of care also means that professional expertise from different locations is indispensable in achieving an optimum quality of care. Home care organizations and GPs have this kind of experience which is badly needed. On the other hand, the more specialized treatment and care of more complex cases in nursing homes is necessary as well.

When it comes to providing high-quality care for a particular client nobody actually disagrees with this. However, when it comes down to formalization of procedures it turns out to be quite another matter. Both sides feel they have the best expertise as well as the authoritative right to care for a particular group of clients. (And of course, both sides are right.) For each new experiment these struggles have to run their course over and over again before an accepted agreement is reached; this is the very core of the innovation process. To get an idea of the problems, here are some examples:

- GPs resent having to turn over to the nursing home specialist the medical responsibility for nursing home clients who were previously treated at home. They never ask for advice of their own accord so the process of developing professional consultation relationships in the form of 'bedside teaching' is thwarted.
- This lack of response to the offer of professional consultation should not only be attributed to resistance. Another reason is that it is very hard for an 'outsider' who does not possess the professional expertise in question, to see that something more can be done than is already provided. A clear example of this emerged when an ergotherapist was added to a home-team consisting of other professionals, and she found a large deficit in ergotherapeutic care, which nobody on the team had noticed before.
- Nursing home officials are doubtful whether the quality of care in experimental situations will be up to their standards, and are eager to prove that the provision of high-quality nursing home care outside nursing homes is too difficult.
- Achieving continuity of care in terms of the same people providing the care is difficult to achieve in the organization of small-scale projects. A small number of employees means less flexibility, so big home-care organizations are necessary to provide continuity of care.
- When either home-care or nursing home organizations provide care in old people's homes they also want responsibility for coordinating it; this creates problems with the project management who claim this responsibility for themselves.
- The structure of home-care organizations is not suited to providing guarantees for round-the-clock care; when this kind of care is needed in an experimental situation they generally say it is impossible to organize and they have enough problems as it is.
- When the boundaries of officially existing institutions are crossed, formal procedures for providing financial support in many cases no longer apply. Because these formal procedures are complex enough as it is, in many cases this proved to be an additional burden in which creative solutions had to be found for the problems that cropped up. This is of course a time-consuming process; and time is a particularly scarce commodity in the experiments.

The ways of dealing with these and many more problems had to be worked out in the experiments while at the same time (on account of being experimental) they were being closely watched for mistakes which in more traditional organizations would probably go unnoticed for some time. Taking into account these difficulties, it is heartening to see how most experiments were able to overcome these difficulties in time with zeal and creativity.

In the course of the experiments, some ways of dealing with these problems turned out to be more effective than others. Although the results are far from fixed, it still seems worthwhile giving the outlines of emerging solutions, as others might profit by them. In the end, they boil down to two guidelines which seem very familiar from the literature on innovation processes.

1 The formalization of new structures is often the hardest part. Therefore it is best to start things going on an informal footing and develop good inter-personal relations as a working base. This goes especially for professionals in the field of medicine and care. Since providing good care for their clients is the core of their professional pride they also are sensitive to the fact that others can make a welcome contribution to this goal. It is not the working together in itself that seems to be the threatening part; it is the handing over of responsibilities in a formalized way. From this it follows that relationships on the operational level can proceed smoothly while people in the meantime get to know and trust each other. When trust is established, the formalizing of procedures is much easier. From this it also follows that negotiations with people who are not involved in the operational process of care but one level higher – in management – are more difficult as they do not have the opportunity to develop respect for the contributions of others. The second rule follows from the first.
2 Start on a small-scale basis and try to work from there, instead of trying to change the world in one big leap. If an innovation turns out to be effective and useful, things will start to open out from there. Moreover, people will tend to feel less threatened because there is little at stake. If, on the other hand, everything has to be worked out beforehand, people will want to cover every eventuality; this slows procedures down to a point where maybe nothing will actually get done.

All the above are findings from the experiments which we monitored from the time they became operational. So, on the operational and tactical level, these findings are applicable. However, a lot of work on the strategic level had been going on before and continued after the experiments started. Although our observational data do not cover this, from trying to piece together the history of the experiments from the beginning, the same principles seem to apply. It is better not to aim for big changes of great complexity; the outcomes are too uncertain on account of unforeseen effects. 'Cutting up' the process of change into manageable pieces and experimenting with them seems (from our experience, but also historically), a better way of doing things. Evaluation and feedback, finding solutions and discarding some of them, are necessarily slow processes which in these experiments have shown good results.

The hard part of innovative strategy is most often the 'unfreezing' of existing structures and procedures. In general, this is so obvious as to seem almost trite. Organizations and people are inherently conservative, and only inclined to change if they are confronted by a problem or a challenge. Innovation takes time; the bigger the innovation, the more resistance is met with and the more time is required.

CONCLUSION

From the experiments it turns out that neither cost nor organizational problems are prohibiting factors in giving nursing home care at other locations than our traditional nursing homes. There is in this respect a wide variety of options available, each with its own particular advantages and disadvantages. However, all these experiments have been going on in particular settings which influenced the outcome to a great extent. Local conditions, quality of management, relationships between different institutions of care-providers, to name but a few, all have their influence. That these factors vary locally, however, does not mean that nothing can be said about the best solution in a particular setting. Quite the contrary. Far too often we tend to frame the options involved in the form of a general dilemma: either this *or* that, instead of framing the question as a decision-making problem.

- Staying at home, even with the best of care, is not always the best solution for the demented elderly because of the risk of loneliness. However, if a living-in partner is well-motivated to keep someone at home, avoiding institutionalization can enhance the joy of life for both partners. Good support from the outside, however, is required to make this a real option.
- Providing an integrated institutional environment, in which the more mentally able are mixed with cases which are worse off, has particular disadvantages for the 'best' cases. These are not outweighed by advantages in the form of a guarantee that they will not be referred to another institution in the event of their own condition deteriorating.
- The most feasible type of small-scale situation, available as an option for care, varies with local circumstances. In a city environment, an old neighbourhood where people have lived all their lives might prove to be a very good option. Newly built premises, mostly located on the outskirts, are only 'next best'.
- The advantages of continuity of medical care with GPs remaining responsible are in general not outweighed by the disadvantages of their lack of geriatric education. For general somatic care and emergency situations, however, GPs are eminently qualified. In rural areas and/or in very small-scale situations, there might be no other option available to fall back on for emergency care. Even in these cases, however, it would be most desirable to have only one or two physicians for the small institution, instead of letting people keep their own GP.

- Small-scale situations, either embedded in a larger institution or on their own, can provide a much-needed home environment in which people can live as much as possible an ordinary home life. These last types in general seem to have the least disadvantages in terms of quality of care and turn out to be not more expensive and in some cases clearly cheaper than traditional nursing homes. They might well be the emerging trend for the care of the demented elderly in the coming decades.

NOTES

1 In The Netherlands, contrary to most other countries, there are two different kinds of institutionalized care for the elderly. 'Old people's homes', in which relatively able elderly have their own apartment and some home help as well as meals, and for the more severe cases what are generally known as 'nursing homes', which are more like hospitals in that people do not have their own rooms and are wholly looked after.
2 For a general discussion on this subject, see, for example, R.K. Yin, *Case-Study Research: Design and Methods*, Sage: Newbury Park, California, 1989.
3 If the figures in this example had been collected in different years, the different figures for the particular years would have been used as a comparison measure.
4 For some of the figures it is doubtful whether the comparison made in this way is methodologically completely valid; e.g. in some cases figures have been constructed by means of averaging BOP scales which have not been constructed to allow for this. However, as the comparison is not meant as a valid 'proof', but rather as an indication, we have chosen to disregard these problems.
5 The expression is taken from the famous experiments in the Hawthorne factories in the US in the 1940s, in which production continued to rise under different conditions by the sheer effect of the attention paid to the situation itself.
6 See e.g. M. Duijnstee, *De belasting van familieleden van dementerenden*, NIZW: Utrecht, 1992.
7 Bowlby first documented this attachment behaviour for the very young. Recently it has been extended to cover the behaviour of the elderly in a process of dementia; evidence to support this explanation came out of recent research. See J. Bowlby, *Attachment, Life-Span and Old Age* (ed. by J.M.A. Munnichs and B. Miesen), Van Loghum, Slaterus: Deventer, 1986; and B. Miesen, *Gehechtheid en dementie*, Versluys: Almere, 1990.
8 B. Miesen, Psychic pain surfacing in dementia: from new to old trauma? Paper presented at the European Colloquium on Therapeutic Work with Older People, University of Stirling, 1995.

Chapter 19

Education about normal forgetfulness and dementia

Kees Commissaris

INTRODUCTION

In Western European and North American countries there has been a sharp increase in the total number as well as in the proportion of aged individuals in the population. In The Netherlands, for example, the number of people aged 65 years and older will increase from 12.5 per cent in 1988 to 24.1 per cent in 2040 (Central Bureau of Statistics, 1989). This development has important consequences, not only for the elderly themselves, but also for society in general and health care in particular. The number of chronic diseases will increase – for example, arthritis, asthma, chronic obstructive pulmonary disease, diabetes mellitus, psychogeriatric disorders and dementia. With advancing years, not only do physical functions diminish, but changes also occur in cognitive functioning. For instance, people experience that their memory is not working as well as it used to. In this chapter, the issue of educating people to accept what is normal forgetfulness and to seek help for abnormal forgetfulness will be considered. An information brochure was developed for this purpose and its content and effectiveness will be described in this chapter.

Normal ageing and forgetfulness

A normal phenomenon of the ageing process is a decrease in the accessibility of information. It not only concerns information that was stored a long time ago, but also information stored in the recent past. Because of this, elderly people are less able to remember relatively minor details of an event, although the event itself can still be recalled. These 'memory problems' are not permanent and most of the time the information can be recalled later. Considering changes in the retrieval processes, it appears that active recall works less 'smoothly' with age. However, research shows that passive recognition of information stored earlier is not decreased (Schonfield and Stones, 1979). This indicates that a recall problem is a consequence of an ineffective search of one's memory, or of an ineffective use of memory strategies (Jolles and Hijman, 1983; Branconnier and De Vitt, 1984).

The study of cognitive ageing is called cognitive gerontology (Rabbitt, 1990). On the basis of large-scale research in the past, most scientists have agreed that different aspects of cognitive functioning decrease during the normal ageing process in healthy individuals (Charness, 1985; Birren and Schaie, 1985; Poon, 1985). The changes that occur in information processing with ageing are fundamentally related to speed. In particular, the storage of new information demands more time in elderly people (Eriksen *et al.*, 1970). Furthermore, we live in an information society with rapid technological changes. Many elderly people are less able to use these new technical aids, such as video-recorders, pin-codes and teletext, in daily life. This increases feelings of impotence and insufficiency (Jolles, 1991). It also appears that skills such as the planning of new activities, problem-solving, making complex decisions and flexibility are considerably decreased (Reese and Rodeheaver, 1985). Paying attention to achieve input, consolidating to achieve storage, retrieving to achieve output may all become more difficult for the old (Job, 1992). With age, people become slower, particularly in conducting tasks under time pressure or in difficult situations. This is mainly caused by changes in the central nervous system (Botwinick, 1984).

People's worries about their memory

Labelling oneself forgetful involves more than simply how frequently one forgets. It is 'a personal response to the interaction between one's forgetting and one's social world' (Cromwell, 1994). The central issue of this chapter is the fact that a large number of people worry about their diminishing memory (Commissaris *et al.*, 1994). They experience cognitive decline as final proof of deterioration. This subjective decline could result in anxiety about becoming demented. Elderly people start to ascribe events of normal forgetfulness to something abnormal. This could lead to a further increase in anxiety and worry, ending in a vicious circle. In most cases, however, people's concern about dementia is unsubstantiated. Research at the Maastricht Memory Clinic showed that there were no signs of dementia in eight out of ten patients who were anxious about developing dementia (Verhey, 1993).

A reasonable estimate is that 5–10 per cent of all people aged 65 years or older are suffering from severe dementia. Estimates for mild dementia are twice as high. In the United States the costs of dementia in terms of nursing homes and other forms of care are calculated at about $40 billion per year (NIH, 1987). Despite the fact that many people are directly or indirectly confronted with this severe and deteriorating disease, the numbers mentioned above also imply that 80–95 per cent of all people of

65 years and older are not suffering from dementia. The forgetfulness many people complain about often does not herald dementia.

People's concern and worries about forgetfulness and dementia are partly caused by difficulties in accepting the fact that one is getting older. Furthermore, people tend to accept changes in the physical area more easily than changes in the cognitive area. In general, people are not worried about the fact that they cannot run as fast or cycle as far as they used to. The fact that information storage and retrieval also demand more time is not as easy to accept for most people.

Memory retraining courses

From research into the characteristics of people who participate in a memory retraining course, it appears that people with subjective memory complaints have more complaints of a depressive nature than people without memory complaints (Zarit, Kenneth and Guilder, 1981b). Other research revealed that participants with and without memory complaints did not differ on actual memory performance (Scogin and Bienias, 1988). However, some research shows that elderly people who complain about their memory have more negative expectations about the functioning of their memory (Zarit, Gallagher and Kramer, 1981a; Scogin et al., 1985). Ponds et al. (1992) concluded that the fact that depression among the elderly is often correlated with memory complaints can be explained by the concept of 'Memory Self-Efficacy' (MSE). MSE is a sub-scale of the 'Metamemory in Adulthood' (MIA) Questionnaire of Dixon et al. (1988) and gives an indication of people's expectations about their own memory performance. The perceived MSE partly determines the extent to which an individual is inclined to put energy in memory-related tasks, regardless of his or her potential memory abilities (Bandura, 1989).

COMMON CAUSES OF NORMAL FORGETFULNESS

As already mentioned, forgetfulness is a normal part of the ageing process and is mainly caused by cognitive changes in, for example, attention, speed and concentration. Memory complaints are also reported by people with depression (McAllister, 1983). Furthermore, several physical and psychological causes can be related to memory problems. The most common causes will be discussed briefly hereafter.

Physical causes

The use of tranquillizers and/or sleeping pills could be one of the physical causes of forgetfulness. The metabolism of medication in the body takes more time in elderly people, which might cause drowsiness and concentration problems, resulting in forgetfulness. Forgetfulness can also be caused by poor eating habits, leading to a vitamin deficiency. The human brain is very sensitive to this and as a consequence functions less well. Alcohol also has a negative effect on the brain, especially in elderly people, who are more sensitive to the effects of alcohol than younger people. Another physical cause of forgetfulness is an inadequately functioning thyroid gland. Hearing problems or eyesight problems can also cause forgetfulness. If it is not possible to store information properly, information cannot be recalled properly either. These people thus give the impression of being forgetful.

These are the most common, reversible, physical causes of forgetfulness. If professional help is provided at an early stage, in most cases an adequate intervention can improve the functioning of a person's memory. In practice, things are not as simple. There is often not just one factor contributing to forgetfulness, but several.

Psychological causes

One of the most common psychological causes of forgetfulness is stress. People who are depressed or melancholic, and people who worry a lot can be so preoccupied with their problems that their minds are 'full'. This can occur when people have lost a loved one, have lost their job, or felt in a crisis after retirement. Elderly people who are hospitalized can give the impression of being forgetful, or even seem to suffer from a dementia syndrome. Too much is going on in their minds at the same time.

Another psychological cause of forgetfulness can occur when people experience too little stress in daily life (sensory deprivation). They participate little in social activities and lack social contacts. Because of this, each day can look the same, without any peaks or troughs and without much to remember. These situations could lead to a vicious cycle of worrying, forgetting things and avoiding social situations. In most cases these people need help in order to change the situation and to improve their cognitive functioning.

WHAT THE PUBLIC SHOULD KNOW

In health education activities for the general public it is important to focus upon the differences between normal forgetfulness and dementia. This is not the place to discuss this subject in detail, but some issues will be mentioned. In the Dutch Alzheimer brochure *Vergeetachtig? of Dement?* ('Forgetful? or Demented?') (Verhey *et al.*, 1992) the following differences are explained to the general public.

• A main difference between forgetfulness and dementia is the difference in their occurrence. Almost everyone is bothered by forgetfulness from time to time. Dementia is less common.

• Another important difference is that although forgetfulness is often annoying, it does not lead to a major disruption of normal daily life. In the case of dementia, a person needs supervision and is dependent on the support of others. The chance that the forgetfulness is based on dementia is very small if someone can still manage his or her own finances, travel, and is able to manage the household.

• Normal forgetfulness is characterized by forgetting the details of an event. In the case of dementia, the whole event cannot be recalled. This is an important difference between normal forgetfulness and dementia. Another difference is that in normal forgetfulness someone has trouble with the active recall of nouns, for example the name of a person or town. The name is stored in the long-term memory and it cannot be recalled, but people recognize the name when they hear or see it. In the case of dementia, there are serious problems with the storage of new information and the retrieval of information.

When to seek help?

People who are worried about their diminishing memory, and/or about incipient dementia, need to know when they need to seek professional help and when they do not. In the case of dementia, early detection is important for both the patient and his or her social environment. Only then can the patient be treated and supported adequately. It is important that people who have close contact with the patient get proper information, emotional support and practical advice. If there is a psychological or physical cause for the forgetfulness, early detection and treatment is important in order to prevent further deterioration and worry. In the case of normal forgetfulness, it is important that people are reassured at as early a stage as possible. This might prevent depression, shopping around for the best medical advice, and a negative influence on the quality of life. Most people with memory complaints first consult their general practitioner. He or she can carry out a physical examination and talk to a relative of the patient, if necessary. The general practitioner can also refer the patient to a psychologist, psychiatrist or a memory clinic for further examination.

Memory clinics

In recent years, special memory clinics have been set up in several countries, for example the UK (Bayer *et al.*, 1987; van der Cammen *et al.*, 1987; Philpot and Levy, 1987), for the evaluation and management of elderly patients with milder cognitive deficits. In order to give an impression of what a memory clinic is, a brief description of the Maastricht Memory Clinic (MMC) in The Netherlands is given.

The Maastricht Memory Clinic opened in May 1986. It was a joint effort of the Department of Neuropsychology and Psychobiology, University of Limburg, and the Departments of Psychiatry and Neurology of the University Hospital of Maastricht. The explicit aims of the MMC are to provide a new service for the diagnosis and treatment of patients with relatively mild memory problems, whether demented or not, and to perform clinical research with particular reference to the very early stages of Alzheimer's disease. The diagnostic approach is multi-disciplinary, with equal input from psychiatry, neurology and neuropsychology. The clinic is not only a centre for diagnosis but also offers specific treatment and care, in order to meet the expectations of the patients. In the MMC, the criteria of the DSM–III–R (APA, 1987) are used for the diagnosis of dementia and other psychiatric syndromes. The criteria of the National Institute of Neurological and Communicative Disorders and Stroke, and the Alzheimer's Disease and Related Disorders Association (NINCDS–ADRDA) are used for the diagnosis of possible and probable Alzheimer's disease (McKahn et al., 1984). Hachinski's Ischaemic Score is used for the diagnosis of vascular dementia. By May 1993 more than 600 patients had been examined in the MMC. Thirty-five per cent of the first 430 patients, mean age 61.7 years, fulfilled the DSM–III–R criteria of dementia, and cognitive impairments could be objectified in another 49 per cent. Sixteen per cent of the patients appeared to have normal cognitive functions on extensive neuropsychological testing (Verhey, 1993).

EDUCATION ABOUT NORMAL FORGETFULNESS AND DEMENTIA

Many elderly people are worried about their diminishing memory. Dutch research revealed that half of the 350 people who attended an information meeting, 'Forgetfulness: often a normal phenomenon', were very worried about their memory (Commissaris et al., 1994). More than half of this group (56 per cent) were also afraid of developing dementia. This uncertainty and concern is mainly caused by a lack of information about normal forgetfulness and dementia and the differences between them. There are many misunderstandings and prejudices about memory problems and dementia, not only among the general public, but also among general practitioners and other health care workers. Among health care professionals, existing misunderstandings and prejudices might be the cause of a less than adequate way of coping with elderly people with memory complaints (Cooper and Bickel, 1984).

One way to increase people's knowledge about dementia and to decrease anxiety and misunderstanding is by carefully planned education campaigns. Research has revealed that current education activities in The Netherlands seem to take place mainly on an *ad hoc* basis, usually as a result of the existing need of a group of elderly people or of professionals who have a lot of contact with elderly people (Commissaris, 1993). Therefore it is important to know where elderly people can get information about normal and abnormal forgetfulness. Important sources of information are the mass media: radio, TV and newspapers. In Dutch daily newspapers there has been a steady flow of information about dementia in the past five years. However, it appeared that the number of articles about memory and forgetfulness was very low in comparison with the number of publications about dementia. The same conclusion could be drawn from research into the information provided for the general public by health care organizations. Emphasis was on dementia (94 per cent) and hardly any attention was paid to normal forgetfulness and memory complaints (6 per cent) (Commissaris, 1993). This lack of information could lead to a further increase in anxiety in people who are already uncertain about the functioning of their memory.

Planning health education activities

Because of the existing uncertainty and taboo, it is worthwhile paying more attention to education about memory, normal forgetfulness and dementia. In order to be effective, education should be carefully planned and systematically evaluated against educational criteria (Mullen *et al.*, 1985). Kok (1992) and Green and Kreuter (1991) discern ten steps for the planning of health education interventions: five planning questions and five evaluation questions.

The five planning questions are:

1 How serious is the problem?
2 What behaviour is involved?
3 What are the determinants of the behaviour?
4 Which interventions might change the behaviour?
5 How can they be implemented?

The five evaluation questions are:

6 Has the implementation been carried out as expected?
7 Has the implementation been received as planned?
8 Have the determinants of the behaviour changed?
9 Has the behaviour changed?
10 Has the problem lessened?

This planning process has mainly been used for interventions aimed at changing risky behaviour, for example, smoking, unsafe sex, not wearing safety belts, etc. Although there is no known relationship between dementia and a certain behaviour, this does not mean that this model cannot be used. Two examples clarify this statement. Secondary prevention of dementia by early detection is only possible when people seek professional help in an early stage. For an intervention aiming at this goal it is important to change 'help-seeking behaviour'. As already mentioned, there are several risky behaviours that are related to normal forgetfulness (using tranquillizers, alcohol consumption and poor eating habits). By aiming at the determinants of these behaviours, it is possible to decrease the number of people 'suffering' from normal forgetfulness that they might themselves confuse with a dementia syndrome.

AN INFORMATION BROCHURE ABOUT NORMAL FORGETFULNESS AND DEMENTIA

In order to provide the general public with information about the differences between normal forgetfulness and dementia, the staff of the Maastricht Memory Clinic developed an information brochure at the request of the Dutch Alzheimer's Association (Verhey *et al.*, 1992). Before national distribution of the brochure in April 1992, its effectiveness was tested among a group of 500 elderly in the province of Limburg, who were worried about their memory.

Objectives

The first objective of the study prior to the national distribution of the brochure was to gain more information about the characteristics of the people who were worried. The second objective was to assess the effectiveness of the brochure. Two specific questions were examined: (a) does the brochure reduce worry among people who are worried unnecessarily about their memory? and (b) does the brochure urge people to seek professional help when this seems advisable? The level of worry was rated on a five-point Likert scale, varying from 'no worries at all' (1) to 'very worried' (5).

The second question was investigated with a short cognitive test battery among 104 of the 463 people who cooperated in the pre-test as well as the post-test. The results of this study will be discussed briefly. More detailed information can be found elsewhere (Commissaris *et al.*, 1995a).

Results

The average age of the respondents was 66.5 years, varying from 30 to 90 years (N = 537). More than 32 per cent were 'worried' about their forgetfulness, and 57 per cent were 'somewhat worried'. Forgetfulness in daily life was predicted as 33 per cent of people's concern. Age, level of education, and locus of control were not correlated. Fifty per cent of the respondents had been worried for more than three years. People were asked to give their opinion about the causes of their forgetfulness. They gave more than one answer. It was striking that 45 per cent mentioned stress and tension as a contributing cause of their forgetfulness. Problems with hearing or eyesight were also mentioned frequently (38 per cent), as was the use of medication (30 per cent) and the use of alcohol (11 per cent). Almost 22 per cent of the respondents were worried or very worried about incipient dementia, 47 per cent were worried somewhat, and 31 per cent were hardly worried or not worried at all.

Of all the 430 people who were concerned about their forgetfulness, 114 (26 per cent) had consulted their general practitioner to discuss their memory complaints. Most people were told that their problems were not serious and were to do with their age. In 24 per cent of all cases people indicated that they had not received any information from their general practitioner with respect to their complaints. Four per cent were told they were suffering from incipient dementia. After reading the brochure, 63 per cent of the 140 respondents who had been worried (a lot) about their forgetfulness said that their worries had considerably decreased or had disappeared. Three per cent became more worried. The information in the brochure reassured 77 per cent of the 99 respondents who had earlier worried (a lot) about possible dementia. These patients indicated that their worries had significantly decreased or had disappeared.

After reading the information in the brochure, 8 per cent of all people who filled in the second questionnaire (N = 450) consulted their general practitioner to discuss their memory problems and 10 per cent indicated that they had changed one or more behaviours that might have had an impact on the functioning of their memory by consuming healthier food, less alcohol, and fewer sleeping pills.

Conclusions after testing

A total number of 104 people were tested with a short cognitive test battery. The brochure enabled most people to find out whether they were worrying unnecessarily or not. However, some people remained (very) worried about possible dementia, despite the information provided and their good test performance. Within this group a relatively high percentage of people had a close relative with dementia. Anxiety about inheriting dementia could be a possible explanation for their concern. Some people with a poor test performance became less worried. This outcome result was not in accordance with the goals of the brochure. This group was characterized by fewer problems in daily life than the people who were justifiably worried. This group also had a higher internal locus of control and therefore a better way of coping with their forgetfulness in daily life.

The results of this study were used to adapt the brochure where necessary and it was distributed on a national level. The brochure certainly met an existing need for information among the general public. In the first two years 40,000 brochures were distributed on request.

CONCLUSIONS AND RECOMMENDATIONS

Up to now hardly any attention has been paid to education about memory, memory problems, and normal forgetfulness. Most emphasis has been on dementia. In future education programmes more explicit information should be given about memory complaints, normal forgetfulness, and cognitive changes in the elderly. The media could make an important contribution towards achieving this goal. An important condition is better cooperation with experts on the subject. Carefully planned education and information campaigns for the general public and health care workers can make an important contribution to the prevention of incorrect diagnoses of dementia and also to the early detection of dementia. However, evaluation research is indispensable for gaining a better understanding of educational activities and intervention programmes. In this way information becomes available about whether the goals of a programme are actually achieved.

The role of the general practitioner

General practitioners can have an important role in patient-education. Because of their key position, they have regular contact with people who complain about their (diminishing) memory. By giving them clear information, it is possible for general practitioners to reassure a large group of people who are worrying unnecessarily. The problem at the moment is that, by and large, general practitioners do not have enough knowledge and skills to give adequate information and explanation to their patients. An information brochure about the differences between normal forgetfulness and dementia can be used as a helpful aid by the general practitioner. In order to be able to accomplish this role, an education protocol should be developed and evaluated to enable general practitioners to provide adequate information to patients with memory complaints. One advantage of providing information to worried patients could be considerable economic saving for the health care system.

In the case of dementia, the general practitioner can have an important role in informing the patient and his or her social environment, especially the husband or wife and the children. The importance of this has been reported in several publications (Chenoweth and Spencer, 1986; Haley et al., 1992; Commissaris et al., 1995b). The more information families and care-givers receive, the better they are able to cope with the problems that might occur as a consequence of the disease. This enables care-givers to keep the patient at home for longer. This also means a saving for the health care system. It is of great importance that interventions in this field are developed.

Information to the general public

It is important that people achieve a better understanding of dementia. An atmosphere of taboo still prevails. People do not know how to respond to the strange behaviour of the dementia patient and they often choose to avoid all contact. Still, it is possible that everyone sooner or later, directly or indirectly, will be confronted with dementia. It is important to know that not every dementia syndrome means that the situation is absolutely hopeless. Seeking professional help is not only of great importance in the case of a dementia syndrome with a reversible cause, but also in the case of a dementia syndrome of an irreversible nature. Treating dementia patients in the best possible way can improve their quality of life. Early detection of dementia can help prevent psychopathology in close relatives of patients.

Future education policies should aim to reduce existing prejudices and misunderstanding about memory problems and dementia. An adequate education policy could improve the quality of patients' lives and their social environment and will reduce costs for the health care system. Interventions aimed at these goals deserve special attention.

SUMMARY

In this chapter, the issue of educating people about the differences between normal forgetfulness and dementia is considered. For this purpose an information brochure was developed and evaluated. Information about this topic is necessary because research reveals that many people, especially the elderly, are worried about their diminishing memory and/or about incipient dementia. However, most people in this group are worrying unnecessarily, which could result in reduced quality of life and in increased costs for the health care system. The effectiveness of the brochure was tested among a group of 500 elderly people in the province of Limburg in The Netherlands who were worried about their memory. An interesting finding was that 45 per cent mentioned stress and tension as a contributing cause of their forgetfulness. The use of alcohol was mentioned by 11 per cent of the respondents as a possible cause. After reading the brochure, the number of people who worried a lot about their memory or incipient dementia decreased considerably.

After testing 104 people with a short cognitive test battery, it appeared that some people remained worried about possible dementia, despite the information in the brochure and their good test performance. A relatively high percentage of people in this group appeared to have a close relative with dementia and their worries could be explained by anxiety about heredity. Some people with poor test results became less worried. This group experienced fewer problems in daily life than the people who were justifiably worried, and there are indications that they have a better way of coping with their forgetfulness in daily life.

In future health education activities on this topic, general practitioners could have an important role in instructing and educating people with memory complaints, because of their key position in the health care system. An education protocol should be developed in order to enable them to accomplish this role adequately. This will lead to considerable savings for the health care system.

REFERENCES

APA (American Psychiatric Association) (1987) *Diagnostic and Statistical Manual of Mental Disorders*, 3rd edition revised (DSM–III–R). Washington: APA.

Bandura, A. (1989) Regulation of cognitive processes through perceived self-efficacy. *Developmental Psychology* 25: 729–735.

Bayer, A.J., Pathy, J., and Twining, C. (1987) The memory clinic, a new approach for the detection of early dementia. *Drugs* 33, suppl. 2: 84–89.

Birren, J.E. and Schaie, K.W. (eds) (1985) *Handbook of the Psychology of Aging* (3rd edition). New York: Van Nostrand Reinhold.

Botwinick J. (1984) *Aging and Behavior* (3rd edition). New York: Springer.

Branconnier, R.J. and De Vitt, D.R. (1984) Early detection of incipient Alzheimer's disease. In: B. Reisberg (ed.). *Alzheimer's Disease* (pp. 214–227). New York: The Free Press.

Cammen, T.J.M. van der, Simpson, J.M., Fraser, R.M., Preker, A.S. and Exton-Smith, A.N. (1987) The memory clinic. A new approach to the detection of dementia. *British Journal of Psychiatry* 150: 359–364.

Central Bureau of Statistics (1989) *Bevolkingsprognose voor Nederland 1988–2050* (Prognosis for the Dutch population in the period 1988–2050). Den Haag: SDU-uitgeverij.

Charness, N. (ed.) (1985) *Aging and Human Performance*. Chichester: Wiley.

Chenoweth, B. and Spencer, B. (1986) Dementia: the experience of family caregivers. *The Gerontologist* 26: 267–272.

Commissaris, C.J.A.M. (1993) Voorlichting over geheugenproblemen en dementie (Education about memory problems and dementia). Doctoral dissertation. Maastricht: University of Limburg.

——, Verhey, F.R.J., Ponds, R.W.H.M., Jolles, J., Damoiseaux, V. and Kok, G.J. (1994) Public information about normal forgetfulness and dementia: Importance and effects. *Patient Education and Counseling* 24: 109–115.

——, Ponds, R.W.H.M., Verhey, F.R.J., Damoiseaux, V., Kok, G.J. and Jolles, J. (1995a) Public education about normal forgetfulness and dementia: Effectiveness of a systematically developed information brochure. *Educational Gerontology* 21: 763–777.

——, Jolles, J., Verhey, F.R.J. and Kok, G.J. (1995b) Perceived problems of caregiving spouses of patients with dementia and the role of education. *Patient Education and Counseling* 25: 143–149.

Cooper, B. and Bickel, H. (1984) Population screening and the early detection of dementing disorders in old age: a review. *Psychological Medicine* 14: 81–95.

Cromwell, S.L. (1994) The subjective experience of forgetfulness among elders. *Qualitative Health Research* 4: 444–462.

Dixon, R.A., Hultsch, D.F. and Hertzog, C. (1988) The Metamemory in Adulthood (MIA) Questionnaire. *Psychopharmacological Bulletin* 24: 671–688.

Eriksen, C.W., Hamlin, R.M. and Breitmeyer, R.G. (1970) Temporal factors in visual perception as related to aging. *Perceptive Psychology* 7: 354–356.

Green, L.W. and Kreuter, M.W. (1991) *Health Promotion Planning, an Educational and Environmental Approach*. Mayfield: Mountain View.

Haley, W.E., Clair, J.M. and Saulsberry, K. (1992) Family care-giver satisfaction with medical care of their demented relatives. *The Gerontologist* 32: 219–226.

Job, E. (1992) The anticipation of memory loss and dementia in old age. In: G.M.M. Jones and B.M.L. Miesen, (eds). *Care-Giving in Dementia. Research and Applications*, vol. 1. London/New York: Tavistock/Routledge.

Jolles, J. (1991) Mogelijke ontwikkelingen in gerontologie en geriatrie gezien vanuit cognitieve invalshoek [Possible developments in gerontology and geriatrics from a cognitive perspective]. *Tijdschrift voor Gerontologie en Geriatrie* 22: 89–91.

—— and Hijman, R. (1983) The neuropsychology of aging and dementia. *Developmental Neurology* 7: 227–250.

Kok, G.J. (1992) Quality of planning as a decisive determinant of health education effectiveness. *Hygie* 11: 5–8.

McAllister, Th.W. (1983) Overview Pseudodementia. *American Journal of Psychiatry* 140: 528–533.

McKahn, G., Drachman, D., Folstein, M., Katzman, R., Price, D. and Stadlan, E.M. (1984) Clinical diagnosis of Alzheimer's disease. Report of NINCDS–ARDRA workgroup on Alzheimer's disease. *Neurology* 34: 939–944.

Mullen, M.D., Green, L.W. and Persinger, G.S. (1985) Clinical trials of patient education for chronic conditions: A comparative meta-analysis of intervention types. *Preventive Medicine*; 14: 753–781.

NIH (National Institute of Health) (1987) Differential diagnosis of dementing diseases. NIH Consensus Development Conference.

Philpot, M.P. and Levy, R. (1987) Memory clinic for the early diagnosis of dementia. *International Journal of Geriatric Psychiatry* 2: 195–200.

Ponds, R.W.H.M., Bruning, H.A. and Jolles, J. (1992) Ouderen en geheugen-klachten. Een onderzoek naar zelfkennis over het geheugen, depressie en geheugenprestaties (Elderly and memory complaints. An investigation of metamemory, depression, and memory abilities). *Tijdschrift voor Gerontologie en Geriatrie* 23: 188–194.

Poon, L.W. (1985) Differences in human memory with aging: Nature, causes and clinical problems. In: J.E. Birren and K.W. Schaie (eds). *Handbook of the Psychology of Aging*, 2nd edition (pp. 187–201). New York: Van Nostrand Reinhold.

Rabbitt, P.M.A. (1990) Applied cognitive gerontology: Some problems, method-ologies and data. *Applied Cognitive Psychology* 4: 225–246.

Reese, H.W. and Rodeheaver, D. (1985) Problem solving and decision making. In: J.E. Birren and K.W. Schaie (eds). *Handbook of the Psychology of Aging*, 2nd edition (pp. 474–499). New York; Van Nostrand Reinhold.

Schonfeld, D. and Stones, M.J. (1979) Remembering and aging. In: J.F. Kihlstrom and F.J. Evans (eds). *Functional Disorders of Memory* (pp. 103–109). New York: Erlbaum and Hillsdale.

Scogin, F., Storandt, M. and Lott, L. (1985) Memory-skills training, memory complaints and depression in older adults. *Journal of Gerontology* 40: 563–568.

Scogin, F. and Bienias, J.L. (1988) A three year follow-up of older adult participants in a memory-skills training program. *Psychology and Aging* 3: 334–337.

Verhey, F.R.J. (1993) Dementia, depression and forgetfulness. Clinical studies of the early diagnosis and the differential diagnosis of dementia. Dissertation. Maastricht: Maastricht University Press.

——, Ponds, R.W.H.M., Jolles, J., Commissaris, C.J.A.M. and Damoiseaux, V. (1992) *Vergeetachtig? of Dement?* (Forgetfulness? or Dementia?). Bunnik: Alzheimer Stichting.

Zarit, S.H., Gallagher, D. and Kramer, N. (1981a) Memory training in the community aged: effects on depression, memory complaint and memory performance. *Educational Gerontology* 6: 11–27.

Zarit, S.H., Kenneth, D.C. and Guilder, R.L. (1981b) Memory training strategies and subjective complaints of memory in the aged. *The Gerontologist* 21: 158–164.

Chapter 20

Ethical issues in the care of the demented elderly

Ilse Warners

INTRODUCTION

The care of people suffering from a dementing process inevitably involves dilemmas concerning fundamental human rights as well as human responsibilities. A central point of discussion is the concept of autonomy, understandably so as dementia affects people's ability to organize their lives according to their own will, insights and beliefs. The decline of organizing skills, however, should not be confused with loss of self-awareness or the need to respond to one's own situation and to give meaning to one's own existence. Expressions of anxiety, agitation or disorientation are often linked with feelings of responsibility.

Ethics can be described as a systematic reflection on responsibility, (de Graaf, 1972). In the history of health care, ethical reflections were mainly concentrated on the responsibilities of the care-givers, not by admonishments to dedicate their knowledge and skills to the support and healing of the sick and the weak, but also by prohibitions on the abuse of their powerful position (Jonsen 1992). Not until the second half of the twentieth century was it recognized that those who were in need of care had something to say for themselves. Autonomy, originally a philosophical and political concept, became an important issue in the relation between, particularly, physicians and patients. The necessity of a formal structure to guarantee the patient's autonomy, however, threatens to obscure the essence of autonomy and responsibility as an inevitable part of being human. Prior to recognition of human rights comes the acceptance of human nature, which forces us, even in utter confusion and bewilderment, to choose, to act, to respond to our situation.

In the next few paragraphs an attempt will be made to shift the concept of autonomy from a juridical sense to the area where the struggle for autonomy becomes concrete and demands systematic reflection on responsibilities. In order to do so, a distinction is made between various levels of autonomy.

The problem of competency is related to dilemmas about autonomy. A well known example is the question whether somebody suffering from depression and wanting to die is competent to control his situation, whether his refusal of food and drink should be respected or whether he should be treated against his expressed wish.

The decision as to whether somebody is competent to understand a problem concerning his or her own situation, to reflect upon the consequences of alternative choices and to make decisions formally belongs to the field of diagnostics and of the law. As Godderis *et al.* state, there is no little discrepancy between the two. According to the law somebody is either competent or he is not, *tertium non datur.* Medical (psychiatric) interpretation of competency implies the possibility of a continuum and moreover of fluctuations in competency, for which jurisprudence leaves little room (Godderis *et al.*, 1992). Apart from differences in legal and medical standpoints, implementation of the concept of competency (or rather incompetency) seems to meet with great difficulties. Up to now formal decisions about the incompetency of individuals with psychogeriatric problems seem to have been limited to questions concerning the execution of a will, management of property and personal affairs, and health care decisions.

Many authors point out that there are different levels of competency (for example Godderis *et al.*, 1992; Davis, 1991). The capacity to manage one's own financial affairs, for instance, is not so common as generally assumed, but no bank is held responsible for encouraging its clients to spend too much. Young men and women are judged competent to volunteer for actions with a high risk of violent death or mutilation. But take the same people, fifty years later, undergoing a revival of their long repressed traumatic experiences, and their death wish is no longer judged rational. It is not, of course. Neither was it, fifty years earlier.

As a matter of fact many important decisions are often not made on a rational basis, but on impulses stemming from phylogenetically older components of the human mind. In the most common forms of dementia the greater part of these older structures seem to stay intact until perhaps the final stage (Vroon, 1989). This may explain the phenomenon of 'contextual awareness' in demented persons (Miesen, 1995). Even in an advanced stage of dementia people are aware of their situation and react accordingly. Many of them somehow adapt to their new situation, make new relations or perhaps transfer old feelings to new relations and thus participate in the human family. As we will see, this may make him or her competent enough to make deliberate choices and accept the consequences.

Ethical questions are closely related to views on humanity. Until very recently there has been little literature in which ethical questions around dementia are raised. If the situation of people suffering from dementia has not been taken into consideration, it may have been caused by the –

unspoken – assumption that dementia strips a person of his humanity. Indeed, the idea that you are no longer fully human in a certain stage of dementia is widespread. One of the reasons may be found in the classic picture of man or woman in his or her prime at about 40 or 50 years old. A second image, sometimes overlapping the former, pictures man or woman in full command of his or her intellectual capacities as the crown of creation. These idealized images are completed with the view of the human course of life as an epic with the protagonist dying at the height of his or her achievements. As most people reaching 40 want to go on living they try to accept a gradual loss of physical strength and skills, but a loss of mental capacities is literally *unthinkable*. Only if we accept that being human has meaning primarily within the community and within history, may we perhaps look at our mental decline from the standpoint of the community or even from the standpoint of our species. Perhaps we may see the phases of our lives in which we are fully dependent on the care of other people, as no less meaningful than our more heroic performances.

Individuals, finally, have a morality of their own, in some respects congruent with their social environment, but all the same rooted in a very personal feeling of right and wrong. Ethics, on the other hand, demands a communal effort to bring different viewpoints, even different beliefs, to a common standpoint. Even if the Church or other authority proclaims a certain moral code, a community which takes upon itself the responsibility for its members can only fully meet that responsibility by continuous systematic reflection upon its own motives, goals and actions.

AUTONOMY

Autonomy is a complex concept consisting of the components '*autos*', self, and '*nomos*', generally translated as law or rule. *Nomos* is related to the verb '*nemein*' which means to take in possession, to reclaim (land), to manage or administer (one's affairs). Autonomy in a philosophical and ethical sense concerns the freedom to direct one's own actions, to give direction and meaning to one's existence. Different levels can be distinguished.

On the primary level, giving direction to one's own life is not a right granted to the individual by the community, but a quality through which the individual is who he or she is. On this level autonomy corresponds to *authenticity*. I am the origin of my perception, my feelings, thoughts and actions. I am the centre of time and place when I speak of past or future. This, that, here and there, define the location of objects with respect to myself as point of orientation. As subject of my perception, my emotions, thoughts, desires, movements, I experience the authenticity of my existence, a feeling of ontological security as Laing puts it (Laing, 1959). From this security as starting point I can communicate with other people. Probably everyone has moments in which he does not feel real nor at ease. Sometimes these feelings are accompanied by dizziness and a black mood. These moments disappear as they come, leaving no trace. There are, however, conditions in which the sensation of unreality repeatedly occurs – some people are more disposed to this sensation than others – or even persists. In that case, communication with other people may be threatening. When you have the feeling of losing your identity, a feeling of ontological insecurity, you are in danger of becoming a plaything in a game of other people's making. The reverse also occurs: being at the mercy of the intentions and actions, even the care, of people by whom you do not feel recognized, may cause sensations of unreality. One needs the recognition of the other to experience the reality of one's own existence (see also chapter 1).

A second level of autonomy is connected with the concept of *privacy*. This concept contains the acknowledgement of a personal territory, into which an individual may withdraw, in which he or she feels safe from the interference of strangers. In a juridical sense the right of privacy is limited to the right of protection of data which, if they come to the knowledge of other people, might harm the person concerned. For example there is the privacy of correspondence or physicians' or lawyers' obligation of confidentiality. Psychologically the individual's need to have his or her privacy respected reaches further. An 83-year-old woman, when asked what privacy meant to her, replied:

It has always been very important to me to have a spot where you can withdraw. I've been in hospital a few times and what I really hated was fellow patients being witness of all kind of intimate things, like when you had to break wind, or when you felt down. But at home too I sometimes needed to be left alone, to have a moment for myself without my husband and my children. As a matter of fact they always claimed my attention during those times when I needed to work things out for myself. Now you may say that I have privacy enough [in an apartment of a service-home], but that is not the same. If you are on your own for days and days you become imprisoned in your thoughts. The question is not one of being alone, but that people respect that you have private thoughts. There are some who constantly watch what you are doing and want to know everything, like that woman two doors from here. 'I did not see your son this week.' She knows exactly when he comes to visit me. Once in a while he has to cancel his visit because he is too busy. Of course that is a disappointment. In my situation a week is a long time, but I should not complain. It is just wonderful that he comes to see me so regularly. He has a very responsible job and often has to work in the evenings or during the weekends. It is wonderful to have him here. We may talk about all kinds of things or just sit and read. Actually that is privacy as I mean it. Just the two of us together; the rest is nobody's business.

Privacy and authenticity are connected. Another person's casual observation of my vulnerability, my naked body, my emotions or my relations forms an intrusion into the space I need in order to accept myself. This space is not firmly confined.

Remarkably, the old lady quoted admitted the interviewer into her vulnerability. By voluntarily sharing her 'secret' with someone else she confirmed her self-esteem.

A third level of autonomy is formed by *the right of self-determination*. The term 'right' implies an agreement between individual and community or society. Through self-determination the individual is responsible. Society starts with the assumption that individuals are able to determine their will and consequently holds them responsible for their actions (Leenen, 1991). The right of self-determination implies the freedom to make choices that may not correspond with dominant social norms, as long as they do not curtail other people's right of self-determination. As an illustration Leenen mentions the individual's right to take his own life, although it might clash with prevailing beliefs within society. Figure 20.1 gives a schematic overview of three levels of autonomy.

The distinction may help us to recognize questions concerning individual autonomy. A different or more extensive analysis, however, may be equally useful, particularly as there is no clear dividing line. It is important that autonomy is only partially a right which has to be protected, but essentially is part of human nature. Moreover, being aware of your situation is not the same as being capable of handling your rights as a citizen or even of organizing your own life according to your own wishes. On two levels it seems meaningful to distinguish awareness of autonomy from legal rights. As is shown in Figure 20.1 it is awareness which forms the link between the three levels.

Protective and constructive measures

If we look at guidelines concerning the right of self-determination, we may notice they are mainly of a *safeguarding* nature, namely protection of the weak against the arbitrariness of the strong. Autonomy seen from other levels may cause someone to wonder if guidelines of an *obligatory* nature are desirable, possible and controllable. Such guidelines would focus on *support* of the autonomy of individuals in a vulnerable position by those on whom they are dependent. Let us consider an example. Within the geriatric setting, physical restraint, for instance to prevent someone getting out of bed or standing up from a chair has been the subject of ethical discussions these last few years. It is clear that restraint is contrary to the right of self-determination, but admissible in spite of that, provided that certain conditions of carefulness are met. Among them are that:

- the measure is accounted for in care-planning and the decision is taken in the (inter-disciplinary) care team;
- an independent commission within the institution is informed of the measure;
- this commission reports to the management (Nationale Ziekenhuisraad, 1990).

The effort of meeting these conditions will no doubt have positive effects, but it does not change anything for the person whose movements are restrained. A review of the literature on the use of physical restraint of the elderly (Strumpf, Evans and Schwartz, 1991) shows that it seems 'to intensify the disorganized behavior of many patients . . . contribute to sensory deprivation and a loss of self-image . . . and decline in central nervous system activity'. What in a legal sense may be considered a *measure of protection* appears to affect the individual's autonomy on a much deeper level.

AUTHENTICITY	**ontological awareness**
	I am
	this is my body
	this has been my life
	this is my life
PRIVACY	**territorial awareness**
	this is my home
	this is between you and me
	this is my property
	these are my private thoughts and feelings
	territorial rights
	domestic peace
	protection of property
	protection of personal data
SELF-DETERMINATION	**legal and political awareness**
	provided it is not harmful to other people, I may believe, prefer or do things my own way, including things which are thought unhealthy, unwise, indecent or eccentric
	legal and political rights
	freedom of movement
	validity of living will
	protection against moral pressure and intimidation
	medical treatment on the basis of informed consent

Figure 20.1 Three levels of autonomy; within each level distinction is made between the dimensions of awareness and formal rights. On the dimension of awareness there is a close connection between the three levels.

Recording of the restraining measure should therefore contain both circumstances such as changes in the staff or commotion in the ward, and the alternatives which were considered. This way certain patterns may appear, which have nothing to do with personal needs, but rather with organizational problems such as shortage of staff, lack of insight and skills, or unrest caused by the change of shifts. In case of circumstantial causes for restraint there certainly is a moral problem, not least for management and society as a whole.

If restraint is necessary for reasons that really concern the person him- or herself, the protocol mentioned above should also contain guidelines to ensure the person's well-being – such as release (at least every two hours), frequent personal contact, guided walks (eventually by wheelchair), variety in the person's surroundings to prevent sensory deprivation and boredom, and activities which he or she likes.

Although it is generally accepted that care-giving institutions operate with resident safety and protection as priorities, most of them do not allow for the residents to have genuine privacy. The impact of an environment that continually forces someone to be alert, to be on the defensive against meaningless stimuli, may be a greater threat to his or her identity than dementia itself.

We may wonder if a collective anti-influenza policy in a nursing home does not interfere with the natural course of life. Fever, formerly used as well as electro-convulsion therapy in the treatment of depression, is replaced by anti-depressives. We do not know which of them, fever or drugs, has the greater impact on someone's authenticity, in this case someone's capacity to find a new balance in life or to die in peace. The same question arises in all those cases where palliative treatment might be a good alternative to curative treatment (see Volicer et al., 1994).

In all these cases protection against some dangers is, ethically, only half of the question. The rest consists of reflection on constructive measures which may help individuals complete the rest of their journey according to their own norms and possibilities.

COMPETENCY

Competency, like autonomy, is a very complex concept, which may be defined from different viewpoints. As soon as moral choices in the field of care-giving have the individual's well-being as a leading principle (which in modern democracies seems to be the case) a distinction should be made between *subjective* and *objective* viewpoints. From a subjective viewpoint, not being able to make the right financial decisions and needing expert advice does not necessarily involve a feeling of incompetence. Another's judgement, however, that one is not capable of handling one's financial affairs may greatly affect one's feelings of dignity. Similarly, practical support in washing and dressing may be accepted with good grace. But if someone feels quite capable of managing their personal hygiene according to their own standards, they may feel offended by offers of help. In most cases, however, resentment is not directed against friendly and considerate assistance, but against the authoritarian attitude of helpers who decide that you have to undress fully before washing your hands and face, or that you need a shower – in short against those who impose their hygienic norms on you.

Three levels of competency

Apart from the difference between an objective assessment or a subjective experience of competency, different levels can be distinguished. In the case of dementia generally the emphasis lies on the capacity to choose and to take decisions in questions involving civil rights, for instance consenting to medical treatment or deciding how much one wants to spend on charity. On another level, competency means the capacity to cope with the demands of daily life, practically as well as socially. On a third and deeper level lies the ability to maintain what Erikson (1983) called ego-integrity.

These levels more or less correspond with Bengston's and Kuypers' (1989) three dimensions of competency as:

- adequate social functioning;
- adapting to and coping with new and unforeseen stimuli;
- the phenomenological experience of being in control of one's own situation.

A dementing process may gradually deprive individuals of their capacity to take decisions in financial matters so that someone else has to look after their interests. Giving up one's house, whether it is owned or rented, is often a particularly sensitive subject. If one has lived there for a significant part of one's life, it is home. It is not only a rational decision that has to be taken, but more a matter of cutting an emotional tie.

Impairments in memory and recognition, and consequently the capacity to make decisions, are often subject to changes: one moment there may be a clear understanding of the situation, the next moment it may be lost. That is more likely to be the case if a decision causes grief and involves a process of adaptation and coping. It often happens that people suffering from dementia deny they have made a decision and accuse other people – partner or children – of improper manipulation. As a matter of fact important decisions are often influenced by some outward pressure, especially when money is involved. The law cannot completely cover this problem as it is difficult to prove one's intentions. The presence of personal interests, however, does not necessarily imply false intent.

Reason and emotion

Important decisions in an individual's life, such as moving house, marrying, having a child or quitting a job, are often not the result of a long process of deciding. No doubt some process precedes the decision, but it does not always take place on a rational level. It is, rather, a matter of growing towards a decision, sometimes even unconsciously – of moving from a state of indecision to suddenly being resolved.

Being competent to take decisions depends partially on cognitive capacities, but much more on someone's emotional development and personality. If, for instance, a decision is required to stop renting a house, or to sell it and get rid of the furniture and other possessions, the individual should be allowed time to come to his or her own resolution. Sometimes people make provisions beforehand, like authorizing someone to guard their interests, or writing down their will. But even in that case one has to confirm one's resolve at the time it becomes actual, provided one's faculties are intact. Nobody can anticipate their own emotions. In the case of dementia the same choices often have to be made again and again, the same emotions experienced over and over. It seems, nevertheless, that a kind of adaptation to the new situation is possible. The following example may illustrate this.

Mrs King had consented to move to a home for the demented elderly. The home was an innovatory project aiming at normal living conditions (Anton Pieckhofje, Haarlem). Just like the other residents, Mrs King had a room of her own, furnished after her own taste with pieces of furniture she was attached to. There was a common living room and kitchen, where the residents, together with a nursing auxiliary, had meals which they prepared themselves, and where they took part in household activities, as far as each wished or was able to. She was free to go to her room whenever she wanted and also to receive visitors there. Her daughter came daily. She could go for a walk in the courtyard with its nice garden and pay a visit to neighbouring living-units.

When I came to visit her she proudly showed me her room. My eye was caught by a picture of her daughter. 'This must be your daughter', I said. She denied this, at the same time telling me that she hardly saw her daughter any more. The last time had been weeks ago, when they had gone to her own house. It was totally empty. 'Sure,' I said, 'because you have all your things here now.' She looked around. 'It was a very difficult decision to take, but I had no choice. I could not manage at home any more. I am all right here, but I shall never feel at home. And now other people are living in my house.' When I was about to leave she invited me to stay for a while and have a cup of tea. Her daughter would come at any moment. She came every day.(The daughter had in fact left some minutes before I arrived.)

Mrs King really had consented to moving. It had taken a long time to accept the facts and to get used to the idea of leaving the house in which she had lived nearly all her adult life, and of spending the rest of it in a totally strange environment, however nice it might be. She had made her choice freely, without any kind of pressure except her own evaluation of the situation. It was a very interrupted process, as her memory often deserted her. Her daughter had to introduce the subject repeatedly, as if it were for the first time. Mrs King was aware of something she had to think about but had forgotten what it was. It felt quite uncomfortable. 'It is as if suddenly my head is empty.' She also confessed that she sometimes could not remember where she was now and that at the moment of realization she felt displaced and homesick. All the same she never doubted that she had taken the right decision.

Informed consent

A patient's informed consent is required for medical tests and treatment. What are the conditions for a person to be considered responsible for his or her decisions? This question still depends heavily on a medical judgement (see, for instance art. 3 van de Wet Bijzondere Opnemingen Psychiatrische Ziekenhuizen en de Wet Geneeskundige Behandelovereenkomst art. 1653 u [Law for Unusual Admissions to Psychiatric Hospitals and Law for Nursing Intervention Policy Agreement]). Choosing and deciding, however, is a process that, for the greater part, does not belong to the field of medicine. Neither does defining responsibility. Indeed, within the field of psychiatry attempts are made to apply standards for specifying competency, but up to now the results are unsatisfactory (see Davis, 1991).

A realistic approach might seem appropiate to determine if a person is capable of understanding questions, but with people suffering from dementia the level of comprehension varies. It is also often very difficult for the interviewer to decide whether the person does or does not understand the question. If comprehension of language is impaired, communication on a rational level seems to become impossible. Yet the capacity to will and to express it may remain intact. This is illustrated in the following case.

Mrs Forester was an educated and emancipated woman. When she was about 50 she had made a living will declaring that in case of dementia, if she got ill, she did not want treatment which might lengthen her life. If euthanasia was legalized by then, she wanted her life to be terminated before she was a total wreck. She knew what she was talking about. At the time she wrote her will, both her mother and an aunt were suffering from dementia.

At the age of 75 Mrs Forester was admitted to a nursing home in an advanced stage of dementia. After some months she contracted pneumonia. The doctor tried to find out from her if she did or did not want treatment with antibiotics. Her response was not clear, for she had almost totally lost her capacity of speech and it was difficult to determine how much she understood. A nursing assistant showed her a capsule in such a way that she could take it or refuse it. She took it eagerly and put it into her mouth. Helping her to drink some water the nurse hugged her and said: 'Get better dear, won't you', at which Mrs Forester smiled.

In spite of the antibiotics she got worse. The way she held the nurse's hands and also the doctor's – who, during his visits to her, purposely wore a white coat which he usually did not – suggested a wish to live. To improve her physical condition a nasogastric tube was inserted. Apparently she had no objections. She recovered from her illness and seemed to be content with life. When, some months later, she died, she looked peaceful.

Social context

When individuals have to make decisions, more often than not they will look for advice and support from their social environment. Even in small matters, such as: 'Is it cold outside? Shall I put on a coat?' or 'What shall we have for dinner?' people will consult each other. In most cases a so-called independent judgement is the outcome of interactions with family, friends, neighbours, etc. A necessary condition, however, for confiding in other people and consulting them, is some ongoing communication.

It is very difficult to determine whether the decrease of interactions during the final stages of dementia is caused by the dementing process itself or is a result of the inability of those around to communicate with the seriously handicapped person. In a one-sided communication – a paradox in itself – an inter-personal exchange tends to be replaced by an intra-subjective 'dialogue'. This may take place in the demented person's mind, and may often be recognized at the beginning of the process, though in later stages it may escape observation. It certainly takes place in care-givers' minds. Ultimately their decisions are made on the basis of projections and assumptions, if not on professional prejudice.

In both cases, Mrs King's as well as Mrs Forester's, the social context appears to be of great importance. The way Mrs King made her own decision and, although grieving for her lost home, stayed with that decision, is not in the end the result of the relation between her and her daughter. Although we do not know what Mrs Forester did or did not understand, and although we have no proof that her gestures were correctly interpreted, there certainly was some kind of communication between her and her care-givers.

In an advanced stage of dementia, and in spite of a serious language problem and poor physical condition, Mrs Forester could express her love of life. It was made possible by the trusting relationship which had developed between her and her nurse. No less important was the fact that the doctor relied on that relationship. Yet it is possible that in the case of Mrs Forester the care-givers interpreted the old lady's attitude according to their own wishes. Her gestures of attachment might have been caused by a feeling of total frustration and abandonment. Care-givers should realize that their definition of the other's needs may result from personal and professional norms. If, for instance, Mrs Forester had pushed away the hand with the medicine, would it have been explained as a refusal, or ascribed to confusion? No doubt care-givers have a preference, however hard they may try to hide or even deny it. Apart from interpreting a person's reaction according to one's own preferences, part of the older person's response may be induced by the care-giver's attitude. It is hardly possible to hide your personal feelings and at the same time show your commitment and care. A neutral attitude in front of somebody in a vulnerable condition may be felt as a lack of interest. So may acting according to a will which was written many years earlier in a different situation. It shows respect for the person he or she was, but the person living now and possibly struggling for life is neglected. Again, perhaps Mrs Forester was not struggling for life, or she may have been caught in the conflicting emotions so many people experience when facing the end of life, but she very clearly showed a wish to be cared for.

In procedures to guarantee optimal respect for the demented person's preferences, partner and children are often referred to as important information providers and representatives of that person. However, they also may project their own ideas and preferences onto their partner or parent. Their assessment of the actual situation will most probably be influenced by the memory of the person he or she used to be.

There may, in addition, be problems of communication related to a breakdown of the social network, as Bengston and Kuypers (1989) point out. Part of this breakdown may be ascribed to latent conflicts which tend to show themselves when the system is out of balance. In such a case the individual's apparent incompetence mirrors disintegrating mechanisms all through the system. Members of such a disintegrating system are hardly capable of representing the best interests of the one who is deemed to be incompetent, without the intervention of professional care-givers.

Two conclusions may be drawn:

1 People who are isolated for a considerable time from social interactions may be expected to show increasing difficulties in expressing their wishes and deciding what to do. Part of care-giving to demented persons consists of supporting their ability to choose in simple matters in order

to involve them in decisions of a more serious nature. It is also an exercise for care-givers themselves to learn the person's preferences and the way he or she expresses them.

2 Support of the individual's capacity to express wishes, to cope with the situation and to feel confident enough includes support of his or her social network. Successful support of the network will result in improving the competency of the system as a whole.

Environment

If the social context contributes to a person's competency and ontological security, so does the personal and material environment. Beside a basic need to see people and communicate with them there is the equally basic need of some place to withdraw, to be alone with one's thoughts. Apart from that, there is a limit to the number of encounters an individual can bear or the time he or she can manage within a crowd. Many people, when moving in a crowd, have a way of withdrawing into themselves and screening off too large an input of stimuli. Although dementia may increase a person's capacity to withdraw, at the same time the subject cannot control it. Selectivity of perception seems to decrease as dementia proceeds.

The territorial needs of demented persons have not been much researched to date. Most nursing homes in The Netherlands, as well as in the UK, have bedrooms for four persons, three or four rooms with two beds and one or two single rooms for terminal care. Dormitories in which eight to twelve demented elderly slept at night and in which in the morning they queued up for the shower on commodes, seem to have disappeared. Obviously the situation was no longer acceptable, although it is not easy to see what caused this change of building policy. If a connection between environmental factors and demented behaviour was researched it certainly did not make headlines in the popular media. Perhaps in the construction of new nursing homes, the reduction of scale which became the trend in the care for the mentally handicapped and in psychiatry, simply took over. Or perhaps the change took place for aesthetic reasons, because the smaller bedrooms, with Christmas greetings and the grandchildren's drawings on the walls looked so much prettier than those huge, impersonal dormitories. There may be various reasons, any one of them good enough. The assumption, however, which justified the large dormitories and which essentially did not change with the building of smaller bedrooms for two or four persons, was never questioned. Even now you can hear statements such as: 'They feel safer at night when they have company', or 'They get confused and anxious when they are alone', or 'They do not notice with whom or with how many they share the room.'

Indeed, for some people the presence of other persons may be reassuring. Sometimes anxiety caused by loneliness is more disturbing than the proximity of other people twenty-four hours a day. All the same applying an occasional experience as a general rule without assessing the individual need for privacy and without extensive research cannot be justified by whatever ethical standard.

Mrs Peters cannot be persuaded to go to bed in the company of room-mates. Bedcurtains offer no solution. She does not want them to be drawn. She cannot express her objections verbally, but in her own way she makes her feelings quite clear. Usually the other women are not allowed to go to bed before Mrs Peters is asleep. In the morning, when she awakes before her room-mates, she sometimes allows herself to be guided to the bathroom, the nurse walking on tiptoe, saying 'Shh, mind the children.' But when the other women are awake at the same time, all hell breaks loose. Screaming, kicking and fighting, Mrs Peters is the living picture of anxiety, confusion and fury.

All the same she is known as a very nice person. During the day she does not avoid company, but talks to people in a friendly, even empathic though incomprehensible way. She smiles a lot and is fond of little jokes. Evidently she is used to having people around. Sometimes, however, she has had enough and then she retires to a quiet corner into herself.

To Mrs Peters and many others the nursing home offers more comfort than the situation at home. Although she strongly resisted going into the nursing home and the first two weeks were very difficult and sad, she somehow adapted to the new situation. Her children, who visited her frequently, found her condition much better than it had been at home and even regretted that they had waited so long before taking the step. The decision, about which they felt guilty, proved all right after all. However carefully a decision is made, we cannot always foretell its effects. But that is quite different from making decisions based on unevaluated assumptions.

Mrs Peters, though aphasic, made it quite clear that she objected to sharing her bedroom with other people. It is hardly surprising, considering that for more than fifty years she shared her bedroom only with her husband and, after his death ten years earlier, with nobody. It was a point often discussed within the nursing team, not only in connection with Mrs Peters but with other residents as well. Although some of the staff assumed that most of the residents would be happier if they had a room of their own, it could not be tested because the few single rooms they had were always occupied by the very sick and the dying.

In many nursing homes the dining rooms have the appearance of restaurants, serving twenty to thirty guests at the same time. There are tables for six with a helper hovering around to serve, to feed, and to prevent catastrophes. There is a lot of movement and noise. Going to a restaurant may be very relaxing if limited to special occasions, but as a daily exercise it has a dulling effect. Not for nothing does the travelling salesman arm himself with a journal at the dining table. So what might be the effect of a daily experience such as this on a dementing person's mind? Apparently, people adapt themselves to the unavoidable, but we do not know at what cost. How much problematic behaviour such as apathy, calling out, aggression or agitation is due to the dementing process and how much to environmental stress?

An ethical approach to care-giving in dementia includes evaluation of physical surroundings and staffing conditions. A frequent comment in discussions about staffing and building conditions is: 'We have to be realistic.' As often is the case, ethics is confused with idealism and wishful thinking, and finance with realism. True realism, however, is based on scrupulous assessment and weighing of all the factors involved. Only then is it possible to take the responsibility for decisions, even if they are to the disadvantage of a number of people. There is hardly any science more realistic than ethics.

Health care rationing in itself does not clash with ethics. On the contrary. We have to decide on priorities in the distribution of public resources. Private rooms for the demented elderly, preferably with a private bathroom, are expensive. Small living groups have consequences for staffing. Within an institution one option may exclude another. On a national level other groups rightfully claim their share in the health care budget and other interests beside health care may be equally important. Taking all interests into consideration, we may conclude that we cannot provide for demented persons according to their needs. It is essential for ethical decision-making, however, that those needs are seriously explored and acknowledged.

It is to be noted that with a movement in national health care policy from institutional towards home care, older people's desire to stay at home has suddenly become a political issue, whereas in an earlier period of almost unlimited growth of nursing institutions the opinion of the demented seemed to be ignored. Resistance and despair were taken as symptoms of dementia and not as a defence of the powerless against a system which threatened to deprive them of their individuality. The present emphasis on home care may suggest a deeper insight into demented persons' needs, but in fact is no more grounded in research and ethical considerations.

QUALITY OF LIFE

In the previous pages autonomy and competency were discussed as leading ethical principles. We concentrated particularly on capacities that remained despite increasing handicaps through cognitive impairment. We also focused on environmental conditions to meet the individual's need for authenticity, privacy and feelings of competency. Yet we have to accept that it is possible that people can become no longer capable of expressing their will or of being understood. In such a situation the principle of autonomy can no longer be a guideline. At the same time the concept of competency, or rather incompetency, though it may justify care-givers acting without a person's consent, does not essentially offer a solution to ethical dilemmas.

During the second half of the twentieth century the term 'quality of life' entered into ethical discussions. Although various attempts have been made to introduce standards for quality of life, the results are pretty meagre. The ethical view in general is that no one can judge someone else's quality of life. Indeed, judging that someone's life is not worth living is considered unethical (Dupuis, Kerkhoff and Thung, 1992). If a person is content with life as it is and somehow feels capable of coping with the problems he or she experiences, no one has the right to deny him or her a place among the living. If, on the other hand, a person feels life is not worth living any more, this feeling should be respected as well. It does not, however mean that we simply step aside and leave it to the individual to handle their death-wish. In many cases it seems possible to enhance someone's feeling of well-being (which may be considered as a general description of quality of life), but in other cases death seems the only way to resolve stress beyond endurance.

In The Netherlands euthanasia and assisted suicide are no longer criminal offences, provided that the actions are carefully reported and strict rules are observed. The first of these rules is that the subject expresses his or her wish clearly and consistently over a period of time and without moral pressure from other people. The second rule is that the suffering involved should be beyond endurance, and that the subject would die in any case within a short time. The second criterion has recently been omitted, because it excluded mental suffering of an enduring kind.

If people cannot describe their suffering nor clearly state their wish to have it ended, euthanasia is not permissible. However, the treatment of 'symptoms' with a certain risk of death is not legally contested as long as the doctor acts within the rules for professional conduct. The following case may illustrate the ethical dilemmas which arise from the 'treatment of symptoms'.

The case of Heather Hofman

Mrs Hofman, a 78-year-old woman, who had lived in a psychogeriatric nursing home for three years, was known as a strong character, very outspoken in her opinions, demanding much of her husband and her daughter as well as of herself. As long as her husband had known her she had 'had her moods'. She could be sombre for days and days and at other times she could be very angry. Most of the time she was cheerful, though tending to sarcasm. During her stay in the nursing home these changes of mood occurred more and more often and sometimes took extreme forms: one moment she assaulted people verbally and even physically, the next moment she was laughing, singing and embracing the whole world. She also got more and more restless at night and might walk the corridors for hours.

Her own house was always scrupulously clean. She was a good cook. 'Mother put her heart into the food', her daughter said. Mother was not accustomed to demonstrate affection in other ways. Later, during her stay in the nursing home, she could be very affectionate towards her daughter, Doreen. 'Nowadays I get more kisses in a week than I had during my whole youth', Doreen said. As was the custom in their village, husband and wife showed no signs of endearment in public, but in the nursing home they often sat or walked hand in hand. It was her husband who suggested she be called by her Christian name as she did not respond to 'Mrs Hofman'. Besides she was known as Heather all through the village.

Heather was a confirmed Catholic and a regular church-goer. In the early stage of Alzheimer's disease – as it was later diagnosed – the frequency of her church-going increased and she sometimes went three times a day. The household did not seem to interest her any longer. Her husband took over preparation of the meals (Doreen had a household of her own), but she often did not have the patience to sit down. More often than not, her husband had to feed her while she was walking. Sometimes she refused food. This pattern continued after she was taken to the nursing home. She did not join the other residents at meals and ate quite irregularly.

Once a week (on Thursdays) a service was held by a local priest and some pastoral assistants, mostly women. It was hoped that Heather would find there what she had so desperately sought before. She did not, however, recognize the priest as such, perhaps because his dress, with the exception of his collar, was pretty informal. Nor did she associate the living room, adapted to the occasion, with a chapel. It even seemed to infuriate her and she once assaulted the priest.

A special bond of mutual attachment developed between Heather and Ann, one of the nurses. When Heather was very agitated, the presence of Ann generally had a calming effect. They might walk together, at first at high speed but gradually slower and slower. Sometimes, when Heather was totally exhausted and could not put one foot in front of the other but nevertheless could not rest, she let Ann help her into a wheelchair and push her round and round the corridors. Ann, who shared a Roman Catholic background though no longer going to confession, used to sing all the familiar hymns and songs, in which Heather sometimes joined until she became sleepy.

Drug treatments, anti-depressives as well as anti-anxiety agents and sedatives were tried a few times, but both the physical and psychological effects were unacceptable. She got more depressed and agitated, became incontinent (which she had not been before) began to fall and would accept help from neither Doreen nor Ann. The drugs were administered without her knowledge, hidden in apple sauce or porridge, because she refused any medication.

After a few relatively peaceful months Heather suddenly got into a state of delirious activity, with signs of anxiety, despair and fury. She did not sleep, nor did she drink or eat. She assaulted other residents and kicked and screamed at her husband, who came every day but could not bear it much longer. She had to be isolated, Doreen and Ann accompanying her by turns as much as possible, but the situation got out of hand. Her state might have been caused by physical problems but a proper diagnosis was impossible, unless force was used to examine her. Formerly Heather had refused any physical examination. Her urine had been regularly checked – that was possible without her knowledge – occasional cystitis had been treated, medicine having been given surreptitiously. Once or twice a sample of blood had been taken against her will, to which she reacted violently. The present situation posed a dilemma for which there seemed to be no satisfying solution.

Finally, after deliberation with the husband, the daughter, the nursing staff and after consulting a colleague who specialized in geriatric medicine, the doctor decided to inject a drug to let her sleep. This way he hoped that further escalation of her psychotic condition might be halted and some inner balance might be restored. Previous experience made everybody well aware of a risk.

Shortly after the injection Heather fell asleep. She never awoke.

DISCUSSION

The case of Heather Hofman raises a series of ethical dilemmas, that is, choices to be made from conflicting moral standpoints. 'A dilemma refers to a moral conflict in which opposite duties, norms and values are involved' (Roelens, 1995). Opposite standpoints concerning the individual care in this case are shown in Figure 20.2.

Other arguments may be added, introducing new points of view. People might question the medication used in the various stages of the woman's suffering, or might prefer quite a different approach to the problems. In other words it could be suggested that some alternatives were overlooked, which might have resulted in a more satisfactory outcome. Principally it does not change the fact that all choices, technological though they may seem, have moral implications. And people act from their own sense of morality which comes from tradition, cultural background, education,

moral obligation to prevent/relieve suffering	respect for patient autonomy
refusal of treatment not based on free will but not rooted in earlier conflict (of religious nature?)	suffering is part of her life-history; though possibly victim to a frustrating moral code, she has found her own way of coping
administration of drugs without her knowing it does not burden her conscience	this is an arbitrary standpoint based on loose assumptions; deception and abuse of trust will damage sincere relationship
symptom-management intended to improve her condition but with a risk of death	disguised euthanasia, the first contrary to any moral standpoint, the latter incompatible with her religion
if no consensus can be reached the doctor decides	if no consensus can be reached the status quo is maintained

Figure 20.2 Opposite standpoints on team level of care

personal experience, and not least from the specific context, which includes the knowledge, the insights, the skills available, as well as group dynamics and all kinds of psychological motives.

With such a variety of attitudes it is difficult to reach some kind of consensus when matters have reached a crisis, involving a choice between life and death. Members of a care-giving team should start with ethical reflections at a much earlier stage, and be aware of moral implications and controversies from the start of a care-giving policy – on an individual level as well as institutional or even national level.

In many cases a demented person's behaviour is only a problem if it is problematic to other people. As long as the behaviour more or less corresponds with patterns care-givers have grown used to and which they can manage, signs of distress or calls for attention can be easily overlooked. This in itself is cause for ethical reflection. A decision may pass unnoticed in one situation but the same decision becomes highlighted in another case. In Heather's case the tragic outcome threw a new light on earlier decisions, which at the time did not seem to be important enough for more than a slight disagreement. If former attempts to treat Heather with medication had had a favourable effect, staff who were against concealment of the drugs would perhaps afterwards have conceded that those in favour were right. If the injection had not been fatal but instead had been helpful, the moral dilemma – if recognized as such rather than as a technical disagreement about treatment policy – would not have been put on the agenda for further reflection.

Ethical reflection does not just belong to the tradition of health care workers. If we look back in history, physicians had their codes of professional conduct of which the Hippocratic oath is the best known. Nurses had their standards of conduct as well, depending on the order to which they belonged or the culture of the institution where they worked. It does not mean that their consciences were not troubled with conflicting questions, but these remained personal and incidental. Ethical considerations have never been a *structural* part of health care practice. Ethics was for philosophers, health care workers are pragmatic.

A pragmatic attitude does not exclude an individual sense of morality. On the contrary, during staff meetings and occasional discussions and certainly during training sessions or symposia moral arguments are prominent. People working in a team are fairly familiar with each other's moral convictions and are inclined to treat them as ideas to be humoured. But in most cases more considered reflection as a normal part of care-planning is absent.

In Heather's case – as in many others – the lack of a structural ethical approach is clear. Everybody involved wanted 'the best' for this woman. Indeed, ethical discussion is based on belief in each other's integrity. 'You want the best for her as well as I do, although we have quite different approaches.' But what is the best?

REFERENCES

Bengtson, V.L. and Kuypers, J. (1989) 'De familie-ondersteuningscyclus: psychosociale problemen in een ouder wordende familie', in J. Munnichs and G. Uildriks (eds), *Psychogerontologie*, Deventer: Van Loghum Slaterus.

Davis, A.J. (1991) 'Ethical issues in gerontological nursing', in W.C. Chenitz, J.T. Stone and S.A. Salisbury (eds), *Clinical Gerontological Nursing*, Philadelphia/ London: W.A. Saunders Company.

Dupuis, H.M., Kerkhoff, A.H.M. and Thung, P.J. (1992) *Voordelen van de twijfel': een inleiding tot de gezondheidsethiek*, 3e herziene druk, Houten: Bohn Stafleu Van Loghum.

Erikson, E. (1983) *The Life Cycle Completed*, New York: Norton.

Godderis, J., van de Ven, L. and Wils, V. (eds) (1992), '*Handboek Geriatrische Psychiatrie*', Leuven: Garant.

Graaf, J. de (1972) *Elementair begrip van de ethiek*, Amsterdam: de erven Bohn.

Jonsen, A.R. (1992) 'The end of medical ethics', *Journal of the American Geriatrics Society* 40: 393–397.

Laing, R.D. (1959) *The Divided Self*, London: Tavistock.

Leenen, H.J.J. (1991) *Gezondheidsrecht*, Houten: Bohn Stafleu Van Loghum.

Miesen, B.M.L. (1995) 'Awareness in Alzheimer's disease patients: consequences for care-giving and research', paper presented at the Third European Congress of Gerontology, Amsterdam.

Nationale Ziekenhuisraad (1990) *'Een wankel evenwicht': zelf-beschikking en paternalisme in de psychogeriatrie*, Utrecht: Dienst Publicaties NZi/NZR.

Roelens, A. (1995) 'Ethische besluitvorming voor de verpleegkunde, naar een geïntegreerd model', *Verpleegkunde* 9: 220–231.

Strumpf, N.E., Evans, L.K. and Schwartz, D. (1991) 'Physical restraint of the elderly', in W.C. Chenitz, J.T. Stone and S.A. Salisbury (eds) *Clinical Gerontological Nursing*, Philadelphia/London: W.A. Saunders Company.

Volicer, L., Collard, A., Hurley A. *et al.* (1994) 'Impact of special care unit for patients with advanced Alzheimer's disease on patients' discomfort and costs', *Journal of the American Geriatrics Society* 42: 597–603.

Vroon, P. (1989) *Tranen van de krokodil*, Baarn: Ambo.

Chapter 21

Care-giving in dementia: the challenge of attachment

Bère M. L. Miesen

INTRODUCTION

Today, most researchers and care-givers all around the world agree about one common goal in dementia. All methods, approaches, techniques or interventions are meant to improve the quality of inter-personal interaction with the sufferer in order to counteract the impending isolation of the sufferer and his family, as the dementia process progresses. They can now be elaborated without becoming competitive, demagogic or religious. The realization that many roads lead to the same goal represents valuable progress. Yet, there is no magic formula for working with the dementing elderly. At the moment we acknowledge that in modelling individual care-giving in whatever setting, we have to consider the aetiology of the disease, the stage of the process, the life-span and the personality of the sufferer, and his or her family system. However, that knowledge and expertise was addressed mainly to care-givers; which implies that the patient is still often considered as an object of the dementia disease. Fortunately, the individual perspective of the sufferer has recently been stressed more and more by many authors. This new view means that the patient is becoming the subject of his or her disease. This changing perspective is enabling us to see, on the one side, the rich panorama of experiences and emotional needs of the patient; and on the other, it has enabled us to enter and discuss the experiences and (un)conscious needs of the care-givers themselves, be they relatives or professionals. In a broader context, the foundations on which care-giving in dementia is grounded, implicitly reflect the basic values and beliefs of our culture and society.

REVIEW

PART I: MODELS AND THEORIES

The concept of personhood and its relevance for a new culture of dementia care (chapter 1)

In this chapter Kitwood reaches into the realm of ethics. The original concept of caring appears to be part of an ethical ideal, wherein, as it were, the interdependence of all human life and the innate need to feel connected to someone are inextinguishable. The author describes two opposite ways of relating, stressed by the German philosopher Martin Buber. He concludes that the concept of personhood is rooted in Buber's 'I–Thou' mode of relating. The need 'to meet the other' is inherent in human nature and, as such, is a normal need of dementing persons. Of course, care-giving can be done without 'meeting' the patient. But that is dangerous because it could lead to dehumanization. If care-giving involves meeting the other person, it protects, preserves and validates his or her personhood until the end of the dementia process. There is no doubt that the concept of personhood is appropriate to many practical issues in dementia care-giving, even environmental ones. Focussing on personhood allows us to follow the sufferer's experience of the disease, instead of attempting futilely to repair what is irreparable. Kitwood formulates the heart of his claims as follows: 'It is a strange and tragic paradox that so much "care" has been practised without real meeting.' Probably, the same assertion holds true for assessing and researching dementia sufferers. If the focus in assessment and research could be shifted or widened, clinicians and researchers could also reap the fruits of this new culture of dementia care.

The dementias in a psychodynamic perspective (chapter 2)

Hagberg argues in this chapter that the cognitive decline in dementia affects the sufferer's personality organization. This thesis is based on a part of the the Lund Longitudinal Dementia study wherein correlations have been found between degree of cognitive decline, adaptive strategy and focal cerebral dysfunctioning in the left hemisphere of the brain. Starting from a psychodynamic frame of reference, the author then considers the multiplicity of secondary symptoms. Using personality theory he emphasizes especially how the organization of the ego, and hence the patient's coping ability, changes during Frontal Lobe Dementia. Although he concludes that the frontal lobes affect in particular the adaptive regulating role of ego-functioning, he explicitly rejects a localization theory of personality. Hagberg links the secondary symptoms of dementia, in terms of personality-related factors, with brain dysfunction, with pre-morbid personality and the degree of maturity of personality. What stands out the most in his research and is of great interest, is his notion that: 'personality related symptoms may be the most sensitive indicator of a dementia process'.

Culture and dementia: effects on care-givers and implications for services (chapter 3)

Now and in the future, no doubt, the family bears the greater part of informal care-giving in dementia, and continues to be the primary source of support. In this chapter Cox shows that culture and ethnicity act as additional factors resulting in variations in felt stress or subjective burden. She investigated various factors mediating the 'subjective burden' in both African and white American care-givers. In the first group of care-givers, informal support and competence contribute to stress; in the second group, lack of knowledge or of information and respite care contribute. Cox concludes that the influence of cultural values and ethnic norms is a strong one, and explains these differences by the stronger adherence to norms of filial responsibility in the African American care-givers. Traditional cultural expectations heighten stress when care-givers feel that they don't reach the expected standards. Instead of delivering quantitative interventions, for example giving more hours of professional help, one must analyse the subjective burden in order to choose adequate assistance. Cox's contribution increases understanding of the nature of the stress felt by informal care-givers. Therefore, if one realizes the consequences of cultural values and ethical norms, this will lead to differentiation in approaches and interventions; and to various ways to relieve the stress caused by 'objective burden'. Formal services which fail to match these subjective needs are missing the target. It is obvious that any interpretation of intercultural research on the care-givers' burden in dementia, must take account of culture, especially in western plural societies. To quote the author: 'Cultural values continue to be important influences in care-giving relationships as they can affect behaviours, expectations, and well-being of care-givers.'

Memory, emotion and dementia (chapter 4)

Every care-giver knows from experience that in parallel with fading cognition, emotional expression sharpens. Mills' chapter holds that dementia sufferers continue to have at their disposal emotional memories, even when the expression of the emotions fails. Her research project demonstrates a carefully executed single case-study methodology. She shows how care-givers of dementia sufferers can both trigger and preserve essential (emotional) memories. When persons in the early stages of dementia tell their life-stories, their general well-being increases. The care-giver's knowledge of these stories increases the ability to help the patient stay in contact with his or her (social) environment in the later stages of the disease. Furthermore, this knowledge could help elicit meaningful key emotional memories. Even when patients can no longer recall memories, they can sometimes recognize and 'feel' them when recounted by another. Undoubtedly, Mills' thesis, rooted in reminiscence theory, leads to a deeper understanding of approaches such as reminiscing, life-review and review counselling. It has implications for both therapy and theory building. She makes a strong plea for cognitive and emotional continuity in care-giving and therapy, for the sufferer and for his or her social support system. It is evident that any adequate approach or intervention is grounded in a strong relationship between memory and emotion.

Awareness in dementia patients and family grieving: a practical perspective (chapter 5)

In the first part of this chapter Miesen extends his POPFiD theory (Parent Orientation and Parent Fixation in Dementia), and consolidates theoretically the concept of 'awareness-context'. He further develops a psychology of secondary symptomatology in dementia by considering it as an extension of normal behaviour, as a normal reaction to potential trauma. In the second part of the chapter he focuses on the feelings and experiences of family care-givers, and argues that they have to deal with a grieving process which implies potential pathology. This is understandable when one considers its similarities with the emotional condition of 'missing' a loved person. The striking resemblance between the dementia sufferer and the dementia family care-giver is that, sooner or later, both experience emotional separation. The attachment theory of the late John Bowlby is an important frame of reference. Miesen uses it for care-giving, care-planning, and therapy. He pleads for (much greater) direct contact between dementia sufferers and other members of society, and between the sufferer and the professional, lay, or family care-giver. Meeting and addressing the sufferer directly, may prevent or delay the experience of trauma, in which isolation and separation are predominant. Counselling both family and professional care-givers, and helping them to overcome the pains of their own past, will facilitate both grieving and coping with the illness of dementia.

PART II: INTERVENTIONS IN CARE FACILITIES

Practical management of frontal lobe dementia: institutional perspectives (chapter 6)

The chapter of Tainsh and Hinshelwood highlights two aspects of Frontal Lobe Dementia (FLD). Its under- and false-diagnosis is particularly detrimental because it requires special management. They distinguish two sub-types of FLD: an 'apathetic' and a 'disinhibited' type. The first sub-type is easier to manage than the second one. The authors contribute especially to differential diagnosis, and give suggestions for management of the symptoms based on their clinical experience. First, the clinical features or characteristics of FLD are described as compared with those of Senile Dementia of Alzheimer Type (SDAT). Early onset of FLD can lead to early admission which can cause difficulties in a setting for the frail elderly. The authors emphasize that a solely cognitive assessment will miss the characteristic changes in behaviour, personality and social skills, because these symptoms precede the memory problems so typical of SDAT. Second, the authors focus on the management of the symptoms of the disinhibited type of FLD. After discussing pharmacological treatment, they suggest non-pharmacological interventions in the area of environment, interaction and activities. Although they mention the family carer's additional problems due to the non-cognitive changes without an awareness-context in the patient, and the contra-indication for group activity interventions, they point out the advantages of the preserved functions (for example learning abilities) which may facilitate behavioral therapy interventions. Recall that Hagberg's perspective on FLD (chapter 2) focuses on the dynamics of personality change, and the usefulness of psychodynamic interventions.

Psychomotor group therapy for demented patients in the nursing home (chapter 7)

In this chapter on Psychomotor Therapy (PMT) Dröes introduces her 'adaptation-coping model', in order to study more thoroughly the process of coping with dementia and institutionalization in mild to moderate SDAT patients. She also presents a general multi-disciplinary procedure to determine individual goals, treatment plans and interventions, translated into different forms of PMT. Thereafter she describes a method to evaluate the effects of PMT on secondary symptoms of dementia. Dröes' research results indicate a positive effect of PMT on the emotional balance of the patient particularly, that is, on satisfaction, aggression and night-time restlessness. The model incorporates social and affective functioning, and builds an individualized care-plan based on life-span factors, such as pre-morbid personality, previous social life and coping habits. She operates from a homeostasis perspective, which implies that each dementia patient keeps moving, be it yesterday in a crisis, or tomorrow in a downward spiral of psychosocial problems, or today in unstable balance. In using-movement oriented activities and/or body-oriented experiences to solve psychosocial problems, she proves, again, the positive effects of psychosocial interventions. She plays down a solely organic explanation of secondary symptoms by showing that they can arise from a patient's appraisal of the consequences of organic dysfunctioning. When other functions are fading, a dementia patient's movement and body can offer the care-giver an alternative way of communicating.

'Snoezelen': a new way of communicating with the severely demented elderly (chapter 8)

The authors of this chapter describe the development and implementation of 'snoezelen', a one-to-one approach to communicating with the demented elderly in the last stage of dementia. Achterberg, Kok and Salentijn describe how to maintain communication with the dementing elderly as they reach the final stages; to stay in contact with the inner world of the sufferer, even when the ability to respond verbally is fading. The 'snoezelen' method offers the authors a motivating technique which immediately decreases their own frustration and feelings of discomfort and impotence. Through connecting with certain preserved senses, care-givers let the severely demented elderly express emotions. The 'snoezelen' method warrants a place in the care-giving field. It should be integrated into care-giving, but can also be carried out as a separate activity. 'Snoezelen' affects care-givers' attitudes positively and guarantees a way of responding to the needs and feelings of the sufferer. In this way, patient and carer can continue to communicate or meet non-verbally late in the course of dementia. Such meeting allows both to stay involved with each other in a personal way, and, therefore, saves both from feeling totally separate and isolated.

Psychosocial treatment for demented patients: overview of methods and effects (chapter 9)

Dröes' second contribution consists of an updated review of the psycho-social approaches presented in the first volume of *Care-Giving in Dementia* (Jones and Miesen, 1992). Her overview confirms the increasing trend of researchers and clinicians to try to move into the dementia sufferer's inner world: to understand their feelings, experiences and manner of coping with a disease they never asked for. Apparently meaningless behaviour on closer examination, is full of meaning. She covers psychotherapy, psycho-motor therapy, behaviour modification, remotivation and resocialization, reminiscence, reality orientation training, and validation. She identifies a development from cognitive oriented methods to more affective/emotional oriented approaches. Her chapter establishes once and for all that thera-peutic nihilism is behind us. The next step that needs taking is to relate the effects of the different approaches and methods with distinctive stages of the dementia process, without losing sight of the individuality and unique identity (the personhood) of the dementia sufferer.

PART III: INTERVENTIONS IN THE COMMUNITY

The homeostasis model and dementia: a new perspective on care-giving (chapter 10)

Extrapolating mainly from research on chronically ill and disabled elderly, van der Plaats argues in this chapter that the dementing elderly have some understanding of their condition. She states that this understanding explains at least a part of their behaviour. 'Dementing patients feel and realize that they are ... losing their skills.' This is fully in line with Droës' chapter (chapter 7) and that of Miesen (chapter 5). She explains that care-givers have to accommodate and compensate the patient's competence; and in doing so, may restore his or her self-image. Passing from a medically oriented approach to care-giving to a psychosocial approach, she relates the consequences of the illness to decreasing well-being, autonomy and self-image. This change in perspective is possible because she expands a physical homeostasis model into a broader one, and assumes that people also try to maintain balance in their psychic and social systems. Besides providing (para)medical and nursing care (that is, curative care), care-givers must make allowance for patients' appraisal of their condition. They must help them to express their feelings and experiences which come from personal understanding of their situations. Based on this estimation, care-givers can help to maintain the psychic and social balance of patients, through 'situational' and 'transforming' care.

Supporting informal care-givers of demented elderly people: psychosocial interventions and their outcomes (chapter 11)

In this chapter Cuijpers and Nies expose the methodological shortcomings of (quasi)experimental research on the effects of informal care-giver interventions. There is no doubt that care-givers run a high risk of developing emotional problems. However, individuals can gain benefits from support interventions. It is obvious that informative counselling without emotional counselling is not effective. Caring for carers is linked directly with caring for the patient. The authors review the research literature on different types of interventions, such as the results of education, consulting and emotional support(groups); respite care, and individual psychosocial intervention. They report that demands for admission are affected positively by some interventions. At the same time they emphasize the necessity of refining research in order to 'address issues such as for whom, at what moment, and how much each intervention is effective on which aspects of individual and social functioning.' On the whole, research on the effects of group support intervention is still at a pioneering stage. The point at which informal care-givers 'press the button' is in particular need of further study.

On the methodological as well as on the explanatory level, Duijnstee's 'intervening factors' are important for future research.

Activation of care-giver coping processes through professional support (chapter 12)

In this chapter Vernooij-Dassen and Lamers present a meta-analysis of two family intervention studies. They address the fact that research has underestimated individual differences in the perceived burden of family care-givers. Here they focus on individual differences in the effects of professional interventions aimed at improving the primary care-giver's perceived competence to care. They compare a study of Duijnstee with a study in which the family-support model of Kuypers and Bengston is used. Professionals often ignore the strengths and the weaknesses of the family. Therefore it is necessary to refine and redefine the assessment of the felt burden. The primary care-giver's perception of the burden and the help they want and need to continue to care, must be researched (see also chapter 16). This implies that the family has to be accepted as a type of professional, as participants in a multi-disciplinary diagnosis of the care-situation. It would be better for professionals to provide a little of what primary care-givers really need, than offer them what they do not need. The care-plan must contain individualized approaches to the patient and to the primary care-giver. Understanding the processes which affect the sense of competence a primary care-giver feels, is part of the psychology of care-giving.

PART IV: INTERVENTIONS FOR THE FAMILY

Attachment, loss and coping in caring for a dementing spouse (chapter 13)

This chapter contains an important key to understanding the way in which the burden of dementia affects the spouse, as primary care-giver, in a unique way. This contribution shows the fruitfulness of Bowlby's attachment theory. Spouses are often confronted with increasing attachment behaviour from the sufferer as the dementia progresses. How a spouse responds to this 'proximity-seeking behaviour' of the sufferer relates to his or her own attachment history, and hence previous attachment to the sufferer. Different attachment types, considered as internalized working models, seem to predict the way a spouse is able to cope emotionally with the gradual loss of a dementing partner. Ingebretsen and Solem demonstrate coping styles of the secure and insecure attachment types (anxious attachment; compulsive care-giving; and independence and self-sufficiency). The insecure attachment types are likely to have coping problems. The response of the spouse partly depends upon how attached the sufferer was to her/his partner before the dementia began. Just as emotional separation is inevitable, likewise grieving ultimately creates even more emotional distance. A spouse must resolve a conflict: a sufferer's attachment behaviour evokes care-giving behaviour while at the same time distancing is occurring. A spouse stays close, while feeling apart. Because continuous care-giving cannot be maintained without some distance, some grieving has to be done to survive. By identifying 'separation' as the origin of the emotional reaction of the spouse, the authors offer a third focus to individual and group family intervention. In addition to problem- and emotion-focused coping, they point to relationship-focused coping.

Understanding the social context of families experiencing dementia: a qualitative approach (chapter 14)

Enhancing personhood and the well-being of the person are major goals for effective care-giving and social service delivery systems for the elderly with dementia. Personhood-enhancement of both sufferer and family care-giver requires a contextualized approach, in which a mapping out of the life-history of both is needed. The story of the patient and the family care-giver must 'be told' to uncover the meaning of their behaviour, and to build meaningful interventions. Staff need to understand more fully the social context of the person and the family. Based on attachment theory and a client-system approach, LeNavenec presents five tools ('visual gestalts') to describe social and life-span contexts: genograms, ecomaps, lifelines, communication pattern diagrams and attachment pattern diagrams. In presenting these tools the author contributes to individualized care-giving which does not omit the story of the family. Professional care-givers often run up against interactions and communication problems between sufferer and family care-giver, as well as between themselves and the family. By interpreting the family's 'difficult' or 'incomprehensible' behaviour in terms of social and life-span inter-dependency, professional care-givers are able to refine their communication patterns with them. Researchers can also benefit from the tools the author describes. Research results can exceed the bare assessment of cognitive functioning, by interpreting dysfunctioning in the perspective of the life-span of the individual.

Carer support groups: change mechanisms and preventive effects (chapter 15)

Today the needs of care-givers are taken more seriously; not only because of the mediative role they play in delaying admission or institutional-ization, but especially because they have been identified as a group of people who themselves can be in need. A support group for care-givers can be an important means of relieving their psychic pain through the reduction and prevention of an increase in their perceived burden. In this chapter Cuijpers, Hosman and Munnichs review the literature and describe from their own quantitative and qualitative research how the beneficial effects of carer groups are obtained and for whom. They are interested in the change mechanisms and preventive effects for which Lazarus' stress and coping theory is a frame of reference. The authors point out that not everyone can be helped through the same intervention. As far as carer groups are concerned, the focus must be on all kinds of support – informative, counselling, normative and emotional. The conclusion that 'those care-givers in particular who feel heavily burdened find benefit in a support group' stresses again, on the one hand, the need to diagnose SDAT as early as possible. On the other hand it emphasizes that family care-givers still suffer silently for years before they ask for help. It will be a challenge to reduce their isolation earlier.

Behind the facts: an insight into the burden on family carers of dementia patients (chapter 16)

In this chapter Blom and Duijnstee link Duijnstee's theoretical views with a practical procedure, to optimize the assessment of 'subjective burden' as experienced by family care-givers. Generally family care-givers face countless practical and emotional problems. The authors point out that research into dementia must not only consider the sufferer, but at the same time look at family and environmental factors in order to understand how subjective burden is connected with personal psychological factors, such as inadequate coping, problems with acceptance, or lack of motivation. It is obvious that different family care-givers may experience the same situation from different perspectives. The same 'objective' burden can be felt quite differently, and, hence, needs distinct interventions. In the second part of the chapter the authors describe a tool to assess subjective burden, an interview schedule directed to patient and carer problems, for mapping out individual variations in subjective burden. This contribution greatly assists case-management in care-giving in dementia. They caution researchers and clinicians not to rely merely on objective estimates of burden by professionals, but to assess carefully the subjective experience of the family care-givers themselves.

Cultural dimensions of dementia and care-giving (chapter 17)

In his chapter King discusses the relevance of cultural frameworks for the conceptualization of care-giving and models of care-giving practice, by analysing the phenomenology of present-day Japanese care-giving from historical and cultural perspectives. 'In short, Japanese care-givers tend to see dementia in inter-personal and collective rather than organic and individual terms.' He argues that it is not enough to use only biomedical parameters to understand care-giving behaviour in different societies. The explanatory power of the biomedical approach and the organization of care-giving interventions based on it, is lacking when cultural dimensions are involved. In Japan care-giving is delineated along generational boundaries. Traditional values and beliefs (especially the Japanese cosmology, wherein 'dependency' in childhood and old age has a high status) collide with western ones. 'Dependency' in western culture is linked with the biological realm of life and also with shame and humiliation. The author carefully exposes the different perceptions of dementia in Japanese and western society. For the latter dementia is a neuropathological agent in the body of an old person which affects his life. For Japanese care-givers dementia means a disruption in the flow of social relations. Family care-giving in Japan is thus constructed as an essential duty to maintain filial continuity and to convey the elder's spirit to the next world. The subjective burden of Japanese care-givers can only be fully understood when viewed from the struggle of trying to balance this spiritual duty with the practical demands of everyday living and care-giving.

PART V: ENVIRONMENT, EDUCATION AND ETHICS

In search of the best environment (chapter 18)

Historically evolved institutions do not always provide the best approaches to the care-giving needs of dementia sufferers. At the same time, staying at home, even with the best care, is not always the ideal solution. In her chapter Fahrenfort questions the institutionalization of institutions. She evaluates five different innovative settings in The Netherlands, intended to be less institutionalized than the average institution in The Netherlands. The aim of her research was to provide 'better care for equal money'. The settings involved a lesser to a greater degree of institutionalization, and were presented as alternatives to general psychogeriatric nursing home care. She evaluates them in terms of patient characteristics, costs, quality of care, and organizational features. The quality of care was measured by the client's satisfaction, the quantity of 'home-like' environment, continuity, and other professional care-givers' estimations. Her conclusion is that a wide variety of options exists. For both the dementia sufferer and relatives, there must always be a choice. Small-scale settings, embedded in a larger centre for psychogeriatic intervention and care, can provide a much-needed 'home' environment in which 'ordinary' life can continue.

Education about normal forgetfulness and dementia (chapter 19)

Commissaris' chapter makes a contribution to the psychological education of the lay elderly public. Undoubtedly, most of them associate (subjective) cognitive decline and diminishing memory with deterioration – which causes them considerable anxiety. They feel as if the sword of dementia is hanging above them, though research shows that four out of five worry needlessly. Subjective memory complaints do not coincide with the objective assessment of poor memory. This concern and worry remains a substantial feature of old age, and explains the great interest the elderly have in memory (re)training courses and visits to memory clinics. The author asks the question: can information about memory, and the difference between normal forgetfulnes and dementia help to decrease these worries? An information brochure was developed and tested in a study. The author found that accurate and concrete information could prevent many older persons from worrying unnecessarily, as well as providing the advantages of early detection. Another aim of the study was to gain more information about the profile of those who were worrying. Having a close relative with dementia (dementia in the family) appeared to explain most complaints about one's forgetfulness. The author points to the responsibilities of the media and the general practitioner. They must not only focus on information about dementia, but much more explicitly on information about the differences between normal and abnormal forgetfulness.

Ethical issues in the care of the demented elderly (chapter 20)

In this chapter Warners, following the definition of ethics as 'a systematic reflection upon responsible conduct', completes the circle which started with Kitwood's contribution. She suggests that the ethical arguments care-givers use in (not) planning care in dementia practice, more often stem from implicit value judgements than from comparing the pros and the cons of a situation. Sooner or later in the dementia process, as in the care-giving process, dilemmas arise from the fact that the decreasing competence of the sufferer does not necessarily mean a fading of autonomy. The author helps care-givers to recognize questions concerning individual autonomy about authenticity, privacy and self-determination. 'What in a legal sense may be considered a *measure of protection*, appears to affect the individual's autonomy on a much deeper level.' She emphasizes that moral choices, both on the micro and macro organizational levels of care-giving, are closely linked to the view one has of optimal 'human' existence in times of limited mental, physical, social and financial resources. She points to the fact that care-givers must accept and reflect on their projections, prejudices and unconscious attitudes. 'Care-givers should realize that their definition of the other's needs may result from personal and professional norms' – certainly in the advanced stages of the dementia process.

PERSPECTIVES

Issues that remain

Undoubtedly, dementia is a disease of the brain for which one must try to trace the causes. Perhaps a drug will be found to stop the process, or even to prevent it. However, the subject of care-giving in dementia is much broader. Fortunately, the interest of researchers in the psychosocial perspectives of dementia is growing. Dementia is a chronic problem. It affects the sufferer in an irreversible way. And it pushes the family into a particularly emotional state. Furthermore, it raises questions about adequate interpersonal interventions for care-giving, by both families and professionals in diverse settings. Bioneurological, medical and psychological knowledge is still insufficient to understand and explain specific behaviour within a variety of dementia syndromes. Last but not least, there is the issue that some will want to end their life of suffering prematurely, and the legal question of how this could be done.

In addition to coping with increasing practical problems, a partner enters into a grieving process. This process is very difficult, because one is losing someone while they are still there. One can only say goodbye completely when the sufferer is dead. The more one succeeds in achieving the necessary distance, the better able one is to see the sufferer in another role and 'adopt' him or her as a person needing care.

The struggle of the sufferer, as well as the grieving process of the family, often go unrecognized. The loss has no status, as it were, because it is invisible. The two are still together; separated, but still together.

In June 1995, at the University of Stirling in Scotland, a European colloquium was held about therapeutic work with the elderly (see Hunt, Marshall and Rowlings, 1997). All participants were involved in counselling the elderly – to do with issues of political violence; of terror or civil evacuation in the Second World War; as survivors of concentration camps; or as war veterans or victims of incest. Counselling concentrated upon the traumatic effects of particular life events. Everyone knows what is meant by traumatic experiences. One may be in an unsafe situation, or dependent entirely upon one's own resources; there may be no one upon whom to rely, either for protection or to get one out of it.

Psychologically speaking the dementia sufferer experiences similar feelings. The continuity in his or her life is gradually lost causing feelings of displacement, separation and alienation. Every dementia sufferer fights against this. This fight can be seen as a kind of grieving process which contains hope, uncertainty, denial, aggression, sadness, depression, etc. But the fight is a losing battle.

Challenges in research

Studies of the differences between the various approaches, stages of dementia and syndromes are being developed for particular groups of sufferers, rather than being borrowed or adopted from elsewhere. Inter-personal interventions are focused more directly on the secondary symptoms, and are defined more in terms of emotional needs than in terms of a more traditional psychiatric vocabulary. For many researchers the rich psychodynamics of the secondary symptoms are beyond dispute. This may contribute to the early detection of dementia where both cognitive and affective signs must be assessed. Both cognitive and affective stress reactions must be of concern in planning long-term care.

The concept of 'awareness-context' implies that sufferers are aware that 'something is not right', an awareness which involves both cognitive and affective aspects. This concept makes the assumption that the sufferer is the subject instead of the object of the disease. The focus shifts to assessing coping methods and to seeing his or her behaviour as quite normal given the dementia. Information about life-history, especially on individual attachment, coping strategy and personality, is crucial. Attachment theory becomes increasingly important in understanding both the behaviour of sufferers, as well as that of professional and family care-givers. Research can be aimed at predicting the coping process, which facilitates and individualizes the planning of stage-specific interventions and care-giving.

An interesting question is whether or not coping and awareness in themselves are related to brain failure. One hypothesis would be to assume that absence of awareness is connected with frontal lobe dementia and the last stage of SDAT, but not with MID or mild/moderate SDAT. Is awareness located in the frontal brain? And what has awareness to do with the maintenance of one's identity or personhood? It is likely to be more complex because 'the person does not only react to damage, but is affected by it in his capacity to organize and integrate new experience' (see p. 33). Is it possible to differentiate between personality changes based on frontal lesions and individual reactions to generalized brain trauma?

In our efforts to collect all possible data to support care-planning, we must not forget that the sufferer can tell his own story, and can supply the care-giver with information that will be useful in the later stages of the disease. From this perspective the personal narrative is an ethical issue, in that impending isolation, decreasing contact, and increasing inaccessibility is dangerous for sustaining personhood.

The emotional situation of family care-givers of dementia sufferers becomes more explicit. Their acceptance of the 'strange' behaviour of the demented relative often lags behind that of professional care-givers, because it is the psychic pain of the whole situation which slows down acceptance. What families often need most is time. Care-givers' expectation that information will help them to know what to do, is sometimes unrealistic if there is no progress through the grieving process. Counselling or psychotherapy may help the explicit grieving which is needed to cope with the problems.

Advice for the future

At present, we can say to the dementia patient:

Perhaps a lot is wrong in your head, but it doesn't mean you are crazy. Try to explain clearly to your loved ones the changes you have noticed in yourself. Let your complaints be investigated by experts as soon as possible. Nothing is worse than the fear uncertainty and doubt bring.

We can say to the family:

It is necessary to stand up for yourselves. Demand attention for the grieving process you are going through. Seek emotional support, confiding in people who are suffering or have suffered the same experience. Caring for yourself is also good for the dementia sufferer. Let your ability to care be sustained by receiving the support from whatever sources of assistance are available. The Alzheimer's Disease Society, the Alzheimer's group in your region, your general practitioner and others can show you the way. Get help quickly for your practical problems, and, in addition, get enough rest.

We can say to the social environment or society:

If you suspect or know someone who is suffering from dementia, do not think that he or she doesn't want to speak to you about it. Such talks are easier than you expect: often you only have to listen. Do not forget to ask the partner or children what the illness means to them. The problems often seem to be greater than at first glance.

And we can say to the professionals:

Try as quickly as possible to complete the diagnosis. Inform both patient and family about the diagnosis. Inform them also about how and where they can go for counselling. Take care to talk to both together which may enable them to share their worries and pain, to help reduce their loneliness, and to facilitate their grieving process.

To be concluded

The evidence which supports the hypothesis that dementia could be considered as a chronic brain trauma causing potential psychotrauma, is increasing. Dementia can reactivate feelings of old trauma in some sufferers. Hence, the core challenge in counselling and care-giving in dementia could be that of the preservation of the personhood of the sufferer and the carers, making them feel respected, and safe. Research in care-giving must increasingly focus upon that.

The chapters on the effects of culture and ethics are impressive. They help me realize that western society, the first fifty years of my life-span, and my personality, continuously affect my clinical work, my counselling, teaching and research in dementia. Permanent awareness of the possible countertransference of these influences is needed to let me genuinely meet the dementia sufferer and his or her family, so as not to increase unnecessarily their isolation and pain. At the same time, it helps me to understand the richness of the contributions of my colleagues in psychogeriatrics or the psychiatry of old age all over the world.

ACKNOWLEDGEMENT

The author is grateful to Gemma Jones for her comments, and to Joy Beddoe for her help.

REFERENCES

Hunt, L., Marshall, M. and Rowlings, C. (eds) (1997) *Past Trauma in Late Life*, London: Jessica Kingsley.
Jones, G.M.M. and Miesen, B.M.L. (eds) (1992) *Care-Giving in Dementia.* Research and Applications, vol. 1. London/New York: Routledge/Tavistock.

Subject Index

abandonment, feelings of 161
absconding, from care 90
abusive behaviour 261
acceptance: behavioural 350; of caring
role 74, 179, 180, 181, 183, 193, 251,
252; and coping 254–6; of dementia
56, 57, 63, 128, 133, 160, 255; of
emotion 63; instinctive 160; of loss
196, 199, 203, 206; and motivation
254–6; of others 55, 58, 61, 134;
problems 253–4; social 55, 160; of
sufferer 139
accusatory behaviour 133, 260
acting-out behaviour 20, 22, 28
activities of daily living (ADL) 90,
122–3, 131, 133–4, 257; dressing 122,
131, 153, 250, 259; washing 122, 123,
131, 250; see also eating and toilet
behaviour
activity: craft work 119, 138; group
137–8; lack of 153; offering 120, 122,
127, 137, 160; optimal 165;
programme 138; restriction, carer 40,
41, 42, 233; self sustained 250, 257,
259–60; snoezelen 121–3; stimulating
107–9, 119, 130–33, 322; see also
passivity
adaptation: 132, 180, 183, 185, 187, 323,
324; carer 253; -coping model 96, 97,
103, 105, 341; to crisis 100, 101, 103,
104; stimulating 133; and support
groups 233–48; see also coping
adaptive strategies 18, 20, 23–6, 32, 33,
96, 158, 160, 338; enhancing 128, 129;
lacking 30, 104; mature 26, 27, 28
adaptive tasks 96, 100, 102–6
adjustment see adaptation
affect see emotion

African American people 38–46, 339
age: appropriate therapy 91; of onset
54, 86
ageing: attitudes to 274; cognitive 303;
and concentration 304, 305; and
cultural factors 36, 37, 274, 275, 276;
and dependency 274; normal
processes of 16, 151, 155, 156, 302;
perspective 26, 32–3, 271, 280, 281,
282; population 302; reactions to
161–2, 274; restrictions of 129, 161;
and mental speed 303, 304
ageism 269
aggressive behaviour 20, 30, 59, 61, 70,
97, 103, 106, 122, 158, 161, 168, 341;
stabilizing 114, 122, 132
agitation 17, 102, 136, 158, 163, 316; see
also restlessness
agnosia see recognition
agraphia see writing
alcohol, and cognitive functioning 305,
310
alienation 349
Alzheimer's dementia 17–20, 30, 67, 68,
76, 87, 133, 341; activity programme
138; pharmacotherapy 88
amae 275–6, 277
amayakasu 275; see also care
American African people 38–46, 339
anger 49, 52, 122, 133, 159, 235; coping
with 245; suppressed 60
anhedonia 85
anti-convulsants 88; see also medication
anti-depressants 88, 322; see also
medication
anticipation, as coping strategy 181,
183, 185

resources 214; satisfaction 182, 254;
self-confidence 244; self-esteem
186, 224; sensitivity 195, 197,
199–201, 207; social contact for 238;
social context of 210–32; stress
37–46, 168, 172, 193, 239, 339;
successes 186; supervision 31;
support for 45, 168–77, 178–88, 198,
233–48, 251, 257, 263–4, 343;
symbiosis 195, 197, 199–201, 207;
tolerance 174; understanding 31,
42–4, 63, 128, 138, 139, 165, 174, 183,
244, 253; well-being 44, 172, 234, 239,
241
case-studies 50–62, 102–3, 122–3, 151,
163, 183, 324–5, 325–6; care-givers
179–85, 239; euthanasia 331–3;
family 213, 214, 217, 226, 252;
marital 196–204; support groups
237–8; *see also* research
catastrophic reactions 33
cathartic *see* release
cerebral functioning *see* brain
change: cognitive 14, 15, 17, 21, 23,
303; mechanisms *see* adaptation;
personality 14, 17, 18, 19, 20, 21,
23–5, 33, 339, 341; sociability 129,
193, 233, 341
chihoushou 279
childlike behaviour *see* regression
China 274
chloripramine 88; *see also* medication
choice *see* decision making
circular (communication) pattern
diagrams (CPDs) 220–2
claiming behaviour 70
clinging *see* attachment
closeness *see* intimacy
coaching 29, 30
cognition: changes in 14, 15, 17, 21, 23,
303; and emotion 49–50, 130;
primitive 317
cognitive: ageing 303; appraisal 96;
-behavioural psychotherapy 129–30;
deterioration 16, 17, 19, 20, 23, 24,
25, 26, 27, 28, 30, 130, 338;
developmental model 21, 34;
functioning 21, 23, 26, 28, 29, 68, 69,
70, 305, 310, 338; gerontology 303;
organization 21; reasoning 23, 24,
278; reduction 17, 19, 20, 23, 24, 25,
26, 27, 28, 30, 129, 130, 132, 137;
rigidity 21, 25, 303; skills 273; speed

17, 19, 20, 23, 303, 304; status 42;
training 164
colour, use of 111
commitment *see* motivation
communication 269: abilities 251;
analysing 128; bodily 121, 124, 270,
271, 273; breakdown 122, 201, 203,
325, 327; evaluating 112; of emotions
67, 272; empathic 110, 128, 139;
facilitating 63, 77, 106, 134, 138, 139,
207; intra-subjective 326; methods of
119–26; movement as 99, 121, 342;
non-verbal 121, 124, 139, 270, 271,
325, 326, 342; patterns 220–2, 345;
problems 71, 103; using sensory
stimulation 121, 122; therapy 92, 128;
verbal 120, 128, 134; *see also*
snoezelen
company, enjoying 260
compassion 76
compensation 33, 181, 183, 186, 343;
for sensory deprivation 136
competence, care-giver 40, 43, 44, 45,
181, 182, 183, 186, 344; sufferer 317,
322–30, 331; *see also* independence
complaining behaviour 161
compulsive: behaviour 88, 89, 158;
care-giving 195, 197, 199–201, 207
concentration 17, 20, 23, 91, 129; and
ageing 304, 305
concrete: behaviour 23; language 24
confabulation *see* intimacy
conflict: carer 184, 206; emotional 16,
154; of values 36; resolving 135, 136,
139; unresolved 129, 138
conformity 181, 183
confusion 136
congruency 181, 183
connecting 5, 6, 7, 8, 11, 120, 125, 152,
338; *see also* social interaction
conscious/unconscious balance *see*
topographic organization
consciousness 271; and mind 278; of
suffering *see* awareness *and*
subjectivity
consent, informed 325–6, 328
consideration 181, 183; *see also*
understanding
contact: bodily 121; *see also*
communication *and* connecting
containment 63
context, social: of care 224–5, 227;
definition 210, 210–32; external 210;

Name Index

Gallagher, D.E. 237, 245
Gibson, F. 62
Gilberson, D.L. 134
Gilleard, C.J. 193
Glaser, B.G. 67, 68
Glosser, G. 237
Godderis, J. 317
Goldfarb, A.I. 128
Golodetz, A. 249
Gonyea, J.G. 173
Gottesman, L. 140
Gow, C.A. 22
Grafström, M. 193
Green, L.W. 308
Gresham, M. 175, 238
Gubrium, J.F. 216

Hagberg, B. 14–35, 338, 341
Haley, W.E. 172, 245
Hanley, I.G. 138
Hartman, A. 214
Hartmann, H. 21, 34
Head, D.M 136
Hepworth, M. 271
Hinshelwood, D. 83–94, 340
Hofman, Mrs Heather 331–5
Holden, U.P. 140
Hosman, C. 233–48, 346

Ingbretsen, R. 191–209, 344
Ingvar, D.H. 26

Janet, P. 8
Janssen, J.A. 134
Johnson, C.L. 193
Johnson, H. 39
Johnson, Mr 76
Johnston, M.M. 224
Jones, Mr 213
Jones, Mrs 76

Keith, J. 277
King, Mrs 324–5, 326
King, C. 269–84, 346
Kitwood, T. 1–13, 49, 338, 348
Kochen, J.A.W. 160
Kok, W. 119–26, 308, 342
Kreuter, M.W. 308
Kurokawa, Y. 281
Kuypers, J. 178, 179, 181, 183, 186, 187, 323, 327, 344

Lajoie, Mr 214

Laing, R.D. 318
Lamers, C. 178–88, 344
Larner, S. 174
Lawton, M.P. 140, 173
Lazarus, R.S. 162, 163, 239, 346
Leahey, M. 210, 220, 222
Ledoux, D. 225
Lee, Mrs 217
Leenen, H.J.J. 320
Leering, C. 158
LeNavenac, C. 210–32, 345
Levy, L.L. 140
Linsk, N.L. 133
Lund dementia group 17
Luria, A.R. 22
Lyman, K.A. 270

Maastricht Memory Clinic 303, 307, 309
Mace, N.L. 249
McFarland, H.N. 278
McGrowder-Lin, R. 138
Maletta, G.J. 129
Mattson, B. 187
Mauss, M. 273
Merriam, S.B. 217
Mertens, F. 165
Mesulam, M.M. 21, 22
Miesen, B.M.L. 61, 67–79, 155, 158, 161, 162, 337–52
Mills, M. 48–66, 339, 340
Montgomery, R.J.V. 238
Morris, L.W. 193
Morris, P. 222
Morycz, R. 40
Mosher-Ashley, P.M. 140
Munnichs, J.M.A. 159, 346
Munnins, J. 233–48
Murphy, E. 187, 188

National Institute of Neurological and Communicative Disorders and Stroke 307
Neary, D. 83
Nehrke, M.F. 135
Neimeyer, G.J. 226
Nell, H.W. 160
Netherlands 130, 239
Neuschatz, S. 135
Niederehe, G. 250
Nies, H. 168–77, 343
Nigel, Mrs 102–3
Norbeck, J. 226